THE CAT ENCYCLOPEDIA

THE CAT
ENCYCLOPEDIA

Contains content previously
published in *The Complete
Cat Breed Book*

LONDON, NEW YORK, MELBOURNE,
MUNICH, AND DELHI

DORLING KINDERSLEY
Senior Art Editor Gadi Farfour
Project Editor Miezan van Zyl
Project Art Editor Amy Child
Editorial Assistant Henry Fry
US Editor Margaret Parrish
Jacket Designer Laura Brim
Jacket Editor Maud Whatley
Jacket Design Development Manager Sophia Tampakopoulos
Producer, Preproduction Francesca Wardell
Producer Mary Slater
Additional Photography Tracy Morgan
Managing Art Editor Karen Self
Managing Editor Esther Ripley
Publisher Sarah Larter
Art Director Phil Ormerod
Associate Publishing Director Liz Wheeler
Publishing Director Jonathan Metcalf

Consultant Editor Kim Dennis-Bryan
Contributors Ann Baggaley, Jolyon Goddard, Katie John

DK INDIA
Senior Editor Monica Saigal
Editor Antara Moitra
Art Editors Neha Sharma, Supriya Mahajan
Assistant Art Editors Namita, Roshni Kapur, Vansh Kohli
Managing Editor Pakshalika Jayaprakash
Managing Art Editor Arunesh Talapatra
DTP Designers Bimlesh Tiwary, Mohammad Usman, Nityanand Kumar
Preproduction Manager Balwant Singh
Production Manager Pankaj Sharma
Picture Research Surya Sankash Sarangi

First American Edition, 2014
Published in the United States by DK Publishing,
4th Floor, 345 Hudson Street, New York, New York 10014

14 15 16 17 18 10 9 8 7 6 5 4 3 2 1
001—193220—Jul/14

Printed and bound in China by South China Printing Company.

DK books are available at special discounts when purchased in bulk for sales
promotions, premiums, fund-raising, or educational use. For details, contact:
DK Publishing Special Markets, 345 Hudson Street, New York, New York 10014
or SpecialSales@dk.com.

Discover more at
www.dk.com

Every effort has been made to ensure that the information in this book is accurate.
Neither the publishers nor the authors accept any legal responsibility for any
personal injury or injuries to your cat or other damage or loss arising from the
undertaking of any of the activities or exercises presented in this book, or from
the reliance on any advice in this book. If your cat is ill or has behavioral problems,
please seek the advice of a qualified professional, such as a vet or behavioral expert.

CONTENTS

1 INTRODUCTION TO CATS

Cat species around the world	**8**
What is a cat?	**10**
From wildcat to house cat	**14**
How domestic cats spread	**18**
Feral cats	**20**

2 CATS IN CULTURE

Cats in religion	**24**
Myths and superstition	**26**
Folklore and fairy tales	**28**
Cats in literature	**30**
Cats in art	**32**
Cats in entertainment	**38**

3 FELINE BIOLOGY

Brain and nervous system	**42**
Cat senses	**44**
The skeleton and body form	**48**
Skin and coat	**50**
Muscle and movement	**54**
Heart and lungs	**58**
Digestion and reproduction	**60**
The immune system	**62**
Understanding breeds	**64**
Choosing the right cat	**66**

4 CATALOG OF BREEDS

Shorthairs   71

Longhairs   185

5 CARING FOR YOUR CAT

Preparing for arrival   256

Living indoors   258

Going outdoors   260

Essential equipment   262

First days   264

First vet check-up   268

Food and feeding   270

Handling your cat   274

Grooming and hygiene   276

Understanding your cat   280

Socializing your cat   282

Importance of play   284

Training your cat   288

Behavioral problems   290

Responsible breeding   292

Inherited disorders   296

A healthy cat   298

Signs of illness   300

Health and care   302

The aging cat   308

GLOSSARY   310

INDEX   312

ACKNOWLEDGMENTS   319

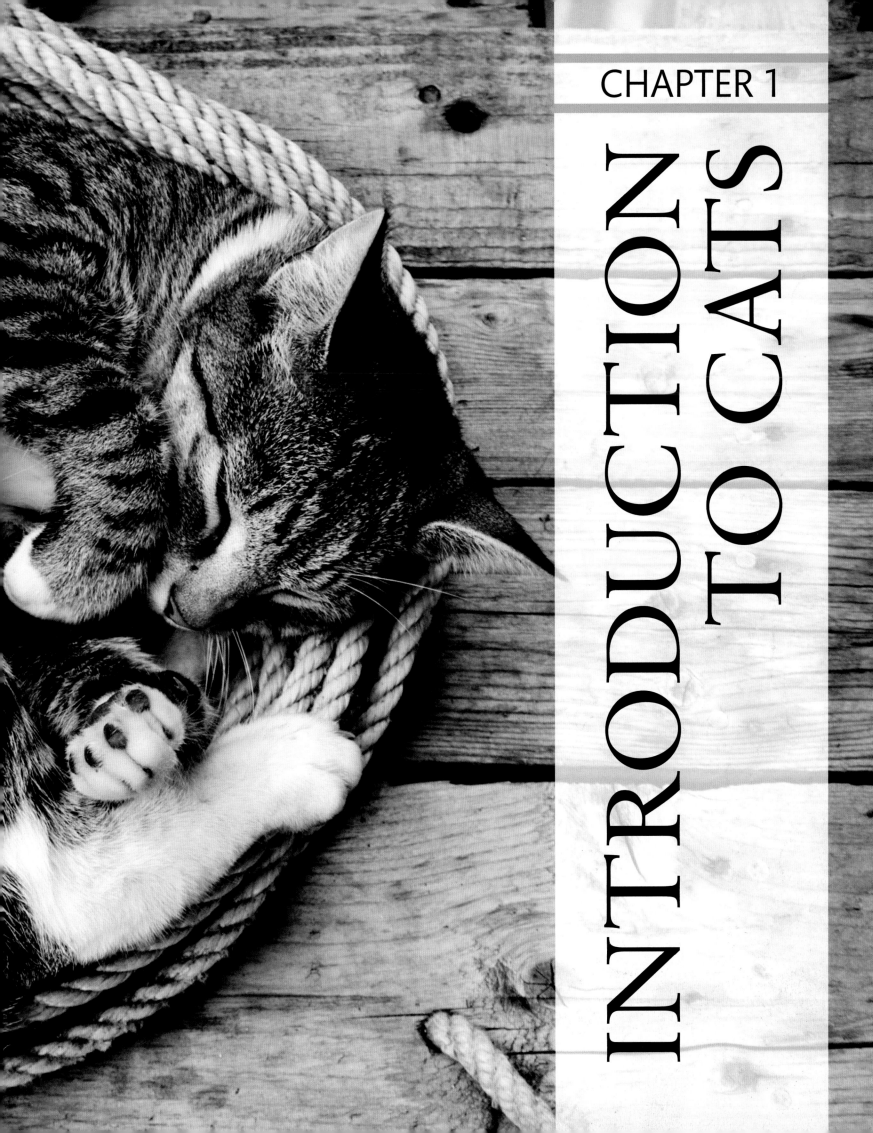

CHAPTER 1

INTRODUCTION TO CATS

Cat species around the world

Elegant, powerful, and elusive, wildcats can be large and may roar like a lion, or small and purr like a domestic cat. They are superb hunters, adapted to be as successful living in a dry sandy desert as they are in a dense tropical forest.

Cats are predatory hunters belonging to the order Carnivora. They are, like all carnivores, adapted for stalking, catching, and eating other animals. For example, they have large canine teeth and powerful jaw muscles.

There are 37 species of cat in the family Felidae. All are similar in having retractile claws, rather blunt, flattened faces, acute hearing, and large eyes that enable them to hunt at night. Those living in open landscapes tend to be sandy colored, while those living in woodland and forest often have spectacular markings that break up their outline and keep them well hidden from their prey.

The cat family is divided into two main groups—the Pantherinae and the Felinae. The pantherines (big cats) have long been distinguished from other cats on the supposition

that they can roar (see panel, below), whereas the smaller cats can only purr. In recent years, genetic evidence has allowed scientists to better understand the relationships between the smaller cats and further subdivide them into seven groups, or lineages.

The world of cats
This map shows the distribution of seven species of the Felinae. Each cat represents one of the seven lineages that has been revealed by recent anatomical and genetic analyses.

Wildcats are successful in evolutionary terms in that they were once widespread and found in many different habitats, but most species are now either endangered or threatened. In contrast, there are an estimated 600 million domestic cats worldwide.

BIG CATS

There are seven species of pantherines, or big cats—the lion, leopard, tiger, snow leopard, two species of clouded leopard, and the jaguar. The lion and leopard have the widest distribution, being found in both Africa and Asia. The tiger, snow and clouded leopards are limited to Asia. The only big cat found in the Americas is the jaguar. Although commonly referred to as the roaring cats, only some, such as lions, can do so. This is because they have more complicated and flexible vocal chords in their larynxes than those found in the smaller cats (see p. 59).

Puma
Puma concolor

The puma is one of three cat species in the puma lineage, the other two being the jaguarundi from South America and the cheetah from Africa and Asia. It is able to survive in remarkably diverse environmental conditions, being found over a wide geographical area and at elevations up to 10,000ft (4,000m). However, it needs large prey, such as deer, to feed on if it is to thrive.

Ocelot
Leopardus pardalis

The ocelot lineage comprises seven species. All belong to the genus *Leopardus* and are found in South and Central America—only the range of the ocelot extends farther north into southwestern Texas. The ocelot feeds mainly on ground-dwelling rodents, which it hunts at night by waiting quietly for a potential victim to pass by.

NORTH AMERICA

SOUTH AMERICA

Eurasian Lynx
Lynx lynx

The lynx lineage is made up of the three species of lynx and the bobcat. The Eurasian lynx is found over most of Eurasia, the Iberian lynx in Spain and Portugal, and the Canadian lynx and bobcat throughout North America. Characterized by their tufted ears and short tails, all feed on rabbits and hares except the Eurasian lynx, which eats small ungulates such as the chamois.

KEY

- — Puma *Puma concolor*
- — Ocelot *Leopardus pardalis*
- — Eurasian Lynx *Lynx lynx*
- — Caracal *Caracal caracal*
- — Marbled cat *Pardofelis marmorata*
- — Leopard cat *Prionailurus bengalensis*
- — Wildcat *Felis silvestris*

Wildcat
Felis silvestris

The domestic cat lineage includes the wildcat and four other *Felis* species. The cats in this group live in Africa and/or Eurasia, but only the wildcat has spread into Western Europe. There are a number of wildcat subspecies, which vary in size and in coat color and pattern. Like many of the smaller cats, the wildcat feeds mainly on rodents but will eat rabbits, reptiles, and amphibians if it can catch them.

Leopard cat
Prionailurus bengalensis

One of five Asian cats comprising this group, the leopard cat has the widest distribution and is the most common of all the small Asian cats, living in forest habitats up to 10,000ft (3,000m) above sea level. Being smaller than a domestic cat, it feeds on a variety of small prey, including rodents, birds, reptiles, amphibians, and invertebrates.

Marbled cat
Pardofelis marmorata

The marbled cat is a forest dweller, as are the bay cat and Asian golden cat that make up this group. As such, it is an excellent climber that feeds predominantly on birds but also catches rodents. Similar in size to a domestic cat, the marbled cat has a very long tail that helps it balance when moving through the trees.

EUROPE

ASIA

AFRICA

AUSTRALASIA

Caracal
Caracal caracal

Found in Africa and western Asia in dry woodland, savanna, and mountains up to 8,000ft (2,500m), the caracal has the widest distribution of the three cats in the caracal group, the serval and African golden cat living only in Africa. The caracal is recognized by its long ear tufts and red or sandy-colored fur. It feeds mostly on small mammals but also catches birds.

What is a cat?

The ancestors of modern cats were much more diverse than today's felines. Big cats were the first to form a distinct group. Smaller cat groups branched out later and at surprising speed. The domestic cat group is the latest addition to the family tree.

The ancestor of the carnivores, or meat-eating mammals, which include the cat family, ate insects and is thought to have resembled a modern tree shrew. It lived more than 65 million years ago during the late Cretaceous period. Called *Cimolestes*, it already showed rudimentary signs of having teeth with a scissorlike cutting action—essential for slicing through flesh and bone—which made it possible to change

from feeding on insects to eating meat. From this tiny animal two groups of carnivorous mammals evolved, both now extinct: the creodonts and the miacids. Creodonts, which appeared first, were the earliest meat-eaters and occupied many of the same ecological niches as would the carnivores yet to come. Later, the miacids took over, and it is from this group that the "true" carnivores, and eventually cats, arose.

EARLY ANCESTORS

The miacids were mammals that lived during the Eocene epoch between 55.8 and 33.9 million years ago. Some were small, weasel-like, predominantly tree-dwelling creatures, while others were more cat- or doglike and spent more time on the ground. The miacids evolved into the first "true" carnivores, which appeared about 48 million years ago and can be divided into two

THE EARLY EVOLUTION OF MODERN CATS

This branching diagram shows how the early meat-eating mammals were derived from insectivores and subsequently gave rise to the ancestral carnivores (viverravines) that evolved into the modern cats. It is superimposed on

a geological timeline to show the sequential appearance of each group and the time periods in which they lived and became extinct. The creodonts, for example, appeared during the late Paleocene and became extinct in the

mid to late Miocene, outliving the miacids by a considerable margin. Extant felids are shown here as a single line—details of the groups within the modern cats and their relationships are shown on p. 12.

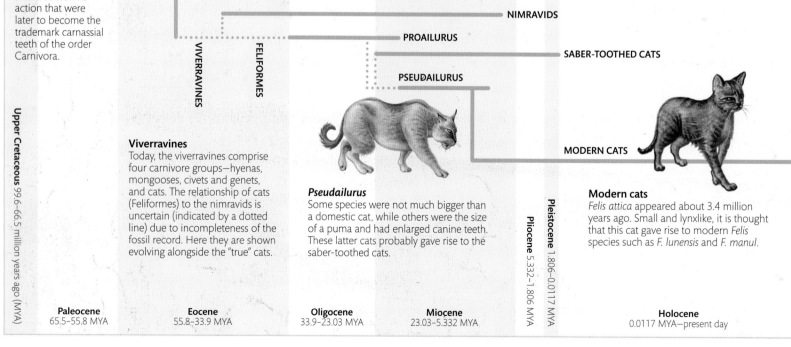

CREODONTS

CIMOLESTES

Cimolestes
This insectivorous mammal was the first to display laterally flattened cheek teeth with a scissorlike action that were later to become the trademark carnassial teeth of the order Carnivora.

MIACIDS

Miacids
This group of mammals is important mainly because some species had features that were characteristic of the doglike carnivores (not shown on this diagram), while others were more catlike and gave rise to the viverravines.

Creodonts
Once thought to be ancestors of the carnivores, creodonts are now known to have evolved differently. They lack the fused wrist bones of carnivores and there are differences in their carnassial teeth.

NIMRAVIDS

PROAILURUS

SABER-TOOTHED CATS

PSEUDAILURUS

VIVERRAVINES

FELIFORMES

Viverravines
Today, the viverravines comprise four carnivore groups—hyenas, mongooses, civets and genets, and cats. The relationship of cats (Feliformes) to the nimravids is uncertain (indicated by a dotted line) due to incompleteness of the fossil record. Here they are shown evolving alongside the "true" cats.

Pseudailurus
Some species were not much bigger than a domestic cat, while others were the size of a puma and had enlarged canine teeth. These latter cats probably gave rise to the saber-toothed cats.

MODERN CATS

Modern cats
Felis attica appeared about 3.4 million years ago. Small and lynxlike, it is thought that this cat gave rise to modern *Felis* species such as *F. lunensis* and *F. manul*.

Upper Cretaceous 99.6–66.5 million years ago (MYA)

Pliocene 5.332–1.806 MYA

Pleistocene 1.806–0.0117 MYA

| Paleocene 65.5–55.8 MYA | Eocene 55.8–33.9 MYA | Oligocene 33.9–23.03 MYA | Miocene 23.03–5.332 MYA | Holocene 0.0117 MYA–present day |

NIMRAVIDS

Also known as false saber-tooths, the nimravids were catlike mammals that lived alongside the ancestors of modern cats. Although they had retractile claws, nimravids differed from "true" cats in the shape of the skull. They first appeared during the Eocene, about 36 million years ago, when woodland covered large areas of North America and Eurasia. As the climate became drier during the Miocene, trees gave way to grassland and nimravid numbers declined. They became extinct in the late Miocene about five million years ago.

Nimravid skull
Hoplophoneus was a genus of nimravid that lived during the Oligocene epoch about 33 to 23 million years ago.

SABER-TOOTHED CATS

Since the time of the primitive cat-ancestor *Cimolestes* in the late Cretaceous, saber-toothed carnivores have arisen on three occasions in three different carnivore groups. The earliest were the creodonts, followed by the nimravids, and finally the saber-toothed cats, including *Smilodon*. None of these are considered to be directly ancestral to the cats living today.

Saber-toothed cats appeared at the start of the Miocene and survived until about 11,000 years ago, which meant that they would have been known to early humans. They had impressive, backward curving canine teeth in the upper jaw that were so long—up to 6in (15cm)—they ran down the sides of the lower jaw outside the mouth when it was closed. To be able to use these teeth effectively, saber-toothed cats had an enormous gape—they could open their mouths about 120 degrees. The "sabers" broke more easily than other teeth because they were so large, but their serrated edges could be used for cutting through tough hide or biting off chunks of flesh.

No one knows why the saber-toothed cats became extinct. Some scientists think a decline in prey led to their demise but there is evidence to refute this. Others suggest

groups. One group, the Old World viverravines, subsequently gave rise to the nimravids, or "false" saber-tooth cats (see panel, above), and the catlike carnivores (including hyenas, civets, and mongooses). The second group, the New World miacines, eventually gave rise to the doglike carnivores, including wolves and bears.

THE FIRST REAL CATS

One of the earliest ancestors of our modern cats is considered to be a meat-eating mammal named *Proailurus* (meaning "before cats"), which appeared in what is now Eurasia during the Oligocene epoch 34–23 million years ago. Little is known about *Proailurus*, but fossil remains show that it was not much larger than a domestic cat and had short legs, a long body and tail, and claws that could have been at least partially retracted. It would have been adept at climbing and probably stalked its prey among the trees.

About 20 million years ago, *Proailurus*, or another species very like it, gave rise to *Pseudailurus* ("pseudo-cat"), a predator considered to be the first of the true cats. More terrestrial than its predecessor, *Pseudailurus* had a long, flexible back and hind legs longer than its forelegs. This early cat is important for two reasons. First, it gave rise to three groups of cats. These comprise the two modern groups—Pantherinae, which includes the big cats, and Felinae, among

which are the smaller wild cats and the domestic cat—and also the now extinct saber-toothed cats (Machairodontinae). Second, *Pseudailurus* was the first cat to migrate to what is now North America by crossing over the Bering land bridge that for a time linked Alaska with Siberia.

In the warmer, drier climate of the Miocene—the epoch following the Oligocene, 23–5.3 million years ago—environmental changes favored the descendants of *Pseudailurus*. The decline of forest ecosystems and an increase in more open habitats such as grassland allowed hoofed mammals to diversify—and so the cats that hunted them diversified, too.

Big bite
About the size of a lion, *Smilodon* was a saber-toothed cat that lived in North America. A hunter of large, slow-moving prey, such as the bison and mammoth, it became extinct about 10,000 years ago.

that they were unable to compete with the more recently evolved pantherines and cheetahs, with which they latterly coexisted. Certainly, the newer cats were swifter hunters and possessed teeth less vulnerable to breaking.

BRANCHING OUT

Among carnivores, the cat family Felidae are the most accomplished killers and are highly specialized anatomically for this purpose. Some species are capable of killing prey larger than themselves. The big cats, or pantherine branch—large, impressive, fast, and ferocious—appeared at least 10.8 million years ago. Later branches gave rise first to the bay cat group in Africa 9.4 million years ago followed by the caracal group in Africa 8.5 million years ago. The ocelot group, which arose about 8 million years ago, crossed into South America when the Panamanian land bridge was formed. This highway permitted small cats from North and Central America (now known only from fossil remains) to migrate and diversify there. Nine of the 10 living cat species of South America belong to the ocelot group, which are unusual in having 36 chromosomes (18 pairs) rather than the more usual felid number of 38.

The lynx group and the puma group evolved 7.2 and 6.7 million years ago respectively and contain species from different continents, suggesting a number of different migrations. These cats include the cheetah, which originated from the puma lineage in North America and subsequently crossed into Asia and Africa where it survives today. The leopard cat and domestic cat groups are the most recent additions to the cat family and both are restricted to Eurasia. The first modern *Felis* species is thought to be *Felis lunensis*, which appeared about 2.5 million years ago during the Pliocene period. It later gave rise to the wildcat *Felis sylvestris*, of which the European strain is the oldest, dating back about 250,000 years. It migrated anywhere that had a suitable habitat and prey to sustain it. The African wildcat, *Felis silvestris lybica*, became distinct about 20,000 years ago and it is from these cats that the domestic cat came into being, probably around 8,000 years ago.

CAVE LIONS

The European cave lion (*Panthera spelaea*) was probably the largest cat that ever lived. Twenty-five percent larger than modern lions, this formidable hunter stood over 4ft (1.25m) at the shoulder. It was one of the most common predators of its time, using its relatively long legs to run down horses, deer, and other large, hoofed animals. The cave lion appeared in Europe about 400,000 years ago and survived there until about 12,000 years ago, toward the end of the last ice age. Similar large cats were known from North America and are thought to have descended from European cave lions that migrated across the Bering land bridge to Alaska.

THE CAT FAMILY

The small and medium-sized cats (Felinae) diversified rapidly in geological terms—taking only about 3.2 million years. The pantherines, or big cats, had branched off at least 1.4 million years earlier. Recent genetic analysis has revealed that

Felinae fall into seven distinct groups, as the diagram shows. The most recently evolved domestic cat and leopard cat groups are seen at the top, the earliest bay cat group just above the pantherines. The domestic and leopard cat groups are more closely

related to one another than either is to the older groups below. The "kink" in the domestic cat line indicates the appearance of *Felis attica* 3.4 million years ago, from which the modern *Felis* species, and therefore the domestic cat, have evolved.

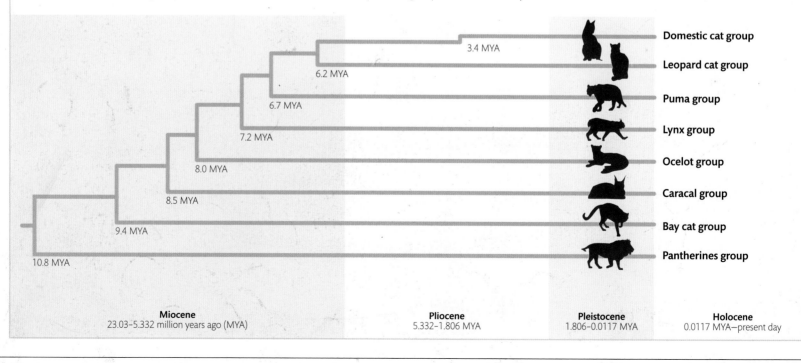

		Group
3.4 MYA		Domestic cat group
6.2 MYA		Leopard cat group
6.7 MYA		Puma group
7.2 MYA		Lynx group
8.0 MYA		Ocelot group
8.5 MYA		Caracal group
9.4 MYA		Bay cat group
10.8 MYA		Pantherines group

Miocene
23.03–5.332 million years ago (MYA)

Pliocene
5.332–1.806 MYA

Pleistocene
1.806–0.0117 MYA

Holocene
0.0117 MYA—present day

Ancestral cat
This African wildcat (*Felis silvestris lybica*) crouching in the grass on a hunting mission, is the final link in the chain between the domestic cat and its prehistoric, and now extinct, ancestors.

From wildcat to house cat

The story of the cat's domestication is one of mutual appreciation, not servitude: early farming communities benefitted from cats' rodent-catching skills, while cats won themselves protection and shelter without losing their independence.

Our relationship with cats reaches back thousands of years, although compared to the domestication of other animals, that of the cat was a somewhat random process. For example, people readily appreciated the advantages of owning horses, cattle, and dogs, because they could be turned to practical use. Through selection of the best specimens and careful breeding for certain traits, such animals were developed for specific purposes and became even more useful. When the first cats wandered in from the wild—because it suited them to live in close proximity to human settlements—they proved their worth as vermin hunters, but they were most probably not otherwise seen as valuable assets.

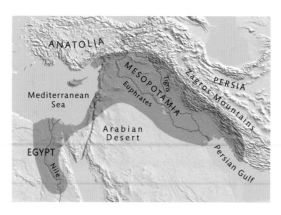

A cat did not provide substantial amounts of meat for food, and although it could be tamed and become accustomed to handling, it could not be trained to obey orders or perform tasks on demand. In the early

Origins of domestication
The ancient region known as the Fertile Crescent, which sweeps in an arc from the Nile to the Persian Gulf, was where the domestication of cats is believed to have originated. This region also corresponds to part of the natural range of the African wildcat, the ancestor of all domestic cats.

history of the cat there are no obvious attempts at deliberate selection for quality or to "improve" behavior or appearance. In fact, the first true house cats probably selected themselves, when some learned to trust people more easily than others and felt secure enough to rear their kittens under a roof shared with humans.

EARLIEST LINKS

Until quite recently, accounts of the history of the domestic cat generally agreed that the earliest evidence of feline cohabitation with humans could be dated to ancient Egyptian societies around 4,000 years ago. However, discoveries in the last few years hint at a much earlier link between cats and people.

In the early 2000s, archeologists excavating a Neolithic village in Cyprus came across a burial site containing the complete skeleton of a cat alongside human remains. As the grave contained various valuable objects such as stone tools and other artifacts, it appeared that the person had been interred with some ceremony. Researchers concluded that the cat, estimated to be about eight months old, was likely to have been deliberately killed and buried because it had some

Cat with tabby markings

Part of the family
A tabby cat appears in a painting (c.1350 BCE) from the tomb-chapel of a minor Egyptian official, Nebamun, shown hunting in the Nile marshes. By this era in Egypt, cats were firmly established as family pets.

special significance. If this is the case, the evidence that people kept cats, either as status symbols or pets, takes a major leap backward to 7500 BCE. The Cyprus cat is similar to the domestic cat's ancestor, the African wildcat, *Felis silvestris lybica* (see p. 9 and pp. 12–13). If it did belong to this species, it was not native to the island and so must have been taken there.

Archeologists have also recently disinterred the bones of small felines at the site of a 5,000-year-old arable farming settlement in central China. Detailed analysis of the bones suggested that the cats had preyed on grain-eating rodents, so they clearly had some association with the human community, although whether by chance or because they had been tamed is impossible to establish.

Fascinating though they are, these newest finds are a long way from representing conclusive proof that the domestication of the cat is an older story than originally believed. However, it is likely that the domestication of the cat progressed through a number of unsuccessful starts.

MOVING INDOORS

Cats probably first put a paw into domestic life when humans made the switch from being hunter-gatherers to being farmers. Growing crops meant storing grain, and granaries attracted swarms of rodents

Personal appeal
Eventually, the cats that came in from the wild lost their distrust of people and took up permanent residence around human settlements. Their appeal as pets and playthings would have helped them gain entry into homes.

DOMESTICATING BIG CATS

Out of all the big cat species, only the cheetah has proved possible to domesticate to any extent. Both the ancient Egyptians and the Assyrians kept tame cheetahs and used them for hunting, as centuries later did the Mogul emperors in India. These beautiful animals can be remarkably tractable when habituated to people—the huntsmen of old trained them to accept a collar and leash, and to return to the huntsmen when the chase was over. However, even among those with the means to keep them, cheetahs never became widespread as pets. This is most probably because until recently people did not understand their breeding behavior well enough for them to reproduce successfully in captivity. Replacement animals were always sourced from the wild and therefore never developed the temperament of domestic pets that are born and raised by people over many generations.

EMPEROR AKBAR OF INDIA, HUNTING WITH CHEETAHS

ready to feast on this new bonanza of food. In turn, this provided an inexhaustible supply of easily caught prey for local populations of wildcats.

The modern house cat has its origins in the very birthplace of agriculture, a swathe of richly productive farmlands known as the Fertile Crescent that extends from the Nile Valley up to the eastern Mediterranean and then southward to the Persian Gulf (see map, opposite). When, more than 2000 years BCE, the ancient Egyptians established the earliest-known organized agricultural societies along the banks of the Nile, the African wildcats of the region were ready to fill a new niche.

Most of the cats that began to visit the Fertile Crescent farming communities would have been small spotted tabbies, very much like many of today's household pets. Although initially these cats arrived

uninvited, eventually farmers began to realize the benefits of having on-site rodent control. The popular theory is that people actively encouraged cats to take up residence in their grain stores by tempting them with food scraps. From there, it is easy to imagine how the increasingly socialized cats would have moved into the house.

Sheltered from the hazards of the wild, including larger predators, cats could now breed prolifically and their offspring had a better chance of surviving to maturity.

A litter of kittens born in a domestic environment, and most likely petted from a very young age, could with little difficulty be absorbed into a family as pets.

As Egyptian civilization rose, so did the status of Egyptian cats, whose eventual progression from household mouser to sacred icon is well recorded in paintings, statues, and mummified remains (see pp. 24–25). However, until cats started to spread out of the Fertile Crescent from about 500 BCE (see pp. 18–19), the concept of the cat as a truly domesticated animal did not extend beyond this region.

Wildcat litter
Although they look like domestic tabbies, these young Indian Desert Cats (*Felis silvestris*) are truly wild. The species has a range that extends from Central Asia to northeast India.

How domestic cats spread

Cats are world citizens and have come a long way from their roots in North Africa and the eastern Mediterranean. While cats do not respect boundaries, and some early house cats probably moved independently, they have mostly traveled where humans have taken them. Even in areas where their wild counterparts have never occurred— such as Australia—domestic cats seem to have effortlessly adopted a new niche.

For more than two millennia, domestic cats remained almost entirely exclusive to Egypt (see pp. 14–15). Here, they became so revered that their export to other countries was, in theory at least, strictly banned. But, with their strongly independent natures, domesticated or at least semi-domesticated Egyptian cats most likely drifted away into other regions. They are thought to have roamed along the trade routes of the Mediterranean, reaching Greece, the region that is now Iraq, and possibly even Europe.

OUT OF EGYPT

When domestic cats first started their world travels in any significant numbers, which seems to have been around 2,500 years ago, their main exit route from the Fertile Crescent, and Egypt in particular, was via the ships of the Phoenicians. It is speculated that this nation of seafarers and colonizers, who for centuries dominated maritime trade in the eastern Mediterranean, may in fact have started transporting cats, tame or otherwise, at a much earlier date.

The cats of ancient Egypt were valuable commodities. The Phoenicians acquired them—perhaps through barter or by smuggling them on board, or even as stowaways—and carried them for sale or exchange on their commercial voyages along the sea routes to Spain, Italy, and the Mediterranean islands. Later, when the Silk Road opened up communications between Asia and Europe, cats went both east and west with merchant adventurers. The ancient Egyptians themselves may have

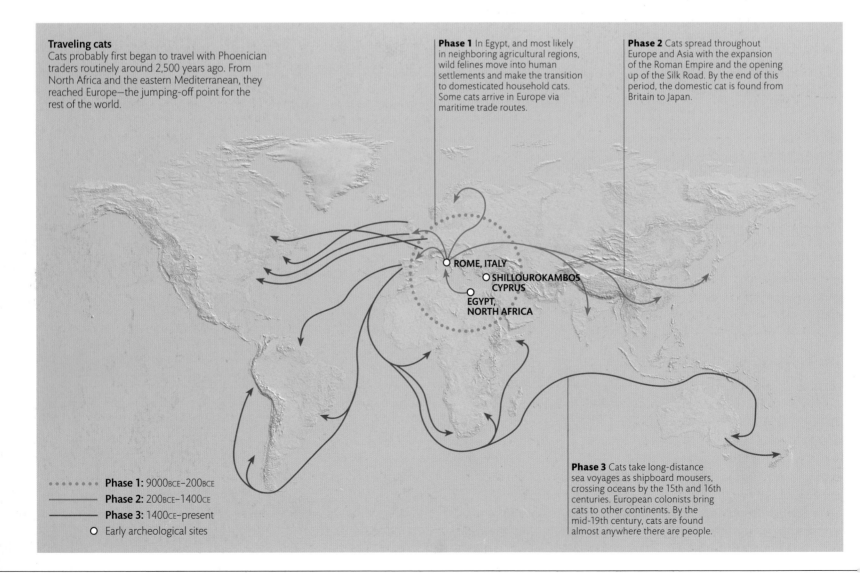

Traveling cats
Cats probably first began to travel with Phoenician traders routinely around 2,500 years ago. From North Africa and the eastern Mediterranean, they reached Europe—the jumping-off point for the rest of the world.

Phase 1 In Egypt, and most likely in neighboring agricultural regions, wild felines move into human settlements and make the transition to domesticated household cats. Some cats arrive in Europe via maritime trade routes.

Phase 2 Cats spread throughout Europe and Asia with the expansion of the Roman Empire and the opening up of the Silk Road. By the end of this period, the domestic cat is found from Britain to Japan.

ROME, ITALY

SHILLOUROKAMBOS CYPRUS

EGYPT, NORTH AFRICA

Phase 3 Cats take long-distance sea voyages as shipboard mousers, crossing oceans by the 15th and 16th centuries. European colonists bring cats to other continents. By the mid-19th century, cats are found almost anywhere there are people.

· · · · · · **Phase 1:** 9000BCE–200BCE
———— **Phase 2:** 200BCE–1400CE
———— **Phase 3:** 1400CE–present
O Early archeological sites

SHIPS' CATS

Cats got where they are today largely by sea travel. From ancient times, when they first left Egypt, they crossed vast distances on ships taking merchants, colonists, and adventurers around the world. Cats were sometimes carried as trade items, but more often as vermin controllers. Wherever people disembarked in new lands, so did the cats. The tradition of a ship's cat continues today only among private sailors. Modern commercial and naval vessels no longer permit cats like "Stripey," seen below on board the British Royal Navy warship HMS *Warspite* in the 1940s.

perhaps presented some of their cats as prestigious gifts to Chinese emperors or to the Romans, who were becoming increasingly powerful in northern Africa.

After domestic cats reached Rome, the advance of the Roman Empire carried them even farther throughout Western Europe. By the end of the Roman Empire, cats were probably widespread in Britain, where they were to enjoy hundreds of years of peaceful coexistence with people until they fell out of favor in the Middle Ages (see pp. 24–27).

ON TO THE NEW WORLD

With the beginning of the great voyages of discovery and colonization that set out from Europe from the 15th century onward, domestic cats crossed the Atlantic for the first time. Taken on board sailing ships to control infestations of rodents, they had ample time on the long sea passages to the Americas to produce kittens. When they arrived at ports of call, many of these burgeoning cat families simply jumped ship,

or were perhaps traded with local communities, while others accompanied pioneering settlers into the interior of the New World.

In the opposite direction, cats headed for Australia on convict ships and alongside colonists. There is a possibly apocryphal story that the first cats to reach Australia were in fact survivors of a Dutch shipwreck in the mid-17th century.

RISE OF THE INTERNATIONAL CAT

By the middle of the 19th century, domestic cats could be found on almost every sizeable landmass in the world and had diversified into distinct types. In Europe and the United States, the import of exotic-looking cats such as the Siamese and Turkish Angora stimulated much interest, and people began to see the taken-for-granted farmyard mouser or house pet in a new light. For almost the first time since the days of the ancient Egyptians, the cat was about to be once again a prized possession and a status symbol.

Like-minded owners began to form cat clubs, where they could enthuse about their particular favorites and argue the merits of one type over another. These cat fanciers—or the "cat fancy" as they came to be known—organized shows that engendered much rivalry and endless competition to produce better-quality cats that conformed to ever-more precise specifications.

The serious breeding of pedigree cats and the perfection of breed standards triggered a new phase of international travel for cats. As getting around the world became easier from the mid-20th century onward, cat enthusiasts, and even ordinary tourists, discovered "new" breeds—for example, the Turkish Van or the bobtailed cats from Japan—that had in fact been developing over many centuries in rarely visited areas. Brought back to the United States and the UK, such cats were used to start enthusiastic breeding programs and transatlantic exchanges. Cats have even been highly

Migrating mutation
The polydactyl (extra-toed) cats common along the east coast of the United States may be descended from those taken across the Atlantic to Boston by 17th-century English Puritan colonists.

mobile within their native countries, moving from relative obscurity in a particular area to nationwide popularity and then—for example, the Devon Rex or the Maine Coon—achieving international recognition.

In the 21st century, cats are still passing back and forth across the Atlantic as one exotic breed after another becomes fashionable. Crosses between such novelties have produced yet further variations. As some of these become recognized outside their country of origin—and not all are—the global migration of cats continues. One of the most recent developments has been a return to the original wildcat template, with breeders creating spotted cats not unlike those that 4,000 years ago became the first pet felines. The domestic cat's extensive travels could be said to have brought it back to its starting point.

Transatlantic cat
One of the modern results of cats interchanging countries, the Elf is a hybrid created by crossing the hairless Sphynx, which originated in Canada and was developed in the Netherlands, with the American Curl.

Feral cats

Cats of domestic descent that have known little or no human contact, or former pets that have become homeless for various reasons, are termed "feral." Although feral cats live in a wild state, they have no relationship to the true wildcat species found throughout the world.

Being resourceful animals, cats that have strayed or been abandoned by their owners often manage to survive on their own once they have reverted to the wild. Most have highly developed hunting instincts that allow them to subsist on small prey such as birds and rodents, and many supplement their diets by scavenging or accepting food handouts from sympathetic cat lovers. Such cats usually learn to become wary of humans, but because they still have a background of domesticity it is sometimes possible to rehabilitate them.

Truly feral cats, which are born wild and never handled, are difficult if not impossible to domesticate as adults. Feral kittens, if rescued at a very early age, can sometimes be socialized with time and patience; but even at a few weeks old they have a natural distrust of humans and may already be beyond the stage where this can be overcome.

STICKING TOGETHER

The majority of domestic cats lead solitary lives and resent or fear competition for food, territory, and shelter. However, two or more cats that share a home can become friends, especially if they are littermates. Others, at best, cease hostilities and settle down together with indifference. Among feral cats there is a much greater degree of sociability. Because food supplies can be scarce and unreliable, any feral cats within one area tend to be drawn to a common food source, such as a garbage dump, a feeding station organized by cat welfare organizations, or an empty building overrun by rats and mice. Out of necessity, these cats tolerate each other and will share resources with minimal aggression.

Where a few feral cats have found shelter, a colony can build up, which over the years can amount to dozens of animals of several interrelated generations. Any unneutered females attract toms—entire males—and frequent matings produce two or more litters of kittens a year for each female.

Established colonies are very much matriarchal societies, with a core population of females that often form close bonds. Female cats have been observed sharing birth dens and cooperatively nursing and raising litters of kittens, taking turns guarding the family when one of the mothers goes out hunting. Feral females have even been known to present a combined front

Among the ruins
A feral cat crouches against the backdrop of the ancient Ionian city of Ephesus, in what is now western Turkey. As a source of titbits, tourist hot spots such as this tend to attract feral cat colonies.

Respite from hunger
These cats lining the waterfront of a Greek harbor may thrive in the summer months, when there are fish scraps to be had from fishing boats, and tourists provide handouts or leave edible garbage. Their lives will be much harder during the winter months.

Farmyard haven
Although they will never be family pets, feral barn cats depend on shelter and human concern for their welfare. The provision of basic care encourages them to stay and help control rodents.

to fight off marauding toms, which are a constant peril with their desire to kill off kittens and so bring the females back into season for further matings.

As a feral colony expands, the dynamic within it changes, with stronger toms ousting weaker rivals that then either hang around the periphery of the group or strike out on their own to find more congenial territory. Occasionally, males born within a colony do become accepted by the senior members simply because of their familiarity, but a strange tom attempting to infiltrate the group is usually rejected vigorously.

CONTROL OF COLONIES

Life in a feral cat colony is hard and tends to be short. While well-cared-for pet cats often live into their teens, a feral cat is lucky to survive beyond about three or four years. Diseases are common and spread rapidly. Nutrition is often inadequate, and as the colony grows there is less food for everyone.

ENVIRONMENTAL THREAT

With the total population of feral cats worldwide estimated at around 100 million, conservationists are concerned about the effect colonies have on local wildlife. Islands are especially high-risk environments, with species such as ground-nesting birds being hunted by cats to the point of extinction. This was nearly the case with the kakapo, a rare flightless parrot native to New Zealand, which was all but wiped out by introduced domestic predators such as cats and ferrets. The few remaining birds, although still critically endangered, are now protected in island sanctuaries that are entirely cat free.

Females weakened by continual breeding are particularly vulnerable and may die, leaving sick and abandoned kittens. Traffic accidents and fighting among rival toms lead to injuries and infections (see pp. 304–05) that never receive treatment.

Most countries now have a policy of managing feral cat colonies, both for humane reasons and to prevent them from becoming an environmental problem. As a more acceptable alternative to wholesale eradication, many cat rescue organizations or animal welfare societies have put a three-part program into practice. This involves trapping the cats without causing injury, neutering them (and ear-tagging them for future identification), and returning them to the colony. Unfortunately, this often proves to be a temporary solution. The numbers of feral cats may fall for a time, but eventually unneutered cats will join the community and even a single breeding pair can restock the colony within a year.

BARN CATS

In rural areas, feral cats are sometimes welcomed by farmers and other landowners as low-maintenance providers of rodent control in stables, barns, and feed stores. Some cat adoption centers have exploited this by offering farmers feral cats that they have collected and taken into care.

Neutering program
While a sedated feral cat is prepared for surgery, a vet shaves an ear ready to cut a small notch that identifies the animal as neutered. On recovery, the cat will be taken back to its home colony.

Properly managed, such programs can be a satisfactory solution to the problem of feral colonies that have become too large or need to be relocated because of health issues. Although the animals concerned are not regarded as pets, the people who "adopt" them must agree to provide minimum shelter, a small daily amount of cat food to augment whatever prey is taken by hunting, and veterinary care if necessary.

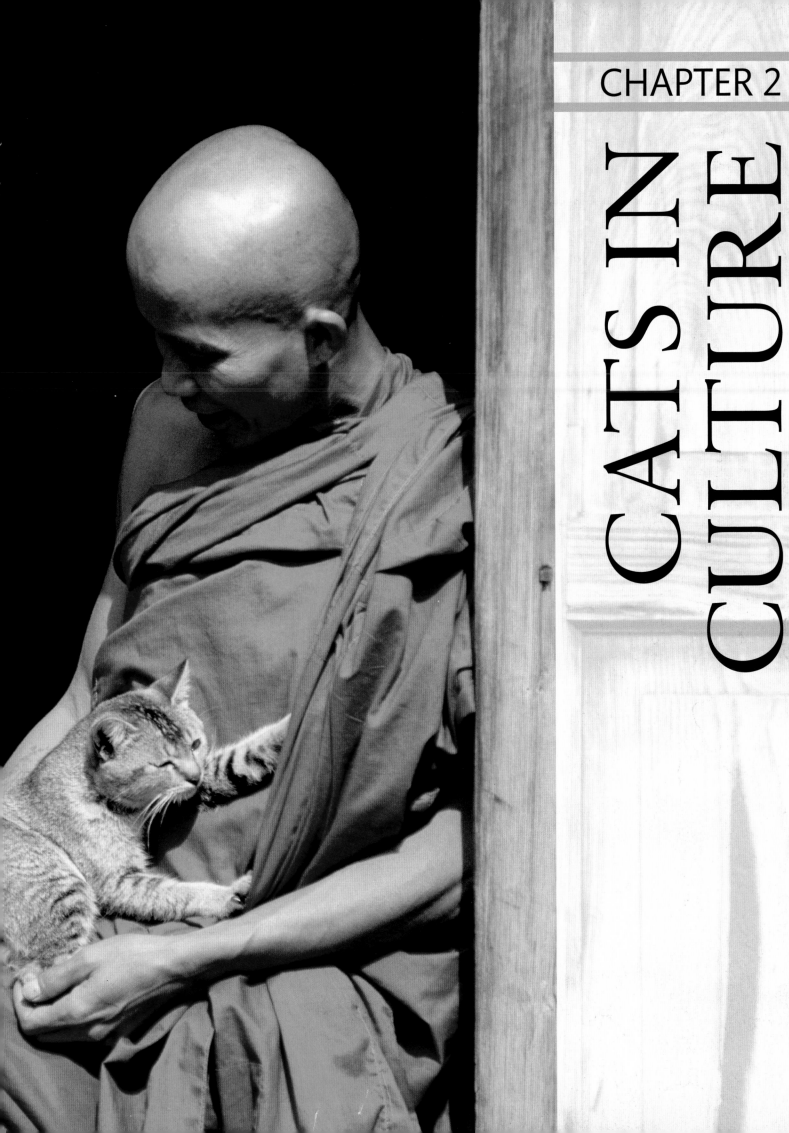

CHAPTER 2

CATS IN CULTURE

Cats in religion

Whether revered, reviled, or simply ignored, cats have in general not been served well by religious beliefs. Being regarded as sacred animals in pagan religions of the past may have placed cats among the gods, but for millions of them it also guaranteed a sacrificial death. With the rise of Christianity it became even more dangerous for cats. Linked with devil worship, cats in Europe were nearly eradicated in the Middle Ages by the Church's campaign of persecution.

EGYPTIAN GODDESS

The earliest historical records linking cats with religion date back thousands of years to ancient Egypt. From around 1500BCE, a cult associated with the cat-goddess Bastet (also known as Bast) began to gain ground. Bastet, originally worshiped as a lion-goddess, achieved enormous popularity in her gentler form and had a devoted following, particularly among women. In statues she was usually represented as a cat-headed woman, sometimes surrounded by a group of small cats or kittens. It is likely that the extreme veneration with which ancient Egyptians came to regard cats had its origins in the Bastet cult.

When a family

Mummified cat c.1st century CE
The preserved bodies of cats, intricately wrapped in linen strips and topped with a head mask, were commonly sold at ancient Egyptian temples as offerings to the cat-goddess Bastet.

cat died, the owners went into extravagant mourning and, if they were wealthy enough, buried their mummified and decorated pet in an elaborate sarcophagus. Anyone who killed a cat, even by accident, risked being put to death.

Paradoxically, such reverence did not stop the mass slaughter of cats for religious reasons. Alongside numerous statuettes of symbolic cats, archeological excavations at ancient Egyptian sites turned up huge cat cemeteries containing mummified cats in their hundreds of thousands. X-ray examination of some of the bodies showed that the cats were young, hardly more than kittens, and had died from broken necks. These were clearly not household pets but victims of deliberate slaughter. Various studies have come to the conclusion that the cats would have been kept by temple priests specifically for sacrificial killing and mummification, then sold to pilgrims as offerings to the gods.

SACRED ICONS

Outside Egypt, cats never achieved comparable religious status, although they have appeared in subsidiary roles in some belief systems. The goddess Freya in the Norse pantheon was

Freya's chariot cats
Norse goddess of love and fertility, Freya had a particular affinity with cats. Modern breeders like to associate the powerful pair that pulled her chariot with today's Norwegian Forest Cat (see pp. 222–23).

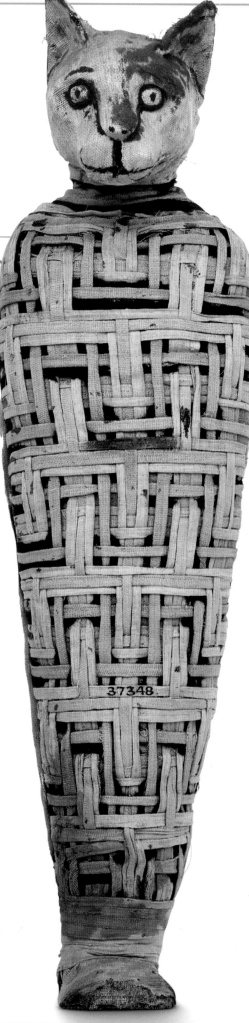

37348.

Walking with lions
In this late-Victorian painting by Sir William Blake Richmond, Venus, the Roman goddess of love, walks with a lion and lioness and turns winter into spring as she passes.

a cat lover and drove a chariot pulled by two enormous gray cats that had been given to her as a gift by Thor, the god of thunder. The ancient Romans were said to be great respecters of cats, the only animals allowed to enter their temples, and sometimes gave them preferential treatment as household gods, symbols of home and safety.

In the Americas, pre-Columbian civilizations knew nothing of domestic cats, which had yet to cross the Atlantic, but some of their deities were associated with big cats. Both the Mayans and the Incas worshiped gods who took the form of jaguars. In today's major religions, cats as sacred icons remain few and far between. One exception is the Hindu goddess Shashthi, worshiped as a protector of children, who is often depicted riding a cat. In some branches of Buddhism, the soul of someone who has attained great spirituality is said on death to enter the body of a cat. There is also an old tradition of cats, especially white ones, being kept by Buddhist monks as temple guardians.

Peruvian puma
This gold artifact depicting a puma had religious significance for the Moche people of Peru, whose society flourished between about 100 and 800CE. Puma gods were common to many early American cultures.

CHRISTIAN PERSECUTION
Unlike many other animals, cats are not mentioned anywhere in the Bible, either for good or evil. In a rare positive association between cats and Christianity, the 7th-century St. Gertrude, abbess of a Benedictine order near Brussels, is regarded as the patron saint of cats; she is sometimes portrayed holding a cat—or surrounded by mice. There is some evidence that Gertrude, presumably thanks to her cats, had a reputation for keeping her abbey miraculously free of mice in an age plagued with vermin. Another happy association is the charming legend that a cat with its litter of kittens was present in the stable at the birth of Jesus,

and was marked with an "M" on its forehead—the classic coat pattern seen in tabby cats—when the Madonna stroked it. The Christian Church's centuries-long, well documented prejudice against cats was probably at least partly driven by a determination to stamp out the remnants of earlier pagan beliefs. Church authorities viewed cats as agents of the Devil, especially when they were kept by people believed to be witches (see pp.26–27), and dealt with them mercilessly—maiming, torturing, hanging, and burning were among the cruelties sanctioned. Persecution of cats reached its height in the Middle Ages and continued, astonishingly, into early modern times.

ISLAMIC BLESSING
Historically, out of all their connections with religions, cats have had the greatest acceptance in Muslim cultures, where treating animals with kindness is an

Temple resident
Many Buddhist temples swarm with street cats like this one, which has found a home at Wat Phra Yai, near Pattaya in Thailand. Such animals are highly respected by the monks, who provide them with food and shelter.

important part of Islamic teaching. The Prophet Muhammad, whose revelations in the 7th century form the text of the Holy Koran, set an example—there are many reports of the care and respect he gave to his own pets. In an Islamic version of the origins of the tabby forehead marking, the "M" is said to have been left by the Prophet's touch.

Myths and superstition

Cats are enigmatic animals and there is a touch of magic about them. For people in the past, the magic was real, and the traits and behaviors that amuse and puzzle the owners of today's indulged pets were once seen as unearthly, often malign. Myths and superstitions about cats, with countless variations, have had a wide currency and a long life, some lingering into modern times. Few countries do not have a tradition of an unlucky (or lucky) black cat.

WITCH'S FAMILIAR

Prowlers of the night—appearing and disappearing in the blink of an eye—cats were long believed to be supernatural creatures that walked with ghosts and evil spirits. The association of cats, particularly black ones, with the forces of darkness was widespread throughout medieval times and lasted into the 18th century. Many a harmless old woman who kept a cat for company was suspected of being a witch; it was believed that every witch had a "familiar"—a demon servant in the form of a small animal, perhaps a toad or a hare, or an owl, but often a cat. Even more alarming, an animal could be a shape-shifting witch in disguise, so it was prudent to guard your tongue in the presence of a strange cat. In Europe, millions of cats suffered the same hideous fate as anyone accused of witchcraft, being subjected to trial by torture and burned alive if found guilty.

LUCKY FOR SOME

Superstitions about black—or in some cultures, white—cats as omens of either good or ill fortune are surprisingly persistent throughout much of the world. The beliefs are often contradictory, varying

Bad reputation
In medieval Europe, cats were believed to be either witches in disguise or magical spirits working as intermediaries in the service of witches. Fear and distrust led to their wholesale slaughter.

from one country or region to another, and can involve complicated conventions. For example, just the way a person encounters a black cat can matter: whether it crosses someone's path from right to left, or vice versa, may make all the difference between a good day and a bad one. And while being approached by the cat brings luck, fortune takes a turn for the worse if the cat stalks off in the opposite direction.

For the superstitious, in some parts of Europe and in the United States black cats are unlucky. Many US rescue centers find it difficult to find them homes. In Britain, black cats are considered lucky, much in favor as a subject for wedding-day keepsakes such as beribboned charms or whimsical ornaments.

Japan is another country where black cats signify good luck, although here they take second place to the much-loved, multicoloured icon Maneki Neko—the "beckoning" cat. Ceramic figurines of this cat, with its doll-like face and raised paw, fill souvenir shops and are commonly placed in doorways to welcome visitors. According to legend, the original Maneki Neko was a temple cat that invited a passing feudal lord to come in and take shelter, thereby saving him from being caught in a violent storm.

REMARKABLE MAGIC POWERS

There are numerous myths linking cats with the weather. It is said that a cat will raise a storm by clawing at the furniture, and can predict rain by sneezing or washing behind his ears. Some of these tales may have originated with sailors, who not only need to keep a constant eye on the weather but also have a long-held reputation for being highly superstitious. Traditionally, seafarers kept a cat on board the ship for protection against the elements. Japanese mariners thought tortoiseshell cats worked best for giving advance warning of storms. A cat shipmate could also turn into a liability unless treated with care. It was the custom never to speak the animal's name, otherwise trouble was guaranteed. If the worst happened and the cat fell overboard, nothing short of gales and sinking could be expected to follow.

The popular saying that cats have nine lives has endured since at least the 16th century. In 1595, William Shakespeare certainly thought it familiar enough to use as one of Mercutio's quips in *Romeo and Juliet*, and at that time the notion was given some credence. Because of their quick reflexes and agility, twisting in midair to right themselves after a fall, cats do seem to have a remarkable ability

Waving for luck
Figurines of the lucky cat Maneki Neko are ubiquitous in Japan. If the cat's right paw is raised it brings good luck; the left paw welcomes visitors or draws customers to a business.

Magical picture
It was once the custom in China to use cats to guard valuable silkworms. A painting with magical properties was believed to work just as well, especially if the cats pictured were lucky tortoiseshells, such as these tortie-and-white cats.

to get themselves out of trouble. To earlier generations, this may well have seemed proof of unnatural powers that enabled a cat to begin a new life after a fatal accident.

Although for much of their domestic history cats have had an image problem, they have occasionally been regarded as protective spirits. This has not necessarily been to their advantage. Across Europe, mummified bodies of cats have been found inside the fabric of old buildings, where they were walled up in the belief that this would deter rats; and in both Europe and Southeast Asia, cats were buried in fields to ensure good crops. Less gruesomely, silkworm farmers in China once used cats, or magical pictures of cats, as guardians of the developing silk cocoons. In rice-growing areas, an old tradition was to carry a cat around in a basket for each household to sprinkle with water to encourage the rains.

St. Cadoc and the cat
There are several old European legends about the Devil building a bridge and claiming the first soul to cross it. Here, the Welsh saint Cadoc foils the Evil One by offering him a cat that crossed over before any human.

Folklore and fairy tales

Clever and helpful, or devious and downright sneaky, the cats in traditional folk tales have a mixed reputation. The way they are represented reflects how people across generations and in various countries have understood, and frequently misunderstood, the character of the average domestic feline. The cat-and-mouse theme is especially prevalent and appears in many cultures in old legends and stories that have proved remarkably enduring.

UNIVERSAL TRUTHS

Early tales about cats appear in the collection of some 200 fables said to have been created by the former Greek slave Aesop (c.620–560BCE). These stories were intended to illustrate universal truths, and the fable of *Venus and the Cat* makes the point that it is impossible to change one's true nature. A cat, desperate to win the affection of a young man, begs Venus, the Greek goddess of love, to change her into a beautiful girl. The wish is granted and a match is made, but after the wedding the bride forgets she is human and pounces on a mouse. Outraged, Venus changes her back into a cat. The old saying "belling the cat"—taking on a dangerous task—comes from another fable attributed to Aesop, *The Mice in Council*. The moral of the tale, as an old mouse points out, is that it is easier to suggest a risky venture than to find someone to carry it out.

Aesop's cats
An 1887 version of Aesop's Fables, told in simple rhymes for young children, included two well-known moral tales featuring cats: *Venus and the Cat* and *The Mice in Council*. The influential English book illustrator Walter Crane (1845–1915) provided the engravings.

FELINE PARTNERS

Cats are included in many of the folk tales collected and rewritten by the German scholars and master storytellers Jacob and Wilhelm Grimm at the beginning of the 19th century. In *Cat and Mouse in Partnership*, the couple of the title set up house together. The Mouse does the chores, while the greedy Cat devises an elaborate scam that involves eating all their winter provisions. "All gone," cries the Mouse, suspicions belatedly aroused, before she, too, is gobbled up. As the story says, "that is the way of the world." However, the collaboration of cat, donkey, dog, and rooster in another Grimm story, *The Musicians of Bremen*, is based on mutual respect. Making music with their own voices, the four companions use the combined uproar—as well as claws, teeth, and feet—to scare off a band of robbers and appropriate their comfortable lodgings. It is not surprising that in so many old stories cats and mice are found together, because until the late 19th century people kept cats primarily for vermin control. In regions as diverse as Europe, Africa, and the Middle East, traditional tales can be found about cats outwitting (and occasionally being outwitted by) mice and rats.

FORTUNE HUNTERS

In fairy tales cats are good at hoodwinking humans, too. The arch-trickster has to be the eponymous *Puss in Boots*. Originally an old French tale (*Le Chat Botté*) by Charles Perrault, and first published in 1697, *Puss in Boots* has

Musical companions
With his back arched, a cat takes his place among the four friends of the Grimm brothers' *Musicians of Bremen*, immortalized in a bronze statue outside Bremen town hall. The landmark by sculptor Gerhard Marcks was installed in 1953.

long been popular as a Christmas pantomime in the UK. Wily Puss manages to pass off his poverty-stricken master as the noble Marquis of Carabas, who, as penniless nobodies so often do in fairy tales, ends up marrying a king's daughter. Through association, Puss himself is set up for life.

Another favorite pantomime was created from the tale of Dick Whittington, a real person born in the mid-14th century who was elected Lord Mayor of London several times. There is no record that Whittington had a cat, but in the story he is accompanied by an intrepid rat-slayer who helps Dick win fame and fortune. On Highgate Hill in London, the statue of a cat marks the spot where Dick, trudging home defeated in his ambitions, supposedly heard church bells telling him to turn around and try again.

Whittington's cat
In an illustration from an edition of the Dick Whittington story published in the mid-19th century, Dick demonstrates his cat's superlative rat-catching skills to the amazement of the king and queen of Barbary.

Postage Puss
A swashbuckling Puss in Boots featured on a French postage stamp issued in 1997. The image was taken from a 19th-century version of the story illustrated by Gustav Doré.

CAT TALES

Some of the most engaging cat legends are interpretations of how and why cats look and behave as they do. The origins of the cat are explained in a tale of Noah's Ark. When Noah begged God to rid the Ark of multiplying rats, God's response was to make the lion sneeze—ejecting the very first cat out of its nostrils. In another Ark legend, the Manx (see pp. 164–65) cat, arriving late on board, lost its tail as Noah slammed the door shut on it.

A fable from old Siam (now Thailand) tells the story of the Siamese cat's tail. At one time, many Siamese cats had a distinctive kink in their tail and crossed eyes, traits that were later bred out as undesirable. According to the story, a Siamese cat guarding a golden goblet for her king clutched the treasure so tightly with her tail and watched it for so long that she developed a kinked tail and a squint.

A traditional Jewish folk tale explains why cats and dogs are age-old enemies. At the beginning of the world, the newly created cat and dog were friends while good times lasted. When winter came, the cat sheltered in Adam's house, but selfishly refused to share lodgings with the dog. Adam, exasperated by their quarreling, foresaw that cats and dogs would never agree again.

Cats in literature

For the most part, cats have been sidelined in adult literature, making appearances as major players largely in books for children. Some literary cats are more realistic than others, but even the most fantastic usually have qualities that are instantly recognizable as feline. Often, the creators of fictional cats have used their own pets as a source of inspiration.

Cheshire Cat grin
Alice holds a confusing conversation with "Cheshire Puss"—as she nervously addresses him—in John Tenniel's immortal illustration for *Alice's Adventures in Wonderland*. The grinning cat, who declares himself mad, is one of the great icons of children's fiction.

CLASSIC CATS

Many cat stories and poems have become accepted as classics, losing nothing of their timeless appeal through translation into dozens of different languages and countless editions. One of the most famous of all fictional felines is the Cheshire Cat in Lewis Carroll's *Alice's Adventures in Wonderland* (1865), the book that changed children's literature forever. This maddening and slightly eerie animal with its semidetached grin makes Alice "quite giddy" as it appears and evaporates at will. The proverbial expression "grinning like a Cheshire cat" was not coined by Carroll, and is known to predate Alice by more than half a century. Other cats—normal ones—have minor roles in the second Alice story, *Through the Looking-Glass* (1871), and a mischievous black kitten gets blamed for the adventure.

The cats and kittens in Beatrix Potter's tales were based on the cats that lived in and around the author's farmhouse in the English Lake District, but their characters probably owed something to the children she knew. In *The Tale of Tom Kitten* (1907), Tom and his sisters end up in disgrace for ruining their best clothes. But Tom fares even worse in *The Tale of Samuel Whiskers* (1908), when he is covered with dough and made into a "roly-poly pudding," destined to be dinner for a pair of rats. Potter's cats—among them, Tom, Tabitha, Miss Moppet, Simpkin from *The Tailor of Gloucester* (1903), and the inefficient shopkeeper Ginger—have shared their familiar names with countless pets.

"The Cat that Walked by Himself," in Rudyard Kipling's *Just So Stories* (1902), is cool, calculating, and self-possessed. "Waving his wild tail and walking by his wild lone," he cleverly persuades a human family to give him a place at the fireside. Unlike the already domesticated dog, horse, and cow, this cat is no friend, servant, or provider, but he knows how to honor a bargain and yet keep his independence.

A modern book that has achieved near-classic status both in Britain and the United States is Barbara Sleigh's *Carbonel* (1955), the story of a royal cat stolen from his rightful kingdom by a witch. Carbonel is arrogant and touchy, and the two children who help him to regain his throne, getting mixed up with magic and catfights along the way, find him a sometimes trying companion. Sleigh wrote two, less-acclaimed, sequels concerning the adventures of Carbonel's offspring.

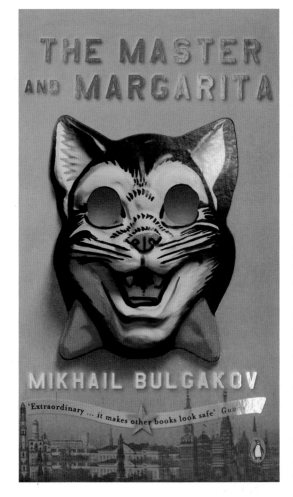

Evil giant
Behemoth, the colossal black cat that stalks on two legs through Bulgakov's satire *The Master and Margarita*, is a not-very-well-respected servant of the Devil. He is named after the monster described in the Bible's Book of Job.

Hemingway's cats
Writer and cat lover Ernest Hemingway kept polydactyl (extra-toed) cats at his home on Key West, Florida. Some 40 or 50 of their descendants, many of them polydactyl, live around what is now the Hemingway Museum.

The Cat in the Hat, the comical creation of Theodor Giesel, who wrote as Dr. Seuss, has taught generations of young children to read. First published in the United States in the 1950s and still going strong, this is one of several books featuring the scraggy anthropomorphic Cat, absurdly dressed in a scarf and a tall, striped hat. A positive lord of misrule, the Cat, whose exploits are told in simple, cantering rhymes, causes wreckage and mayhem just to provide amusement for a couple of bored children on a rainy day.

DEMONS AND DETECTIVES

In fiction for adult readers, cats as major characters are rare. Of the few memorable examples, there can be none more frightful than the gigantic, demonic, gunslinging Behemoth in Mikhail Bulgakov's chaotic and witty satire *The Master and Margarita* (published posthumously in 1967). And for sheer horror, there is little to beat Edgar Allan Poe's short story "The Black Cat" (1843), in which a murdered cat haunts the drunken master who killed it.

A subgenre of the detective novel with a feline twist has become immensely popular in recent decades. Known loosely as "cat mysteries," series after series of books, mostly variations on the theme of the small-town amateur sleuth with a canny cat partner, have been flooding bookshelves alongside conventional crime fiction.

CATS IN POETRY

Poets rather than novelists have found inspiration in cats. Thomas Gray mourned a pet in "Ode on the Death of a Favorite Cat Drowned in a Tub of Gold Fishes" (1748), while John Keats in "Sonnet to a Cat" (c.1818) paid affectionate tribute to a battered and asthmatic old reprobate, and William Wordsworth (1770–1850) was moved to versify about a kitten playing with leaves. More likely to be quoted than any of these is Edward Lear's nonsense rhyme "The Owl and the Pussycat" (1871), or the best-known

modern cat poems collected in *Old Possum's Book of Practical Cats* (1939) by T. S. Eliot. Like Lear, Eliot was writing for children, but his shrewd and amusing portrayals of feline personalities are enjoyed by all ages.

THE WRITER'S MUSE

Many writers, Eliot included, have kept cats for company in their solitary working lives. The favorite of Dr. Samuel Johnson, famed for his English dictionary (1755), was Hodge, who is immortalized in a statue outside Johnson's house in London. In his novels, Charles Dickens (1812–70) sees cats as fit associates for some of his nastier characters, but he was nevertheless a cat lover, apparently keeping the stuffed paw of a much-missed pet on his desk. Ernest Hemingway (1899–1961) did not stuff a paw from his six-toed cat Snowball, but her descendants live on as tourist attractions at the writer's house, now a museum, in Key West, Florida.

Dr. Johnson's "Hodge"
With scattered oyster shells—the remains of his usual meal—at his feet, a bronze statue of Dr. Samuel Johnson's favorite cat, Hodge, sits outside his master's house in a quiet London square.

Cats in art

Cats have appeared intermittently in symbolic and sacred art since the time of the ancient Egyptians, but it was not until the 18th century that they were portrayed as domestic pets. For a long period, Western artists struggled, and largely failed, to capture the elusive nature of felines in drawings and paintings. It was Eastern art that led the way in portraying cats as they really are. In modern times, interpretations of the cat are as broad as artists' imaginations.

One of the least popular domestic animals in the Middle Ages in Europe, because of its association with wickedness (see p. 26), the cat was poorly represented in European art until the beginning of the modern age. A few early images of cats are found in medieval carvings in churches and cathedrals, where they can be seen preying on rats and mice around galleries or on misericords. Some of the most beautiful cat illustrations of the Middle Ages occur in bestiaries, illuminated manuscripts describing animals both real and fantastic. These texts were not medieval field guides but were used to teach moral principles rather than natural history. Cats also turn up in the illustrated margins of medieval Psalters (books of psalms) and books of hours (prayer books).

RENAISSANCE DETAILS

The great artists of the Renaissance occasionally included cats as a minor detail in their work. In the triptych *Garden of Earthly Delights* painted by Dutch artist Hieronymus Bosch (c.1450–1516), a spotted cat carrying a rat in its mouth can be found among the crowded allegorical scenes. In another of Bosch's works, *The Temptation of St. Anthony*, a cat emerges from beneath some drapery to seize a fish. With its gaping mouth and long, pointed ears, this animal looks more like a small demon than a cat.

Leonardo da Vinci (1452–1519) was fascinated by the way

Japanese woodblock print
Utagawa Kuniyoshi (1798–1861), one of Japan's most celebrated painters, often included cats in his beautifully colored prints. Until modern times, Japanese artists showed a superior ability when it came to painting cats with character.

Renaissance cat
Caring for the Sick (c.1440), a fresco by Domenico di Bartolo, is typical of Renaissance paintings in which cats appear as minor figures. Here, doctors and patients in the hospital of Santa Maria della Scala in Siena ignore an imminent cat-and-dog fight.

animals move—in a sheet of drawings of various animals (including a small dragon), he sketched cats playing, fighting, washing, stalking, and sleeping. Leonardo also added a cat to his drawing of the *Virgin and Child*, possibly a study for an intended painting. Here, the infant Christ, seated on his mother's lap, clutches a cat that is doing its best to struggle free.

The cat in medieval religious paintings—perhaps lurking behind a chair leg or hiding under a table—is usually interpreted as a symbol of sin, such as lust, deceitfulness, and heresy. However, viewing these pictures with a modern eye, it is difficult not to suppose that the artists might have included them simply because cats were a normal part of any domestic scene. Even if they were not regarded with any particular

The Cat's Lunch
This cat being waited on was painted by Marguerite Gérard (1761–1837), sister-in-law of well-known Rococo artist Jean-Honoré Fragonard. Like many artists of the time, Gérard failed to bring cats to life, despite the almost hair-by-hair detail.

affection, they were readily available as models. Certainly, the cat romping around an urn in *The Wedding at Cana*, a painting by the Venetian Paolo Veronese (1528–88) based on one of the miracles of Christ, looks merely playful rather than wicked.

FELINE COMPANIONS

By the 18th century, cats were beginning to gain ground as house pets rather than as just catchers of vermin. As a popular subject for portraits, they still trailed a long way behind dogs and horses, but were given at least passing attention by some of the major artists of the day, particularly in England. William Hogarth (1697–1764) included a family tabby in his portrait *The Graham Children*, and in one of his London street scenes a pair of fighting cats, strung up by their tails from a lamppost, are a reminder of the cruelty that was then casually accepted. George Morland (1763–1804), who specialized in rustic scenes, painted his own, clearly well fed, cat; and the kitten portrayed by master animal painter George Stubbs (1724–1806) is much in demand as a reproduction in the 21st century. In France, Jean-Honoré Fragonard (1732–1806), whose work was much favored among the upper classes, sometimes found cats useful as accessories in portraits of young women.

The 18th century also saw a proliferation of cats in run-of-the-mill portraits by lesser-known artists. These cats were often the companions of children, and in scenes intended to be humorous were shown suffering such indignities as being dressed up in dolls' clothes or made to dance. Fluffy snow-white cats, similar to today's Angoras, seem to have been among the most popular models. In the majority of such portraits, although the cats' fur and features are rendered competently enough, the subtleties of feline character and movement have clearly eluded the artists. The animals remain strangely static and have neither grace nor beauty.

EASTERN EXPRESSION

Cats have been important in Eastern art for centuries. Generally treated with great respect in Asia, even throughout the periods when they were disliked and mistrusted elsewhere, cats began to be depicted with sympathy and understanding much earlier in the East than in the West. Some of the most exquisite cat paintings and prints are those by the artists

True to life
Simply executed but highly realistic, this overfed and self-satisfied tabby is an amusing example of the delightful cat portraits produced by Asian artists. It was painted around the mid-19th century.

of 18th- and 19th-century Japan. Executed with the lightest of touches in watercolors on silk and parchment, or printed from woodblocks, these Japanese cats play amid flowers, bat at toys with their paws, get up to mischief, and are petted or scolded by beautiful women. Awake or asleep, they are very real animals, expressing all the natural feline liveliness and mystique so lacking in European art of the same period.

Bosch's cat
The cat making off with a rat in one corner of the allegorical painting *Garden of Earthly Delights* (c.1500) adds a small, recognizably domestic touch to the scenes of wild fantasy created by Hieronymus Bosch.

Three Cats (1913)
The powerful geometric lines and vivid colors of Expressionist artist Franz Marc's cats are repeated in the background, making an inseparable whole. Bold and dramatic, the painting is a startling portrayal of the endless variations of feline form and movement.

IMPRESSIONIST CATS

From about the middle of the 19th century, artists began to look at cats differently, concentrating more on character than fur and whiskers and bringing the animals to life. One of the most celebrated artists of the French Impressionist movement, Pierre-Auguste Renoir (1841–1919), successfully painted cats many times. Despite most of his subjects looking distinctly drowsy—like the tabby in *Sleeping Cat*—Renoir's cats still manage to convey the unmistakable self-possession that comes naturally to all felines. Another French artist, Edouard Manet (1832–83), whose work contained elements of both Impressionism and Realism, put his own cat into some of his paintings. This comfortable cat, the epitome of respectability, is seen, for instance, in *La femme au chat*, a portrait of Manet's wife. However, the black cat in Manet's *Olympia*, a painting that scandalized the public when first shown in 1863, is part of a very different picture. Standing uneasily with arched back at the feet of a reclining and naked prostitute, it suggests a return to the depiction of cats as a symbol of lust.

As the 19th century moved into its last decades and the post-Impressionist movement gathered momentum, artists continued to be beguiled by the charm and character of cats. Their interpretations were highly individual, although some well-known cat paintings are conventional enough, such as the delightful *Mimi et son chat* by Paul Gauguin (1846–1903) in which a chubby toddler plays with a ginger and white cat. The cats painted by Henri Rousseau (1844–1910) were mostly big ones—wild-eyed lions and tigers inhabiting exotic, dreamworld jungles. But Rousseau's subjects also included more homey animals, such as the stolid-looking pet tabbies in *The Tiger Cat* and *Portrait of Pierre Loti*.

MODERN FELINES

By the beginning of the 20th century, cats in art saw an even more dramatic change in style. There is nothing reassuringly domestic about *The White Cat* painted by Pierre Bonnard (1867–1947). This humorously weird creature hunches on exaggeratedly long, stiltlike legs, narrowing its eyes to sinister slits. The German Expressionist painter Franz Marc (1880–1916) superbly captured feline form and movement but using vibrant blues, yellows, and reds and curvy geometric shapes. Pablo Picasso (1881–1973) loved cats and they are a recurring presence in his work, their killer instincts acknowledged in gruesome paintings of cats ripping birds to pieces. The cat as hunter was a theme explored by other modern artists, including Paul Klee (1879–1940), who made it obvious in *Cat and Bird* that the stylized cat glaring from the canvas has the thought of a bird very much on its mind.

Andy Warhol (1928–87), leader of the Pop Art movement of the 1960s, was the enthusiastic owner of numerous cats (all apparently sharing the name "Sam"). He was another artist who loved bright colors, and his series of rainbow-tinted cats in various poses, which he painted working from photographs, are among his most popular prints today.

Not all cats in modern art are stylized or unconventional, although some appear in disturbing contexts. For example, the perfectly ordinary cats lolling and prowling around the adolescent girls painted by the French artist Balthus (1908–2001) do much to heighten the erotic atmosphere of the

Portrait of Pierre Loti (1891)
The idiosyncratic style of self-taught painter Henri Rousseau perfectly captures the forthright personalities of both cat and man in this dual portrait of French writer Pierre Loti and his companion.

portraits. Balthus also painted a self-portrait that he called *The King of Cats,* presenting himself as an arrogantly slouching young man with a massive tabby cat fawning around his legs and a lion-tamer's whip in handy reach. But possibly few cat paintings are as unsettling as the one in *Girl with Kitten* by Lucian Freud (1922–2011). The girl of the portrait, modeled by Freud's first wife, Kitty Garman, is rigid with tension and seems to be unaware that she has a stranglehold grip around the neck of her blank-eyed, unresisting kitten.

Alongside such provocative images, "Percy," the white cat temporarily given that name for the double portrait *Mr. and Mrs. Clark and Percy* by David Hockney (born 1937), seems to be in a reassuringly normal situation, perched on Mr. Clark's lap. However, that has not stopped commentators from attaching symbolic meanings to Percy's presence, including the age-old suggestion of infidelity.

POSTER ICONS
Paintings and drawings of cats have by no means been confined to mainstream art. Cats have long been a favorite subject for illustrators of ephemera such as posters and greetings cards. One of the most prolific cat artists for the popular market in the late Victorian era was Louis Wain (1860–1939). His vast output of amusing and fanciful cat and kitten paintings for cards, books, and magazines are still much sought after by collectors. Wain's best-known work typically features anthropomorphized cats wearing clothes, playing games, and generally enjoying a human-style social life.

Another popular illustrator whose work has endured for over a century was the Swiss painter Theophile Steinlen (1859–1923). He often painted cats and made some exquisite naturalistic sketches, but is most famous for his poster art. Steinlen's Art Nouveau "*Le Chat Noir*" advertisement for a 19th-century Parisian nightclub and artists' salon is a familiar icon on tote bags, postcards, and T-shirts.

21ST-CENTURY MUSES
Cats are still acting as artists' muses in the 21st century. Conventional, kitsch, weird, and whimsical, they appear in paintings, prints, photographs, and videos. Major art galleries devote exhibitions to "cat art" from all centuries. For a modest fee, any cat owner can commission an animal portraitist to immortalize a favorite pet in any chosen style. Much fun with felines is also provided by an internet craze for digitally altering world-famous paintings to include a cat. Masterpieces "improved" by the addition of a colossally fat ginger cat range from Leonardo's *Mona Lisa* and Botticelli's *Birth of Venus* to Salvador Dali's *Dream,* in which the surrealist's leaping, snarling tigers have become something much more benign.

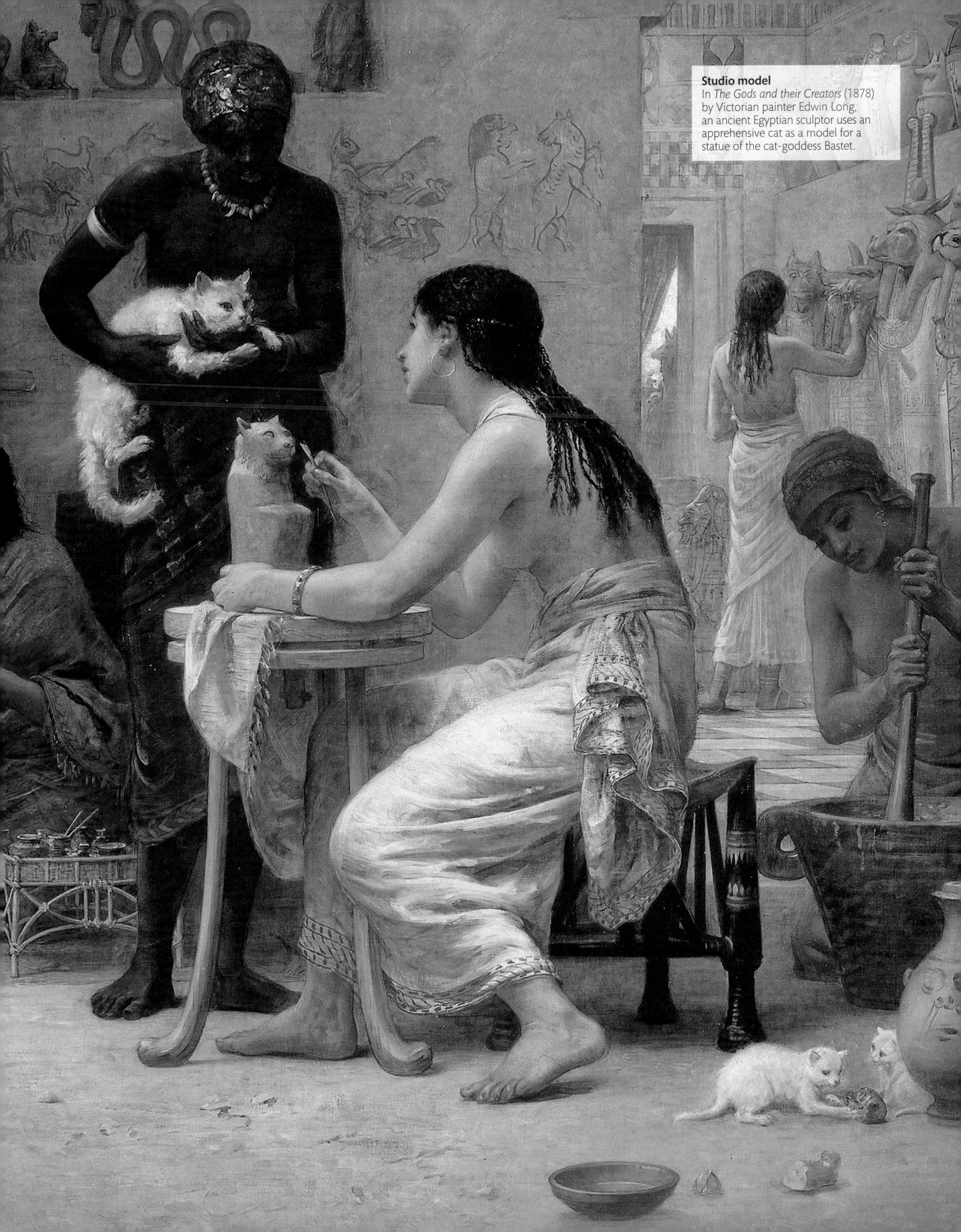

Studio model
In *The Gods and their Creators* (1878) by Victorian painter Edwin Long, an ancient Egyptian sculptor uses an apprehensive cat as a model for a statue of the cat-goddess Bastet.

Cats in entertainment

Charming though they are, cats have not achieved superstardom in the entertainment world in the same way as dogs, being far less cooperative than their canine counterparts. Nevertheless, their personalities and foibles have made cats a source of inspiration for cartoon caricatures, and their visual appeal has not been lost on the creators of marketing campaigns. The rise of a new generation of "internet cats" is the feline success story of the 21st century.

FELINES ON FILM

It is not in feline nature to act to order, and what cats do best is simply being themselves. Filmmakers have not missed opportunities to use this talent, and many actors have shared the screen with a cat that steals the scene just by putting in an appearance. A classic example is the memorable ginger tom befriended by good-time girl Holly Golightly (played by Audrey Hepburn) in *Breakfast at Tiffany's* (1961). More recently, another ginger—fluffy, snub-nosed Crookshanks—scored a big hit for his minor role in the Harry Potter series of films, first appearing in *Harry Potter and the Prisoner of Azkaban* (2004). Crookshanks was, in fact, played by two cats; most feline actors share their roles, sometimes with as many as four or five look-alike cats.

One well-worn film cliché is to combine cats and villains. A staple character of several James Bond films, including *You Only Live Twice* (1967) and *Diamonds are Forever* (1971), is the sadistic, murdering Ernst Blofeld, who cuddles his beautiful white Persian cat while masterminding global domination. The cat-and-baddie theme is parodied in the Austin Powers spoof spy films (1997, 1999, and 2002), with the hairless Sphynx cat Mr. Bigglesworth (who must never be upset) as the pet of the megalomaniac, and equally bald, Dr. Evil.

CARTOON CHARACTERS

While real cat stars are scarce, plenty of cartoon cats have earned a place in movie history. The prototype was Felix the Cat, an odd little character that became famous in silent animated films of the 1920s and remains popular in comic books and on television. Felix was followed by the clownish black-and-white Sylvester featured in Looney Tunes, a series of short cartoons produced by the Warner Brothers studio between the 1930s and the late 1960s. Sylvester, characterized by billowing side-whiskers and a spluttering lisp, wastes much energy trying to catch the canary Tweety Pie. Equally hapless is Tom, the cat forever outwitted by Jerry the mouse in countless episodes of Tom and Jerry from 1940 to the 2000s. Probably the most famous cartoon cats of all are the wicked Siamese pair in *Lady and the Tramp* (1955). In their big scene, they casually trash a sitting-room, leaving the spaniel Lady to take the blame. Strictly for adult audiences

The cat with no name
In the film *Breakfast at Tiffany's*, the stray cat that becomes the chance roommate of Holly Golighty (Audrey Hepburn) has no name. The lovable ginger—called "Orangey" in real life—was a seasoned actor with many roles to his credit.

Beauty and beast
Arch-villain of several James Bond movies, Ernst Stavro Blofeld (played here by Charles Gray in *Diamonds are Forever*) may have been a crazed and cold-blooded killer, but he was also a cat lover. His trademark pet was a glamorous white Persian.

with its overtly political and sexual content, the hugely successful *Fritz the Cat* (1972) is a much darker cartoon comedy about a free-living New York feline. *Puss in Boots* (2011) is a modern reimagining of the old fairy tale (see pp. 28–29) in which the swashbuckling cat encounters other storybook characters such as Humpty Dumpty and Jack of beanstalk fame.

THEATER CATS

Cats are as unlikely to be given leading roles on stage than they are in films. But the cats brought spectacularly to life by actors in Andrew Lloyd Webber's award-winning musical *Cats* have enchanted theatergoers since the show opened in London in 1981. Based on T. S. Eliot's *Old Possum's Book of Practical Cats* (see p. 30), the production has toured the world to rave reviews.

In another sense, the "theater cat" has a long tradition, as at one time nearly every leading theater had a resident mouse catcher. Loved by actors and stage staff alike, these cats helped to keep down the numbers of rodents attracted by litter-strewn auditoriums. There are many stories of theater cats casually strolling on stage during a performance and washing themselves in the footlights, or causing mayhem in the "props" room. Today, vermin are controlled in different ways and the very few old troupers that linger on as theater cats are usually firmly denied access to the stage.

In a relatively new, and controversial, development in feline show business, touring "cat circuses" are becoming particularly popular in the United States and Moscow. One of the largest of the Russian companies has about 120 cats trained to perform acrobatic tricks. The glitzy circus routines, which are set to various themes, include cats tightrope-walking, riding rocking horses, and balancing on top of balls. The ethics of making cats perform for entertainment, however humane their treatment, has aroused considerable debate.

BALLET ROLES

With their lithe bodies and graceful movements, it is perhaps surprising that cats have not been represented more often in either classical or contemporary ballet. Two of the few cats in the ballet repertoire appear in the final act of Tchaikovsky's *The Sleeping Beauty* (first performed in 1890) when, among other fairy-tale characters, Puss in Boots dances a *pas de deux* with a white cat at the wedding festival of newly awakened Princess Aurora. In *Alice's Adventures in Wonderland* (2011), the huge Cheshire Cat that drifts creepily on and off the stage is not a dancing role—the head and body comprise a series of disjointed parts worked by puppeteers.

Black Cat brand
A black cat may seem an odd choice of image for a brand of fireworks—most cats are terrified of the bangs—but as a lucky symbol it appears to have worked. The manufacturers are one of the largest and most successful fireworks producers in the world.

SELLING POWER

Advertising campaigns have been using cats for more than a century. As early as 1904, a black cat was adopted as the image for a brand of cigarette. Today, two enormous black cat sculptures sit at the entrance of the tobacco company's former factory in London. Cats of all types label pet foods; and as they also make excellent images for suggesting ease and comfort, they are a natural choice for promoting deep-pile carpets, luxurious furniture, and home-heating systems. In fashion shoots, slinky pedigree felines, the epitome of style and grace, are a perfect complement to elegant models advertising designer perfumes, clothes, and accessories.

ON THE NET

A 21st-century phenomenon is the proliferation of cat photos and videos on the internet. What began as a craze for posting clips of bizarre and amusing cats has, for a few, turned into big business, especially in the United States. Certain videos went viral, and cats with particularly striking features— as well as one with a talent for "playing" a keyboard—became overnight celebrities. They gained a following of devoted fans and, in some cases, a million-dollar earning power thanks to lucrative advertising deals, TV shows, and personal appearances. Also immensely popular on the internet are the simple animated films in the series *Simon's Cat* (shown from 2008 on). These small comedy sketches record the trials of a put-upon owner and his attention-seeking pet cat.

Double act
The best-known cat and mouse in cartoon history, Tom and Jerry have been engaged in a battle of wits, with a few brief interludes of friendship, since the 1940s.

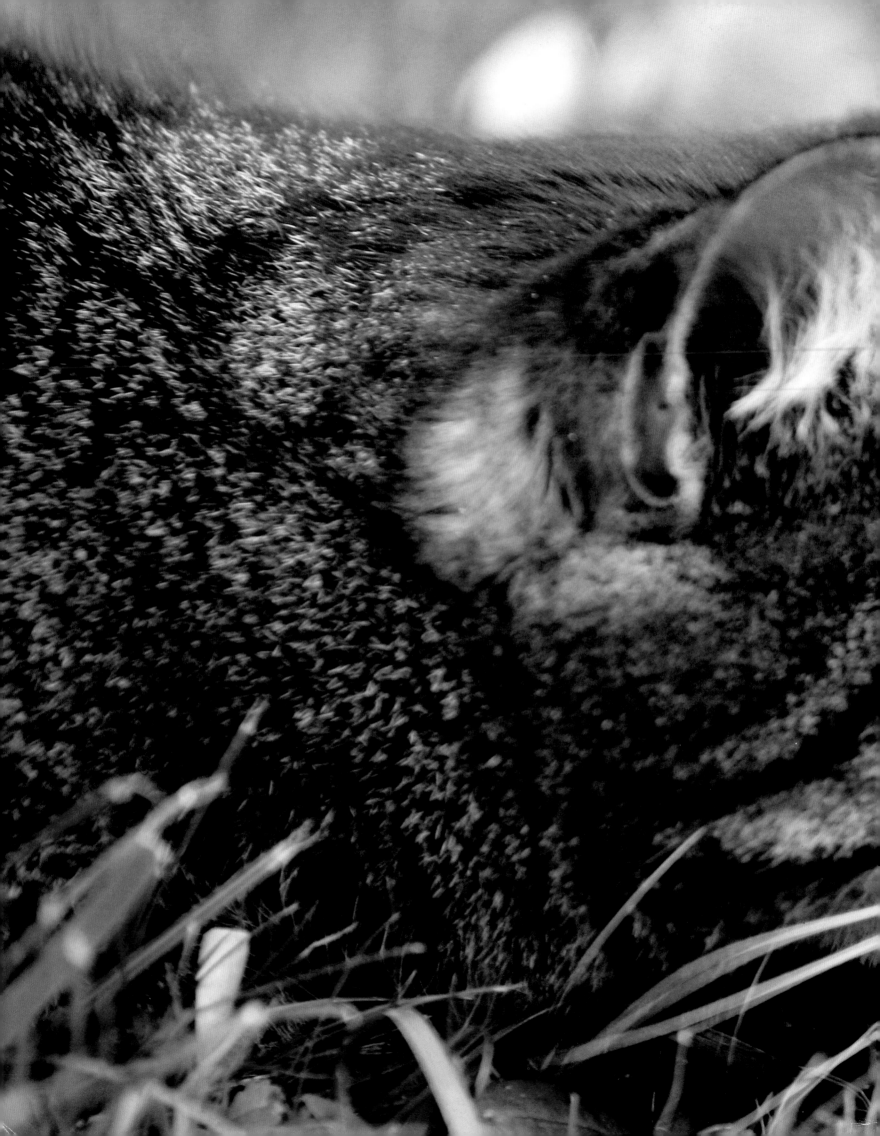

CHAPTER 3

FELINE BIOLOGY

Brain and nervous system

The nervous system controls and regulates a cat's body. It is made up of nerve cells (neurons) and their fibers, which transmit impulses, or electrical signals, between parts of the body. The brain analyses information from stimuli gathered by the sensory organs, such as the cat's eyes and ears, and from inside a cat's body, too. It then makes changes by stimulating muscle activity or causing the release of chemical messengers called hormones that can alter body chemistry.

The anatomical structure of a cat's brain is similar to that of other mammals. Its largest part, the cerebrum, governs behavior, learning, memory, and the interpretation of sensory information. It is divided into two halves, or cerebral hemispheres, each made up of lobes with their own functions. The cerebellum, at the back of the brain, fine-tunes body and limb movements. Other structures within the brain include the pineal gland, hypothalamus, and pituitary body, which are also part of the endocrine system.

The brainstem connects the brain to the spinal cord, which runs inside the vertebral column, or spine.

CORTICAL FOLDING

A cat's brain weighs up to about 1oz (30g), which is just under 1 percent of its total body weight. That's relatively small compared to a human brain (2 percent of body weight) or even that of a dog (1.2 percent). The domestic cat's brain is also about 25 percent smaller than that of its closest relative, the wildcat. This reduction in size is mainly because the regions of a wildcat's brain used to map an extensive hunting territory are no longer needed in the domestic cat, which gradually came to depend on humans for most of its food. The cerebrum of a cat's brain has a higher degree of folding in its outer layer (cortex) than that of a dog. Cortical folding significantly increases the amount of the cerebral cortex, which contains the cell bodies of neurons (also known as "gray matter"), allowing many more cells to be packed into the confined space of the skull.

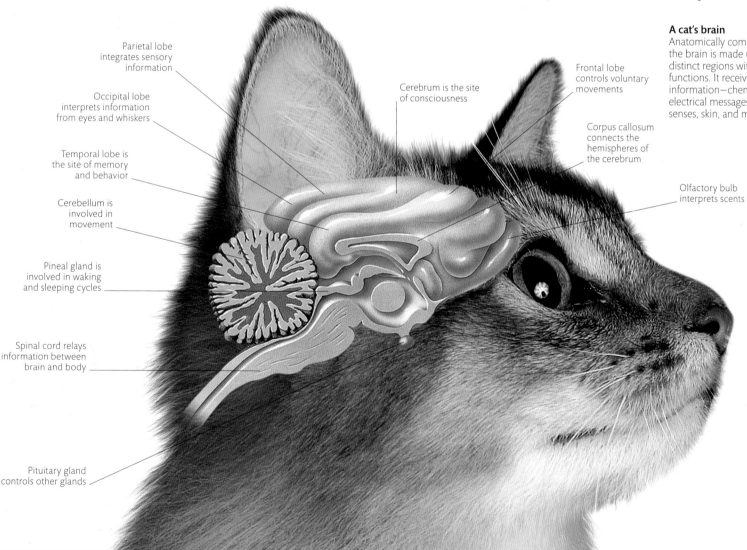

Parietal lobe integrates sensory information

Occipital lobe interprets information from eyes and whiskers

Temporal lobe is the site of memory and behavior

Cerebellum is involved in movement

Pineal gland is involved in waking and sleeping cycles

Spinal cord relays information between brain and body

Pituitary gland controls other glands

Cerebrum is the site of consciousness

Frontal lobe controls voluntary movements

Corpus callosum connects the hemispheres of the cerebrum

Olfactory bulb interprets scents

A cat's brain
Anatomically complex, the brain is made up of distinct regions with separate functions. It receives constant information—chemical and electrical messages—from the senses, skin, and muscles.

A cat's cerebral cortex contains about 300 million neurons. That is almost double the number in a dog's cerebral cortex. A high degree of cortical folding is linked to increased brain processing and what we humans think of as intelligence.

HIGHLY DEVELOPED REGIONS

The areas of the brain involved in interpreting sensory information are particularly well developed in cats. For example, the feline visual cortex, which receives input from the eyes, contains more neurons than the equivalent area of a human brain. Vision is a cat's key sense when it hunts. The regions that control paw movements and grip are also intricate, allowing cats to be surprisingly dextrous with their paws. They can use their paws almost like human hands when seizing and manipulating objects, such as items of prey and toys. This skill and other hunting behaviors, such as stalking, pouncing, and biting, appear to be hardwired into a cat's brain. Kittens instinctively begin to practice hunting when playing with their littermates, and indoor cats without access to wild prey will continue to hone their predatory skills on toys.

A cat's brain has an built-in directional compass. A frontal area of the brain contains iron salts that are sensitive to the Earth's magnetic fields. This compass helps cats navigate their territory and may also explain how some cats have managed to travel hundreds of miles back to their home after being moved away. The cat's brain also registers the different times of the day from the movement of the sun. From this internal clock, a cat soon learns when to appear each day for its dinner.

CNS AND PNS

Together, the brain and spinal cord (which contains bundles of nerve fibers) are known as the central nervous system (CNS). The rest of the nervous system—nerve fibers branching off from the CNS and associated groups of cells called ganglia—is known as the peripheral nervous system (PNS). The PNS connects the CNS with the limbs and body organs. Some nerve fibers of the PNS transmit electrical signals to the CNS for analysis; others carry signals in the opposite direction to cause a change in the body. Some parts of the PNS are under voluntary, or conscious, control, such as the nerves that allow a cat to wave its tail to show annoyance or to pounce on a mouse; other parts of the PNS are involuntary, subconsciously affecting internal processes such as regulation of heartbeat or digestion.

Peripheral nerves
Nerve fibers from the skin, muscles, and other internal body parts send electrical messages to the central nervous system (CNS) for analysis. The CNS then sends back messages with instructions.

Facial nerves control expression

Cranial nerves control head

Radial nerve is a major nerve in front leg

Rich supply of nerves to paws

Spinal cord is part of the CNS and is encased in spine

Peripheral nerves carry information to and from the CNS

Paired spinal nerves

Sacral and lumbar nerves supply the hindquarters

Caudal nerves help move tail

Pudendal nerve innervates genitals

Femoral nerve is a major nerve in back leg

HORMONES

The nervous system works closely with the endocrine system. Hormones made by the pituitary gland in the brain control the production of many other hormones, including those regulating metabolism, response to stress, and sexual behavior.

Biofeedback
As soon as a cat detects a potentially dangerous scent, it becomes primed for a fight-or-flight response by a chain of hormonal reactions. Once the danger is over, the hormone cortisol suppresses—via a biofeedback loop—the hormone that originally triggered the response.

Adrenal gland releases cortisol

Kidney

Cortisol suppresses hormones in brain via biofeedback loop

Unknown scent initiates fight-or-flight response

Danger message passed on through brain activity

Hormone travels in blood to adrenals

Light sleepers
Cats are notorious for the amount of time they sleep — up to 16 hours each day. During about 70 percent of this time, the brain continues to register sounds and smells, which allows the cat to jump into action should danger or prey appear.

Cat senses

Like humans, cats rely on the five senses of vision, hearing, smell, taste, and touch to tell them about the surrounding world. These senses gather information and send it, via nerves, to the brain for interpretation. Cat senses evolved over millions of years to suit their pre-domesticated way of life: that of a nocturnal hunter with exemplary night vision and extraordinary senses of hearing and smell.

VISION

Cats have very large eyes that work most effectively at night, when mice, a main source of prey, are most active. Rods—photoreceptors responsible for black-and-white vision in dim light—outnumber cones (responsible for color vision) in the cat's retina by 25:1 (in humans the ratio is 4:1). Cats do have color vision, but it is not as important to them as their night vision. They can see blues and yellows, but reds and

Super senses
Cats are renowned for their super senses: eyes that see in the dark; ears that detect high-pitched noises inaudible to humans; a powerful sense of smell; and whiskers that allow them to sense their way in pitch darkness.

greens probably appear as grays. In daylight, the pupils shrink to vertical slits to protect the eyes from glare.

Cat vision is much less sharp than that of humans. Focusing such large eyes takes effort and cats are generally farsighted, unable to see clearly within about 1ft (30cm) of their eyes. Their vision is much more attuned to detecting movement. Like many other predators, cats have forward-facing eyes. Their total field of vision is about 200°, with an overlap between the eyes of 140°. This overlap gives the cat binocular vision, allowing it to see in depth and to judge distances accurately, which are essential for success when hunting.

HEARING

Cats have superb hearing, with a range that extends from 40 to 65,000 hertz. That is two octaves higher than humans can hear (up to 20,000 hertz) and into the ultrasound region. This wide range covers all the sounds important to cats, including the vocalizations

NIGHT VISION

In the dark, a cat's pupil expands to an area three times larger than a human's dilated pupil, allowing the tiniest glimmer of light to enter the eye. A cat's night vision is further enhanced by a reflective layer behind the retina called the tapetum lucidum. Any light entering the eye that is not caught by the retina bounces off the tapetum and travels back through the retina, increasing the eye's sensitivity by up to 40 percent.

After dark
The tapetum appears as a bright golden or green disk when a source of light strikes a cat's eye at night.

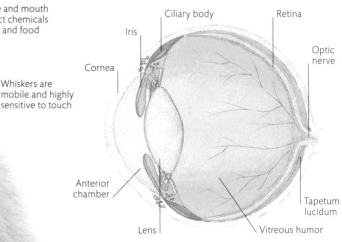

Eyes have a wider field of vision than humans

Ears are moved by more than 20 muscles

Nose and mouth detect chemicals in air and food

Whiskers are mobile and highly sensitive to touch

Ciliary body

Retina

Iris

Cornea

Optic nerve

Anterior chamber

Tapetum lucidum

Lens

Vitreous humor

Eye and vision
A cat's eye is a hollow ball filled with clear jelly, or humor, that lets light pass through. Light rays are focused by the cornea and lens and form images on the light-sensitive retina.

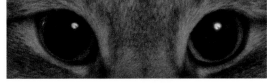

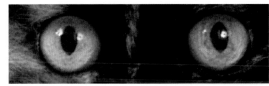

ALMOND-SHAPED AND BLUE

SLANTED AND GREEN

ROUND AND GOLD

ROUND AND ODD-COLORED

Eye colors and shapes
Cats' eye colors come in orange, green, and blue tones. Some cats have odd-colored eyes. Eye shape varies from round to slanted, with some Eastern breeds having very pronounced slants.

ROUNDED TIPS

POINTED TIPS

FOLDED

CURLED

Ear shapes
Most cats have upright ears, with either pointed or rounded tips. A few breeds, including the American Curl and Scottish Fold, have unusual ear shapes, as a result of genetic mutations.

of other cats and enemies, and the rustling of rodents and their high-pitched squeaks. Cats can independently swivel the external parts of the ear, the pinnae, up to 180° to pinpoint the source of a sound. The pinna's design also allows cats to determine the height from which a sound emanates, which is very useful for an animal that climbs. The inner ear contains the vestibular apparatus, or the

organ of balance. It registers changes in direction and speed and allows a cat to right itself when falling (see pp. 54–55). Cats also use their ears to communicate their mood: for example, rotating the ears back and flattening them indicates anger or fright. Cats are extremely sensitive to loudness, about 10 times more so than humans. That is why they dislike noisy environments and become agitated by disturbances such as fireworks.

SMELL AND TASTE
Cats have a powerful sense of smell, not as strong as a dog's but much more acute than a human's. The sensory membrane inside the nasal passages where smells are trapped is five times bigger than the same region in humans. Cats recognize each other by smell and use it to help track prey. They also employ scents from urine, feces, or glands to mark their territory, warning other cats to keep away or advertising their sexual status. Smell is closely linked to taste. A cat will usually smell its food—to check that it is edible—before eating. Taste buds on the upper surface of the tongue mostly respond to bitter, acidic, and salty chemicals

in food. Cats can also recognize sweet tastes, but as strict carnivores they have little need for sugar.

Cats have a sensory organ in the roof of the mouth called the vomeronasal, or Jacobson's, organ. Using this, a cat produces an open-mouthed grimace—"flehman response"—as it laps up scents, usually those of a sexual nature left by other cats.

TOUCH
The hairless parts of a cat's body—the nose, paw pads, and tongue—are highly sensitive to touch, as are the whiskers. Technically known as vibrissae, whiskers are deeply embedded modified hairs. The most prominent whiskers are on the sides of the nose. Smaller whiskers are on the cheeks, above the eyes, and on the back of the forelegs. Whiskers help cats navigate in the dark and also to "see" nearby objects that the eyes cannot focus on. The whiskers on the head also help to judge the width of gaps through which their body can pass.

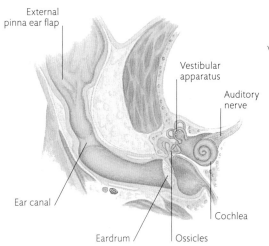

Ear and hearing
Sound funneled into the ear canal travels across the eardrum and ossicles to the cochlea, where nerve impulses are triggered and sent to the brain.

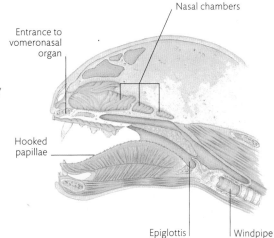

Taste and smell
Chemicals in food are detected by taste buds on the tongue's papillae. Odor molecules are caught in the olfactory membrane in the nasal chamber and the vomeronasal organ.

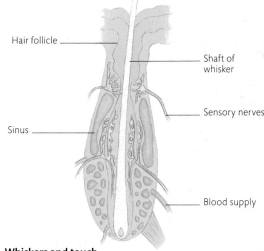

Whiskers and touch
When a whisker brushes against an object, its deeply embedded base, surrounded by a capsule of blood (sinus), sends information to the brain via sensory nerve endings.

Keen senses
Cats are well equipped to be efficient hunters, with good night vision, a strong sense of smell, acute hearing, and sensitive whiskers to help them pinpoint prey with great accuracy.

The skeleton and body form

The cat's skeleton is a lightweight but robust frame designed for speed and agility. The skull has characteristics of a hunting animal, and the limbs are adapted for pouncing and bursts of speed. The highly flexible spine and maneuverable limbs allow a cat to reach most parts of its body when grooming with its paws, tongue, or teeth. Variances occur in body form among different breeds in cats but nowhere near the extent seen in dogs.

SKELETON

A cat skeleton, like that of all mammals, is a collection of bones connected by joints that allow different amounts of movement and are modified to suit its lifestyle as a carnivore. It provides a framework for the muscles that move the bones and also gives the cat its characteristic shape. Other functions include the protection of delicate internal organs such as the heart and lungs.

The skull contains the brain and houses the sense organs—eyes, ears, and nose—that, among other things, help the cat to detect prey effectively. The orbits are very large and often open posteriorly to allow for the powerful jaw muscles that attach to the skull just behind them. The cat's head can turn 180° to groom the back. The hyoid bone sits in the throat where it supports the tongue and voice box (larynx) and is thought to be involved in purring (see p. 59).

A cat has seven neck, or cervical, vertebrae—the same number as is seen in nearly all mammals, but it has a long back for its size, with 13 thoracic vertebrae to which the ribs are attached. The number of vertebrae and their structure increases spinal flexibility, as does the size of the intervertebral spaces, which are occupied with pads of gristly cartilage and allow some movement between adjacent bones. The tail, an extension of the spine, is made up of about 23 bones in most cat breeds and aids balance when climbing. The rib cage, connected to the spine in the chest region, protects the heart, lungs, stomach, liver, and kidneys.

The cat's forelimbs are "floating": the clavicle is greatly reduced in size and the shoulder blade is supported only by muscles and ligaments. This arrangement gives the shoulders a great range of

Cat skeleton

A cat's skeleton is lightly built, compact, and highly flexible, especially in the neck, spine, shoulders, and forelimbs. The long limbs are adapted for speed.

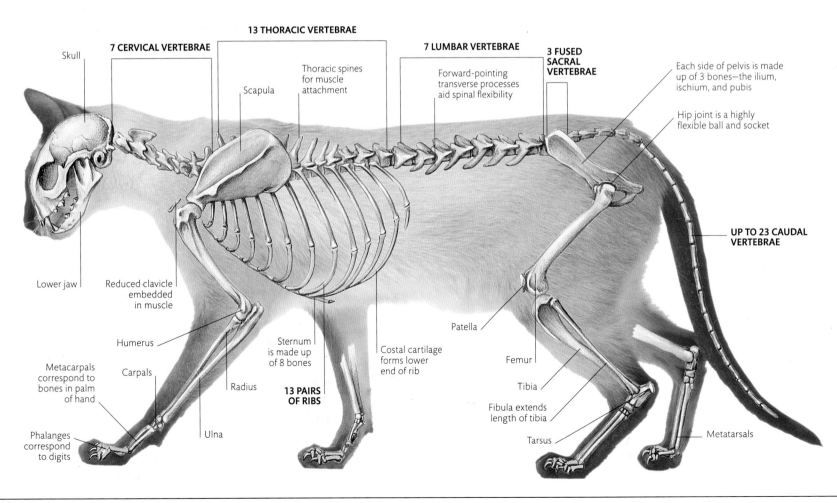

7 CERVICAL VERTEBRAE

13 THORACIC VERTEBRAE

7 LUMBAR VERTEBRAE

3 FUSED SACRAL VERTEBRAE

Skull

Thoracic spines for muscle attachment

Scapula

Forward-pointing transverse processes aid spinal flexibility

Each side of pelvis is made up of 3 bones—the ilium, ischium, and pubis

Hip joint is a highly flexible ball and socket

UP TO 23 CAUDAL VERTEBRAE

Lower jaw

Reduced clavicle embedded in muscle

Humerus

Patella

Sternum is made up of 8 bones

Costal cartilage forms lower end of rib

Femur

Metacarpals correspond to bones in palm of hand

Carpals

Radius

13 PAIRS OF RIBS

Tibia

Fibula extends length of tibia

Phalanges correspond to digits

Ulna

Tarsus

Metatarsals

SKULL

A domestic cat's skull is broad with a short nose. It is made up of 29 bones that fuse together as a cat matures and stops growing. The eye sockets, or orbits, are very large and face forward, which allow hunters to judge distance accurately when pouncing on prey. The lower jaw of the cat is relatively short compared to their wild relatives, especially big cats such as the leopard and lion. It is connected to the skull by a hinge joint that limits movement to the vertical plane and is controlled by strong masseter muscles that provide a powerful bite so that a cat can maintain its hold on struggling prey.

ROUNDED, WEDGE-SHAPED FACE

LONG, WEDGE-SHAPED FACE

ROUNDED, FLAT FACE (FRONT)

ROUNDED, FLAT FACE (SIDE)

Head shapes
Most cats resemble their wild ancestors, having a round head with a wedge-shaped face. Some breeds, however, have an elongated wedge shape, while others have a rounded, flat "doll face."

movements and allows a cat to squeeze effortlessly through gaps wide enough to accommodate its head. Like all carnivores, three of the wrist bones are fused into what is known as the scapholunar bone. It is thought to be an adaptation for climbing that appeared in the early ancestors of the group. Powerful, long hind limbs are attached to the pelvis with ball-and-socket joints and provide drive when running and pouncing.

BODY FORM
The body form of different types of cat is remarkably uniform when you consider the range of shapes and sizes in dogs. This is partly due to the fact that their function was solely pest control, whereas dogs were used for many different purposes, such as hunting and herding; and partly due to the fact that the genes that control size are not as easy to manipulate. There are, however, some feline exceptions, such as the tailless Manx (see pp. 164–65) and the short-legged Munchkin (see pp. 150–51 and p. 233). The smallest cats, such as the Singapura (see p. 86), reach an adult weight of 4–9lb (2–4kg) and the largest breeds, such as the Highlander (see p. 158), range from 10–25lb (4.5–11kg). The adult weight among dog breeds, on the other hand, can range from 3–175lb (1–79kg).

The relatively large size of some of the new hybrid breeds may be influenced by the genes from their wild cat ancestors. For example, the Savannah (see pp. 146–47) is derived from a serval-domestic cat cross and the Chausie (see p. 149) from a jungle cat-domestic cat cross. Some variety does occur, however, within the head (see above) and body (see below) shapes of domestic cats. Oriental breeds, such as the Siamese (see pp. 104–09), tend to have a slender, highly sinuous build, long, thin limbs and tail, and a wedge-shaped head. Western breeds, such as the British Shorthair (see pp. 118–19), have a stocky shape, with a compact, muscular body, relatively short legs, a thicker tail, and a rounder head. Of course, many breeds, such as the Ragdoll (see p. 216), fall between these two extremes of body shape, and the head and body forms can be combined in different ways by the different cat breeders. Body forms also tend to vary around the world, depending on the climate of a region.

Body shapes
Eastern breeds tend to have a slender body shape best suited to warm climates. They have a higher surface area to volume ratio to aid cooling. Western breeds tend to be stocky and prefer a temperate climate. They have a low surface area to volume ratio, which helps to retain heat. Some breeds have a body shape that falls between these two extremes.

Tail shapes
Most cats have a long tail, which they use for balance and communication. A few breeds, such as the Manx and Bobtails (see pp. 161–63), have a short, stumpy tail or no tail at all. One breed, the American Ringtail (see p. 167), has a curl in its tail.

SLENDER ATHLETIC BODY

INTERMEDIATE BODY

STOCKY BODY

LONG TAIL

RING TAIL

BOBTAIL

Skin and coat

The skin is an organ, like the heart or liver. In fact, it is the largest organ of a cat's body, enveloping and protecting the animal from environmental threats and diseases. The soft fur coat, which grows from the skin, is composed of different types of hair and also plays a protective role. The ancestors of the domestic cat were shorthaired, but selective breeding has produced other coat types, ranging from silky longhaired to almost hairless.

The cat's skin has many roles: it acts as a barrier against disease-causing agents, or pathogens; it forms a waterproof layer, preventing vital fluids from leaking out of the body; its blood vessels help regulate internal body temperature; and it makes vitamin D, which is necessary for healthy bones. Cats have loose skin that complements their natural flexibility

Skin structure
This cross-section of a cat's skin and coat shows the outer protective epidermis, made of dead, toughened cells, and the inner dermis, rich in blood vessels, nerves, glands, and hair follicles that form the coat.

of movement. This looseness also helps when fighting, because it allows a cat to turn to some degree and defend itself, even when its skin is held.

TWO LAYERS
The skin has two layers: the outer layer is called the epidermis, and the inner, the dermis. The epidermis is mainly composed of layers of dead, flattened cells containing a tough protein called keratin and water-resistant chemicals. The hair and claws are also made largely of keratin. The deepest, or basal, layer of the epidermis is only about

four cells thick and consists of living cells. These cells divide repeatedly to replenish the outer layers, which are constantly shed from the body's surface. The epidermis also contains immune cells that fight pathogens.

The inner layer, the dermis, is more complex and contains connective tissue, hair follicles, muscles, blood vessels, sebaceous and sweat glands, and millions of nerve endings that detect heat, cold, light touch, pressure, and pain. Cats do not produce sweat to cool the skin. Instead, they produce oily secretions from the sweat glands that condition and protect the skin and coat. A cat's skin is pigmented—except in areas where the fur is white—and is the same color, although slightly paler, as the hair that grows from it. Glands in a cat's skin also release a scent, which is a vital component in feline communication (see p. 281).

TYPES OF HAIR
Cats have four kinds of hair: down, awn, guard, and sensory hair. Down hair is fluffy, short, and thin and provides insulation for warmth. Awn hair is intermediate in length, has thickened tips, and provides warmth, but is also protective. Guard hair forms the outer

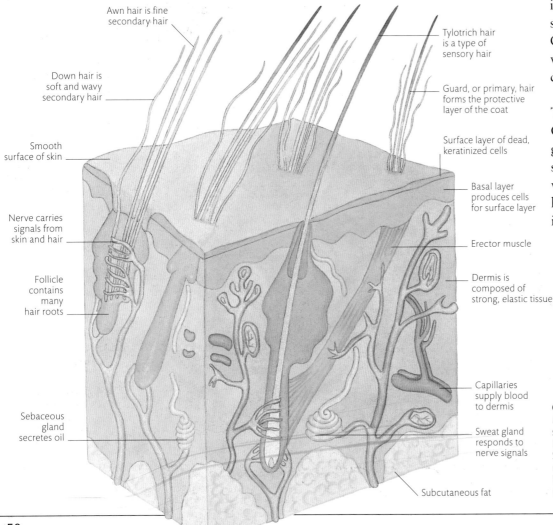

Awn hair is fine secondary hair

Down hair is soft and wavy secondary hair

Smooth surface of skin

Nerve carries signals from skin and hair

Follicle contains many hair roots

Sebaceous gland secretes oil

Tylotrich hair is a type of sensory hair

Guard, or primary, hair forms the protective layer of the coat

Surface layer of dead, keratinized cells

Basal layer produces cells for surface layer

Erector muscle

Dermis is composed of strong, elastic tissue

Capillaries supply blood to dermis

Sweat gland responds to nerve signals

Subcutaneous fat

Coat types
Most cats are shorthairs, but some have other types of coat. Hairless breeds, such as the Sphynx, have almost no hair; rexed cats have curly hair; and longhaired breeds have hair up to 5in (12cm) long.

HAIRLESS

Communicating by scent
Cats have a phenomenal sense of smell. They deposit scent produced by sebaceous glands in the skin to communicate with other cats without meeting face to face. Scent, which contains chemicals called pheromones, allows cats to recognize friends and enemies, different territories, and the sexual status of other cats.

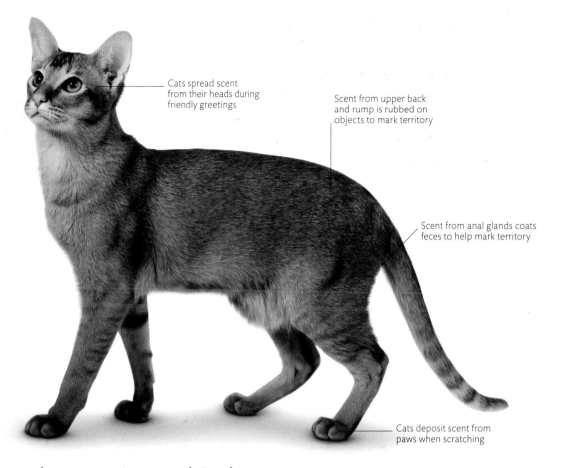

Cats spread scent from their heads during friendly greetings

Scent from upper back and rump is rubbed on objects to mark territory

Scent from anal glands coats feces to help mark territory

Cats deposit scent from paws when scratching

coat, which protects the cat against the elements. These straight hairs, which taper toward their end, are the thickest and longest of the three types of coat hair. They are more dense on the back, chest, and abdomen.

Whiskers, or vibrissae, are long, thick sensory hairs found on the cat's head, throat, and forelegs. These touch sensors help a cat to explore in the dark and to detect nearby objects (see p. 45). Other sensory hairs, called tylotrichs, are scattered throughout the coat and have a role similar to that of the whiskers.

Cats have compound hair follicles, which means that many hairs, but only one guard hair, grow from a single follicle. This creates a thick coat—one square millimeter of cat skin can contain as many as 200 hairs. Hair itself is made of overlapping scales, which are the remains of keratin-packed cells. Each follicle has a sebaceous gland, which produces oil to waterproof and condition the coat, and a small muscle that raises the hair when the cat is angry or excited, making it appear larger and more daunting to enemies.

The sensory hairs are by far the least numerous of all types of hair. The other types of hair occur roughly in the ratio of 100 down: 30 awn: 2 guard hairs. However, selective breeding has altered this proportion and lengths in many breeds to produce a variety of coats. For example, the Maine Coon's (see pp. 214–15) longhaired

coat does not contain any awn hairs; the Cornish Rex's (see pp. 176–77) coat does not have any guard hairs, just curly down and awn hairs; and the apparently hairless Sphynx (see pp. 168–69) has a light covering of down, but lacks whiskers.

Coats come in a bewildering range of patterns and colors (see pp. 52–53). Coat color is produced by two forms of the pigment melanin: eumelanin (black and brown) and phaeomelanin (red, orange, and yellow). Except for white hair, all colors are the result of varying amounts of these two pigments on the hair shaft.

UNDERSTANDING COAT COLORS

Pigmentation in cat fur varies from an even distribution along the hair shaft, which produces a solid coat, to no pigment at all, which gives white fur. A solid coat's color varies with the density of pigment in the coat hairs. For example, dilute black gives blue. If just the end part of each hair holds color, the coat is tipped, shaded, or smoke (see p. 52). Ticked shafts have alternating dark and light bands and give a color called agouti.

Solid color

One-eighth holds color

One-quarter holds color

SOLID

TIPPED

Half of the hair holds color

Band of color

SHADED

Band without color

SMOKE

TICKED

SHORT-COATED

CURLY-COATED

LONG-COATED

SOLID COLORS

Black and red and their dilute forms, blue and cream, are known as Western colors because they traditionally occurred in European and American breeds, such as the British Shorthair and Maine Coon. Solid-white and bicolored are also considered Western. Coat colors traditionally found in breeds with origins east of Europe, such as the Siamese and Persian, are known as Eastern colors. They are chocolate and cinnamon, and their dilute forms, lilac and fawn. All colors now occur globally.

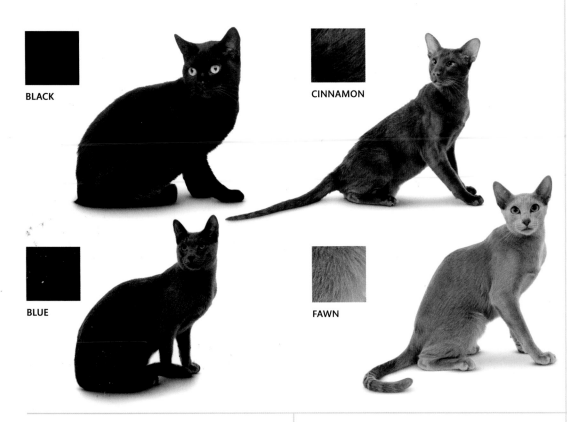

BLACK

CINNAMON

BLUE

FAWN

TIPPED FUR

When just the tip of each hair is heavily pigmented, the effect is known as tipping, chinchilla, or shell. The unpigmented section of the hair is usually white, or silver, although undercoats with yellow or reddish coloring can occur.

LIGHT CHOCOLATE TIPPED

BLUE-TIPPED SILVER

SHADED FUR

The upper quarter of each hair is colored in shaded fur. Shaded fur appears darker on the back, where the fur lies flat. When the cat moves, shading produces a rippling effect. A coat in which the shaded part of the hair is red or cream is called a cameo.

SMOKED FUR

When about half of the uppermost hair shaft is colored, the coat is known as smoke. Cats with smoked fur often appear to have a solid coat. When the cat moves, however, the paler roots become more visible and the coat "shimmers."

TICKED FUR

The hair shafts have alternating pigmented and paler bands in ticked coats. The tips of each hair are always pigmented. Also known as agouti, ticked fur occurs in many wildcats and other mammals because it provides excellent camouflage.

CREAM SHADED CAMEO

SILVER SHADED

BLACK SMOKE

BLUE SMOKE

SILVER RED

RUDDY

PARTI-COLORS

A parti, or parti-colored cat, has two or more colors in its coat. Partis include bicolor and tricolor cats and are found in many breeds, both shorthair and longhair. Partis also include torties (see right) and tabbies (see below, right) with white patches. When torties have a high proportion of white fur, the pattern is described as "calico" or "tortie and white."

TORTIE COLORS

Tortoiseshell, or tortie, coats have patches of black (or chocolate or cinnamon) and red fur either closely mingled or in distinct patches. Dilute forms of the coats also appear: blue, lilac, or fawn with cream fur. Patches of red or cream fur always have some tabby markings, and if the other color patches are tabby, too, the cat is known as a patched tabby. Tortie cats are almost always female.

POINTED

Coats in which the extremities are dark and the body paler are called pointed. In the Siamese and Persian Colorpoint, this pattern is controlled by a heat-sensitive enzyme involved in producing hair pigment. The enzyme works only in the cooler extremities of the body, hence the darker fur. The pointed coat of the Turkish Van, with dark fur on the head and tail only, is a form of white spotting.

PARTI-COLOR BRITISH SHORTHAIR

PARTI-COLOR RAGDOLL

ASIAN TORTIE

BRITISH SHORTHAIR TORTIE

SOLID-POINTED SIAMESE

TURKISH VAN

WHITE SPOTTING

Patches of white in a cat's coat are produced by a dominant gene that suppresses the production of colored fur. The result is a parti-colored coat (see above). The patches vary from just one small area to an almost all-white coat.

WHITE-SPOTTED MAINE COON

NONPEDIGREE SHORTHAIR WITH WHITE BIB AND MITTENS

TABBY PATTERNS

Swirls, stripes, or spots of black, brown, silver, or red solid fur mixed with paler areas of ticked fur form tabby coats. There are four main patterns: spotted; classic (blotches or swirls); mackerel (striped); and ticked.

SPOTTED

MACKEREL

CLASSIC

TICKED

Muscle and movement

There are about 500 muscles attached to a cat's flexible skeleton. They allow the cat to use various gaits (patterns of locomotion) and to make an amazing range of graceful movements, suitable for an athletic hunter of small rodents and birds. The cat's muscles are adapted not only for the short bursts of speed necessary to chase down prey, or to escape from danger, but also for the barely imperceptible movements the cat makes before pouncing on prey.

Muscles allow a cat to move, eat, breathe, and pump blood around the body. Cats, and other vertebrates (animals with a backbone), have three types of muscle. Cardiac muscle is found only in the heart and works tirelessly to pump blood; smooth muscle occurs in the walls of many body structures, such as blood vessels and the digestive tract; and skeletal muscle is attached to the bones by tendons and allows a cat to move body parts, such as the limbs, tail, eyes, and ears, and maintains posture. Skeletal muscle is also

Striated muscles
Skeletal muscle is controlled by the nervous system. This muscle moves bones or parts of the body, such as the eyes and tongue, or helps a cat maintain posture. It usually works in pairs or groups across movable joints.

called striated, or striped, muscle because of its appearance under a microscope. These muscles often work in antagonistic pairs across joints—one contracts while the other relaxes—allowing a body part, such as a section of a limb, to alternately bend and flex.

TYPES OF MUSCLE FIBER
Skeletal muscle tissue is made of bundles of long muscle cells called fibers. There are three types of fiber, depending on how quickly they work and tire. The most common type, "fast-twitch fatiguing" fibers contract and tire rapidly, and are used for short bursts of activity, such as sprinting and leaping. Much less common, "fast-twitch fatigue-resistant" fibers work similarly but tire slowly, and are more prevalent in the

RETRACTABLE CLAWS

Cats use the sharp, curved claws at the ends of their toes for fighting, defending themselves, gripping, climbing, and scratching to leave scent marks. Most of the time, they are hidden away in protective flesh sheaths. To expose, or bare, the claws, digital flexor muscles in the legs contract, tautening tendons and ligaments between the last two bones of the toes and pushing out the claws.

Claws out
At rest, a cat's claws are retracted, avoiding wear and tear and remaining sharp. Tautening the ligaments and tendons in the toes forces the claws out.

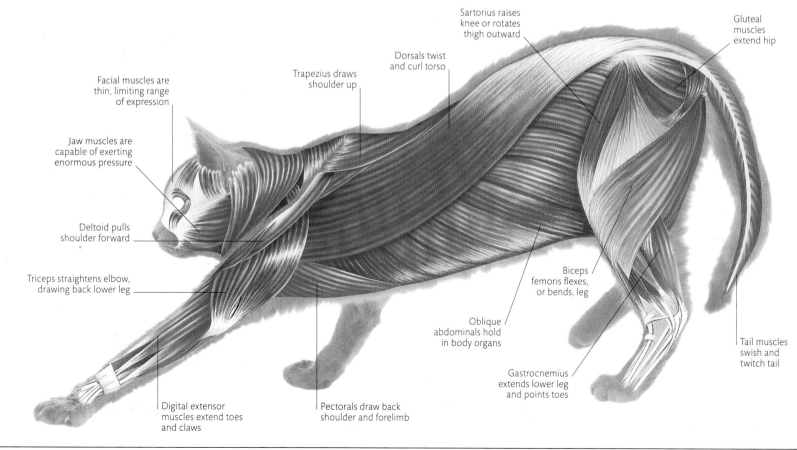

Facial muscles are thin, limiting range of expression

Jaw muscles are capable of exerting enormous pressure

Deltoid pulls shoulder forward

Triceps straightens elbow, drawing back lower leg

Digital extensor muscles extend toes and claws

Pectorals draw back shoulder and forelimb

Trapezius draws shoulder up

Dorsals twist and curl torso

Sartorius raises knee or rotates thigh outward

Gluteal muscles extend hip

Biceps femoris flexes, or bends, leg

Oblique abdominals hold in body organs

Gastrocnemius extends lower leg and points toes

Tail muscles swish and twitch tail

muscles of endurance hunters such as dogs. After a burst of running, a cat has to stop and pant to cool down. "Slow-twitch" fibers contract and tire slowly and are used for precise, stealthy movements when stalking or remaining stock still before the pounce.

GAITS

Unlike humans, who walk on their feet, cats walk on their toes. This type of locomotion of a cat is called *digitigrade* (Latin for "toe walking") and enables them to move quickly and quietly. The forward thrust for all of their gaits (walking, trotting, and running) comes from the powerful muscles in the back legs.

When cats walk, the limbs move sequentially; right rear, right front, left rear, left front. The front legs swing inward, with the paws landing one after the other almost in a line under the cat's body. The hind limbs swing inward, too, but not to the same extent. This gait enables a cat to walk along branches or narrow fence tops with confidence and ease. At such times, the tail is held aloft, helping the cat balance.

If the pace quickens to a trot, limbs that are diagonally opposite, such as the left forelimb and right hind leg, move together.

The floating forelimbs (see pp. 48–49) have extra maneuverability, helping to extend the cat's stride. When running, the cat makes a series of bounds. The back legs push off together, with the airborne

Lithe body
The firm musculature and compact bone structure of the feline form are always on display in hairless breeds, such as the Sphynx (see pp. 168–69) and this Bambino (see pp. 154–55).

cat's front legs touching down first, followed by the hind legs. When the cat stops, the front legs act as brakes.

Cats are adapted for short bursts of speed. Some domestic cats can run as fast as 30mph (48kph). By comparison, the fastest human can manage 27.79mph (44.72kph). Cats are not endurance hunters. The muscles in the cat's back legs are powerful, but they tire quickly. They prefer to stalk their prey and can remain motionless for long periods, waiting for the right moment to pounce.

FLEXIBILITY

A highly flexible body and musculature offer a range of other movements, too. The supple spine enables the cat to arch when stretching (or when trying to appear bigger, such as when threatened), or curl into a circle when the cat is sleeping. Flexibility is useful for grooming, too—the cat's paws and tongue are able to reach almost all parts of the body.

Strong hind leg muscles allow the cat to jump as high as 6½ft (2m) from a standing start, often twisting its body in midair to land safely. This movement is useful for catching birds as they try to make an airborne escape.

When climbing trees, the cat uses outstretched forelegs and claws like crampons, while the hind legs provide the power, propelling the animal up the tree. Descending, however, is a rather clumsy affair, with the cat scrabbling down backward in order to allow the forward-curving claws to be able to maintain a grip on the tree bark. The cat will finish the descent by turning its head and dropping the last metre or so to the ground. Most cats do not like getting wet, but there are some cats that tolerate swimming, their stroke similar to doggy paddle.

RIGHTING REFLEX

If a cat loses its footing and falls from a tree, it has the innate ability to twist the right way up before it lands. Within one-tenth of a second, the vestibular apparatus of the inner ear, which monitors balance, senses disorientation. A reflex reaction rotates the head so that the cat is looking downward. The front legs and then the hindquarters twist round, too, and the cat arches its back. Soft paw pads and flexible joints act as shock absorbers as the cat lands.

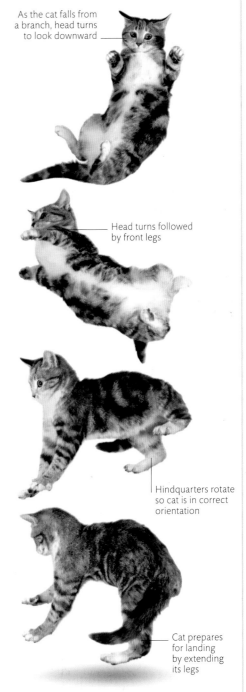

As the cat falls from a branch, head turns to look downward

Head turns followed by front legs

Hindquarters rotate so cat is in correct orientation

Cat prepares for landing by extending its legs

Landing safely
The righting reflex allows cats to twist instinctively their body around into a safe position for landing when falling from a height. A cat's flexible body amazingly rights itself in midair, without anything to push on.

Heart and lungs

The heart and lungs make sure that oxygen is delivered–via airways and blood–to every cell in the body. Oxygen, which makes up about 21 percent of the air, reacts with nutrient molecules, such as the sugar glucose, in body cells to release energy. This energy is then used to power biochemical activities in cells. As air travels to and from the lungs, it passes through the larynx, the source of a cat's vocalizations, including its purr.

The airways and lungs comprise the respiratory system. Air inhaled through a cat's nose is humidified in the nasal passages and drawn along the trachea (windpipe), which branches into two air passages called bronchi, one for each lung. Within the lungs, the bronchi divide into smaller tubes called bronchioles, which end in tiny air sacs called alveoli. Gas exchange occurs inside the alveoli. Oxygen diffuses across the thin walls of the millions of alveoli into tiny blood vessels called capillaries, where it is picked up by red blood cells. The waste gas carbon dioxide travels in the opposite direction, out of the blood and into the alveoli, to be exhaled.

At rest, cats breathe in and out about 20–30 times a minute. During exercise, when the muscles need more oxygen, the rate increases. Muscles between the ribs and a sheet of muscle below the rib cage, called the diaphragm, power breathing.

CARDIOVASCULAR SYSTEM

The heart and the blood vessels form the cardiovascular system. The cat's heart is a four-chambered pump, about the size of a walnut, made of special non-tiring cardiac muscle. It beats between 140 and 220 times each minute, depending on the level of activity, and its resting heartbeat of 140–180 beats per minute is about double that of a resting human. The heart pumps blood around the body in two separate circuits. The pulmonary circuit takes stale, or deoxygenated, blood to the lungs to pick up oxygen. This freshly oxygenated blood then returns to the heart to be pumped around the body to all its organs and tissues in the larger circuit.

Arteries have muscular walls that expand and contract as bright-red oxygenated blood surges through them with each heartbeat. This creates a pulse that can be felt at various points of the cat's body. Darker deoxygenated

BLOOD TYPES

The most important blood group system in cats has three groups, or types: A, B, and AB. The percentage of cats in each group varies among breeds and geographies. Group A is by far the most common type. A few breeds, including the Siamese (see pp. 104–09), are exclusively type A. Type B is relatively low in many breeds, but in some, such as the Devon Rex (see pp. 178–79), it is 25–50 percent. Type AB is rare in all breeds.

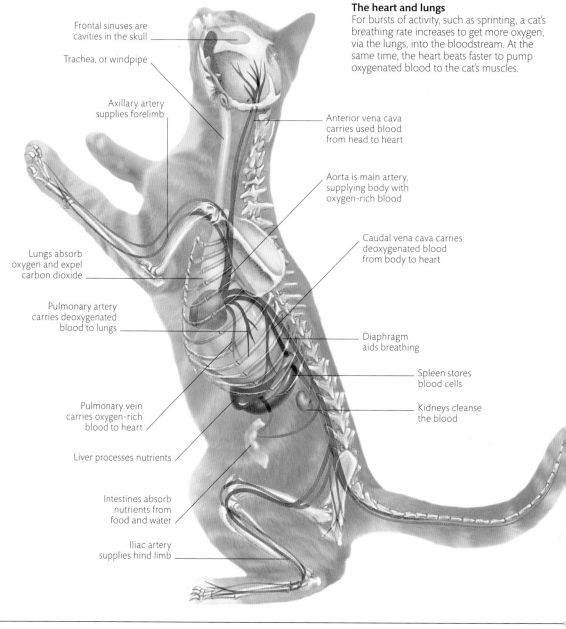

The heart and lungs
For bursts of activity, such as sprinting, a cat's breathing rate increases to get more oxygen, via the lungs, into the bloodstream. At the same time, the heart beats faster to pump oxygenated blood to the cat's muscles.

Frontal sinuses are cavities in the skull

Trachea, or windpipe

Axillary artery supplies forelimb

Lungs absorb oxygen and expel carbon dioxide

Pulmonary artery carries deoxygenated blood to lungs

Pulmonary vein carries oxygen-rich blood to heart

Liver processes nutrients

Intestines absorb nutrients from food and water

Iliac artery supplies hind limb

Anterior vena cava carries used blood from head to heart

Aorta is main artery, supplying body with oxygen-rich blood

Caudal vena cava carries deoxygenated blood from body to heart

Diaphragm aids breathing

Spleen stores blood cells

Kidneys cleanse the blood

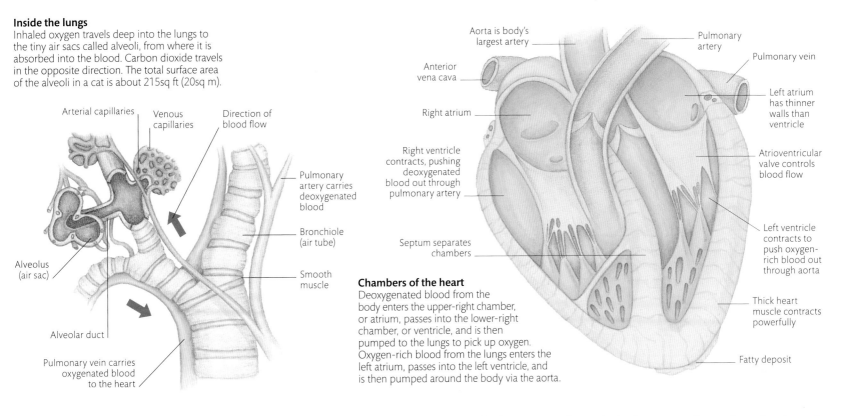

Inside the lungs
Inhaled oxygen travels deep into the lungs to the tiny air sacs called alveoli, from where it is absorbed into the blood. Carbon dioxide travels in the opposite direction. The total surface area of the alveoli in a cat is about 215sq ft (20sq m).

Arterial capillaries

Venous capillaries

Direction of blood flow

Pulmonary artery carries deoxygenated blood

Bronchiole (air tube)

Smooth muscle

Alveolus (air sac)

Alveolar duct

Pulmonary vein carries oxygenated blood to the heart

Aorta is body's largest artery

Anterior vena cava

Right atrium

Right ventricle contracts, pushing deoxygenated blood out through pulmonary artery

Septum separates chambers

Pulmonary artery

Pulmonary vein

Left atrium has thinner walls than ventricle

Atrioventricular valve controls blood flow

Left ventricle contracts to push oxygen-rich blood out through aorta

Thick heart muscle contracts powerfully

Fatty deposit

Chambers of the heart
Deoxygenated blood from the body enters the upper-right chamber, or atrium, passes into the lower-right chamber, or ventricle, and is then pumped to the lungs to pick up oxygen. Oxygen-rich blood from the lungs enters the left atrium, passes into the left ventricle, and is then pumped around the body via the aorta.

blood returns to the heart in thin-walled veins, which contain valves to maintain blood flow in one direction only. A network of microscopic blood vessels called capillaries lies between the arteries and veins. Here, oxygen and other molecules, such as glucose, pass from the blood into surrounding cells and tissues. Wastes, such as carbon dioxide, pass in the opposite direction.

The brain makes up only 0.9 percent of a cat's weight, but it receives up to 20 percent of blood flow. Muscles at rest receive 40 percent of blood flow, but this amount can rapidly increase to up to 90 percent during short bursts of exercise.

An averaged-sized cat of 11lb (5kg) has about 11fl oz (330ml) of blood in its body. By volume, blood is about 54 percent plasma, a watery liquid that carries food molecules such as glucose, salts, wastes, hormones, and other chemicals around the body. Biconcave, disk-shaped red blood cells, which carry oxygen picked up from the lungs, account for another 46 percent of volume. The remaining 1 percent contains white blood cells, which fight infection, and cell fragments called platelets, which help blood clot at sites of injury.

VOCALIZATION PROCESS
Purring was once thought to be the sound of turbulent blood flow in the vena cava, the

large vein that carries blood into the heart. More recent research, however, suggests that it is produced in the larynx (voice box), which connects the back of the throat with the trachea. The vocal cords, two infoldings of membrane in the larynx, vibrate as exhaled air passes over them, to make vocalizations, such as meows and screeches. During purring, however, the muscles that control the vocal cords vibrate, causing the cords to bang into each other repeatedly. Air passing

through the larynx as the cat breathes in and out produces bursts of noise, 25 times a second, known as purring. Other cat species, such as the bobcat, cougar, and cheetah, can purr, too. Big cats of the genus *Panthera*, such as lions and tigers, roar rather than purr. They can do this because of their enlarged larynx. Folds in their vocal cords vibrate to produce sound, while the hyoid bone lowers the pitch and increases the resonance of the roar.

PURRING

We associate the rhythmic chug of a cat's purr with contentment—and in many cases it is a sign of a happy cat. However, cats may also purr when they're anxious, giving birth, or injured. Kittens learn to purr at about one week old (before their eyes open), and biologists believe that it developed as a way for kittens to communicate to the mother that she needs to be still while they are feeding. The mother may join in, too, to reassure her young.

Cats also produce an urgent, "solicitous" purr, which they use when wanting to be fed by their owners. This sound is a mixture of the low-pitched rumble of a regular purr and a higher-frequency meow. Analysis of the meow element shows that its frequency is

similar to that of the cry of a human baby, which may help explain our willingness to feed an insistent cat.

Among older cats, purring may also communicate nonaggression, vulnerability, or a request from one cat grooming another for it to stay still.

STROKING A CAT CAN MAKE IT PURR

Digestion and reproduction

Strict carnivores, cats have a digestive system that has evolved to suit a diet of small animals such as mice. They have sharp teeth designed to kill and cut up prey, and relatively short intestines for digesting meat. The kidneys clean the blood, removing wastes and eliminating them from the body. Queens tend to give birth in spring and summer when food is likely to be plentiful for the kittens once they are weaned.

Cats have one of the narrowest diets of all carnivorous mammals. Their diet must include certain vitamins, fatty acids, and amino acids, as well as a chemical called taurine, which is found only in meat. Cats cannot make these nutrients, or taurine, themselves nor get them from other sources of food, such as plants, and they cannot survive without them.

Unlike vegetable matter, meat is relatively easy to break down into nutrients in the intestines. Cats, therefore, have a relatively short, simple digestive tract compared to that of herbivores such as sheep and horses.

DIGESTION

The domestic cat's digestive tract is a little longer than that of its wildcat ancestor. This suggests that the cat's digestive system has been adapting to the increased plant matter in its diet (probably from scavenged scraps of human food containing both meat and cereal) since it first began to associate with humans several thousand years ago. Cats eat little and often. The transit of food—from eating to defecating—takes about 20 hours. The first stage of digestion is the physical breakup of food in the mouth by the teeth. The mouth produces saliva to lubricate the food, which, on being swallowed, passes down the esophagus into the stomach, where further physical digestion as well as some chemical breakdown by enzymes occurs. The strong acid in a cat's stomach is powerful enough

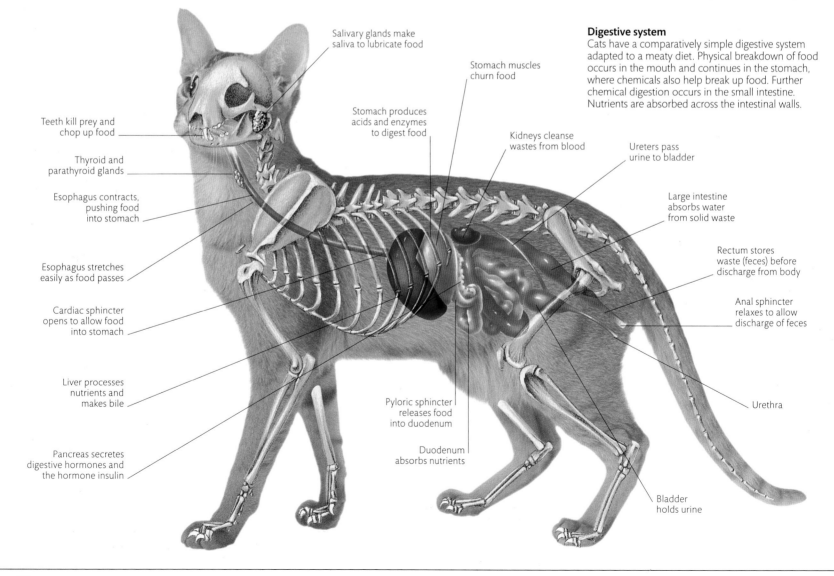

Digestive system
Cats have a comparatively simple digestive system adapted to a meaty diet. Physical breakdown of food occurs in the mouth and continues in the stomach, where chemicals also help break up food. Further chemical digestion occurs in the small intestine. Nutrients are absorbed across the intestinal walls.

Salivary glands make saliva to lubricate food

Stomach muscles churn food

Stomach produces acids and enzymes to digest food

Kidneys cleanse wastes from blood

Ureters pass urine to bladder

Teeth kill prey and chop up food

Thyroid and parathyroid glands

Esophagus contracts, pushing food into stomach

Esophagus stretches easily as food passes

Cardiac sphincter opens to allow food into stomach

Liver processes nutrients and makes bile

Pancreas secretes digestive hormones and the hormone insulin

Pyloric sphincter releases food into duodenum

Duodenum absorbs nutrients

Large intestine absorbs water from solid waste

Rectum stores waste (feces) before discharge from body

Anal sphincter relaxes to allow discharge of feces

Urethra

Bladder holds urine

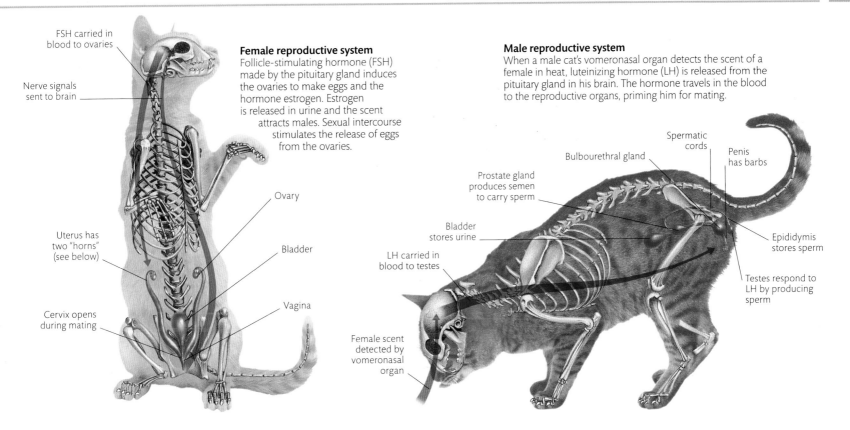

Female reproductive system
Follicle-stimulating hormone (FSH) made by the pituitary gland induces the ovaries to make eggs and the hormone estrogen. Estrogen is released in urine and the scent attracts males. Sexual intercourse stimulates the release of eggs from the ovaries.

FSH carried in blood to ovaries

Nerve signals sent to brain

Uterus has two "horns" (see below)

Cervix opens during mating

Ovary

Bladder

Vagina

Male reproductive system
When a male cat's vomeronasal organ detects the scent of a female in heat, luteinizing hormone (LH) is released from the pituitary gland in his brain. The hormone travels in the blood to the reproductive organs, priming him for mating.

Spermatic cords

Penis has barbs

Bulbourethral gland

Prostate gland produces semen to carry sperm

Bladder stores urine

LH carried in blood to testes

Female scent detected by vomeronasal organ

Epididymis stores sperm

Testes respond to LH by producing sperm

to soften swallowed bones. (Any bones, hair, and feathers that cannot be digested are usually regurgitated later.)

Partly digested food leaves the stomach through the pyloric sphincter and enters the first section of the small intestine, the duodenum, where most of the chemical digestion takes place. Bile, produced by the liver and stored in the gall bladder, and a mix of enzymes from the pancreas enter this small loop of intestine and digest fats, proteins, and carbohydrates. Nutrients are then absorbed across the wall of the small intestine into the bloodstream. They travel to the liver to be processed into useful molecules. Water is absorbed in the colon, and waste matter is passed out through the anus as feces.

ELIMINATION OF WASTES

Besides solid feces, waste from the liver is processed by the kidneys. Their major role is to cleanse the blood, removing potentially harmful metabolic wastes, such as urea. The kidneys also control the composition and volume of fluids in a cat's body. Waste substances leave the kidneys, dissolved in water as urine. The urine flows along narrow ureters—one from each kidney—to be stored in the bladder. This balloonlike organ holds up to 3½ fl oz (100ml) of urine, which exits the bladder through the urethra. The urine of unneutered cats can be especially pungent and is used to mark territory and advertise sexual status.

REPRODUCTION

Cats usually become sexually mature between 6–9 months, although in some Oriental breeds it may be earlier. As daylight hours increase during spring, hormonal changes in an unaltered female, or queen, make her receptive to finding a mate. She is then said to be "in heat" or "in season." She produces scents that attract intact males, or toms, and she may also call to them. Sexual intercourse is painful for the female. A tom's penis has a band of 120–150 backward-pointing hooks that abrade the female's vagina as he withdraws, causing her to yowl loudly and lash out. However, this does not seem to have a lasting effect because she mates many times while in heat, often with several toms.

The pain also triggers the release of eggs from the ovaries about 25–35 hours after the first mating. The eggs travel along the two "horns" (see above) of the uterus. The period of heat then eases off. If no pregnancy occurs, the queen will go into heat again a couple of weeks later. If mating is successful, pregnancy lasts for about 63 days. The average litter size is 3–5 kittens and can be as high as 10.

TEETH

Kittens have 26 milk teeth, which erupt before 2 weeks of age and begin to fall out at about 14 weeks. Cats have 30 permanent teeth. Small incisors at the front of the jaws are used for grasping prey, while the canines, or fangs, kill prey by severing the spinal cord. Cats cannot chew very well; instead, their back teeth chop up food into smaller pieces before it is swallowed. The carnassial teeth (the upper jaw's back premolars and the lower jaw's molars) are especially effective in slicing through food with a scissorlike action. When eating, the cat's rough tongue—which is covered in little barbs—can rasp meat from the bones of prey animals.

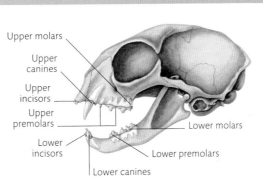

Upper molars

Upper canines

Upper incisors

Upper premolars

Lower incisors

Lower canines

Lower molars

Lower premolars

Keeping clean
A cat's teeth are naturally cleaned by the bones of its prey, which scrape the teeth as the cat eats. Unless owners regularly brush their cats' teeth, they are vulnerable to decay.

The immune system

Cats are at risk of infection from bacteria, viruses, and other infectious agents. To keep healthy they have a powerful immune system with protective white blood cells that recognize "foreign" invaders, quickly destroying them before they multiply. Sometimes the immune system reacts inappropriately, causing allergies or autoimmune disorders. The immune system weakens as a cat ages.

PROTECTION AT BIRTH

When kittens are born, their immune systems are not fully developed and they are at risk of infections. They do, however, receive help from their mother's milk, specifically the first milk she produces after the kittens are born. This thick yellowy milk (colostrum) is made for only about 72 hours after birth and is rich in external antibodies that protect the kittens against infections to which the mother is already immune. This protection lasts for 8–10 weeks, by which time kittens are able to make their own antibodies. Recent research has shown that receiving colostrum is crucial in the first 18 hours of a kitten's life. During that time, the antibodies cross the wall of the kitten's intestine and are absorbed into the bloodstream. Thereafter, the kitten's body loses the ability to absorb antibodies passed on from the mother cat.

A CAT'S IMMUNE SYSTEM

The immune system includes any part of a cat's body that protects it against infection. The body's surface—the skin and mucous membranes—acts as a physical barrier to disease-causing germs (pathogens). The strong acid in the cat's stomach kills many of the germs that enter through the mouth or nose. Those that do manage to enter the body through a cut or tear face attack from the major component of the immune system: white blood cells, also known as leucocytes. Millions of white blood cells, made by bone marrow, are found in the bloodstream and in the lymphatic system. This system is a network of vessels throughout the body that collect and drain a watery fluid called lymph from body organs. Its vessels are dotted with small nodes packed with white blood cells. The nodes filter the lymph, and the white blood cells attack any trapped germs. The tonsils, thymus, spleen, and the lining of the small intestine are also part of the lymphatic system.

There are several types of white blood cell, each with a different role. They identify and attack pathogens, such as bacteria, viruses, fungi, protozoa, and parasites, as well as any harmful chemicals (toxins) they may produce. White blood cells include:

- Neutrophils, which engulf and destroy bacteria and fungi at the site of the infection, such as a wound.
- T-cells, or T-lymphocytes, which have a variety of roles, including the regulation of B-lymphocytes and attacking virus-infected and tumor cells.
- B-lymphocytes, which produce proteins called antibodies that attach to and neutralize pathogens.
- Eosinophils, which target parasites and are also involved in allergic responses.
- Macrophages, which engulf and digest the pathogens marked out by other white blood cells.

ALLERGIES, AUTOIMMUNITY, AND IMMUNODEFICIENCY

Cats can suffer from allergies, producing a range of symptoms, including itchy skin (and redness if the cat has been persistently scratching itself), sneezing, asthmatic wheezing, vomiting, diarrhea, and bloating. Allergies occur when the immune system overreacts to a foreign substance, usually harmless, leading to the release of an inflammatory chemical such as histamine in the body. Common triggers include: fleabites; food—usually proteins in meats such as beef, pork, or chicken; airborne

Exposure to infection
Outdoor cats are at greater risk of infection than indoor cats because they can pick up parasites through contact with other outdoor cats. They are also at risk of swallowing poisons, attacks from other animals such as dogs, and traffic accidents.

STRESS

Cats are easily stressed. A change at home is often the cause, such as the arrival of a new pet or baby, or even the rearrangement of furniture. Stress causes the release of hormones such as epinephrine (adrenalin) and cortisol (see p. 43). In the short term, these hormones increase awareness and energy but if their release is prolonged, they dampen the immune system, impairing a cat's ability to protect itself against infections and cancer and to recover speedily after illness.

Chemicals called endorphins are released by the brain when a cat is highly excited, such as during a fight with another cat or animal. In such cases, endorphins have a protective role because they are natural painkillers, lessening the discomfort of any teeth and claw wounds inflicted.

particles such as pollen; and contact with a substance such as wool or detergent. The surefire way to treat an allergy is to remove the trigger, but it may be difficult to find the exact cause. A vet may prescribe antihistamines, which relieve itchy skin. Pest control is necessary if fleabites are the cause.

Autoimmune disorders are caused by an overactive immune system, which attacks the body's own tissues. Although rare in cats, they include a group of skin diseases known as pemphigus complex and the multisystem disorder systemic lupus erythematosus (SLE). The immune system may also be underactive or weakened with age. Certain feline infections attack cells of the immune system, making the cat vulnerable to other infections and cancer. Such pathogens include the feline immunodeficiency virus (FIV), which attacks certain T-cells, and feline leukemia virus (FeLV), which may cause cancer of white blood cells.

VACCINATIONS

Immunization can help protect the cat against some infectious diseases. Vaccinations trigger the production of antibodies against certain microorganisms, making a cat immune to many diseases without causing the symptoms of the disease. For example, cats can be vaccinated against feline infectious enteritis, feline herpes virus, and feline calcivirus.

Immunization
A vet will advise which vaccinations are appropriate for the region and the cat's lifestyle (for example, if it is an indoor or outdoor cat). Initial vaccinations should begin when cats are kittens, with annual boosters for the rest of their lives.

A cat's immune system
The immune system is made up of a defensive network of cells, tissues, and organs spread throughout the body. White blood cells, found in the lymphatic system and bloodstream, have the greatest role in fighting infection.

Tonsils defend against inhaled or ingested germs

Lymphatic system is a network of vessels and nodes

Intestinal walls contain lymphatic tissue

Lymph nodes filter lymph

Skin and coat act as a barrier to germs

Spleen contains white blood cells

Bone marrow produces white blood cells

Understanding breeds

Like other domesticated animals, there are different breeds of cat. Well-known breeds include the Siamese, Abyssinian, Manx, Persian, and Maine Coon. Cats began to be categorized into breeds in the 19th century with the advent of cat shows. Today, there are over 100 cat breeds and varieties recognized by one or more of the official cat registries. Most pet cats, however, do not belong to any breed; they are random-bred, or just ordinary house cats of mixed breed.

WHAT IS A BREED?

A breed is a type of domestic animal that is bred in a controlled way to produce offspring with consistent features. This holds true for most breeds of cat, but sometimes outcrossing (mating with another breed) is allowed for health reasons or to introduce or refine a feature such as the coat. Cat breeds have been developed relatively recently. As cat fancy took off in the 19th century, registries were established to keep records of show cats and their genealogies. These registries define the characteristics, or "breed standards," of each breed. Major ones include the Cat Fanciers Association (CFA) and The International Cat Association (TICA), the Fédération Internationale Féline (FiFe), and the Governing Council of the Cat Fancy (GCCF).

CHARACTERISTICS

Cat breeds are defined by their appearance: their coat—its color, pattern, and length; head and body shape; and eye color. Unusual features, such as absence of tail, short legs, and folded ears, also define certain breeds. Coat colors and patterns are particularly varied (see pp. 50–53), with some breeds, such as the Chartreux (see p. 115), having just one color, and others, such as the British Shorthair (see pp. 118–19), being permitted many coat colors and patterns.

HOW BREEDS DEVELOP

Some breeds, such as the British Shorthair, developed naturally from isolated groups of cats, their restricted gene pool resulting in a typical appearance. Other natural breeds arose because they had a characteristic that helped them survive, such as the long coat of the Maine Coon (see pp. 214–15), which is indispensable for cold, northern winters.

In small, isolated populations, a trait caused by a genetic mutation—which would probably only rarely appear in a larger population—can become common over generations of inbreeding. This genetic influence is called the "founder effect" and accounts for the taillessness of the Manx (see pp. 164–65), for example. Breeders exploit the founder effect to create new breeds from cats with novel characteristics caused by a mutation. Such breeds include the Scottish Fold (see pp. 156–57), Munchkin (see pp. 150–51), and Sphynx (see pp. 168–69).

THE ROLE OF GENETICS

Breeders of pedigree cats use their understanding of genetics to pinpoint characteristics that are caused by dominant

DOMESTIC CAT HYBRIDS

■ The diagram shows the relationship between the domestic cat and other members of the cat family, particularly the small cats that have been crossed with the domestic cat to produce new breeds such as the Bengal and Chausie. The closer a wild species is to the domestic cat on this diagram, the more closely they are related.

■ A domestic cat's genetic material, or DNA, is carried on 38 chromosomes (19 pairs), as it is in several of the wild felids. It is therefore possible to cross domestic cats with small wildcats despite differences in gestation periods between the species. Often, the fertility of early generations, particularly first crosses (F1 generation), is considerably reduced, but by backcrossing this can be improved.

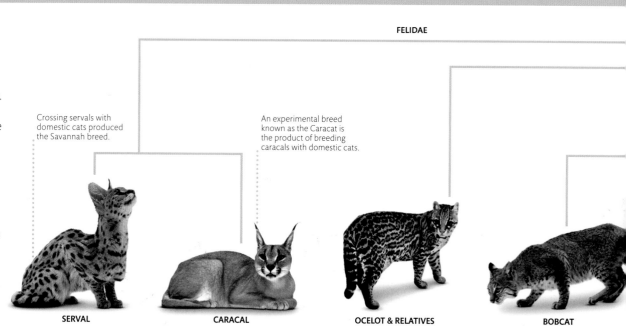

FELIDAE

Crossing servals with domestic cats produced the Savannah breed.

An experimental breed known as the Caracat is the product of breeding caracals with domestic cats.

SERVAL

CARACAL

OCELOT & RELATIVES

BOBCAT

DOMINANT AND RECESSIVE TRAITS

Cats with a dark coat have at least one copy of the dominant dense pigment gene known as *D*. This gene produces hair that is packed with pigment. The recessive form of this gene, called *d*, reduces the level of pigment in the hair, diluting the color of the cat's fur when two copies are present. If two black-coated cats, both with two copies of the black coat gene (*B*), have one copy of the dense (*D*) gene and one copy of the dilute (*d*) pigment gene, there is a one-in-four chance that their kittens will have blue (diluted black) fur.

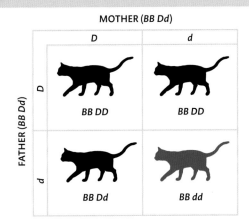

MOTHER (*BB Dd*)

	D	d
D	BB DD	BB DD
d	BB Dd	BB dd

FATHER (*BB Dd*)

or recessive genes. They can then predict how the offspring of different parents will look. Dominant genes require just one copy from either parent to produce an effect. For example, the gene that produces a tabby coat is dominant over the gene causing a non-tabby coat. Recessive genes need two copies—one from each parent—to have an effect. Long hair is another recessive characteristic.

OUTCROSSING

Cat registries stipulate in their breed standards what outcrosses, if any, are permissible for each breed. Crossbred kittens are registered according to their appearance. Outcrossing is also used to develop new breeds, such as longhaired versions of shorthaired breeds.

Outcrossing is also necessary for the health of certain breeds; for example, Scottish Folds are usually a cross between a Fold and a British or American Shorthair with normal ears. This pairing keeps kittens from

Handsome hybrid
A 21st-century designer cat, the Savannah was developed from a cross between a Siamese (see pp. 104–09) and a serval, and has retained the huge ears, long legs, and spotted coat of the serval.

receiving two copies of the fold mutation, because such kittens suffer from a debilitating disease affecting bone development.

HYBRIDS AND FUTURE BREEDS

In recent decades, domestic cats have been crossed with other species of small wildcats to create new breeds, usually with striking "exotic" coats. These hybrids include the Bengal (see pp. 142–43), Chausie (see p. 149), and the Savannah (see pp. 146–47).

New breeds—arising purely from other domestic cats—are always being developed, but it can take years for them to be accepted by cat registries. Pipeline breeds include the Arctic Curl—a shaggy-haired cross between the Selkirk Rex (see pp. 174–75 and p. 248) and the Angora (see p. 229)—and the Benedictine, a longhaired Chartreux with DNA from the Persian (see pp. 186–205).

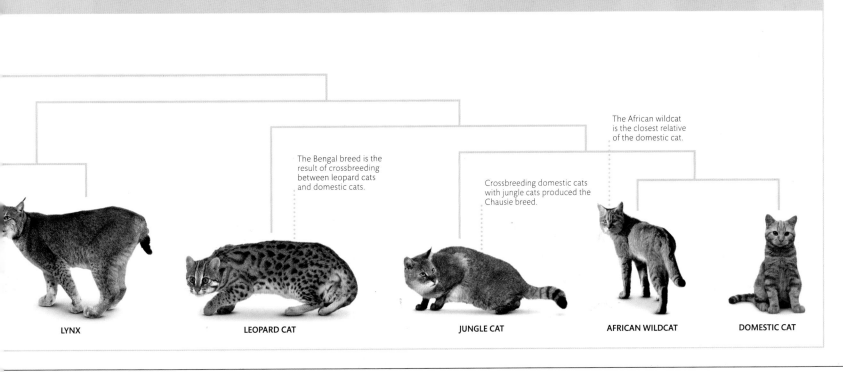

The Bengal breed is the result of crossbreeding between leopard cats and domestic cats.

Crossbreeding domestic cats with jungle cats produced the Chausie breed.

The African wildcat is the closest relative of the domestic cat.

LYNX

LEOPARD CAT

JUNGLE CAT

AFRICAN WILDCAT

DOMESTIC CAT

Choosing the right cat

The needs of cats vary depending on the breed. For example, slender breeds, such as the Siamese, are usually very active and love being part of a family; stockier breeds, such as the British Shorthair, tend to be more laid-back and prefer a quieter life. One way to find a pedigree is to contact a reputable breeder. Pedigrees can sometimes be found in rescue shelters, too, but most cats in such places will be non-pedigree.

A particular breed may be desirable purely for its appearance: for example, the rich brown coat of the Havana (see p. 102) or the thick blue-gray fur of the Chartreux (see p. 115) are captivating to many. Some cat lovers are drawn to the ancient mystique of the Egyptian Mau (see p. 130) or the eye-catching wild look of the Bengal (see pp. 142–43). Size, temperament, and coat length are also important factors when choosing a breed.

Alternatively, an owner may be happy with a non-pedigree cat, which will be easier to find (more than 95 percent of cats fall into this category) and significantly cheaper to buy.

SIZE AND BUILD

Unlike dogs, cat breeds do not vary greatly in size, but some variety among the breeds does exist. If the cat is to remain indoors in a flat or small home, try one of the smaller breeds. The smallest breeds are the Singapura (see p. 86), Lambkin Dwarf (see p. 153), and Bambino (see pp. 154–55), all of which have the short stature of the Munchkin (see pp. 150–51). These cats have an adult weight of as little as 5lb (2kg). Other small breeds tend to have a slender Oriental build and include the Bombay (see pp. 84–85), Havana, and Cornish Rex (see pp. 176–77). At the other end of the scale, the heavyweight of breeds is the

Highlander (see p. 158), which can reach an adult weight of 25lb (11kg). Other large breeds include the Maine Coon (see pp. 214–15), Turkish Van (see pp. 226–27), and Savannah (see pp. 146–47). These large cats need plenty of space and are not suitable as exclusively indoor pets.

ACTIVE OR DOCILE

Different breeds have different temperaments. Sleek-bodied Oriental cats, such as the Siamese (see pp. 104–09), Tonkinese (see p. 90), Burmese (see pp. 87–88), Sphynx (see pp. 168–69), Bombay, and Abyssinian (see pp. 132–33), are more active, playful, and inquisitive than othercat breeds. These

Making new friends
If kittens have been socialized from a young age, they will be friendly and playful, rather than aggressive and fearful, when meeting new people or other pets.

Rare breeds
Some cats are popular in the region where the breed developed, but are not well-known elsewhere in the world, such as the Kurilian Bobtail (see pp. 242–43), which is popular in Japan and Russia, but rare in other countries.

breeds are generally thought to be more intelligent and more likely to learn tricks or to be trained to walk on a harness and leash. Many of these breeds are noisy, or "talkative," too.

More laid-back, quieter breeds are generally those with a thickset, or stocky, body form, such as the British Shorthair (see pp. 118–28), Persian (see pp. 186–205), and Norwegian Forest Cat (see pp. 222–23). The Ragdoll (see p. 216) and Ragamuffin (see p. 217) are particularly docile. These are wonderful to pet, but should be treated with care, since they may not let you know when they are in discomfort.

LONGHAIR OR SHORTHAIR?

Cat breeds are broadly divided into shorthairs and longhairs. Shorthairs, which include the Siamese, Russian Blue (see pp. 116–17), and the Bengal, need grooming just once or twice a week. Longhairs, especially the doll-faced Persian with its long, silky fur, are a greater commitment, requiring daily grooming to keep their coat free of mats and tangles, which become a health risk if left unattended. Other well-known longhairs include the Birman (see pp. 212–13), Ragdoll, and Siberian (see pp. 230–31).

DESIGNER CATS

Novelty, or designer, breeds are becoming increasingly fashionable, but are expensive—kittens may cost up to and over $1,500. These breeds include: cats with unusual ears, such as the Scottish Fold (see pp. 156–57) and American Curl (see pp. 238–39); hairless breeds, such as the Sphynx and Peterbald (see p. 171), which need to live in a centrally heated home in temperate or cold regions; and cats with kinky or curled fur, such as the American Wirehair (see p. 181), LaPerm (see pp. 250–51), and various Rexes. The short-legged Munchkin is much sought

after, as well its "spin-off" breeds. These include the curled ear Kinkalow (see p. 152), the curly coated Skookum (see p. 235) and Lambkin Dwarf, the hairless Bambino, and longhaired Napoleon (see p. 236).

Cats with a beautiful coat that resemble the pelt of small wild cats (see pp. 8–9) are also increasingly popular. Some of these breeds, such as the California Spangled (see p. 140), Egyptian Mau, and Sokoke (see p. 139), arise purely from domestic cats; others, including the Bengal, Savannah, and Chausie (see p. 149), were developed from hybrids of the domestic cat and other feline species. Hybrids are generally active and may bully other cats.

GETTING A CAT

Whatever breed you choose, the first step is to find a reputable breeder. To find a pedigree kitten, begin by contacting a cat club or a breed registry, or visit a cat show where the people showing their cats may suggest a

Rescue me
It is worth checking rescue centers when buying a pedigree cat, especially when looking for an adult pet. Pedigrees needing a new home sometimes find their way into these centers, and they are usually considerably cheaper to buy than from a breeder.

Special care
Many of the cats in rescue centers are elderly, having survived the death of their owner, for example. If you choose an elderly or disabled cat, the center may help pay for the pet's ongoing health care.

breeder or be breeders themselves. The local vet may also be able to recommend breeders in your area.

The breeder will be able to answer questions about your chosen breed and its needs, and you should be able to meet and observe the kitten and its mother before buying it. A good breeder will question a prospective owner about provision and care of the kitten and, if all goes well, arrange for the new owner to be able to collect a socialized, wormed, and vaccinated kitten when it is 12 weeks old.

Many excellent pets may be found in rescue centers or cat shelters, and it is worth looking at these places, too, especially when searching for an older cat with an established personality. These mostly nonprofit organizations usually charge an adoption fee, which helps cover food and veterinary costs for the cats that are housed there. Pedigree cats, especially the more popular breeds, sometimes turn up in rescue centers, but these places are ideal for those not particularly interested in owning a pedigree cat; most of the cats housed are random-bred (see pp. 182–83 and pp. 252–53), but all are in need of a loving home.

CATALOG
OF BREEDS

SHORTHAIRS

Most cats have short hair, whether they are large or small, wild or domestic. This is an evolutionary development that makes sense for a natural predator relying on stealth and the occasional burst of speed. A hunting cat is more efficient in a short coat because it can glide unhampered through dense terrain and move freely for a lightning pounce in a tight corner.

DEVELOPING THE SHORTHAIR
The first cats to be domesticated, possibly over 4,000 years ago, had short hair, and their sleek-coated look has been popular ever since. In a short coat, colors and patterns are clearly defined and the feline form appears to full advantage. Dozens of shorthaired breeds have been developed, but there are three main groups: British, American, and Oriental Shorthairs.

The first two are essentially ordinary domestic cats refined by decades of breeding programs. They are sturdy, round-headed cats, with short, dense, double-layered coats. The strikingly different Oriental group has little to do with the East, being created in Europe through crosses with the Siamese. They have short, close-lying, fine coats with no woolly undercoat.

Other much-loved shorthaired cats include: the Burmese; the plush-furred Russian Blue, which has a very short undercoat that lifts the top guard hairs away from the body; and the Exotic Shorthair, which combines unmistakably Persian looks with a shorter, more manageable coat.

Short hair is taken to extremes in several hairless breeds, including the Sphynx and the Peterbald. These cats are usually not totally hairless—most have a fine covering of body hair with the feel of suede. Another variety of short hair is seen in rexed cats, which have wavy or crimped coats. Among the best known of these are the Devon Rex and the Cornish Rex.

EASY MAINTENANCE
A great advantage for owners of shorthaired breeds is that the coat requires little grooming to keep it in good condition, while parasites and injuries are easy to see and treat. However, keeping a shorthaired cat does not guarantee hair-free carpets and sofas. Some breeds shed heavily, especially during seasonal loss of thick undercoats, and even single-coated varieties such as the Orientals always lose a certain amount of hair.

Familiar face
The Exotic Shorthair's face clearly shows the large eyes, flat face, and full cheeks that it has inherited from the Persian breed. It also has a thick coat that is unique among shorthairs.

Exotic Shorthair

ORIGIN US, 1960s
BREED REGISTRIES CFA, FIFe, GCCF, TICA
WEIGHT RANGE 8–15lb (3.5–7kg)

GROOMING 2–3 times a week
COLORS AND PATTERNS Almost all colors and patterns.

CUDDLY TEDDY

With its rounded, plush-furred body, snub nose, and big eyes, the Exotic Shorthair lives up to its popular nickname of the "teddy bear cat," and most breeders do not fail to make the comparison in their advertisements. The extra-soft, thick double coat is quite unlike that found in any other shorthaired breed. It has an underlayer of long downy hairs, inherited from the Exotic's Persian forebears, that lifts the topcoat away from the body.

This affectionate breed, which has an endearing nature, is a low-maintenance version of the longhaired Persian cat.

The first Exotics were bred in the US in the 1960s, and by the 1980s there was a popular British version as well. These cats were created through breeding programs that crossed the Persian with the American Shorthair (see p. 113) to improve the coat of the latter. Later, crosses were also done with the Burmese (see pp. 87–88), Abyssinian (see pp. 132–33), and British Shorthair (see pp. 118–27). Early breeders aimed to create a shorthaired cat with a silvery coat and green eyes, like a Persian; later, the goal was to breed cats with a Persian-type face and body but short hair.

KITTEN

Exotics combine the Persian's round-faced look and quiet temperament with a thick, soft, but short coat that requires less grooming than its longhaired counterpart; for this reason they are sometimes called "the lazy man's Persian." These gentle cats have the quiet, docile nature of their Persian ancestors. They are happy as indoor pets and are always pleased to have someone around to play with or offer a lap. They have soft voices and rarely make a noise, but they love attention, and many will sit in front of people and gaze up beseechingly for a hug.

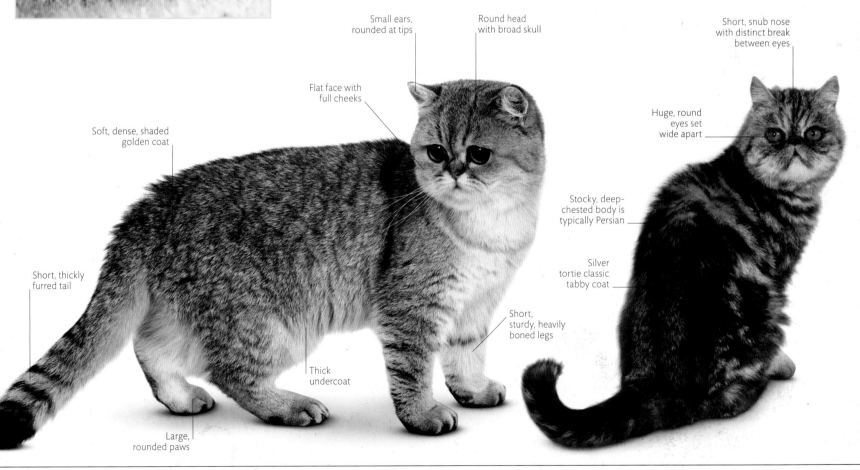

Small ears, rounded at tips

Round head with broad skull

Flat face with full cheeks

Soft, dense, shaded golden coat

Short, thickly furred tail

Thick undercoat

Large, rounded paws

Short, sturdy, heavily boned legs

Short, snub nose with distinct break between eyes

Huge, round eyes set wide apart

Stocky, deep-chested body is typically Persian

Silver tortie classic tabby coat

Khao Manee

ORIGIN Thailand, 14th century
BREED REGISTRIES GCCF, TICA
WEIGHT RANGE 6–12lb (2.5–5.5kg)

GROOMING Weekly
COLORS AND PATTERNS White only.

An extroverted and intelligent breed, this cat is highly curious and will eagerly explore its surroundings.

The "white jewel," as the name translates, is native to Thailand. Cats apparently of this type are recorded in Thai poetry as early as the 14th century, and were described as pure white, having "eyes of clear mercury." Khao Manees were favorites of the Thai royalty (see panel, right) and not seen outside their native country until the 1990s, when a US breeder imported a pair. Now they are attracting attention elsewhere, especially in the UK and the US. In 2013, The International Cat Association (TICA) granted the Khao Manee "Advanced New Breed" status. This aristocratic cat is noted for its variety of eye colors: it may have both eyes the same color, have odd-colored eyes, have eyes the same color but of varying shades, or even have eyes that are each bicolored. The coat is all white, although some kittens are born with a dark spot on the head. Khao Manees are bold, friendly, mischievous, and also sometimes loud-voiced. These extroverts are said to enjoy the company of humans, whether playing with their family or meeting visitors to the home.

Tail is same length as body and tapers to tip

Sparse hair on ears

Wide, wedge-shaped head

Chiseled face with high cheekbones

Prominent nose with pink leather

Shiny white coat has a slightly loose texture

KITTEN

Muscular, well proportioned body

ROYAL FAVORITE

For most of their history, Khao Manee cats were considered so special that they could be owned only by royalty. In Siam (now Thailand), one of the country's greatest rulers, King Chulalongkorn, known as Rama V (1868–1910), gave his son permission to start developing the breed. Many generations of these cats were kept guarded within the royal palace, and it is said that a Khao Manee was ceremonially carried in a coronation procession in 1926.

Odd-colored eyes

Pink skin around eyes

Broad, level back

Paw pads are pink

Korat

ORIGIN Thailand, c.12th–16th century
BREED REGISTRIES CFA, FIFe, GCCF, TICA
WEIGHT RANGE 6–10lb (2.5–4.5kg)

GROOMING Weekly
COLORS AND PATTERNS Blue only.

This enchanting cat has a long and proud history and makes a good family pet, but it can be strong-willed and assertive.

Few cat breeds can truly be described as being of ancient origin, but the Korat from Thailand is one of them. It appears in a book titled *The Cat Book Poems*, which dates back to the Ayudhya period (1350–1767), in what was then Siam. Long prized in its native country as a symbol of good fortune, the Korat was virtually unknown in the West until the mid-20th century, when a breeding pair was sent to the US. This graceful, silvery blue cat makes a very special pet. Usually highly active, the Korat has its peaceful moments, too, and is gentle and affectionate with its owners. With heightened senses, the breed is easily startled by loud noises or abrupt handling.

Large ears flare at base

Oval paws

THE **FOUNDATION** OF THIS **BREED IN** THE **US** WAS A **PAIR FROM THAILAND** NAMED **NARA AND DARRA**.

Lithe, muscular body

Very large, round, green eyes

Distinctive heart-shaped head

Nose leather is heart shaped

Close-lying, blue coat with no undercoat

Silver-tipped coat hairs

Chinese Li Hua

ORIGIN China, 2000s
BREED REGISTRIES CFA
WEIGHT RANGE 9–11lb (4–5kg)

GROOMING Weekly
COLORS AND PATTERNS Brown mackerel tabby only.

One of the earliest known breed of domestic cat, this perky cat needs an active owner and sufficient space to roam.

Cats fitting the description of the Li Hua, or Dragon Li, as it is also called, appear to have been common in China for centuries. In the wider world, however, this cat is a newcomer, recognized as an experimental breed only since 2003, although it is beginning to attract international interest. The Chinese Li Hua is a large cat with a muscular build and a beautifully marked tabby coat. Although not particularly demonstrative, it makes a friendly and faithful pet. This active cat, which has a reputation as a clever hunter, needs space to exercise and is not suited to a confined life in an apartment.

Long, straight nose

Black spot at corner of mouth

Lower jaw slightly shorter than upper

Lighter hairs on belly

IN CHINA, ONE OF THESE CATS WAS **TAUGHT** TO **FETCH** THE **MORNING PAPER.**

Sturdy, rectangular body

Ticked hairs form mackerel pattern

Bright yellow eyes

Tail has ring marks and black tip

Unticked beige hairs on chin and chest

Straight, muscular legs

Asian—Burmilla

ORIGIN UK, 1980s
BREED REGISTRIES FIFe, GCCF
WEIGHT RANGE 9–15lb (4–7kg)

GROOMING 2–3 times a week
COLORS AND PATTERNS Many shaded colors, including lilac, black, brown, blue, and tortie, with silver or golden ground color.

An enchanting cat with delightful looks and temperament, this breed gets along well with children and other pets.

When the accidental mating of a lilac Burmese (see p. 87) with a Persian Chinchilla (see p. 190) in 1981 produced a litter of kittens with exceptionally beautiful coats, their owner was encouraged to experiment with further breeding. The result was the Burmilla, a cat of elegant Asian proportions, with large, appealing eyes and a delicately shaded or tipped coat; a longhaired version also occurs. Although still uncommon, this charming and intelligent breed is becoming increasingly popular. It possesses something of the zany character of the Burmese, modified by the quieter nature of the Chinchilla. The Burmilla enjoys games but will readily settle on a lap for a peaceful snooze.

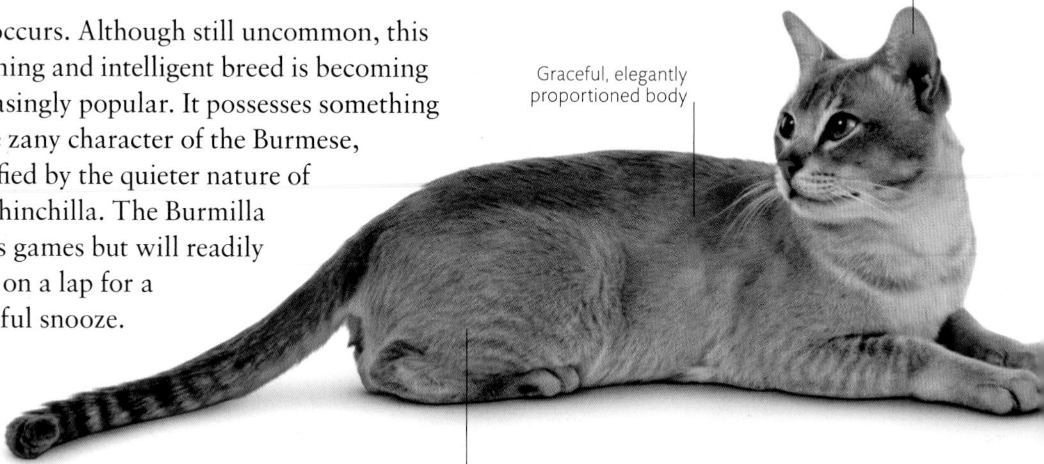

Broad-based ears, slightly rounded at tips

Graceful, elegantly proportioned body

Lilac shaded coat

Lilac shaded silver coat

Face and legs may have slight shading

Slight dip in nose

Large, expressive green eyes

Silky textured, close-lying coat

Silvery white ground with chocolate tipping

Medium-to-long, slightly tapered tail

Vestigial tabby markings

Slender but strong legs

Asian—Smoke

ORIGIN UK, 1980s
BREED REGISTRIES GCCF
WEIGHT RANGE 9–15lb (4–7kg)

GROOMING 2–3 times a week
COLORS AND PATTERNS Any color topcoat, including tortie, with a silvery undercoat.

This inquisitive, playful, and intelligent breed is responsive to attention, and it may be friendly with strangers.

Originally known as the Burmoire, this graceful cat is a cross between the Burmilla (see opposite) and the Burmese (see p. 87). The Asian Smoke has one of the most attractive coats of all the Asian breeds: a deep, often solid color on top, the fur ripples apart when the cat moves or is stroked to reveal glimpses of a gleaming, silvery undercoat. An athletic, playful cat with an outgoing personality, the Asian Smoke is highly curious and loves to investigate everything. Asian Smokes are happy kept as indoor cats as long as they have plenty of human companionship, amusement, and affection.

Black smoke coat

Large eyes slant toward nose

THIS BREED OF THE ASIAN HAS THE INHIBITOR GENE, WHICH RESTRICTS THE COLOR IN THE HAIR SHAFT.

Tail tapers to tip

Medium-to-large ears, rounded at tips

Slender, muscled body

Chocolate smoke coat

Strong, straight back

Silvery rings around eyes

Wide jaw tapers to a blunt muzzle

Brown smoke with silvery white undercoat

Hind legs longer than forelegs

Neat, oval paws

Happy accident
The unintended mating that created the
Asian Burmilla resulted in a cat that is
extroverted but easygoing, exotic but
not extreme, and equally happy to have
boisterous fun or quiet quality time.

Asian—Solid and Tortie

ORIGIN UK, 1980s
BREED REGISTRIES GCCF
WEIGHT RANGE 9–15lb (4–7kg)

GROOMING 2–3 times a week
COLORS AND PATTERNS All solid colors and various torties.

Alert and active, this loving cat will appeal to people looking for a loyal and devoted companion.

The result of experiments to create what is essentially a Burmese cat (see pp. 87–88) with different coat colors, this British breed includes an all-black version known as the Bombay. The latter is easily confused with an American-bred black cat also called Bombay (see pp. 84–85), which has a different breed history. The Asian Solid may be less inclined to create an uproar in the household than its Burmese relation, but it can nevertheless make its presence known with an insistent voice when it wants attention, which is most of the time. This friendly, affectionate cat likes to follow its owner around with doglike devotion.

Obvious nose break

Medium to large ears with rounded tips

KITTEN

THE **SOLID-COLORED ASIAN** BREED HAS **NO TABBY MARKINGS**.

Medium-long tail carried gracefully

Golden eyes set wide apart

Straight back from shoulders to rump

Pink nose leather

Short, fine, close-lying red coat

Cream sepia Burmese variant

Elegant, firmly muscled body

Neat, oval paws

Hind legs slightly longer than forelegs

Asian—Tabby

ORIGIN UK, 1980s
BREED REGISTRIES GCCF
WEIGHT RANGE 9–15lb (4–7kg)

GROOMING 2–3 times a week
COLORS AND PATTERNS Spotted, classic, mackerel, or ticked tabby patterns, in various colors.

This charming cat has a friendly disposition, making it a good choice for a family home, despite its inquisitive nature.

This member of the Asian group of cats comes in four different tabby patterns: classic, mackerel, spotted, and ticked. The variety of stripes, swirls, rings, and spots occur in a wide range of beautiful colors. The most commonly seen pattern is the ticked tabby, in which each individual hair has contrasting bands of color. Like all its relations, the Asian Tabby has the graceful, muscular lines and extrovert personality of the Burmese cats (see pp. 87–88) used in its development, blended with the quieter nature of the Persian Chinchilla (see p. 190). This breed makes a lovely family pet and is growing in popularity.

Medium to large ears set well apart

KITTEN

Prominent cheekbones

Amber eyes set at a slant

Blunt, wedge-shaped head

"M" marking on forehead

Short, thick, glossy, brown mackerel tabby coat

Straight-backed, muscular body

Rounded chest

Delicate, oval paws

Bombay

ORIGIN US, 1950s
BREED REGISTRIES TICA, CFA
WEIGHT RANGE 6–11lb (2.5–5kg)

GROOMING Weekly
COLORS AND PATTERNS Black only.

This pint-sized "black panther" has glossy fur and striking copper eyes; it is not as vocal as other Asian cats.

Created specifically for its appearance, the Bombay is a cross between a sable American Burmese (see p. 88) and a black American Shorthair (see p. 113). Sleek and glossy, this breed comes only in black, with large, gold or copper-colored eyes. The Bombay may look like a panther, but it is a true homebody and few cats are more loving and sociable. Bombays are intelligent and easygoing; they want to be with their owners all the time and are likely to mope if left alone too long. Having inherited the inquisitive and playful nature of the Burmese, these cats are no couch potatoes. Bombays enjoy games and are ready to be entertained—or to entertain their owners. They get along well with children and other pets.

PERFECTLY BLACK

Achieving perfection took Nikki Horner, original American breeder of the Bombay, through many attempts and failures. The deep copper eye color that she sought to set off the gleaming black fur proved particularly elusive. Even when Horner's dream cat had finally been created, it was many years before the Bombay was given official recognition and the breed was permitted to compete in official show classes.

KITTEN

Wide-set eyes are copper color

Head with softly rounded contours

Coal-black coat has deep sheen

Full face

Tip of nose slightly rounded

Round-tipped ears tilt forward

Broad, rounded muzzle

Nose has moderate stop

Sturdy, muscular body

Rounded feet

Not shy
The lithe and gleaming Bombay is a cat that feels confident in company. This breed is prepared to make overtures to anyone who is likely to provide entertainment or a lap to sit on.

Singapura

ORIGIN Singapore, 1970s
BREED REGISTRIES CFA, GCCF, TICA
WEIGHT RANGE 4–9lb (2–4kg)

GROOMING Weekly
COLORS AND PATTERNS Sepia agouti: seal brown ticking on ivory ground color.

This friendly cat loves to be the center of attention and will always be there with you to welcome your guests.

The distinctive ticked coat of this little cat caught the eye of an American scientist, Hal Meadow, while he was working in Singapore in the 1970s. Meadow and his wife started a breeding program for the Singapura, which they carried out both in Singapore and the US. By the 1990s, British breeders were also taking an interest in this cat. Singapuras are now known worldwide, although they are still very rare. Small in size but big in personality, these cats are prying and mischievous, happiest when exploring the world at a high level from a shelf or an owner's shoulder.

Sepia agouti coat paler on chin, chest, and underbelly

Long, strongly muscled legs

Large, deeply cupped ears

Enormous almond-shaped eyes, set wide apart

Firm, muscular body

Each hair of its fine, silky coat has alternate light and dark banding

Dark facial markings on cheekbones

Medium-long, slender tail has dark seal-brown tip

Darker barring on inner forelegs and hind legs

KITTEN

European Burmese

ORIGIN Burma (Myanmar), 1930s
BREED REGISTRIES CFA, FIFe, GCCF, TICA
WEIGHT RANGE 8–14lb (3.5–6.5kg)

GROOMING Weekly
COLORS AND PATTERNS Self and tortie colors include blue, brown, cream, lilac, and red. Always in sepia pattern.

Confident and inquisitive, this cat thrives on companionship and will be happy to participate in everything you do.

This breed was first developed in the US in the 1930s, using a foundation cat introduced from Southeast Asia. In the late 1940s, several Burmese cats were sent from the US to the UK, where the breed acquired a different look. The European Burmese is slightly longer in the head and body than its American counterpart, and it comes in a greater variety of colors. This sweet-natured cat has plenty of affection to offer and needs to be a full member of a loving family. A Burmese is not well suited to a home where it will be left to its own devices for long periods.

THE **FIRST BLUE BURMESE** IN THE **WORLD** WAS **BORN IN** ENGLAND IN **1955**.

Head slightly rounded at top and tapers to blunt wedge

Very fine, satiny chocolate coat

Elegant, muscular body

Back level from shoulders to rump

Nose with noticeable stop

Wide cheekbones

Yellow eyes, set well apart and slanting toward nose

Strong jaw and chin

Slender legs with small, oval paws

Lilac coat

KITTEN

87

American Burmese

ORIGIN Possibly Burma (Myanmar), 1930s
BREED REGISTRIES CFA, TICA
WEIGHT RANGE 8–14lb (3.5–6.5kg)

GROOMING Weekly
COLORS AND PATTERNS All solid and tortie colors in sepia pattern.

Always ready to give and receive affection, these cats will seek out warm laps and gentle petting and stroking.

There are several conflicting accounts of how the Burmese cat came to the West. All that is known for certain is that a Southeast Asian cat of this type, belonging to a Dr. Thompson, appeared in the US in the 1930s and was used to found a new breed. The first recognized American Burmese cats were all a rich brown in color. Later, further colors were accepted, although not as many as in the European version of this breed, which also has a more Oriental appearance. The Burmese is a lovely family pet that can never have enough company and attention.

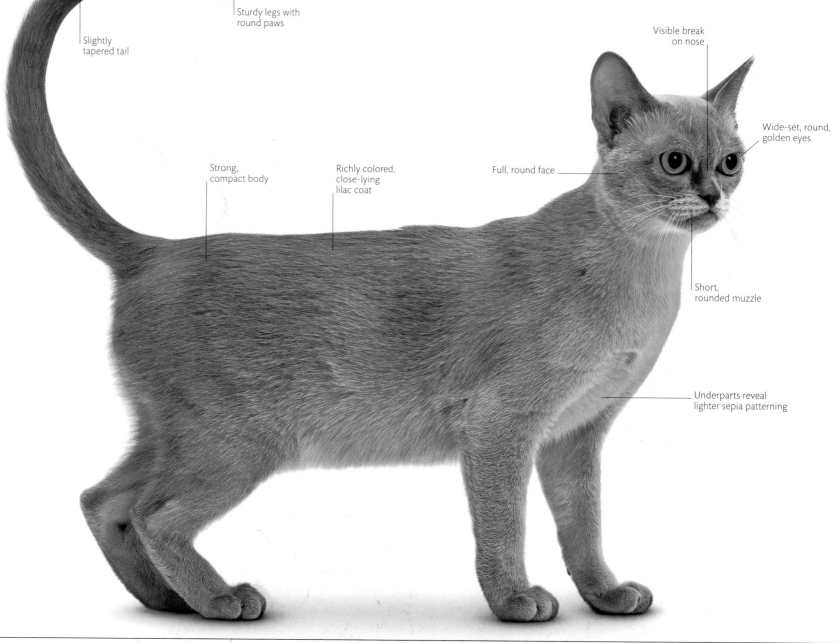

Sturdy legs with round paws

Slightly tapered tail

Visible break on nose

Wide-set, round, golden eyes

Strong, compact body

Richly colored, close-lying lilac coat

Full, round face

Short, rounded muzzle

Underparts reveal lighter sepia patterning

Mandalay

ORIGIN New Zealand, 1980s
BREED REGISTRIES FIFe
WEIGHT RANGE 8–14lb (3.5–6.5kg)

GROOMING Weekly
COLORS AND PATTERNS Many solid colors and patterns, including tabby and tortie.

This glossy-coated beauty is playful and fearless and may be seen attempting feats beyond its capabilities.

In the 1980s, two breeders in New Zealand discovered independently that accidental matings between Burmese cats (see pp. 87–88) and domestic cats produced promising kittens. From these litters, they both went on to develop what is now known as the Mandalay, which has the same breed standard as the Burmese but a greater variety of coat colors. Sleek, glossy, and golden-eyed, this lovely cat is best known in its native country. The Mandalay is very alert and active, and its lithe frame is packed with muscle. It is warmly affectionate toward its own family but inclined to be cautious with strangers.

Top of head is slightly rounded

Strong, round chest

THE MANDALAY IS A **HIGHLY INTELLIGENT** CAT **KNOWN FOR** ITS **STRENGTH** AND **ENDURANCE**.

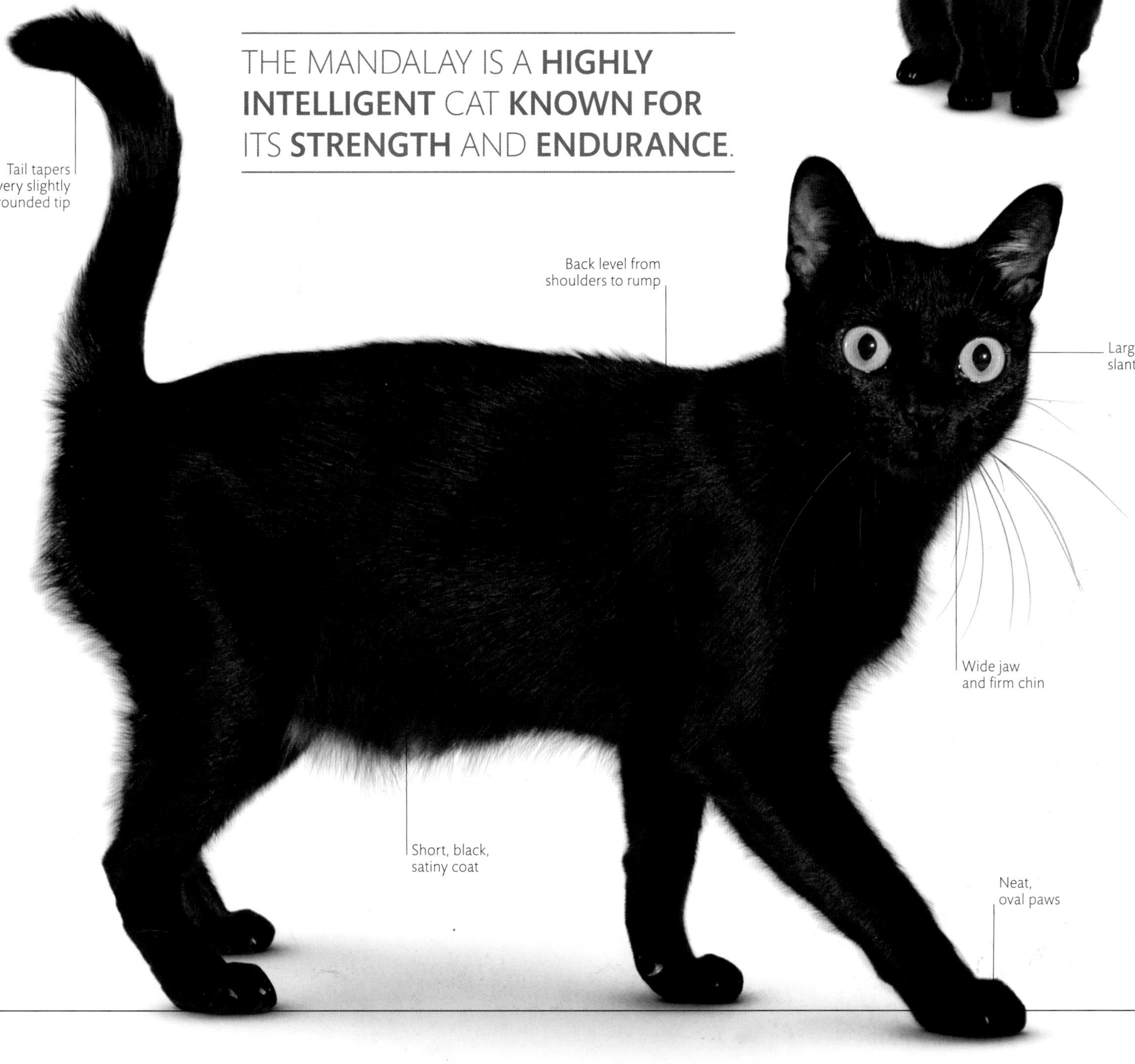

Tail tapers very slightly to rounded tip

Back level from shoulders to rump

Large amber eyes slant toward nose

Wide jaw and firm chin

Short, black, satiny coat

Neat, oval paws

Tonkinese

ORIGIN US, 1950s
BREED REGISTRIES CFA, GCCF, TICA
WEIGHT RANGE 6–12lb (2.5–5.5kg)

GROOMING Weekly
COLORS AND PATTERNS All colors except cinnamon and fawn, in patterns including pointed, tabby, and tortie.

A chic and sleek but strongly muscled cat with plenty of substance, this breed is perfect for people who want a lap cat.

This hybrid cat, created by crossing the Burmese with the Siamese, blends the coloring of both breeds but has a more compact body than many cats of Asian ancestry. It has achieved considerable popularity both in the US, where it was created, and in the UK. The Tonkinese has an independent spirit and would rule the household if it could, but it also has a loving nature and is gratifyingly eager to climb on laps. Playing games, socializing with other pets, and welcoming strangers to the home are all things that the Tonkinese loves to do.

THIS **BREED** WAS **DEVELOPED** UNDER THE NAME **GOLDEN SIAMESE**.

Brown shaded coat

Darker brown legs, tail, and face

High cheekbones

Almond-shaped deep-colored eyes

Well-balanced body, neither long nor stocky

Sleek, close-lying chocolate tortie coat darkens with age

Blunt muzzle

Slight stop on nose

Round-tipped ears set to sides of head

Lilac coat

Patterning continues into belly

Slender legs with oval feet

Oriental—Foreign White

ORIGIN UK, 1950s
BREED REGISTRIES CFA, FIFe, GCCF, TICA
WEIGHT RANGE 9–14lb (4–6.5kg)

GROOMING Weekly
COLORS AND PATTERNS White only.

This dainty, aristocratic cat with a sparkling white coat is very loving, making it an active and loyal companion.

Development of this breed began in the 1950s, with crosses between the Siamese and white shorthaired cats. In the UK the first of these hybrids had either orange or blue eyes, but selective breeding produced cats with blue eyes only, which were given the name of Foreign White. Elsewhere, either green or blue eyes are permitted, and the cat is regarded as a solid-colored variant of the Oriental Shorthair, known as the Oriental White. This striking breed has the characteristic elongated lines and vibrant personality of the Siamese. Many blue-eyed white cats have a genetically linked tendency to deafness, but the Foreign White is free from this defect.

THE FOREIGN WHITE IS THE **ONLY ORIENTAL** BREED THAT **CANNOT BE BRED** WITH **OTHER** ORIENTALS.

Almond-shaped blue eyes

Neat oval paws

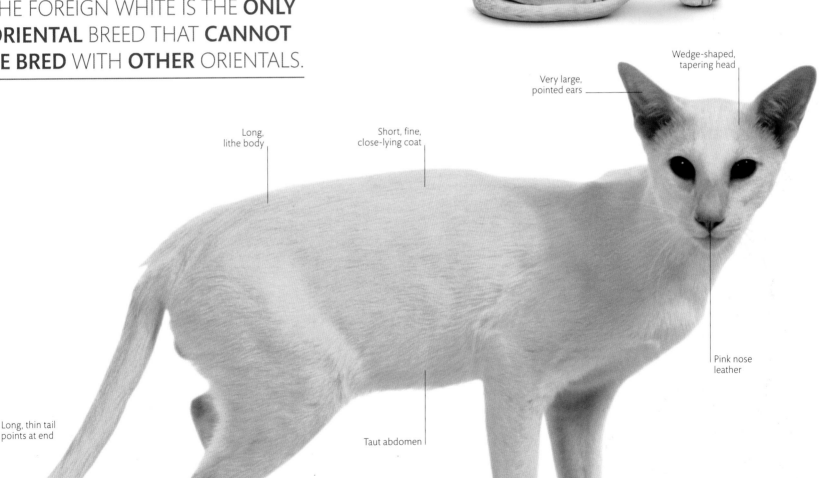

Very large, pointed ears

Wedge-shaped, tapering head

Long, lithe body

Short, fine, close-lying coat

Pink nose leather

Long, thin tail points at end

Taut abdomen

Slender legs

Attractive hybrid
The Tonkinese is midway between the ultra-lean Oriental cats and the typically stocky shorthair. In early breeding programs, it was first known as the Golden Siamese.

Oriental—Solid

ORIGIN UK, 1950s
BREED REGISTRIES CFA, FIFe, GCCF, TICA
WEIGHT RANGE 9–14lb (4–6.5kg)

GROOMING Weekly
COLORS AND PATTERNS Colors include brown (known as Havana), ebony, red, cream, lilac, and blue.

Fine-boned but muscular body

Lilac coat

Bred to combine Siamese lines with traditional solid colors, this cat is highly curious and loves to explore its surroundings.

Solid-colored Oriental Shorthairs were developed in the 1950s, initially by crossing Siamese cats (see pp. 104–09) with other shorthaired cats to eliminate the typical Siamese colorpoint pattern. The first of the Oriental Shorthairs had coats in a rich dark shade of brown and were known as Havanas. In later years, these cats were used to develop a separate breed (see p. 102), called the Havana Brown, in the United States. Decades of further selective breeding introduced a wide range of other solid colors to the Oriental Shorthair, starting with a dilute version of the Havana referred to as lilac in the UK and lavender in the US.

Long, straight nose

Slightly slanting green eyes

Pink nose leather

Long, elegant neck

Color is uniform from root to tip of each hair

Red coat has satiny texture

Hips should not be wider than shoulders

Hind legs longer than forelegs

Oriental—Cinnamon and Fawn

ORIGIN UK, 1960s
BREED REGISTRIES CFA, FIFe, GCCF, TICA
WEIGHT RANGE 9–14lb (4–6.5kg)

GROOMING Weekly
COLORS AND PATTERNS Cinnamon and fawn with no trace of white.

This beautiful, intelligent, and agile cat with a doglike devotion comes in two unusual color versions.

These variations of the Oriental Shorthair are rare because it has proved difficult for breeders to produce their subtle colors. The first Cinnamon was a kitten born in the 1960s to a male Abyssinian (see pp. 132–33) and a female seal point Siamese (see pp. 104–05). The attractive and unusual shade of this kitten's coat—a lighter, reddish-tinged version of the rich brown Oriental solid-coloring known as Havana—inspired its breeder to develop a new line. Fawn Orientals, which were developed slightly later, are an even more diluted brown and their coats have a mushroom-pink or rosy tint, especially when seen in sunlight.

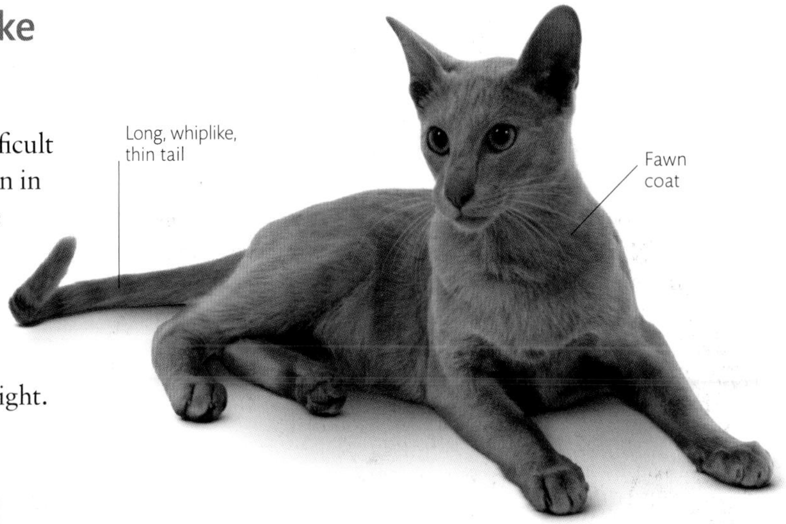

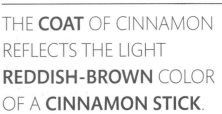

Long, whiplike, thin tail

Fawn coat

Vivid green eyes

Typical Oriental body shape; lean and muscular

THE **COAT** OF CINNAMON REFLECTS THE LIGHT **REDDISH-BROWN** COLOR OF A **CINNAMON STICK**.

Fine, close-lying cinnamon coat

Color of nose leather coordinates with coat

Fawn coloring has warm pinkish tinge

Long, slender legs

Dainty paws

Oriental—Smoke

ORIGIN UK, 1970s
BREED REGISTRIES CFA, FIFe, GCCF, TICA
WEIGHT RANGE 9–14lb (4–6.5kg)

GROOMING Weekly
COLORS AND PATTERNS Oriental solid colors
and tortie and patterns.

A combination of curiosity and intelligence, this striking Oriental is always prepared for a good chase.

In 1971, a cross between a shaded silver hybrid cat and a red-point Siamese produced a litter of kittens in mixed colors. One kitten, which had the coat pattern known as smoke, inspired breeders to create a new-look Oriental. Each hair of a Smoke's coat has two color bands. The top band may be either a solid color—including blue, black, red, and chocolate—or tortoiseshell; beneath this, the hair is very pale or white for at least one-third of its length. The pale hair shows through the darker color and is particularly noticeable when the cat moves.

Vivid green eyes slant down toward nose

"Ghost" tabby markings

Ears with rounded tips continue wedge-shaped line of head

Long, tapering tail

Black smoke coat is short, fine, and glossy

Slender, graceful neck

Hind legs longer than forelegs

Taut belly

Legs with same color tone as face

Oriental—Shaded

ORIGIN UK, 1970s
BREED REGISTRIES CFA, FIFe, GCCF, TICA
WEIGHT RANGE 9–14lb (4–6.5kg)

GROOMING Weekly
COLORS AND PATTERNS All colors
and tabby patterns, except white.

This delicately patterned cat with an unusual beauty is a natural entertainer, full of energy and enthusiasm.

The chance mating between a chocolate-point Siamese (see pp. 104–05) and a Persian Chinchilla (see p. 190) produced a litter that included two kittens with shaded silver coats. This aroused breeders' interest and so began the slow progress toward a new range of Oriental cats. In a shaded Oriental, the coat is essentially a modified tabby pattern, in which the darker markings occur only on the upper ends of the hairs. These markings, which can appear as ticked, spotted, mackerel, or classic tabby patterns, may be quite pronounced in kittens, but as the cat matures the pattern becomes less distinct and in some cats is barely visible.

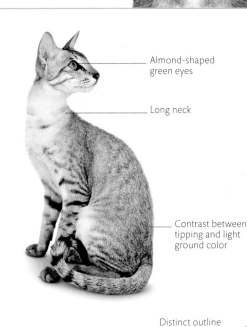

Almond-shaped
green eyes

Long neck

Contrast between
tipping and light
ground color

A SHADED CAT HAS A **WHITE UNDERCOAT** AND THIS IS **ONE OF** OVER **300 COLORS** OF THE **ORIENTAL CAT**.

Distinct outline
around eyes

Huge ears very
wide at base

Chocolate silver
tabby coat has
glistening sheen

Wedge-shaped muzzle

Silvery-white
throat

Tabby markings more
pronounced on tail,
legs, and face

Small, oval paws

Oriental style
With its svelte body and striped or spotted coat, the Oriental Shorthair tabby has more than a touch of the jungle about it. All the traditional patterns and colors are accepted.

Oriental—Tabby

ORIGIN UK, 1970s
BREED REGISTRIES CFA, FIFe, GCCF, TICA
WEIGHT RANGE 9–14lb (4–6.5kg)

GROOMING Weekly
COLORS AND PATTERNS All colors and shades in tabby and patched tabby patterns. Also with white.

NAME CONFUSION

When the Oriental was developed, this new breed needed a name. Initially, in the UK, only tabbies and torties were referred to as Orientals, while solid colors, except fo brown (then known as the Havana), were called Foreign. Ideas of calling the spotted tabby "Mau" were dropped because the name caused confusion with the Egyptian Mau (see p. 130) breed. Now all variations are known as Orientals (as they always have been in the US)—except for the Foreign White (see p. 91).

SILVER SPOTTED TABBY

This lively cat combines streamlined looks with a range of beautiful tabby patterns and does not like to be ignored.

Like the rest of the Oriental group, Oriental Tabbies come in a wide range of coat colors and patterns. Following the rising popularity of self-colored Oriental Shorthairs, breeders turned their attention to producing a line of Oriental tabbies. Early attempts involved crosses between nonpedigree tabbies and Siamese. The first of these patterned Orientals, officially recognized in 1978, was a modern copy of the Siamese-type spotted tabbies believed to be the ancestors of today's domestic cats. Spotted tabbies have round, solid-colored spots on an agouti coat, with striped legs. By the 1980s Orientals with ticked (agouti body, barred legs), mackerel (stripes along the spine and around the body), and classic tabby coats (marbled dark pattern) had also been developed. The patched-tabby Oriental, typically with a mixture of black, red, and cream, was a further addition to the color palette. Despite their aristocratic appearance, these are athletic, mischievous cats who enjoy playing.

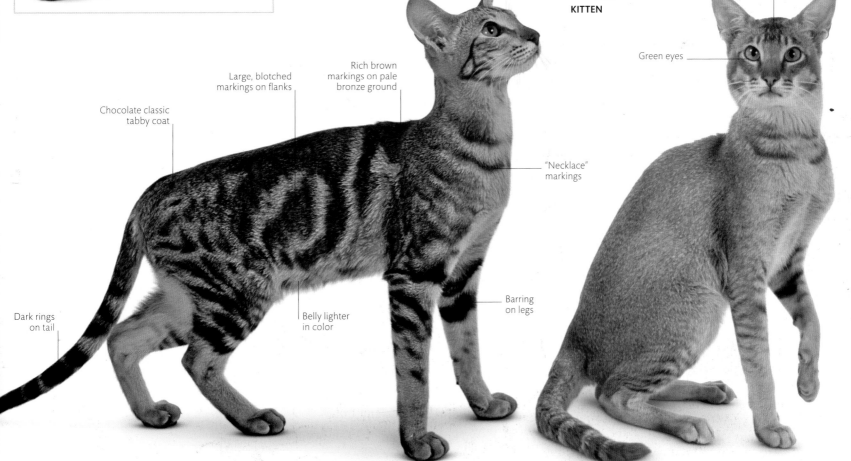

KITTEN

Lines run from top of head to back of neck

Green eyes

Rich brown markings on pale bronze ground

Large, blotched markings on flanks

Chocolate classic tabby coat

"Necklace" markings

Dark rings on tail

Belly lighter in color

Barring on legs

Oriental—Tortie

ORIGIN UK, 1960s
BREED REGISTRIES CFA, FIFe, GCCF, TICA
WEIGHT RANGE 9–14lb (4–6.5kg))

GROOMING Weekly
COLORS AND PATTERNS Ground colors are black, blue, chocolate, lilac, fawn, cinnamon, and caramel; tortoiseshell pattern.

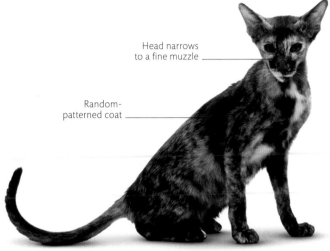

Head narrows to a fine muzzle

Random-patterned coat

This breed has a patterned coat and is affectionate, bold, and almost always playful.

According to an illustrated manuscript, *The Cat Book Poems*, which may date back to the old kingdom of Siam (Thailand), tortie (tortoiseshell) patterned Oriental cats have a long history. Development of the modern Oriental Tortie began in the 1960s, with matings between solid-colored Orientals (see p. 94) and red, tortie, and cream point Siamese (see p. 104–05). The breed eventually gained official recognition in the 1980s. The Tortie coat comes in several ground colors mingled with contrasting patches of cream, or red and cream, depending on the base color. Due to the distribution of tortoiseshell genes, torties are nearly always females; the rare males are usually sterile.

Chocolate tortie coat is warm brown mixed with red shades

Thin, tapering tail

Green eyes

Firm, medium-sized body

Dainty, oval paws

Fine bone structure

Oriental—Bicolor

ORIGIN US, 1970s
BREED REGISTRIES FIFe, GCCF, TICA
WEIGHT RANGE 9–14lb (4–6.5kg)

GROOMING Weekly
COLORS AND PATTERNS Various solid colors, shades, and patterns, including tabby, tortie, and some colorpoints, always with white areas.

This lithe and slender cat with an often dramatic coloring has a strong personality, and it can be quite talkative.

Breeders in the US initially developed this exciting addition to the Oriental Shorthair group through crosses that included a Siamese (see pp. 104–09) and a bicolor American Shorthair (see p. 113). In Europe, further programs experimented with other crosses to achieve the "right" look. The first Oriental Bicolor in the UK arrived in 2004. This striking cat comes in a wonderful range of colors splashed over the coat in an endless variety of patterns; there is even a colorpointed, or Siamese, version. The breed standard requires the white patching to cover at least one-third of the cat and to include the legs, underside, and muzzle.

BICOLORS CAN HAVE **GREEN-**, **BLUE-**, OR **ODD-COLORED** (ONE BLUE AND ONE GREEN) EYES.

Red and white coat

Small oval paws

Triangular head ending in fine muzzle

Large, erect ears

Slanting blue eyes

Long, slim, whiplike tail

Long, slender body

Slender, graceful neck

Black smoke and white

Fine-textured black smoke and white coat lies close to body

Long, slim legs

Firm belly

Havana

ORIGIN US, 1950s
BREED REGISTRIES CFA, TICA
WEIGHT RANGE 6–10lb (2.5–4.5kg)

GROOMING Weekly
COLORS AND PATTERNS Rich brown and lilac.

Vivid
green eyes

Brown whiskers
match coat color

Muzzle narrows
behind whiskers

A gentle, playful cat, this breed enjoys an indoor life and adapts to any situation with poise and confidence.

A rare breed with a confusing background, the Havana (originally known as the Havana Brown) was developed to have two different looks, both with a rich brown coat. In the UK, the cat was produced through crosses with the Siamese (see pp. 104–09) and domestic shorthairs. This version, which had the long, lean Siamese conformation, was eventually classified as a solid-colored Oriental Shorthair (see p. 94). In North America, breeders did not use the Siamese, resulting in a cat with a rounder face and less elongated body (shown here). The stunning Havana is hard to ignore, but if it does not receive attention it will certainly seek it. This affectionate cat likes to be close to people at all times.

THE PHRASE **CHOCOLATE DELIGHT** IS OFTEN
USED BY HAVANA ENTHUSIASTS TO DESCRIBE
THIS CHARMING **CHOCOLATE-BROWN** CAT.

Brown nose leather
has rosy tinge

Large, round-
tipped ears

Narrow head with
rounded muzzle

Firm, well
muscled body

Straight, slim legs
with oval feet

Sleek, rich
chestnut-brown
coat with no other
color markings

Thai

ORIGIN Europe, 1990s
BREED REGISTRIES TICA
WEIGHT RANGE 6–12lb (2.5–5.5kg)

GROOMING Weekly
COLORS AND PATTERNS Any point colors, including tabby and tortie, with pale ground color.

Long, flat forehead typical of breed

Rounded, curving cheekbones

Highly intelligent and curious, this talkative breed loves people and requires a lot of attention from its owner.

Lithe and elegant, with points that come in many colors, the Thai was bred to resemble the traditional Siamese cat of the 1950s, before it began to develop a more extreme, elongated appearance. The defining feature of the Thai is its head, which has a long, flat forehead, rounded cheeks, and a tapering, wedge-shaped muzzle. This cat is very active and intelligent, investigating everything and following its owner everywhere. It is good at communicating both vocally and in actions, and will persist in getting a response. The breed is not suitable for a home where it will be left alone for long periods.

KNOWN AS THE *WICHIENMAAT* IN THAILAND, THIS BREED IS **SIMILAR TO** THE **OLD-STYLE SIAMESE**.

Fairly large, almond-shaped blue eyes

Ear tips point outward

Tapering muzzle with rounded end

Long, graceful body

Long, tapering tail

Short, close-lying coat with minimal undercoat

Chocolate points on feet, face, ears, and tail are evenly matched

Siamese—Solid-Pointed

ORIGIN Thailand (Siam), 14th century
BREED REGISTRIES CFA, FIFe, GCCF, TICA
WEIGHT RANGE 6–12lb (2.5–5.5kg)

GROOMING Weekly
COLORS AND PATTERNS All solid colors in pointed patterns.

Its unique looks and personality make this intelligent and extroverted breed one of the most recognizable cats.

The history of the Siamese includes more myths and legends than hard facts, and the true tale of this "Royal Cat of Siam" is now lost in time. It is certainly thought to be a very old breed; a cat with dark points is pictured in *The Cat Book Poems*, a manuscript produced in Siam (now Thailand) that possibly dates back to the 14th century. The first Siamese cats definitely known in the West appeared at cat shows in London during the 1870s, and in that same decade a cat was sent from Bangkok to the US as a gift for President Rutherford B. Hayes's wife. In the breed's early years of development, on both sides of the Atlantic, all Siamese cats were seal points, and it was not until the 1930s that new colors—blue, chocolate, and lilac—were introduced, and later others were added. The appearance of the Siamese has also changed in other ways over the years.

Traits such as crossed eyes and a kinked tail, which were once common in the Siamese, have been bred out and are now seen as faults in terms of show standards. More controversially, modern breeding has taken the elongated body and narrow head of the Siamese to extremes, producing an ultra-lean and angular look. With a supersized ego and a loud voice that it uses to demand attention, the Siamese is the most extroverted of all cats. This highly intelligent breed is full of fun and energy and makes a wonderful family pet, as ready to give affection as to receive it.

Lean, elongated body

Thin tail tapers to a point

Points on legs slightly lighter than on tail and head

FORGOTTEN SHAPE

Before about the 1970s, the Siamese had the typical appearance of most shorthaired cats, with a rounded head and moderately sturdy body (as shown in a champion Siamese from the 1900s, below). Then, breeders began to develop a dramatic new image, and the Siamese changed almost beyond recognition. With the breed standard altered to reflect the exaggerated outline now preferred, old-style Siamese can no longer hold their own in the show ring against their modern counterparts. However, they are still bred by enthusiasts who prefer the traditional look.

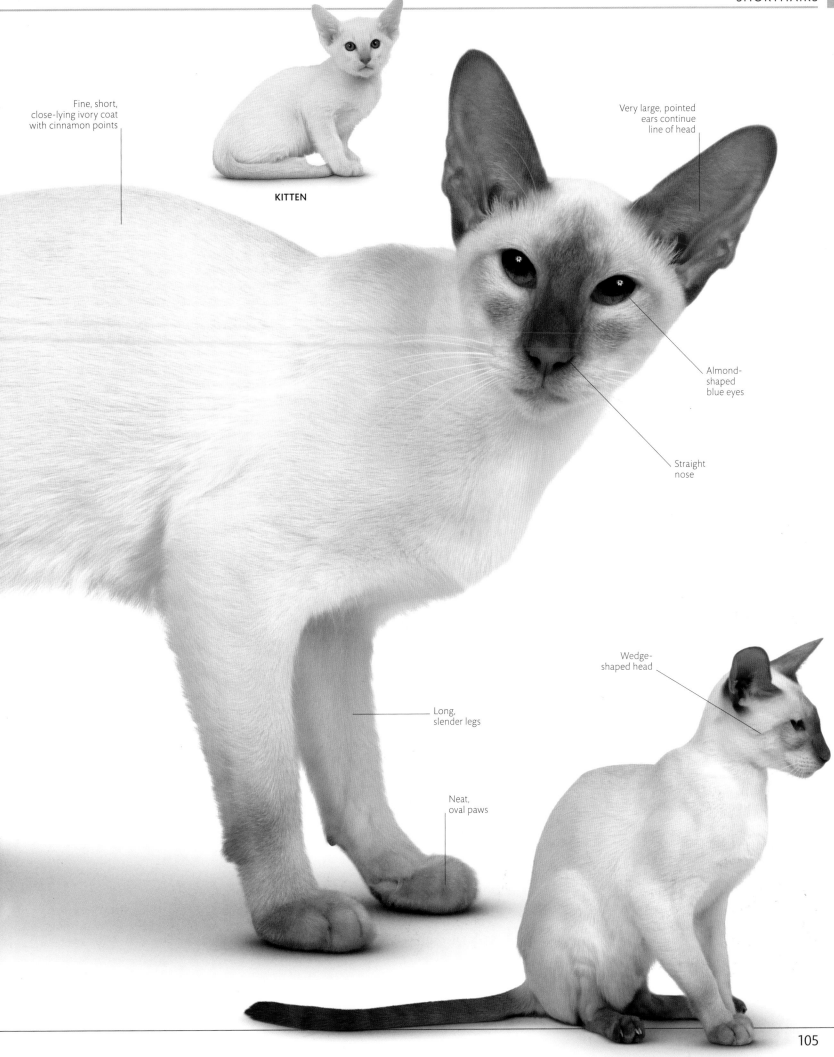

Fine, short,
close-lying ivory coat
with cinnamon points

KITTEN

Very large, pointed
ears continue
line of head

Almond-
shaped
blue eyes

Straight
nose

Long,
slender legs

Neat,
oval paws

Wedge-
shaped head

Siamese—Tabby-Pointed

ORIGIN UK, 1960s
BREED REGISTRIES FIFe, GCCF, TICA
WEIGHT RANGE 6–12lb (2.5–5.5kg)

GROOMING Weekly
COLORS AND PATTERNS Many tabby point colors, including seal, blue, chocolate, lilac, red, cream, cinnamon, caramel, fawn, and apricot; also various tortie tabby point colors.

This stunning variation of the world's most famous cat is playful and content to spend long hours on its own.

A few Siamese cats with tabby points are mentioned in early 20th-century records, but selective development of this new variation did not begin until the 1960s. The first tabby point Siamese to attract the attention of breeders is said to have been a kitten born to a solid-point female Siamese as a result of an unplanned mating. It was some years before the Siamese Tabby-Pointed was recognized and officially named as a breed in the UK; in the US this cat is known as a Lynx Colorpoint. Originally, only seal tabbies appeared, but many other beautiful tabby colors have now been added to the breed standard.

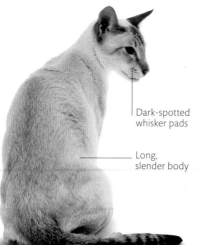

Dark-spotted whisker pads

Long, slender body

Deep blue eyes

Red tabby point coat

Tail has well-defined rings and solid-colored tip

Ears outlined in same color as mask

Well-defined tabby stripes on mask, including typical tabby "M" mark

Nose leather pink with darker rim

Ivory-colored body with chocolate points

Faint stripes on legs

Siamese—Tortie-Pointed

ORIGIN UK, 1960s
BREED REGISTRIES GCCF, TICA
WEIGHT RANGE 6–12lb (2.5–5.5kg)

GROOMING Weekly
COLORS AND PATTERNS Various tortie point colors: seal, blue, chocolate, lilac, caramel, cinnamon, and fawn.

Naughty and mischievous, this cat retains its kittenlike playfulness for a long time and is easily bored.

Producing tortie (tortoiseshell) color points in the Siamese involves a complicated breeding process that introduces the gene for orange coloring. This gene causes random changes in solid colors such as seal, blue, or fawn, resulting in a mottled pattern in which shades of red, apricot, or cream are evident. In some variations there may be striping as well. In kittens the full mixture of colors emerges gradually and may take up to a year to develop fully. The Seal Tortie-Pointed was the first color to be granted official status as a Tortie Siamese in the UK in the late 1960s.

Large, pricked ears follow contours of head

Blue tortie point coat

Slender, graceful body

Delicate muzzle

Long, whiplike tail

Color of nose leather coordinates with points

Intensely blue eyes

Color points contrast with ivory-colored body

Pale coat with seal tortie points

Each tortie point is broken up with cream

Colorpoint Shorthair

ORIGIN US, 1940s/1950s
BREED REGISTRIES CFA
WEIGHT RANGE 6–12lb (2.5–5.5kg)

GROOMING Weekly
COLORS AND PATTERNS Various solid, tabby, and tortie point colors.

This loving, playful cat with a "look-at-me" attitude is intelligent and more easily trained than other breeds.

Developed specifically for its beautiful color combinations, this breed was created during the 1940s and 50s, initially by crossing a Siamese with a red tabby American Shorthair (see p. 113). If not for its different range of colors, the Colorpoint Shorthair would be impossible to distinguish from the Siamese, since it possesses the same elongated body, slender head, outsized ears, and brilliant blue eyes as its relative. Intelligent, sociable, and highly vocal, this cat likes to be the center of attention. A Colorpoint Shorthair needs family life—the more fun going on, the better—and is not suitable for owners who are out of the home for long periods.

THIS BREED WAS FIRST **CREATED** BY INTRODUCING **RED** TO THE **POINT COLORS** OF THE SIAMESE.

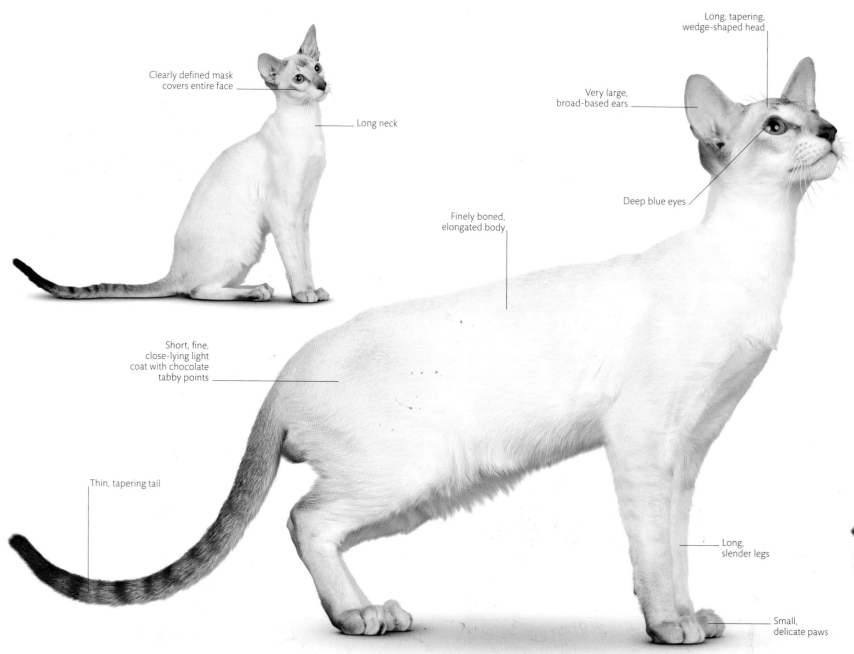

Clearly defined mask covers entire face

Long neck

Long, tapering, wedge-shaped head

Very large, broad-based ears

Deep blue eyes

Finely boned, elongated body

Short, fine, close-lying light coat with chocolate tabby points

Thin, tapering tail

Long, slender legs

Small, delicate paws

Seychellois

ORIGIN UK, 1980s
BREED REGISTRIES FIFe, TICA
WEIGHT RANGE 9–14lb (4–6.5kg)

GROOMING Weekly
COLORS AND PATTERNS White ground color with solid, tortie, and tabby contrast markings. Always bicolor and in pointed pattern.

A lively, energetic, overtly loving, and outgoing cat, this breed is not for owners who prefer a quiet life.

Deep blue, almond-shaped eyes

Strongly contrasting seal huitiéme markings

This comparatively new breed, not yet recognized worldwide, was specially created in the UK to resemble the distinctively patterned cats found in the Seychelles. The first crosses were between a Siamese (see pp. 104–09) and a calico Persian (see pp. 202–03); later, Oriental cats were added to the breeding program and the mix produced a graceful, long-headed, big-eared cat in both shorthaired and longhaired versions. According to the extent of its dramatic color markings, the Seychellois is classified into three types, known as neuviéme (with the least color), septiéme, and huitiéme (with the largest color patches). With a reputation for ditziness, the Seychellois is said to be a demanding, although highly affectionate, companion.

WHEN THE **PIEBALD GENE** CAUSES **WHITE PATCHES** IN **SIAMESE** CATS, THEY ARE CONSIDERED TO BE **SHORTHAIRED SEYCHELLOIS**.

Large, pointed ears

Wedge-shaped head with a long, straight nose

Slim, elongated body with chocolate septiéme markings on coat

Long neck

Short, shiny coat with minimal undercoat

Long, thin, darker colored tail

Long, slender, strongly muscled legs

Small, oval white paws

Snowshoe

PLACE OF ORIGIN US, 1960s
BREED REGISTRIES FIFe, GCCF, TICA
WEIGHT RANGE 6–12lb (2.5–5.5kg)

GROOMING Weekly
COLORS AND PATTERNS Typical Siamese colors in pointed pattern, with white feet. Blue or seal most common.

This aptly named colorpointed cat with distinctive white feet is talkative, easygoing, and enjoys being around people.

The white feet that define the Snowshoe were originally a "mistake," first seen in a litter of kittens born to a normal colorpoint Siamese. Their American breeder, Dorothy Hinds-Daugherty of Philadelphia, liked them enough to develop the striking new look, using crosses between Siamese (see pp. 104–09) and the American Shorthair (see p. 113) to produce the Snowshoe. Intelligent, responsive, and full of character, these cats love a home atmosphere and usually prefer to keep their family in sight. Most Snowshoes get along very well with other cats. Their steady temperament makes them a good choice for first-time cat owners.

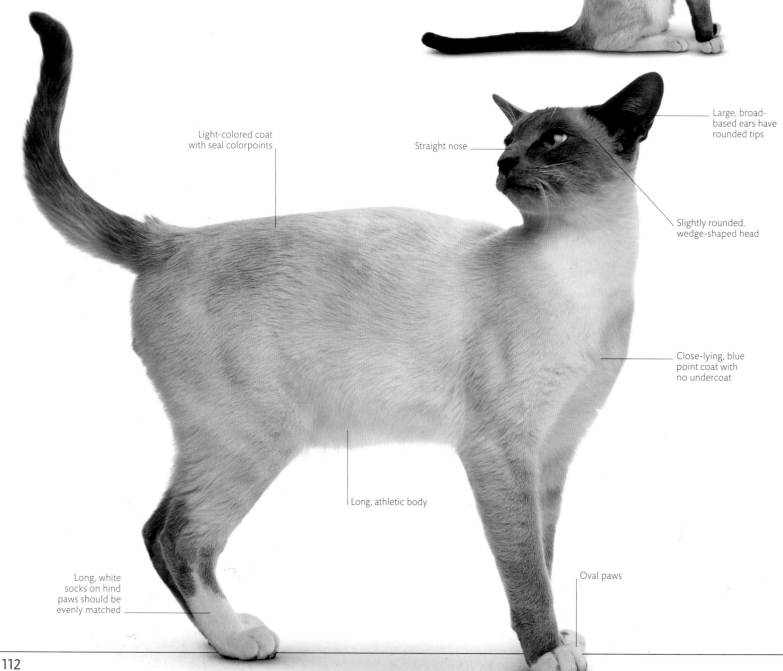

Walnut-shaped blue eyes

High, rounded cheekbones

Light-colored coat with seal colorpoints

Straight nose

Large, broad-based ears have rounded tips

Slightly rounded, wedge-shaped head

Close-lying, blue point coat with no undercoat

Long, athletic body

Long, white socks on hind paws should be evenly matched

Oval paws

American Shorthair

ORIGIN US, 1890s
BREED REGISTRIES CFA, TICA
WEIGHT RANGE 8–15lb (3.5–7kg)

GROOMING 2–3 times a week
COLORS AND PATTERNS Most solid colors and shades; patterns include bicolor, tabby, and tortie.

A robust, easy-care cat, this breed is known for its sweet personality and amiability with children, dogs, and other pets.

The first domestic cats in the US are said to have arrived with the early pilgrims in the 1600s. Over the following centuries, sturdy, workmanlike cats spread all over the US, most of them kept as efficient mousers rather than as house pets. But by the beginning of the 20th century, a more refined form of the farmyard hunter, known as the Domestic Shorthair, began to emerge. Careful breeding further improved the Domestic, and by the 1960s—now renamed the American Shorthair—it was attracting attention at pedigree cat shows. Healthy and hardy, American Shorthairs are perfect family cats that fit in with almost any type of household.

Ears slightly rounded at tips

Sturdy, powerful body

Square muzzle and strong jaws

Broad, rounded head

Round paws with heavy pads

Classic silver tabby coat

Large head with full face

Short, thick, resilient coat

Tail tapers to blunt end

Straight, muscular legs

European Shorthair

ORIGIN Sweden, 1980s
BREED REGISTRIES FIFe
WEIGHT RANGE 8–15lb (3.5–7kg)

GROOMING Weekly
COLORS AND PATTERNS Various colors and bicolors in solid and smoke; patterns include colorpoint, tabby, and tortie.

A fine domestic cat with an air of quality, this breed is calm and reserved and is said to be easy to train.

At first glance, the European Shorthair looks very much like a typical house cat. Very popular in Scandinavia, it was developed in Sweden from ordinary domestic cats, but careful breeding programs ensured that only the best foundation stock, selected for quality of color and conformation, were used.

Unlike most cats of similar type, including the British Shorthair (see pp. 118–19), this breed has not been outcrossed to other lines. Robust and sturdily built, the European Shorthair is a dependable pet that thrives both indoors and out. It is sociable but retains an air of independence and can be a little aloof with strangers.

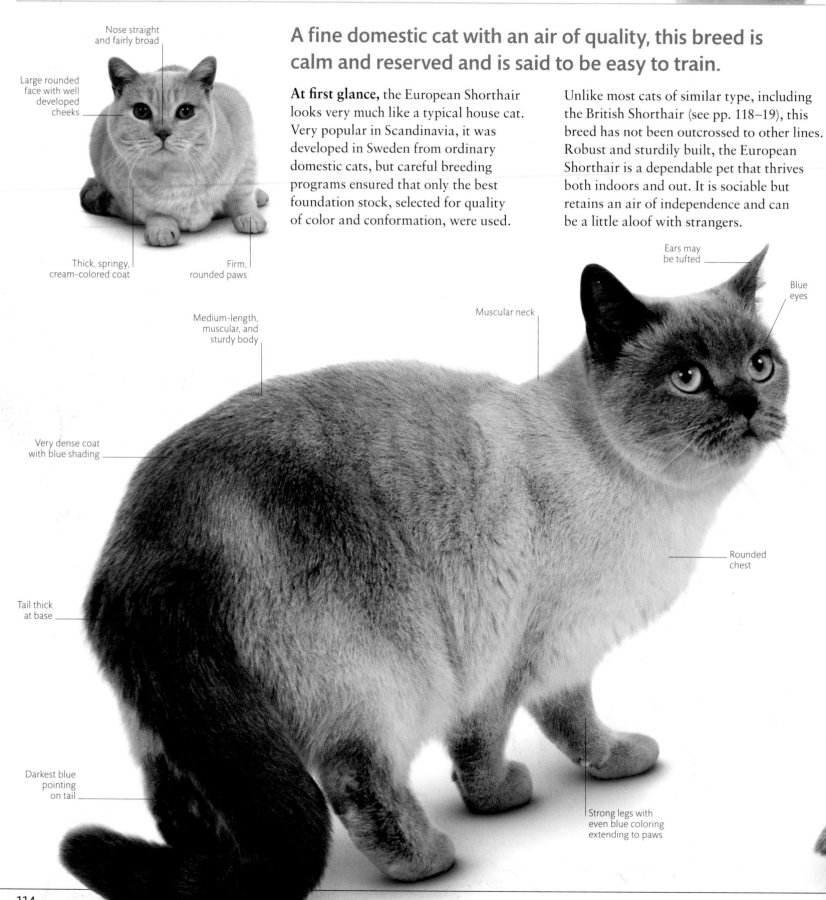

Nose straight and fairly broad

Large rounded face with well developed cheeks

Thick, springy, cream-colored coat

Firm, rounded paws

Ears may be tufted

Blue eyes

Muscular neck

Medium-length, muscular, and sturdy body

Very dense coat with blue shading

Rounded chest

Tail thick at base

Darkest blue pointing on tail

Strong legs with even blue coloring extending to paws

Chartreux

ORIGIN France, pre-18th century
BREED REGISTRIES CFA, FIFe, TICA
WEIGHT RANGE 7–17lb (3–7.5kg)

GROOMING 2–3 times a week
COLORS AND PATTERNS Blue-gray only.

A chunky but agile breed with a "smiley" expression, the Chartreux is loyal and makes a great companion.

Just how far back the history of this very old French breed goes is open to debate. The Chartreux was first named in the mid-18th century and some legends link it to the Carthusian monks, makers of the renowned Chartreuse liqueur, although there is no proof that they ever kept woolly coated blue cats like this one. With its calm, undemanding personality and soft voice, this breed is an unobtrusive yet affectionate house cat. It enjoys quiet play and occasionally explodes in a burst of extra energy when in a hunting mode.

Blue-gray nose straight with slight stop

Round golden eyes

Narrow, tapering muzzle with "smiling" expression

Weather-resistant coat is slightly woolly in texture

Short, dense blue-gray coat

Round head with full cheeks

Short neck

Blue lips

Body solid and muscular but not stocky

Sturdy, fine-boned legs

Plush fur
The Russian Blue's coat, with its rich pile and silvery sheen, is a distinguishing feature of the breed. As the name suggests, blue is the only accepted coat color for this handsome cat.

Russian Blue

ORIGIN Russia, pre-19th century
BREED REGISTRIES CFA, FIFe, TICA
WEIGHT RANGE 7–12lb (3–5.5kg)

GROOMING Weekly
COLORS AND PATTERNS Blue of various shades.

This graceful, friendly but self-sufficient cat does not demand too much attention and can be shy around strangers.

The most widely accepted version of this breed's ancestry suggests that it originated around the Russian port of Archangel, just below the Arctic Circle. Supposedly brought to western Europe by sailors, the Russian Blue was attracting interest in the UK well before the end of the 19th century, featuring in the first cat shows, and it had also appeared in North America by the early 20th century. British, American, and Scandinavian breeders developed the bloodlines for the modern

Russian Blue. With its gracious air, green eyes, and lustrous, silvery-blue coat, it is not surprising that the Russian Blue is now highly popular. Reserved with strangers, this cat has a soft voice, a gentle nature, and an abundance of quiet affection to give its owners. It may bond with one household member more than the rest. It is curious and playful, but not intensely demanding. Differently colored forms of the breed have been developed under the name Russian Shorthair (see panel, right).

KITTEN

COLOR MIXTURE

The coat color of the Russian Blue is created by a diluted version of the gene that produces black hairs. Mating two Blues guarantees a litter of blue kittens. If a Russian Blue is bred to a black Russian Shorthair, both blue and black kittens can result. Mating a blue with a white cat leads to kittens that may be white, black, or blue. All colors have the Russian Shorthair's characteristic green eyes.

Straight nose

Thick, plush blue coat

Long, finely boned legs

Small rounded paws

Long, tapering tail

Long, lithe body

Relatively large, wide-set ears, very thin at tips

Bright green eyes

Dense fur gives broad-faced appearance

Silver-tipped guard hairs

British Shorthair—Solid

PLACE OF ORIGIN UK, 1800s
BREED REGISTRIES CFA, FIFe, GCCF, TICA
WEIGHT RANGE 9–18lb (4–8kg)

GROOMING Weekly
COLORS AND PATTERNS All solid colors.

This cat combines good looks with an easygoing temperament and is affectionate, although not overly demonstrative.

Originally developed from the best examples of ordinary British domestic cats, the British Shorthair was one of the first pedigree cats to appear in shows during the late 19th century. In the following decades, the Shorthair was all but eclipsed by longhaired cats, particularly the Persian, but survived by a narrow margin to enjoy a revival from the mid-20th century onward.

A descendant of cats that worked for their living, keeping down vermin on farms and homesteads, the British Shorthair is now something of a blueprint for the perfect fireside cat. The breed is highly popular in Europe and is steadily gaining a following in the US, where it is less well-known.

Many decades of careful selection have produced a well proportioned cat of superb quality. Powerfully built, the British Shorthair has a medium-to-large, tightly knit body carried on sturdy legs. The massive, round head, broad cheeks, and large, open eyes are characteristic features of the breed. The British Shorthair has a short, dense coat that comes in a variety of colors and has a deep pile and firm texture.

In temperament, this cat is as calm and friendly as its chubby-cheeked, placid expression appears to suggest. It can be kept equally well as a town or country cat. Strong, but not athletic or hyperactive, a British Shorthair prefers to keep its paws on the ground and is perfectly happy to stay indoors and commandeer the sofa. However, it also enjoys time outside and readily uses the hunting skills that made its ancestors such an asset in the past.

Quietly affectionate, the Shorthair likes to stay near its owner. Although alert to what is going on in the household, this cat is not overly demanding of attention.

British Shorthairs generally have robust health and can have a long life. They are easy to care for, since the thick coat does not mat or tangle and regular combing is all that is required to keep it in good condition.

Short, dense black coat with no white markings

Large, powerful body

Tail tapers slightly

KITTEN

Firm, round paws

SETTING STANDARDS

The first organized cat show, held in London, England, in 1871, was the brainchild of Harrison Weir, a British Shorthair enthusiast, who was highly rewarded when his own tabby won Best in Show. Known as the "father of the cat fancy," Weir encouraged interest in selective breeding of cats to set standards of excellence. Among his many books was *Our Cats*, which introduced and illustrated various types and breeds.

HARRISON WEIR

Short, strong neck

Small ears set wide apart

Large, round golden eyes

Massive head with full cheeks

Medium-short, strongly boned legs

British Shorthair— Colorpointed

ORIGIN UK, 1800s
BREED REGISTRIES FIFe, GCCF, TICA,
WEIGHT RANGE 9–18lb (4–8kg)

GROOMING Weekly
COLORS AND PATTERNS Various point colors, including blue-cream, seal, red, chocolate, and lilac; also with tabby and tortie patterns.

Blue-cream tortie mask

Round blue eyes

This traditional breed, with a new look, loves children and gets along with dogs, making it an ideal housecat.

The most recent of the British Shorthair variations, the Colorpoint was recognized only in 1991. This unusual cat is the result of experimental crossbreeding to produce a British Shorthair with the pointed coat pattern of the Siamese. Various attractive colors have been developed and, like the Siamese, all types have blue eyes, although the stocky build and round head typical of the Shorthair remain unchanged. Because of the similarities in name, the British Shorthair Colorpoint is sometimes confused with an Oriental-type American breed called the Colorpoint Shorthair (see p. 110).

Pale ground color with blue-cream highlights

Typically full, rounded face

Powerful shoulders

Tortie pattern more evident on tail

Short neck

Chunky body

Blue points broken with cream markings

British Shorthair— Bicolor

ORIGIN UK, 1800s
BREED REGISTRIES CFA, FIFe, GCCF, TICA
WEIGHT RANGE 9–18lb (4–8kg)

GROOMING Weekly
COLORS AND PATTERNS Black and white, blue and white, red and white, and cream and white.

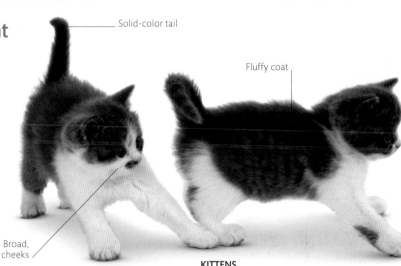

Although undemanding and gentle, this elegant cat may be intolerant of being handled.

Black-and-white British Shorthairs were much valued in the 19th century when this breed had its beginnings, but they were never common. The Bicolor as it is today, which comes in several combinations of white and another color, was not fully developed until the 1960s. At that time, almost impossibly high breeding standards required the color patches to be distributed over head and body with complete symmetry. The rules have since been relaxed, but the best Bicolors still have strikingly even markings.

Solid-color tail

Fluffy coat

Broad, rounded cheeks

KITTENS

Large, powerful body

White blaze on face

Symmetrically distributed blue markings

Pink nose leather

Large, rounded golden eyes

Straight, well boned forelegs

Rounded paws

White on legs and underside

British Shorthair—Smoke

ORIGIN UK, 1800s
BREED REGISTRIES CFA, FIFe, GCCF, TICA
WEIGHT RANGE 9–18lb (4–8kg)

GROOMING Weekly
COLORS AND PATTERNS Smoke pattern in all solid colors, and in tortie and pointed patterns.

This breed's hidden silver undercoat creates a distinctive effect, making it a popular showcat.

A Smoke cat can look as though it is just one color, until it moves or its fur is parted to reveal a narrow silver band at the base of the hairs. This is the effect of the "silver" gene, which inhibits the development of color in the coat, and which British Shorthair Smokes inherited from the silver tabbies in their ancestry. Smoke coloration is even more subtly attractive in the tortie version, which has two colors in the topcoat.

Round orange eyes

Large, firm, rounded paws

Tail tapers to rounded tip

Ears rounded at tips

Rounded forehead

Black nose leather

Prominent whisker pads

TO CREATE A **SMOKE COAT** WITHOUT ANY **GHOST TABBY** MARKINGS **IS DIFFICULT AND** MAKES THIS A **RARE** BRITISH SHORTHAIR COLOR.

Black smoke topcoat conceals silver undercoat

Deep chest

Strong, medium to short legs

British Shorthair—Tabby

ORIGIN UK, 1800s
BREED REGISTRIES CFA, FIFe, GCCF, TICA
WEIGHT RANGE 9–18lb (4–8kg)

GROOMING Weekly
COLORS AND PATTERNS All traditional tabby patterns with many colors, including silver variations; patched tabby in various colors, including silver variations.

One of the largest breeds of cat, this British favorite has been developed in a variety of attractive colors.

Although the British Shorthair is the most even tempered of cats, this variation is a reminder of its wild tabby-patterned ancestors. Brown tabbies were among the first British Shorthairs to appear in cat shows in the 1870s, and red and silver versions became popular early on in the breed's history. This cat now comes in a wide range of additional colors, with three traditional tabby patterns: classic (or blotched) tabby, with markings arranged in broad whorls; mackerel, with narrower markings; and spotted. In the Patched Tabby, the coat has a second ground color.

Large, round golden eyes

Brick-red nose leather

Vertical line runs down spine

Even, unbroken rings on tail

Ground color even over whole body

Typical tabby "M" mark on forehead

Narrow markings on cheeks

Necklace of stripes around neck

Legs barred with darker bracelets

Red classic tabby coat

British Shorthair—Tipped

PLACE OF ORIGIN UK, 1800s
BREED REGISTRIES CFA, FIFe, GCCF, TICA
WEIGHT RANGE 9–18lb (4–8kg)

GROOMING Weekly
COLORS AND PATTERNS Various, including black-tipped on white or golden undercoat; red-tipped on white undercoat.

This delicately colored cat with a sparkle to its coat is loving and enjoys being around children and other pets.

In a tipped cat a pale undercoat is overlaid with what appears to be a light dusting of color. This effect is produced by the ends of the top hairs being colored to about one-eighth of their length. The Tipped British Shorthair—originally called the Chinchilla Shorthair—comes in various color forms. These include silver (white undercoat with black tipping), golden (warm golden or apricot undercoat with black tipping), and the rare red (white undercoat with red tipping), which is known as Shell Cameo in the US.

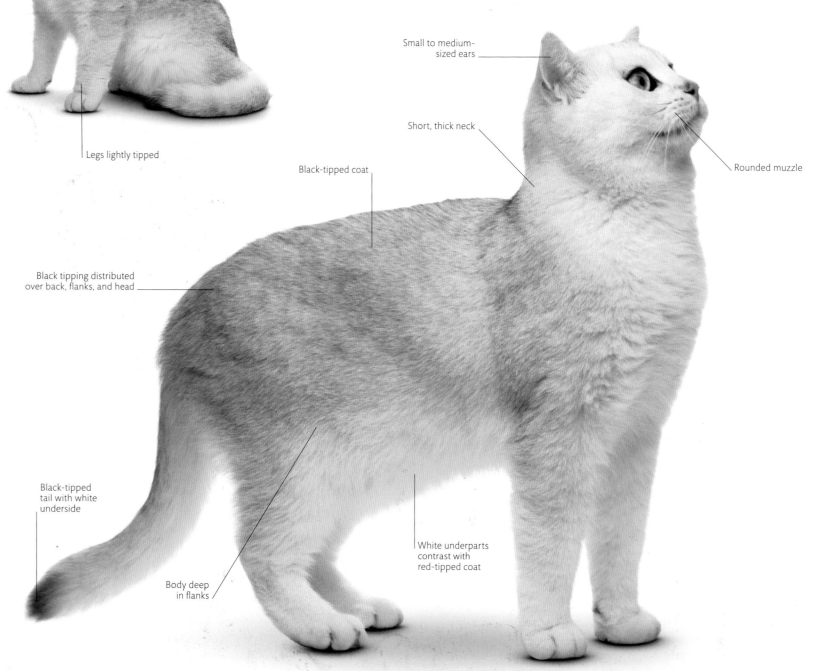

Red nose leather outlined with black

Legs lightly tipped

Small to medium-sized ears

Short, thick neck

Black-tipped coat

Rounded muzzle

Black tipping distributed over back, flanks, and head

Black-tipped tail with white underside

Body deep in flanks

White underparts contrast with red-tipped coat

British Shorthair—Tortie

PLACE OF ORIGIN UK, 1800s
BREED REGISTRIES CFA, FIFe, GCCF, TICA
WEIGHT RANGE 9–18lb (4–8kg)

GROOMING Weekly
COLORS AND PATTERNS Blue-cream, chocolate, lilac, or black tortoiseshell (with white patches in the calico).

Areas of tortie patterning clearly defined

White paws

White markings cover a third of the body

The mingled colors in this cat's coat give the breed an unusual marbled appearance.

In a tortoiseshell (tortie), two coat colors are softly blended. There are many variations, but the most common is black mixed with red—the first tortie color to be developed in British Shorthairs. Blue-cream tortoiseshell, in which black is replaced by blue and red by cream, is another of the older colors, recognized since the 1950s. In the Calico (known as Tortie and White in the UK) the colors are more clearly defined as patches. For genetic reasons, torties are nearly always female and the few males are sterile.

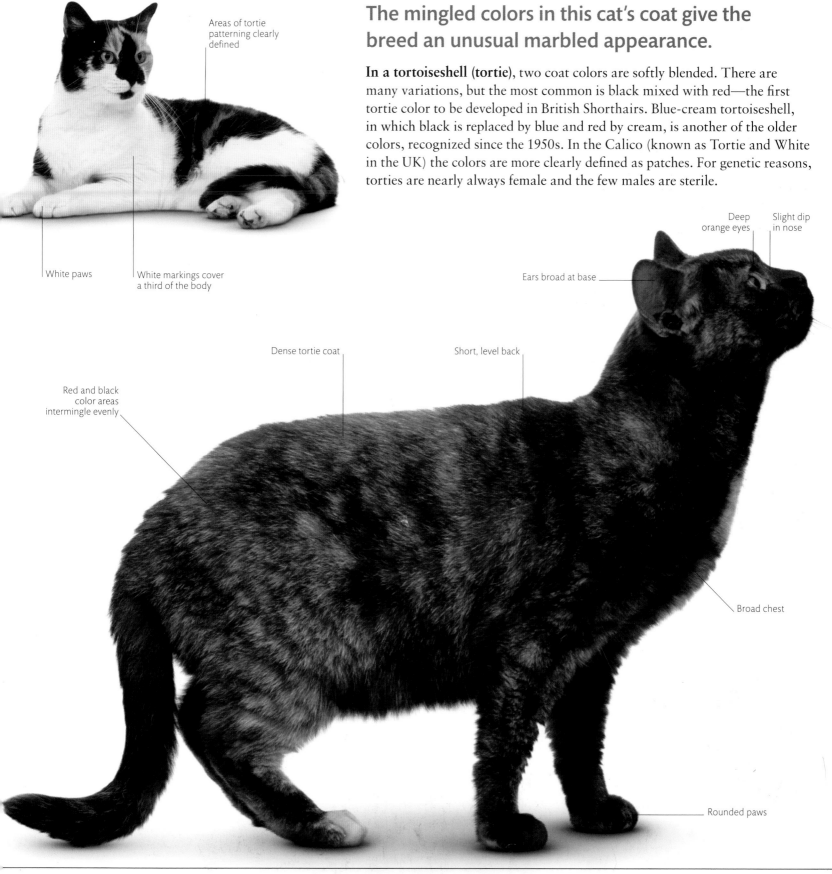

Deep orange eyes

Slight dip in nose

Ears broad at base

Dense tortie coat

Short, level back

Red and black color areas intermingle evenly

Broad chest

Rounded paws

Turkish Shorthair

ORIGIN Turkey, pre-1700s
BREED REGISTRIES None
WEIGHT RANGE 7–19lb (3–8.5kg)

GROOMING Weekly
COLORS AND PATTERNS All colors except chocolate, cinnamon, lilac, and fawn, and all patterns except pointed.

This little-known breed is affectionate and easygoing with people, especially if socialized from an early age.

The history of the Turkish Shorthair is uncertain, but this cat occurs naturally in various regions of Turkey and has probably existed there for a considerable time. Also known as the Anatolian or Anatoli and the Anadolu Kedisi in Turkey, the breed is similar to the longer-haired Turkish Van cat, with which it has often been confused. The Anatolian is rare even in its native country, but breeders, particularly in Germany and the Netherlands, are working to increase its numbers. This strong, agile cat has a great liking for playing in or with water and is known to enjoy a bath.

THIS BREED IS THE **SHORTHAIRED EQUIVALENT** OF THE **TURKISH ANGORA**.

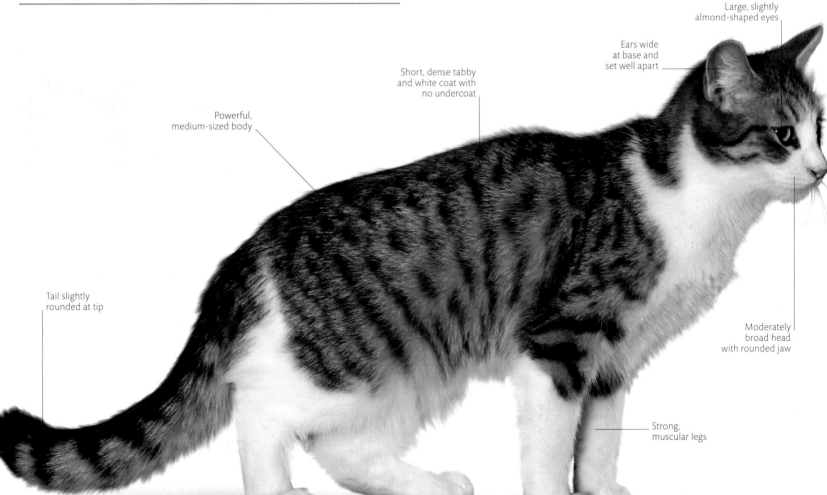

Muscular neck

Calico coat

Neat, round paws

Large, slightly almond-shaped eyes

Ears wide at base and set well apart

Short, dense tabby and white coat with no undercoat

Powerful, medium-sized body

Tail slightly rounded at tip

Moderately broad head with rounded jaw

Strong, muscular legs

Ojos Azules

ORIGIN US, 1980s
BREED REGISTRIES TICA
WEIGHT RANGE 9–12lb (4–5.5kg)

GROOMING Weekly
COLORS AND PATTERNS All colors and patterns.

A newcomer on the pedigree cat scene, this rare and enigmatic cat is active, friendly, and easy to maintain.

First discovered in New Mexico in 1984, the Ojos Azules (the name means "blue eyes" in Spanish) is one of the rarest cats in the world. The stunning eye color is particularly unusual in that it appears with any coat color or pattern, in one or both eyes, including in the longhaired version. Currently, geneticists are monitoring the development of the Ojos Azules, as serious health problems, including skull deformities, have come to light. Because so few have been bred, little is yet known about the traits of this pretty and graceful cat, although it is said to be affectionate and friendly.

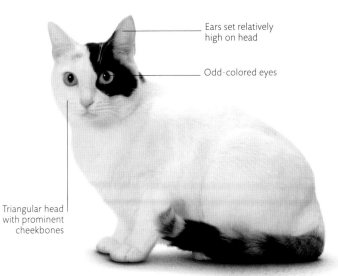

Ears set relatively high on head

Odd-colored eyes

Triangular head with prominent cheekbones

OUTCROSSING TO OTHER SHORTHAIRED CATS MAY HELP TO AVOID THE HEALTH PROBLEMS SEEN IN PUREBRED OJOS AZULES.

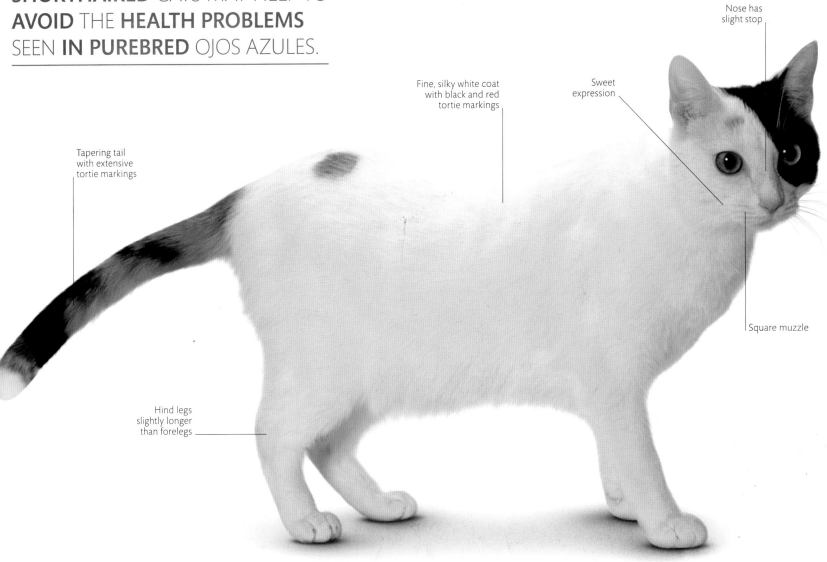

Nose has slight stop

Fine, silky white coat with black and red tortie markings

Sweet expression

Tapering tail with extensive tortie markings

Square muzzle

Hind legs slightly longer than forelegs

Egyptian Mau

ORIGIN Egypt, 1950s
BREED REGISTRIES CFA, FIFe, GCCF, TICA
WEIGHT RANGE 6–11lb (2.5–5kg)

GROOMING Weekly
COLORS AND PATTERNS Bronze and silver in spotted tabby pattern. Black smoke has "ghost" tabby markings.

This strikingly patterned cat, with an alert expression and royal bearing, is the only naturally spotted domestic breed.

This cat bears a certain resemblance to the long-bodied, spotted cats seen in the tomb paintings of ancient Egyptian pharaohs, but it cannot claim direct descent. The modern Egyptian Mau was developed by Natalie Troubetzkoy, a Russian princess in exile, who in 1956 imported several spotted Egyptian cats to the US from Italy. Here, the number of breeding cats remained small for many years, until new imports late in the 20th century reinvigorated the gene pool. Maus are affectionate cats but are also inclined to be sensitive and shy. They need thoughtful socializing at an early age and are probably best suited to an experienced cat owner. However, once a Mau bonds with its family, it stays devoted for life.

THE **EGYPTIAN MAU** IS SAID TO BE THE **FASTEST** OF ALL **DOMESTIC CAT** BREEDS.

Tail has dark rings and dark tip

Broad-based, fairly large ears

Medium-long, wedge-shaped head

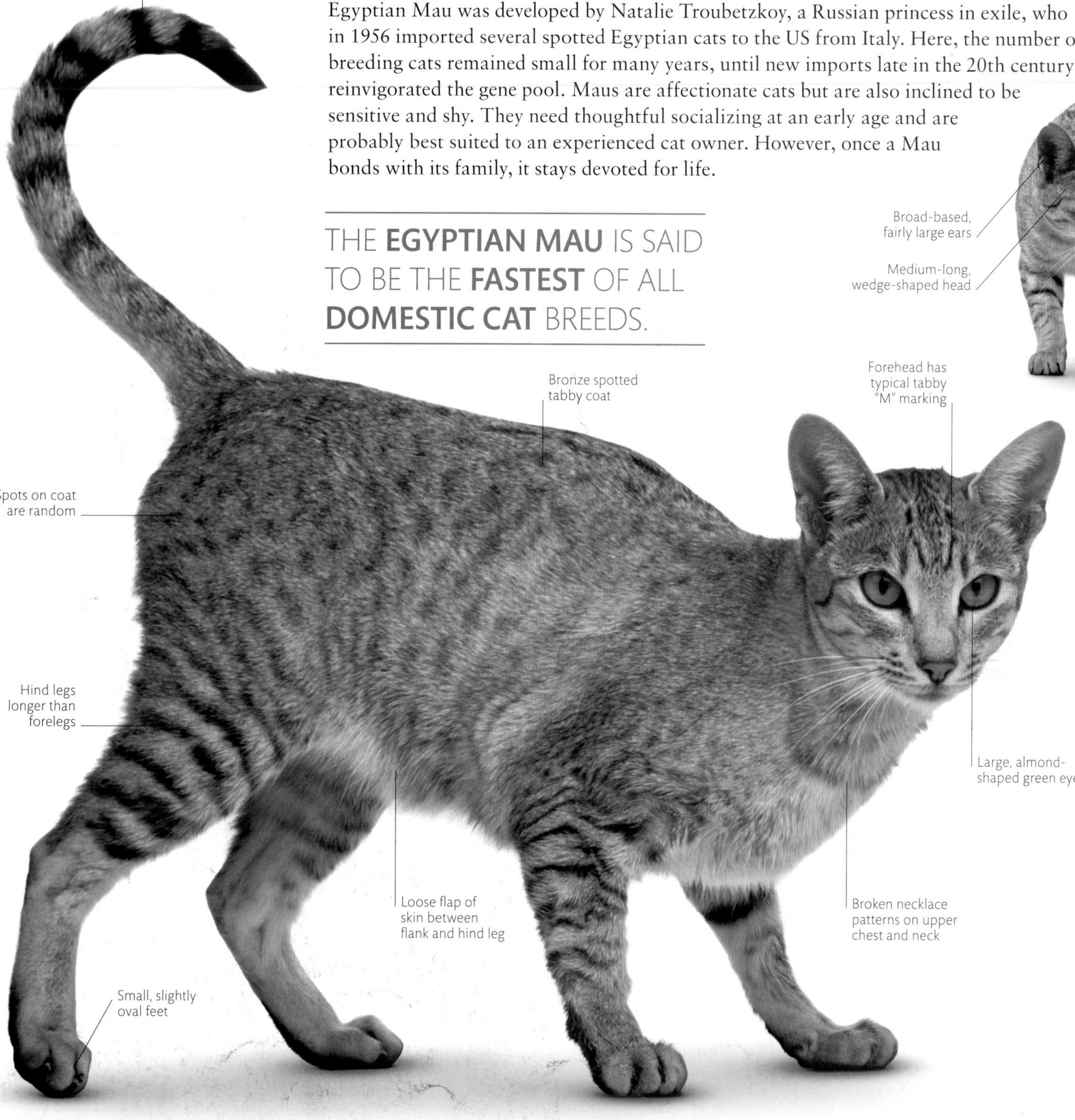

Forehead has typical tabby "M" marking

Bronze spotted tabby coat

Spots on coat are random

Hind legs longer than forelegs

Large, almond-shaped green eyes

Loose flap of skin between flank and hind leg

Broken necklace patterns on upper chest and neck

Small, slightly oval feet

Arabian Mau

ORIGIN UAE, 2000s (modern breed)
BREED REGISTRIES None
WEIGHT RANGE 7–15lb (3–7kg)

GROOMING Weekly
COLORS AND PATTERNS Various solid colors and patterns, including tabby and bicolor.

A desert cat that is well adapted to home life, this breed is active and curious and retains its natural hunting instincts.

A breed native to the Arabian Peninsula, this cat was a desert dweller that migrated to city streets when human populations encroached on its habitat. In 2004, breeding programs to develop the Arabian Mau were started, with the goal of preserving the cat's original traits and natural hardiness. With its high energy levels and need for mental stimulation, this breed can be a handful and will not be content to spend much time lazing around. The Arabian Mau is, however, both loyal and affectionate, and sympathetic owners usually find it a highly rewarding pet.

Large, pointed ears

Slightly slanted, oval eyes

Nose slightly concave

Prominent whisker pads

Necklace markings

Spotted pattern continues on to underside

Long legs with oval paws

Banding on legs

White solid coat

Medium-to-large, muscular body

Single mackerel tabby coat has firm texture

THE **CLOSE-LYING COAT** OF THIS BREED **LACKS** AN **UNDERCOAT**.

Abyssinian

ORIGIN UK,19th century
BREED REGISTRIES CFA, FIFe, GCCF, TICA
WEIGHT RANGE 9–17lb (4–7.5kg)

GROOMING Weekly
COLORS AND PATTERNS Several color forms, all with distinct ticking and facial markings.

A loyal and loving pet, this slinky, graceful cat is curious, full of energy, and needs space to play and explore.

There are various accounts of the Abyssinian's history, including the attractive but highly improbable story that it descends from the sacred cats of ancient Egypt. A more plausible version suggests that its forerunners (see panel, right) might have been brought back from Abyssinia (now Ethiopia) by British soldiers when the Abyssinian War ended in the late 1860s. However, genetic studies have shown that the Abyssinian's ticked coat pattern may have originated in cats from coastal areas of northeastern India. What is certain is that the modern breed was developed in the UK,

most probably by crossing tabby British Shorthairs (see p. 125) with a more unusual, possibly imported, breed. With its athletic build, aristocratic bearing, and beautiful ticked coat, the Abyssinian is a striking cat with a hint of "wild" about it—like a small mountain lion. The original, known as "usual," color is a rich, earthy reddish brown; other colors include fawn, chocolate, and blue. Intelligent and affectionate, Abyssinians make wonderful companions but they like an all-action life, with plenty of human company through the day.

"USUAL"-COLORED KITTEN

ZULA

A story widely repeated in accounts of the Abyssinian's history suggests that the breed's founder may have been "Zula," a cat brought to England by an army officer returning from the 1868 British military campaign in Abyssinia (now Ethiopia). Abyssinians were exhibited at Crystal Palace, London, in the early 1870s, but there is no record that they were descendants of Zula. A drawing of this cat, published in 1876, shows little resemblance to the modern breed, other than a ticked coat.

ILLUSTRATION OF ZULA

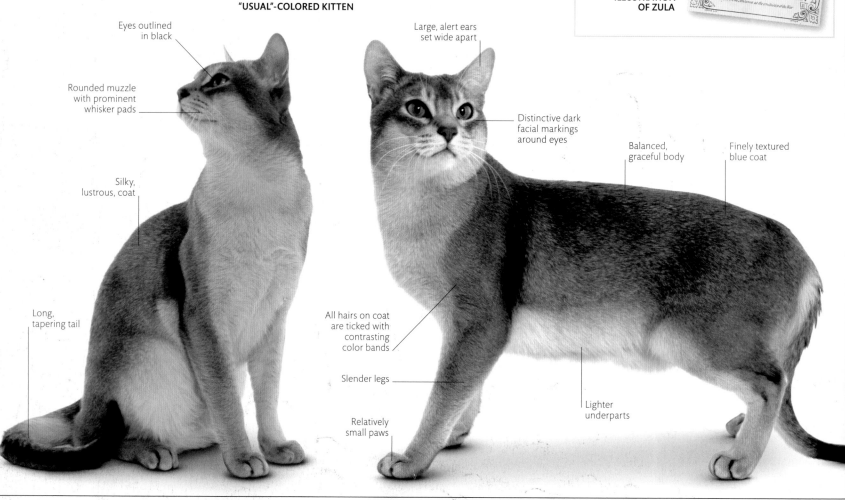

Eyes outlined in black

Rounded muzzle with prominent whisker pads

Silky, lustrous, coat

Long, tapering tail

Large, alert ears set wide apart

Distinctive dark facial markings around eyes

Balanced, graceful body

Finely textured blue coat

All hairs on coat are ticked with contrasting color bands

Slender legs

Relatively small paws

Lighter underparts

Bright-eyed
All ears and eyes, Abyssinians are alert and perpetually on the go. Almost everything engages the interest of these hyperintelligent cats, and they need plenty of regular stimulus.

Australian Mist

ORIGIN Australia, 1970s
BREED REGISTRIES GCCF
WEIGHT RANGE 8–13lb (3.5–6kg)

GROOMING Weekly
COLORS AND PATTERNS Spotted or marbled tabby, misted by ticking; colors include brown, blue, peach, chocolate, lilac, and gold.

This affectionate cat has a beautiful coat and a steady temperament that makes it an excellent pet for anyone.

The first pedigree cat to be developed in Australia, this breed was created from crosses between Burmese (see pp. 87–88), Abyssinian (see pp. 132–33), and Australian domestic shorthair cats. Formerly known as the Spotted Mist, it comes in a range of attractive spotted and marbled patterns and colors, all enhanced by ticking that produces a delicate "misted" effect. It can take up to two years for the full coat color to develop. The Australian Mist is extremely popular in its native country and has earned a reputation as a particularly easy pet to keep. The breed is known for being healthy and even-tempered. It has a loving nature, lives happily indoors, and is equally suitable as a playmate for children or a faithful companion for the less active owner. Its striking appearance and sociable nature have also helped to win the Australian Mist increasing popularity in the show ring.

CREATING A CAT

It took breeder Dr. Truda Straede nine years to create the Australian Mist and achieve official registration for her new cat. Dr. Straede combined the qualities of the cat breeds she loved best. For the foundation cats she chose Burmese (see pp. 87–88) to provide beautiful muted colors and an easy-going nature; Abyssinians (see pp. 132–33), for a tick-marked coat and bright personality; and domestic shorthairs, which not only added variations in pattern, such as a marbled coat, but a wide mix of genes for robust health.

MARBLED KITTEN

KITTEN (SPOTTED PEACH COAT)

Long tail thick in proportion to body

Short, sleek, spotted tabby coat

Medium-large, firm body

Ears wide at base and tilt slightly forward

Broad, slightly rounded head

Nose broad with slight stop

Green eyes with straight upper lids

Prominent whisker pads

Broken necklace markings

Broad, rounded chest

Paler underparts

Neat, oval paws

Ceylon

ORIGIN Sri Lanka, 1980s
BREED REGISTRIES None
WEIGHT RANGE 9–17lb (4–7.5kg)

GROOMING Weekly
COLORS AND PATTERNS Manila (black-ticked on sandy-gold ground color); various other markings and tickings, including blue, red, cream, and tortoiseshell.

Friendly and attentive, this fine-boned cat is playful and energetic and has an attractive ticked coat.

Named after its native home (now Sri Lanka), the Ceylon was imported to Italy in the early 1980s, where the breed was developed. It is now found worldwide and, if not as widely known as other breeds, has achieved some popularity in Italy. With its beautiful ticked coat and sandy coloring, this cat is similar in appearance to the Abyssinian (see pp. 132–33), although the two are not related. The Ceylon has a distinctive pattern on its forehead called the "cobra" mark, which is much valued. Breeders praise the cat's friendly nature and its responsiveness to attention.

Yellowish green eyes with dark rims

Large ears set high on head

Defined stripes on legs

Distinctive "cobra" mark on forehead

Darker lines on cheeks and forehead

Sandy-colored, black-ticked coat

Necklace markings around throat

Broad chest

Clearly defined ticking on body

Short, fine-haired coat with minimal undercoat

Fine-boned but muscular legs

KITTEN

Ocicat

ORIGIN US, 1960s
BREED REGISTRIES CFA, FIFe, GCCF, TICA
WEIGHT RANGE 6–14lb (2.5–6.5kg)

GROOMING Weekly
COLORS AND PATTERNS Black, brown, blue, lilac, and fawn in spotted tabby pattern.

Adaptable and confident, the Ocicat is a curious and playful breed that responds well to training.

Despite its name, this spotted beauty is not a cross between the domestic cat and the ocelot—the native jungle cat of South and Central America—but it looks as though it ought to be. The Ocicat was actually the surprise product of an attempt in 1964 to breed a Siamese (see pp. 104–09) with colorpoints that matched the ticked coat of the Abyssinian (see pp. 132–33). The first spotted kitten that appeared was kept solely as a pet, but others produced later were used to create the new breed. The inclusion of American Shorthairs (see p. 113) in the Ocicat's development program introduced greater size and substance. Ocicats have a delightful temperament, love company, and are easy to manage.

Silver-spotted tabby coat

Large, almond-shaped eyes with dark rims

Darkest coloration appears on tip of tail

Dark lines on cheeks

Broad, slightly square muzzle

KITTEN

Characteristic tabby "M" mark on forehead

Lighter markings around eyes and on chin

Powerful, athletic body

Short, shiny chocolate tabby coat marked with silver "thumbprint" spots

Necklace pattern around neck

Long, slightly tapering tail

Oval paws

Ocicat Classic

ORIGIN US, 1960s
BREED REGISTRIES GCCF
WEIGHT RANGE 6–14lb (2.5–6.5kg)

GROOMING Weekly
COLORS AND PATTERNS Classic tabby pattern in various colors, including silver.

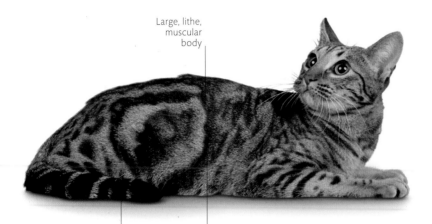

Large, lithe, muscular body

Tail has dark rings along its length

Dark tabby markings on ticked brown fur

This large, beautifully marked tabby is very affectionate and makes a devoted companion.

A version of the Ocicat with markings in the classic tabby pattern rather than spots, this cat was recognized as a separate breed only comparatively recently, and is still not yet accepted as such by all breed authorities. The Ocicat Classic has the same history as its spotted cousin (see p. 137), being a mixture of Siamese (see pp. 104–09), Abyssinian (see pp. 132–33), and American Shorthair (see p. 113). It is an energetic cat, with an enthusiasm for games and getting up on to high places. The breed has an excellent temperament and is highly sociable. An Ocicat Classic will not stay happy for long on its own, and is best-suited to a house full of people and action.

Large, broad-based ears

Traditional tabby "M" marking on forehead

Unbroken line of dark color runs from shoulders along spine

Large, almond-shaped eyes are angled slightly toward base of ears

Long, broad muzzle

Evenly spaced bracelet markings on legs

Sokoke

ORIGIN Kenya, 1970s (modern breed)
BREED REGISTRIES FIFe, TICA
WEIGHT RANGE 8–14lb (3.5–6.5kg)

GROOMING Weekly
COLORS AND PATTERNS Ticked brown tabby only.

This rare breed with a ticked tabby pattern has a peaceful nature but can be possessive of home and family.

A native of the coastal Arabuko Sokoke Forest in Kenya, this spectacular tabby was discovered in the late 1970s, when a British Kenyan resident adopted two feral kittens with distinctive markings and used them for breeding. Sokokes were later imported to Europe and the US, and new bloodlines were introduced in the 21st century. The modern Sokoke combines the traits of what are known as the Old and New Lines. These cats develop close family bonds, and some have a natural talent for communicating vocally with their owners. They remain fairly active beyond kittenhood and enjoy playing games.

A **UNIQUE PATTERN** COMBINED WITH THE **GROUND COLORING** GIVE THE COAT A **SEE-THROUGH EFFECT**.

Eyes outlined with black

Prominent whisker pads

Large, broad-based, upright ears

Black tip to tail

Classic tabby pattern on coat is blurred by ticking

Skull almost flat at top

Long, whiplike tail has firm feel

Chinstrap marking on throat

Long, slender, fine-boned legs

Long hind legs give a tiptoe gait

California Spangled

ORIGIN US, 1970s
BREED REGISTRIES None
WEIGHT RANGE 9–15lb (4–7kg)

GROOMING Weekly
COLORS AND PATTERNS Spotted tabby; ground colors include silver, bronze, gold, red, blue, black, brown, charcoal, and white.

Although this cat has exotic "jungle" looks and strong hunting instincts, it has a far from fierce personality.

This designer cat is a miniature reproduction of wild cats such as the leopard and ocelot. It was created by a conservation enthusiast, Paul Casey, specifically to discourage the killing of wild animals for their fur. Casey reasoned that if people related spotted fur to their own pet cats they would feel distaste for the destruction of wildlife in the name of fashion. The California Spangled was bred by using a variety of domestic cats, and it has no wild cat species in its makeup. Hunting and playing are what this active cat enjoys most, but it is also sociable, affectionate, and easy to handle.

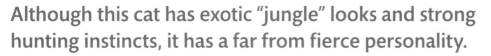

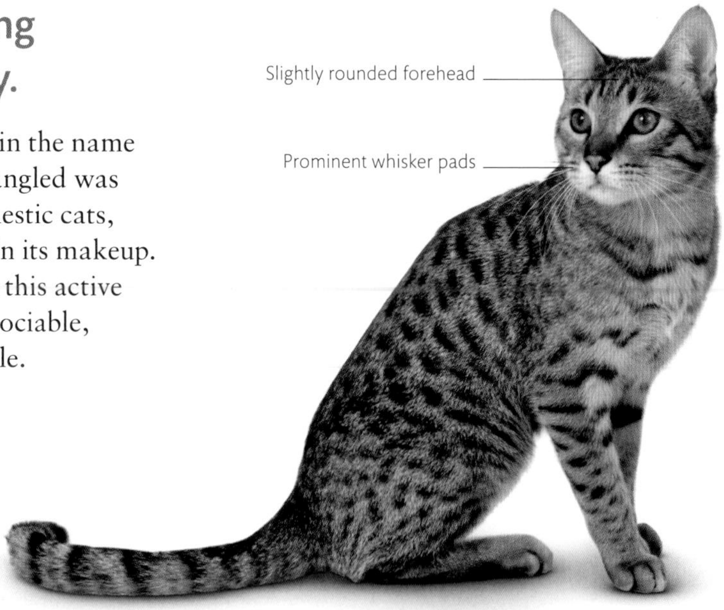

Slightly rounded forehead

Prominent whisker pads

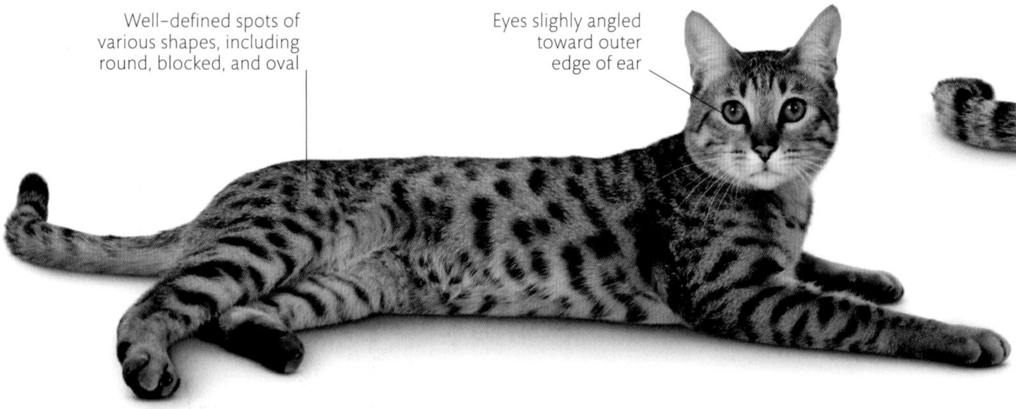

Well-defined spots of various shapes, including round, blocked, and oval

Eyes slighly angled toward outer edge of ear

Gold spotted tabby coat has soft, velvety texture

Ears set high on head

Tail has dark rings and dark tip

Wide cheekbones

Dark bars on legs

Long, lean, muscular body

140

Toyger

ORIGIN US, 1990s
BREED REGISTRIES TICA
WEIGHT RANGE 12–22lb (5.5–10kg)

GROOMING Weekly
COLORS AND PATTERNS Brown mackerel tabby only.

This companionable and intelligent breed is a stunningly beautiful designer cat with a laid-back personality.

A breed developed in the 1990s by crossing a striped, shorthaired cat with a Bengal (see pp. 142–43), the Toyger has a tiger-marked coat with random vertical stripes that are quite distinct from any other tabby pattern. Well built and muscular, this unique "toy tiger" moves with the flowing power and grace of a big jungle cat. The Toyger is confident and outgoing but has a relaxed attitude to life, which allows it to fit in well with any household. Although active and athletic, this cat is easy to handle and can be taught to play games and to walk on a leash.

Long, broad head

Short, lush, glittery coat

Small, rounded ears are thickly furred

KITTEN

Butterfly markings on head

Round eyes have deep color

Muscular neck

Long, strong body carried low to the ground

Long, muscular, low-set, ring-marked tail

Powerful forequarters

Brown mackerel tabby coat

Bengal

ORIGIN US, 1970s
BREED REGISTRIES FIFe, GCCF, TICA
WEIGHT RANGE 12–22lb (5.5–10kg)

GROOMING Weekly
COLORS AND PATTERNS Brown, blue, silver, and snow colors in spotted and marble classic tabby patterns.

This cat has a strikingly beautiful spotted coat and a vibrant personality and is curious, playful, and very energetic.

In the 1970s, scientists crossed the small, wild Asian leopard cat (see panel, below) with shorthaired domestic cats in an attempt to introduce the wildcat's natural immunity to feline leukemia into the pet population. The project failed, but the resulting hybrid caught the interest of several American fanciers. In a series of selective breeding programs, crosses were achieved between these hybrids and various pedigree domestic cats, including the Abyssinian (see pp. 132–33), Bombay (see pp. 84–85), British Shorthair (see pp. 118–27), and Egyptian Mau (see p. 130). The outcome was the Bengal, originally called the Leopardette, which was officially accepted as a new breed in the 1980s.

With its magnificently patterned coat and large, muscular frame, this cat brings more than a hint of the jungle into the living room. Despite its wild ancestry, there is nothing unsafe about the Bengal—it is delightfully affectionate—but it does have a lot of energy and is best suited to an experienced cat owner.

Friendly by nature, a Bengal always wants to be at the heart of its family. It needs company and both physical activity and mental stimulation. A bored Bengal will be unhappy and possibly destructive.

Long and substantially built body

Thick, low-set tail

WILD RELATIVE

The Asian Leopard Cat (*Prionailurus bengalensis*), which was used to create the Bengal, occurs throughout India, China, and much of Southeast Asia, including Indonesia. Its spotted coat has several regional color variations, some of which have been introduced into Bengal breeding programs. The species' striking appearance has made it vulnerable to both commercial fur traders and the wild pet trade. As a result, its total population is declining, and some subspecies of Leopard Cat are considered to be endangered.

WILDCAT POSTAGE STAMP

KITTEN

Luxurious
snow-spotted, dense
coat is silky to touch

Head longer
than it is wide

Prominent
cheekbones

Round-tipped,
relatively short ears
with wide bases

"Mascara"
markings
around eyes

Strong, muscular legs

Large, round paws

143

Wildcat elegance
A Kanaani is a natural athlete, its power and gracefulness clearly evident when the cat is in motion. The sleek, spotted coat resembles that of its wildcat ancestors.

Kanaani

ORIGIN Israel, 2000s
BREED REGISTRIES None
WEIGHT RANGE 11–20lb (5–9kg)

GROOMING Weekly
COLORS AND PATTERNS Spotted and marbled tabby patterns with various ground colors.

This athletic and muscular, yet elegant cat is very active and retains some of the wild nature of its ancestors.

Developed to have a close resemblance to the spotted African wildcat, the Kanaani (as in the Biblical name "Canaanite") is rare. First bred by a sculptor in Jerusalem, this new breed was registered by the World Cat Association only in 2000, and many authorities do not yet accept it as a breed. It is slowly becoming better known, with breeders in Germany and the US. Until 2010, the breeding program for the Kanaani allowed outcrosses with the African wildcat, Bengal (see pp. 142–43), and Oriental Shorthair (see pp. 91–101)—provided all these had spotted coats. All kittens born since 2010, however, must have Kanaani parents only. With its large, slender body, long legs, long neck, and tufted ears, the Kanaani looks like a wild desert cat. This cat has a gentle and affectionate temperament but at the same time retains some of the independence of its wild ancestor and is also an excellent hunter.

CHANGING PATTERN

When Doris Pollatschek (pictured below) set out to breed the Kanaani, her intention was to create a cat that looked authentically wild, with a spotted tabby coat like that of *Felis silvestris lybica* (see p. 9) on which it was modeled. However, the breed standard for the Kanaani now also permits a marbled tabby pattern, which does not occur naturally in *F. silvestris*. Breeders remain conservative in not introducing the silver variation that is so popular in similar breeds such as the Bengal (see pp. 142–43) and Savannah (see pp. 146–47).

Large, almond-shaped green eyes

Broad, triangular-shaped head

Brick-red nose leather

Long, slender, muscular body

Short, coarse-textured, seal-spotted tabby coat

Black-tipped tail has at least three black rings

KITTEN

Spots softened by ticking

Characteristic "M" marking on forehead

Large ears with tufted tips

Long neck

Compact, oval paws

Savannah

ORIGIN US, 1980s
BREED REGISTRIES TICA
WEIGHT RANGE 12–22lb (5.5–10kg)

GROOMING Weekly
COLORS AND PATTERNS Brown-spotted tabby, black silver-spotted tabby, black, or black smoke. Ghost-spotting may be visible in black or black smoke.

A tall, graceful cat with a strikingly unusual appearance, the Savannah is highly curious and can be very demanding.

One of the newest cat breeds, the Savannah was officially recognized only in 2012. It originated from the chance mating of a male serval, a wildcat of the African plains (see pp. 8–9), with a female domestic cat. The Savannah has inherited many of the serval's features—including a spotted coat, long legs, huge, upright ears, and often a "tear" mark extending from each eye, like that seen in a cheetah. This adventurous and athletic cat can jump up to 8ft (2.5m) in the air. It is permanently on the lookout for amusement, which might include playing with water, exploring the contents of a cupboard, or opening doors. It is also loyal and sociable, much like a dog. Because a Savannah can be quite assertive and demanding, the breed is not best suited to first-time cat owners.

Some countries and states impose restrictions on owning and breeding Savannah cats, especially early-generation animals.

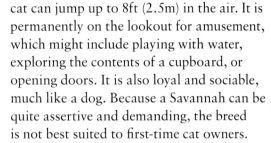

KITTEN

GENERATION CHANGES

As is the case with many crosses between different species, the fertility of first generation (F1) hybrid offspring is compromised. In the case of the Savannah, the males tend to be infertile until the serval genes in the fertile female offspring are further diluted—usually by the fifth (F5) or sixth (F6) generation. However, once these F5 and F6 males are successfully crossed back to a female serval, the kittens produced are much more like a serval, particularly with regard to the clarity of their coat markings.

SIXTH GENERATION SAVANNAH

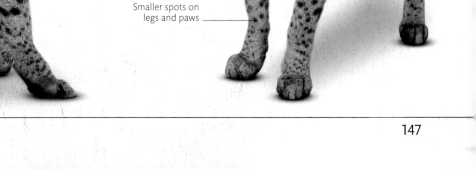

Brown-spotted tabby coat lies flat and has slightly coarse texture, although spots feel softer

Long, slender, athletic body

Brow slightly hooded

Very long, muscular legs

Long neck

Triangular head small in proportion to body

Extremely large, upright ears set high on head

Smaller spots on legs and paws

Serengeti

ORIGIN US, 1990s
BREED REGISTRIES TICA
WEIGHT RANGE 8–15lb (3.5–7kg)

GROOMING Weekly
COLORS AND PATTERNS Black solid color; spotted tabby in any shade of brown or silver (silver ground color with black spots); and black smoke.

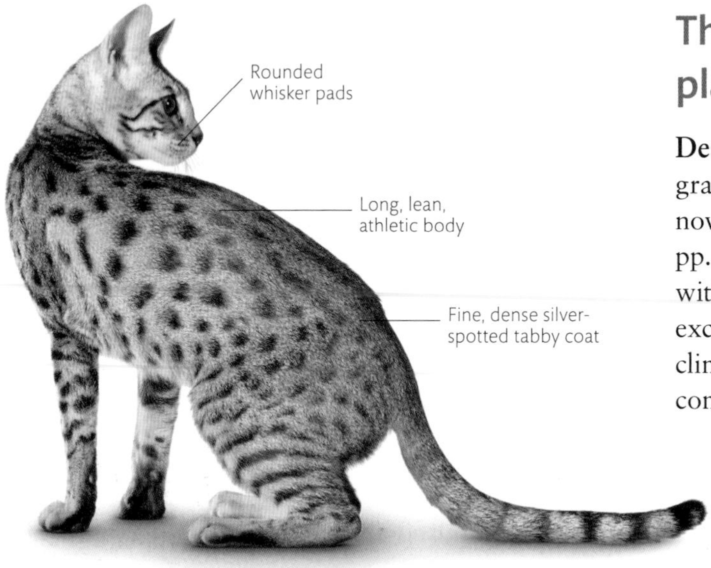

Rounded whisker pads

Long, lean, athletic body

Fine, dense silver-spotted tabby coat

This tall and elegant breed loves to climb to high places, and has a gentle but outgoing temperament.

Designer-bred to resemble the serval—a small, leggy wild cat of the African grasslands—the Serengeti was created in California in the mid-1990s and is now also known in Europe and Australia. The result of crossing a Bengal (see pp. 142–43) with an Oriental (see pp. 91–101), this breed stands out among others with its long neck and legs, and upright stance. Most conspicuous are the Serengeti's exceptionally large ears, which are the same length as its head. This agile cat enjoys climbing and exploring high places. It bonds closely with its owner and is an ideal companion for someone who spends a lot of time at home.

SERENGETIS FORM **LONG-LASTING BONDS** WITH THEIR OWNERS AND WILL **FOLLOW** THEM **ANYWHERE**.

Head longer than broad

Exceptionally large, wide-based ears with rounded tips

Large, round eyes

Long neck in proportion to body

Distinct, widely spaced spots

Dark tail tip

Very long legs

Chausie

ORIGIN US, 1990s
BREED REGISTRIES TICA
WEIGHT RANGE 12–22lb (5.5–10kg)

GROOMING Weekly
COLORS AND PATTERNS Black solid and ticked tabby pattern in brown and grizzled black.

A slender and slinky cat, this charismatic breed is energetic and needs an owner who can give it plenty of attention.

Although the wild jungle cat and the domestic cat could, and probably did, interbreed naturally in the past, the Chausie originated from hybrids created during the 1990s. Initially, the jungle cat was crossed with a variety of cats, but today, to maintain consistency of the Chausie's shape and coat color, only the Abyssinian (see pp. 132–33)

and certain domestic shorthairs are used. Like other hybrid cats, the Chausie is very active and enjoys exploring. It is intelligent and insatiably curious—a Chausie quickly becomes adept at opening doors to pry into cupboards. This cat requires an experienced owner who is able to spend plenty of time at home to provide companionship.

THE BREED'S NAME IS **DERIVED FROM** THE **LATIN** NAME FOR THE **JUNGLE CAT**, *FELIS CHAUS*.

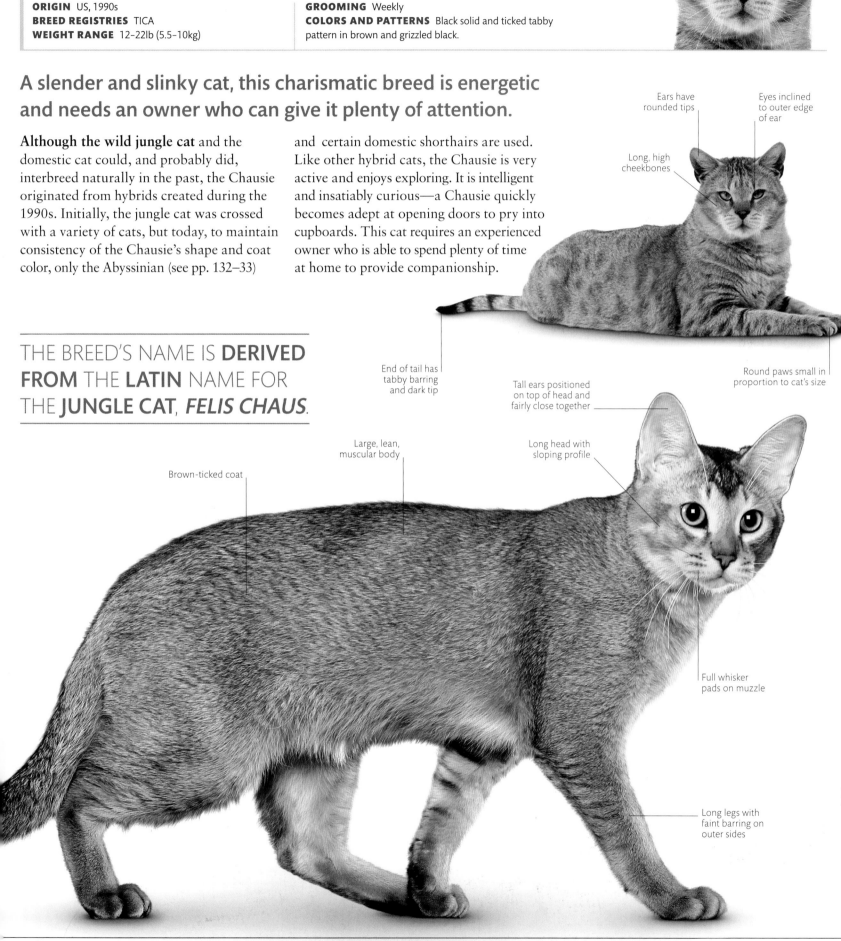

Ears have rounded tips

Eyes inclined to outer edge of ear

Long, high cheekbones

End of tail has tabby barring and dark tip

Round paws small in proportion to cat's size

Tall ears positioned on top of head and fairly close together

Large, lean, muscular body

Long head with sloping profile

Brown-ticked coat

Full whisker pads on muzzle

Long legs with faint barring on outer sides

Munchkin

ORIGIN US, 1980s
BREED REGISTRIES TICA
WEIGHT RANGE 6–9lb (2.5–4kg)

GROOMING Weekly
COLORS AND PATTERNS All colors, shades, and patterns.

Friendly and sweet in temperament, the short–legged Munchkin is highly sociable and loves playing with toys.

KITTEN

The feline equivalent of Dachshunds, Munchkins are instantly recognizable by their short legs and low-slung bodies. The first Munchkins were bred in Louisiana in the 1980s. The exceptionally short legs arose as a random mutation—short-legged cats have occurred naturally in various countries for many years (see panel, below). This feature has been preserved by Munchkin breeders, and the breed is officially recognized by The International Cat Association (TICA). However, although Munchkins are now becoming popular in both shorthaired and longhaired versions (see p. 233), they are not accepted by many other breed organizations. The short legs do not greatly hamper movement; Munchkins are said to run like ferrets and sit up on their hind legs like rabbits and kangaroos.

In addition, the gene for short legs does not seem to affect health or longevity. This little cat may not have the jumping ability of its taller cousins, but it still manages to climb on to furniture and is lively and playful. Muchkins do, however, need help with grooming. The Munchkin has been used to create other short-legged breeds such as the Minskin (see p. 155).

KANGAROO CATS

Although the development of the Munchkin began only in the 1980s, cats with ultra-short legs are not a recent phenomenon. Accounts of feral cats with this trait date back to at least the 1930s. Some reports dubbed them "kangaroo cats" because their forelegs were noticebly shorter than their hind legs, giving the cats the appearance of a kangaroo grazing. Early sightings also noted mixed litters of short- and normal-legged kittens, a common occurrence in Munchkins today. The pair shown below are litter brothers.

High,
well-defined
cheekbones

Rounded
chest

Tail may be as
long as body

Flat forehead

Broad-based
ears set on
top of head

Dense, weather-
resistant mink
colorpoint coat

Rounded, wedge-
shaped head

Walnut-shaped,
yellow eyes

Slight nose
stop

Legs about half
the average length
of other breeds

151

Kinkalow

ORIGIN US, 1990s
BREED REGISTRIES TICA
WEIGHT RANGE 6–9lb (2.5–4kg)

GROOMING Weekly
COLORS AND PATTERNS Many colors and patterns, including tabby and tortie.

This new and rare breed is said to be intelligent and playful, and it enjoys an owner's lap.

A designer dwarf cat, the Kinkalow was deliberately created in the 1990s by crossing the Munchkin (see pp. 150–51) with the American Curl (see p. 159). This still-experimental breed ideally should have the small, compact body and ultra-short legs of the Munchkin, combined with the turned-back ears of the Curl. Not all Kinkalow litters inherit these extreme traits, however, which are due to genetic mutations, and some kittens are born with both normal-length legs and straight ears. The development of the Kinkalow and the establishment of its breed standard are ongoing projects. So far, this miniature cat appears to be free from specific health problems and unhampered by its short legs.

Soft, sleek black coat

Rounded paws

THIS **SHORT-STATURED** BREED WAS **FOUNDED BY** AMERICAN BREEDER **TERRI HARRIS**.

Short, compact body feels heavy for size

Silky red-and-black tortie coat

Tail long in comparison with body

Curled-back ears inherited from American Curl

Pink nose leather

White chest

Forelegs particularly short

Lambkin Dwarf

ORIGIN US, 1980s
BREED REGISTRIES TICA
WEIGHT RANGE 5–9lb (2–4kg)

GROOMING 2–3 times a week
COLORS AND PATTERNS All colors, shades, and patterns.

Sweet and easy-to-keep, this cat is very gentle, active, and a good jumper, despite having very short legs.

This little-known hybrid dwarf cat is a cross between the short-legged Munchkin (see pp. 150–51) and the curly-coated Selkirk Rex (see pp. 174–75). It is sometimes known as the Nanus (meaning "dwarf") Rex. Still regarded as experimental, the Lambkin Dwarf is rare because it is extremely difficult to breed to type. In a single litter, some kittens may inherit both the mutant genes that pass on the short stature of one parent and the curly coat of the other, while other kittens may be short-legged and straight-haired, long-legged and straight-haired, or long-legged and curly-haired. These cats are reputed to have the docility of the Rex with a touch of the Munchkin's impishness.

THIS IS A **RARE BREED** BECAUSE IT IS **DIFFICULT** TO **MATCH** THE BREED **STANDARD**.

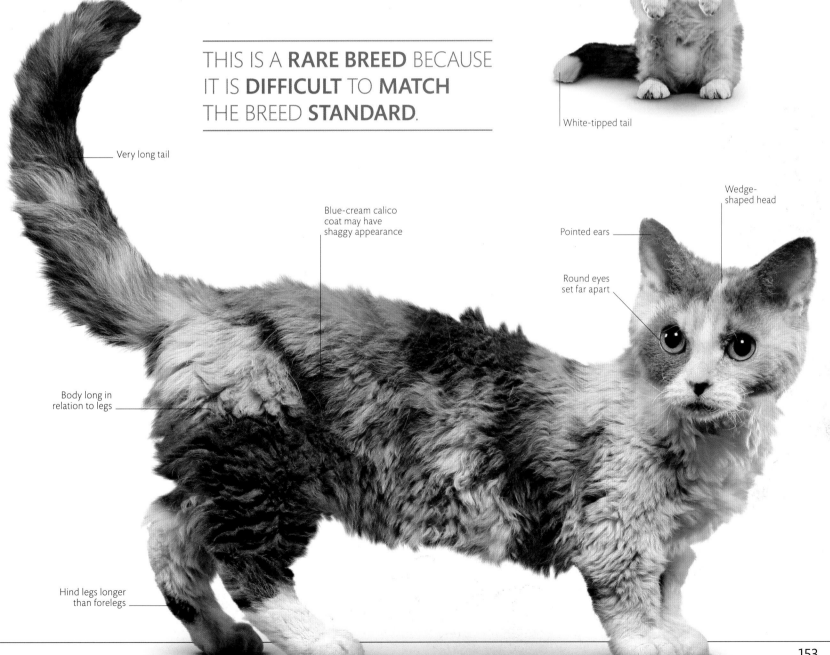

Pink nose leather

Soft-textured coat

White-tipped tail

Very long tail

Blue-cream calico coat may have shaggy appearance

Wedge-shaped head

Pointed ears

Round eyes set far apart

Body long in relation to legs

Hind legs longer than forelegs

Bambino

ORIGIN US, 2000s
BREED REGISTRIES TICA
WEIGHT RANGE 5–9lb (2–4kg)

GROOMING 2–3 times a week
COLORS AND PATTERNS All colors, shades, and patterns.

This strange-looking new breed is gentle but lively, has an affectionate personality, and makes an amusing companion.

This 21st-century experimental dwarf breed is one of the most extraordinary of all designer cats. Developed in the US as a hybrid of the Munchkin (see pp. 150–51) and the hairless Sphynx (see pp. 168–69), the Bambino is extremely short-legged with large ears and a heavily wrinkled skin that looks entirely naked, although it is usually covered with very fine peach-fuzz hair. Both short-legged and long-legged kittens can be born in the same litter. Despite its dainty appearance, this cat is strong and athletic, with firm muscles and a sturdy bone structure, and is able to run, jump, and climb. It is also intelligent and highly sociable. However, the lack of fur means

that the Bambino is vulnerable to strong sun and low temperatures, and must be kept as an indoor pet. Grooming should consist of regular bathing to prevent a buildup of natural skin oils.

KITTENS

THE MINSKIN

In another twist on the Munchkin–Sphynx cross, an American breeder, Paul McSorley, developed another short-legged cat, which he called the Minskin. The breed's name derives from the combination of miniature and skin. Although the name implies a lack of fur, this cat has fine fuzzy body hair, aside from a bald belly. It differs from the Bambino in having dense fur-points on the head and ears, legs, and tail. McSorley introduced Devon Rex (see pp. 178–79) and Burmese (see pp. 87–88) cats into the mix until he achieved his goal. The Minskin comes in all color variations, including tabby and colorpoint.

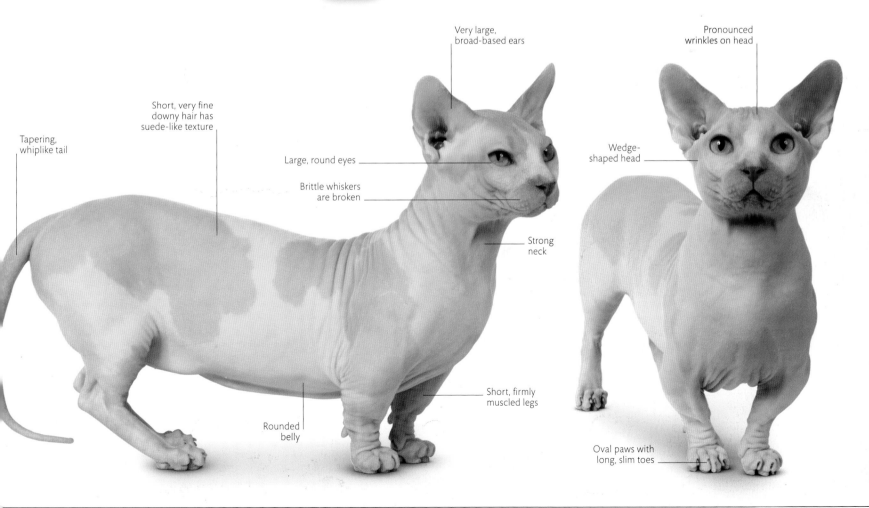

Very large, broad-based ears

Pronounced wrinkles on head

Short, very fine downy hair has suede-like texture

Tapering, whiplike tail

Large, round eyes

Brittle whiskers are broken

Wedge-shaped head

Strong neck

Short, firmly muscled legs

Rounded belly

Oval paws with long, slim toes

Scottish Fold

ORIGIN UK/US, 1960s
BREED REGISTRIES CFA, TICA
WEIGHT RANGE 6–13lb (2.5–6kg)

GROOMING Weekly
COLORS AND PATTERNS Most colors, shades, and patterns, including pointed, tabby, and tortie.

This quiet and companionable breed with unique folded ears is very loyal and gets along well with children.

Round, well padded body

Due to a rare genetic mutation, the ears of this breed fold forward to fit like a cap over the skull, producing a unique round-headed look. The first Fold cat to be discovered was an all-white, long-haired female, known as Susie, that was born on a Scottish farm in the 1960s. At first, this cat and the folded-ear kittens she produced attracted only local interest, but then geneticists began taking notice and some of Susie's descendants were sent to the US. Here, the breed was established, using crosses between Folds and British (see pp. 118–27) and American Shorthairs (see p. 113). During the development of the Scottish Fold, a long-coated version (see p. 237) also emerged. These cats need careful breeding to prevent certain skeletal problems linked with the gene responsible for ear folding, and due to this risk they do not meet with the approval of all breed authorities. Scottish Folds are always born with straight ears that, in kittens carrying the folded-ear gene, begin to flatten forward within about three weeks. Cats that remain straight-eared are known as Scottish Straights. The Scottish Fold is still something of a rarity, more likely to be seen at shows than as a housecat. The breed is known, however, for its loyal nature, and Scottish Folds that do become pets adjust easily to any type of family, making quiet and affectionate companions.

Fairly long tail tapers to rounded tip

KITTEN

TRAVELING COMPANION

American writer Peter Gethers boosted the popularity of this breed with a biographical trilogy about his adventures with his Scottish Fold cat Norton, published in 2009 and 2010. Presented with a kitten as a gift, Gethers became an instant cat fanatic. Norton traveled the world with his owner, accompanying Gethers on long-haul flights and sitting beside him in restaurants. When the cat died, at the age of 16, he had become well-known enough to merit an obituary in the *New York Times*.

THE INTERNATIONAL BESTSELLER
Forever norton
The Perfect Cat, his Flawed Human and Life's Greatest Lesson
'Witty and warm' Vicki Myron, author of DEWEY
PETER GETHERS

Neat, round paws

Short, dense blue coat
stands away from body

Unique ears
fold downward
and forward

Large, round
golden eyes

Short neck

Short, broad,
slightly curved nose

Highlander

ORIGIN North America, 2000s
BREED REGISTRIES TICA
WEIGHT RANGE 10–25lb (4.5–11kg)

GROOMING Weekly
COLORS AND PATTERNS All colors in any tabby pattern, including colorpoints.

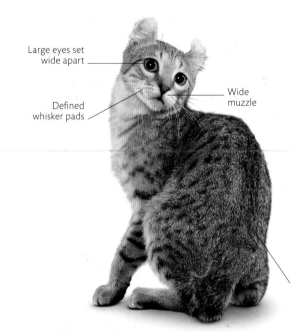

Large eyes set wide apart

Defined whisker pads

Wide muzzle

Spots merge into stripes along top of back

This active, energetic, and playful breed loves to be the center of attention and provides plenty of entertainment.

This recently developed breed, which also comes in a longhaired version (see p. 240), is still extremely rare. It has distinctive looks, with a big body, short tail, and dense coat. Most noticeable of all are the Highlander's large, curled ears; often thickly tufted, they add to the cat's air of wildness.

Although not yet popular, the breed is beginning to earn recognition as a delightful housecat with a very special personality. Highlanders are ready to love everyone and make devoted companions. They have an irrepressible sense of fun, always want to play, and are said to be easy to train.

Distinctive ears curl back loosely at tips, no more than 90 degrees

Broad, muscular shoulders

Broad nose

Short, thick tail

Brown-spotted tabby coat

Large, round paws

American Curl

ORIGIN US, 1980s
BREED REGISTRIES CFA, FIFe, TICA
WEIGHT RANGE 7–11lb (3–5kg)

GROOMING Weekly
COLORS AND PATTERNS All colors, shades, and patterns.

Elegant and engaging, this cat is curious and exuberant, and its kittenlike personality makes it a loving companion.

The first American Curls were longhaired (see pp. 238–39) like the founding female of the breed, which was discovered in California. The shorthaired version was developed later and is essentially the same cat in a different coat. Big-eyed and elegantly proportioned, the American Curl is extremely attractive.

The curled ears, which may appear within a week of birth, add a touch of designer chic, although the mutation is an entirely natural phenomenon. This breed, noted for its sweet temperament, forms a close attachment to its family and always wants to know what is going on in the household.

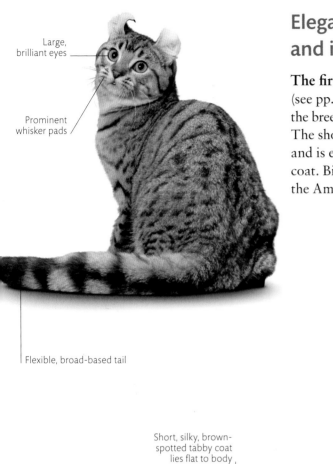

Large, brilliant eyes

Prominent whisker pads

Flexible, broad-based tail

Ears turn smoothly back at least 90 degrees

Wedge-shaped head

Rectangular, moderately muscled body

Short, silky, brown-spotted tabby coat lies flat to body

Rounded paws

Japanese Bobtail

ORIGIN Japan, c.17th century
BREED REGISTRIES CFA, TICA
WEIGHT RANGE 6–9lb (2.5–4kg)

GROOMING Weekly
COLORS AND PATTERNS All colors and patterns, including tabby (except ticked), tortie, and bicolor.

This charming cat has a beautiful voice, a unique pom-pom tail, and is playful, spirited, and people-oriented.

In its native Japan, this cat is said to bring good luck and is a popular subject for ceramic ornaments. The Japanese Bobtail was spotted in the 1960s by an American enthusiast, who sent a number of the cats to the US to begin a breeding program. This shorthaired version won recognition in the late 1970s, followed a decade or so later by the longhaired version (see p. 241). An attractive and beautifully proportioned cat, the Japanese Bobtail is outgoing and intelligent. It has a charmingly melodious voice and fond owners like to claim that it talks, or even sings, to them.

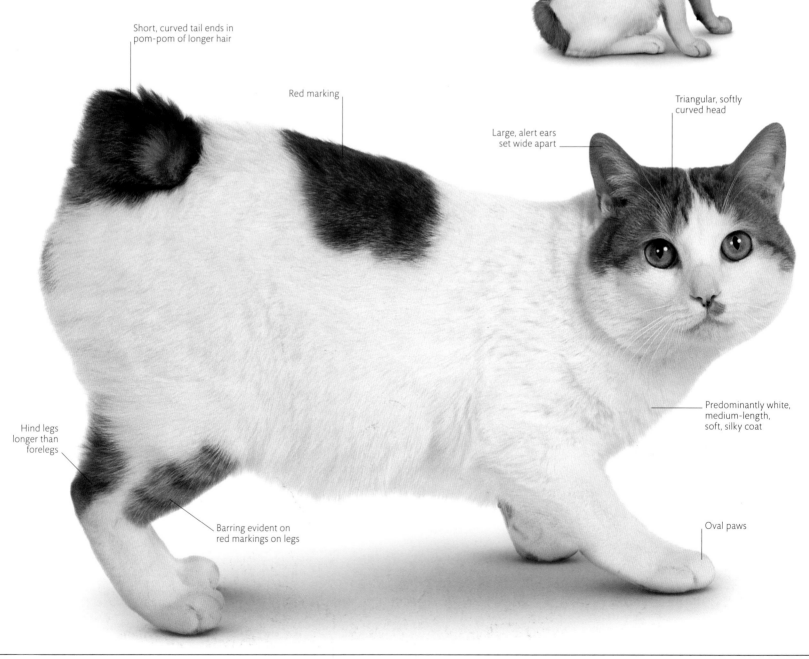

Gold eyes

Broad muzzle with obvious whisker pads

Muscular but slender, well-balanced body

Short, curved tail ends in pom-pom of longer hair

Red marking

Triangular, softly curved head

Large, alert ears set wide apart

Hind legs longer than forelegs

Barring evident on red markings on legs

Predominantly white, medium-length, soft, silky coat

Oval paws

Kurilian Bobtail

ORIGIN Kuril Islands, North Pacific, 20th century
BREED REGISTRIES FIFe, TICA
WEIGHT RANGE 7–10lb (3–4.5kg)

GROOMING Weekly
COLORS AND PATTERNS Most solid colors and shades in bicolor, tortie, and tabby (except ticked) patterns.

This sturdy, strong-limbed cat with a quirky tail is clever and sociable.

Native to the Kuril Islands, which form a chain between the North Pacific and the Sea of Okhotsk, off Siberia, the Kurilian Bobtail first became popular as a domestic cat in mainland Russia during the 20th century. Since the 1990s this breed, in longhaired (see pp. 242–43) as well as shorthaired versions, has also been appearing regularly at Russian cat shows but it is little known elsewhere. The curious tail is a natural mutation and differs from one cat to another; it always has a number of kinks and may curl or bend in almost any direction. Kurilian Bobtails are relaxed, sociable cats, and said to be superb mouse catchers.

Muscular compact body

Broad, straight nose

Triangular ears tilt slightly forward

Short, kinked tail at least two vertebrae long

Close-lying brown mackerel tabby coat has minimal undercoat

Slightly angled, large eyes

Broad, slightly rounded chin

Well-developed thighs

Strong legs with solid bone structure

Mekong Bobtail

ORIGIN Southeast Asia, pre-20th century
BREED REGISTRIES Other
WEIGHT RANGE 8–13lb (3.5–6kg)

GROOMING Weekly
COLORS AND PATTERNS Colorpoints as Siamese
(see pp. 104–9).

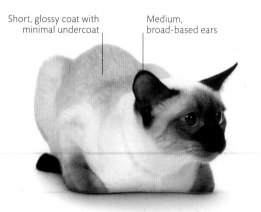

Short, glossy coat with
minimal undercoat

Medium,
broad-based ears

This little-known breed with an attractive Siamese-pointed coat is active and affectionate, and it makes a good pet.

Named after the great Mekong River that flows through China, Laos, Cambodia, and Vietnam, this short-tailed cat occurs naturally over a wide area of Southeast Asia. The Mekong Bobtail was developed as an experimental breed in Russia and has been recognized by some authorities since 2004,

although worldwide it is not particularly well-known. It is a strongly built cat with the brilliant blue eyes and colorpointed coat of a Siamese. The Mekong Bobtail is active and agile, and is good at jumping and climbing. It is said to be a quiet breed with a friendly, well-balanced personality.

ACCORDING TO **EASTERN LEGENDS,** THE MEKONG BOBTAILS WERE **ROYAL CATS** AND THE **GUARDIANS** OF **ANCIENT TEMPLES**.

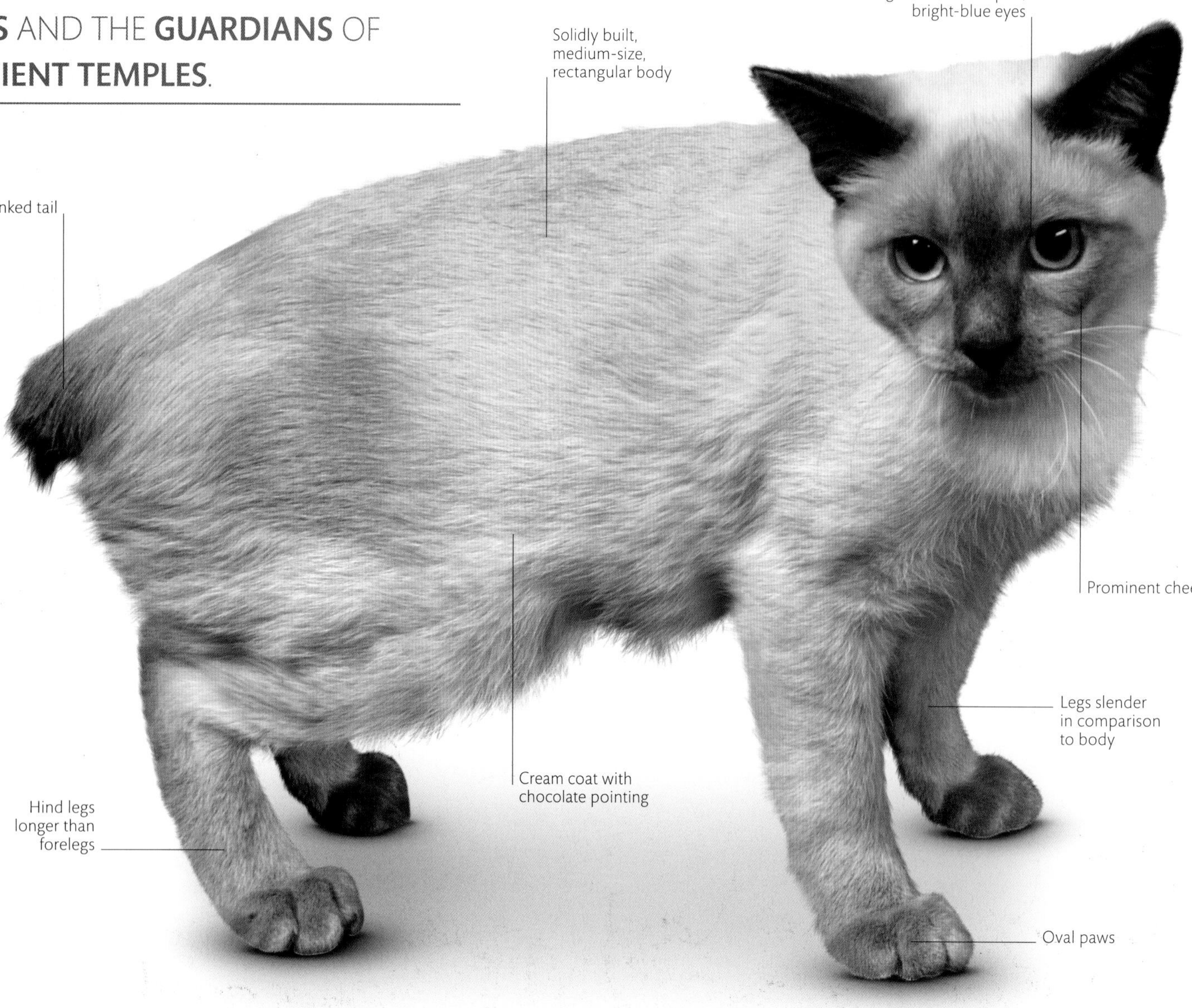

Large, almond-shaped,
bright-blue eyes

Solidly built,
medium-size,
rectangular body

Short, kinked tail

Prominent cheekbones

Legs slender
in comparison
to body

Hind legs
longer than
forelegs

Cream coat with
chocolate pointing

Oval paws

American Bobtail

ORIGIN US, 1960s
BREED REGISTRIES CFA, TICA
WEIGHT RANGE 7–15lb (3–7kg)

GROOMING Weekly
COLORS AND PATTERNS All colors, shades, and patterns, including tabby, tortie, and colorpoint.

Big and beautiful, this cat is an excellent and highly adaptable companion, without being too demanding.

The breeding of domestic bobtail cats native to the US has been reported several times since about the middle of the 20th century, but so far only this one has been fully recognized. There is also a longer-haired version (see p. 247), and both types have the naturally occurring shortened tail that gives the breed its name. The American Bobtail is a substantially built cat, with powerful muscles and large bones. It is intelligent, alert, and reasonably active, but also enjoys quiet times. This cat is happy to be among people, without overwhelming them with its attentions, and it fits in comfortably with any type of household.

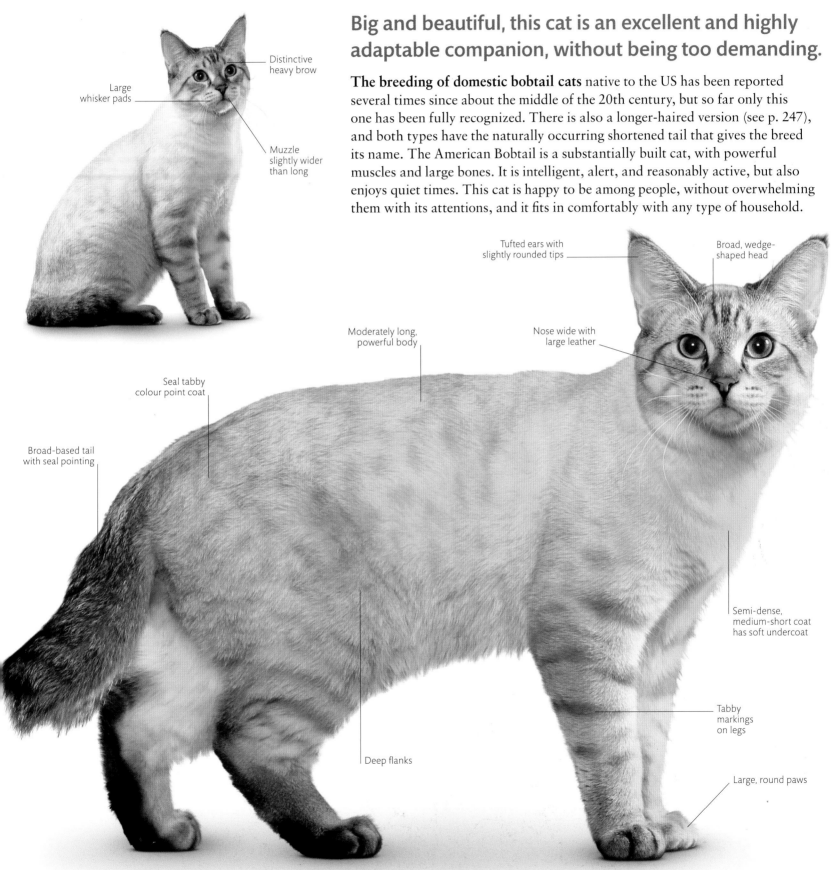

Distinctive heavy brow

Large whisker pads

Muzzle slightly wider than long

Tufted ears with slightly rounded tips

Broad, wedge-shaped head

Moderately long, powerful body

Nose wide with large leather

Seal tabby colour point coat

Broad-based tail with seal pointing

Semi-dense, medium-short coat has soft undercoat

Deep flanks

Tabby markings on legs

Large, round paws

Tail types
Manx cats are classified according to tail length. Categories include "rumpy" (completely tailless); "stumpy" (the tail has from one to three vertebrae); and "longy" (the tail is almost normal length).

Manx

ORIGIN UK, pre-18th century
BREED REGISTRIES CFA, FIFe, GCCF, TICA
WEIGHT RANGE 8–12lb (3.5–5.5kg)

GROOMING Weekly
COLORS AND PATTERNS All colors, shades, and patterns, including tabby and tortie.

THE "CABBIT" MYTH

It was once thought that Manx cats were "cabbits," the result of matings between cats and rabbits. It is not difficult to see how the misconception arose in the days before such crossbreeding was known to be biologically impossible. With its rounded rump, long back legs, and stumpy tail, a Manx has distinctly rabbitlike traits. Astonishingly, animals identified as "cabbits" are still occasionally reported in the 21st century.

Best known of the tailless cats, this breed is popular for its quiet charm and makes a great family companion.

Few breeds have as many stories about their origins as the tailless Manx. Among the more colorful legends, this cat is supposed to have lost its tail in an accident on Noah's Ark. In reality, it is native to the Isle of Man, in the Irish Sea, and its lack of tail is a natural mutation. Another legend has it that the Manx is a hybrid between a cat and a rabbit (see panel, left). The Manx has interested cat fanciers since the early 20th century and, together with its longhaired relation, the Cymric (see p. 246), is known worldwide. Both tailless and partial or full-tailed cats can occur, even in the same litter, although only the tailless ones are eligible for showing. Breeding is carefully controlled to avoid the spinal problems sometimes associated with tailless cats. The Manx is gentle, calm, intelligent, and loyal to its owners. It can be trained to play "fetch" or walk on a leash. Traditionally kept as a working cat, the Manx is still an efficient hunter when given the chance.

KITTEN

Short tail stump

Rump has characteristic rounded appearance

Eyes angled slightly toward nose

Round head with full cheeks

Large whisker pads

Red classic tabby coat has clearly delineated texture

Sturdy, compact body with deep flanks

Heavily boned legs

Heavily muscled hind legs much longer than forelegs

White paws

Pixiebob

ORIGIN US, 1980s
BREED REGISTRIES TICA
WEIGHT RANGE 9–18lb (4–8kg)

GROOMING Weekly
COLORS AND PATTERNS Brown-spotted tabby only.

Despite its fierce looks, this hefty and muscular cat has a sweet temperament and is very affectionate and social.

Like the mountain bobcat from which it derives its name, the Pixiebob has a thick coat, tufted ears, a pointed face, and a powerful body, and it moves with loose-limbed grace. A common feature of this breed—which, unusually, is accepted in the breed standard—is the occurrence of extra toes (polydactylism, see p. 245) on one or more paws. Both the Pixiebob shorthair and a longhaired variant (see pp. 244–45) have richly colored, spotted coats that complete the illusion of a wildcat. Despite appearances, the Pixiebob is entirely domestic in character, loves family life, clings to its owners, plays with children, and good-naturedly accepts other pets.

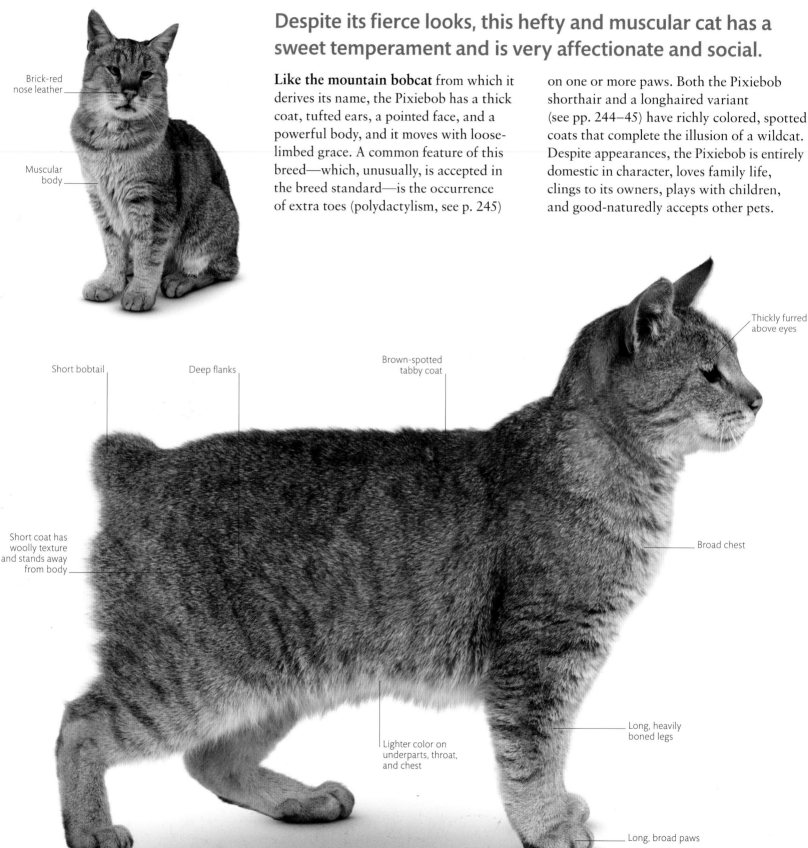

Brick-red nose leather

Muscular body

Short bobtail

Deep flanks

Brown-spotted tabby coat

Thickly furred above eyes

Short coat has woolly texture and stands away from body

Broad chest

Lighter color on underparts, throat, and chest

Long, heavily boned legs

Long, broad paws

American Ringtail

ORIGIN US, 1990s
BREED REGISTRIES CFA, TICA
WEIGHT RANGE 7–15lb (3–7kg)

GROOMING Weekly
COLORS AND PATTERNS All colors, shades, and patterns.

This athletic and plush-coated cat with a twist in its tail is friendly, but it can be reserved with strangers.

No other cat possesses this breed's unique tail, which is carried in a flexible curl over the back or flank. The American Ringtail was discovered by chance in California and, so far, its development has included the introduction of Oriental-type lines. These cats are still few and far between, but interest among breeders is gradually increasing. There is also a longhaired version. Ringtails love games, climbing, and nosing around anything that appeals to their strong sense of curiosity. The soft trilling sounds that they make gave them their original name of Ringtail Sing-a-Ling.

Soft, dense brown classic tabby coat with plush texture

Flexible tail carried in a ring over back

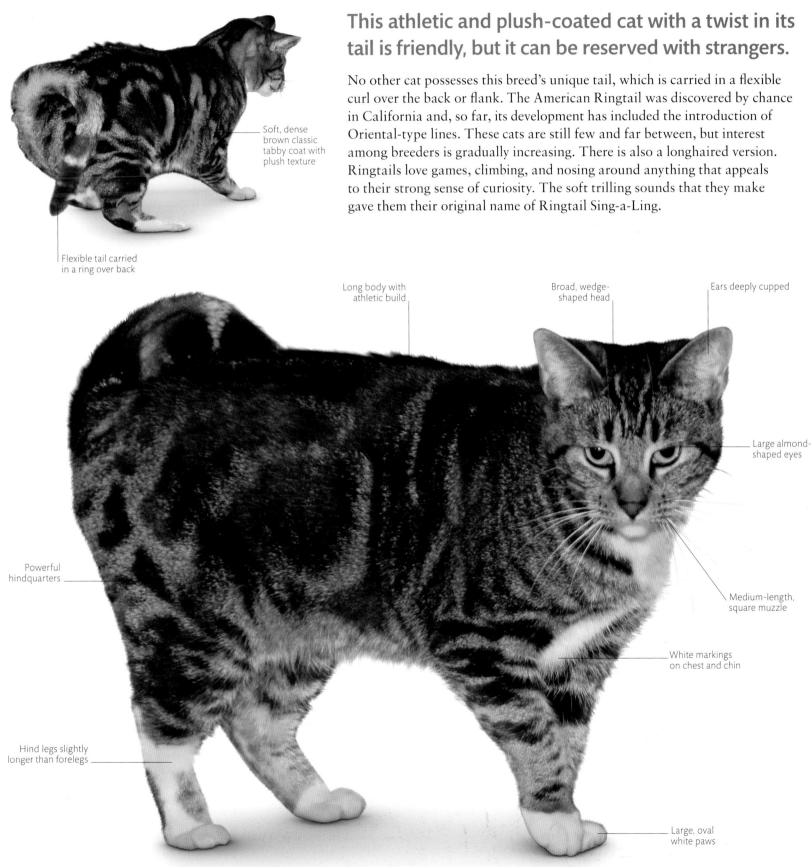

Long body with athletic build

Broad, wedge-shaped head

Ears deeply cupped

Large almond-shaped eyes

Powerful hindquarters

Medium-length, square muzzle

White markings on chest and chin

Hind legs slightly longer than forelegs

Large, oval white paws

Sphynx

ORIGIN Canada, 1960s
BREED REGISTRIES CFA, FIFe, GCCF, TICA
WEIGHT RANGE 8–15lb (3.5–7kg)

GROOMING 2–3 times a week
COLORS AND PATTERNS All colors, shades, and patterns.

This hairless cat has an endearingly impish character, and its dedication to its owner makes it a great companion.

Probably the best known of the hairless cats that have appeared around the world, the Sphynx originated in Canada and was named for its supposed resemblance to the ancient Egyptian sculpture of the mythical Sphinx. The cat's hairlessness is a natural mutation, and interest in its development dates from the birth of a hairless male kitten produced by a short-coated farm cat in Ontario in 1966. This kitten, along with other hairless kittens that appeared over the following decade, was used to found the breed. Although hairlessness is commonly accompanied by other mutations, careful selective breeding, including outcrosses to Cornish Rex (see pp. 176–77) and Devon Rex (see pp. 178–79) cats, has ensured that the Sphynx is relatively free of genetic problems. Sphynx cats are not completely bald—most have a coating of fine, suedelike fuzz on their bodies and often a little thin hair on their heads, tails, and paws. Undeniably an extraordinary looking cat, with its enormous ears, wrinkled skin, and rounded belly, the Sphynx does not appeal to everyone, but its delightfully sociable and loving nature has made more than a few converts. It is easy to live with but needs to be kept indoors and protected from temperature extremes. Lack of a normal coat also means that excess body oils cannot be absorbed, so regular washing is required. Cats used to baths from an early age are unlikely to object.

Muscular, rounded rump

MR. BIGGLESWORTH

A Sphynx shot to fame after appearing as Mr. Bigglesworth, feline companion to the appalling Dr. Evil in the Austin Powers' trilogy of comedy spy movies, the first of which was screened in 1997. The cat that played the role was a championship winner named Ted Nude-Gent. Accustomed to being in the public eye at cat shows, Ted remained unfazed by the noise and activity of a movie set and, like many Sphynxes, responded exceptionally well to training.

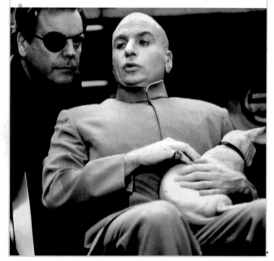

KITTEN

Whiplike tail tapers to fine point

Thick paw pads

Very large,
broad-based,
upright ears

Body has fine
"peach fuzz," black
tortie and white coat

Prominent
cheekbones

Wrinkled skin
around head
and shoulders

Rounded belly

Slightly
arched neck

Pronounced
whisker pads
lack whiskers

Donskoy

ORIGIN Russia, 1980s
BREED REGISTRIES FIFe, TICA
WEIGHT RANGE 8–15lb (3.5–7kg)

GROOMING 2–3 times a week
COLORS AND PATTERNS All colors, shades, and patterns.

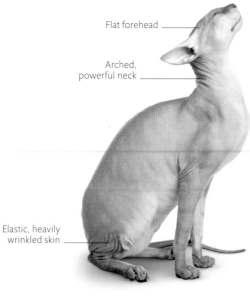

Flat forehead

Arched, powerful neck

Elastic, heavily wrinkled skin

Despite its otherworldly looks, this active breed is gentle and extremely friendly, and has a lovable nature.

The founder of this breed (also known as the Don Sphynx) was an mistreated kitten rescued from the streets in the Russian city of Rostov-on-Don. This stray lost its apparently normal coat as it matured, and it produced offspring with the same mutation. Various coat types occur in the Donskoy—some individuals are truly hairless, while others have a partial coat that can be fuzzy or even wavy. Uniquely, the hairless types may develop temporary fur patches in winter. With wrinkled skin and oversized ears, the Donskoy does not have universal appeal, but aficionados praise its gentleness, sparkling personality, and social ease. Grooming consists of regular bathing to remove excess oil from the skin.

THESE **HIGHLY SOCIAL** CATS WITH **PEAR-SHAPED** BODIES CAN BE **TRAINED** TO FOLLOW **VOICE COMMANDS**.

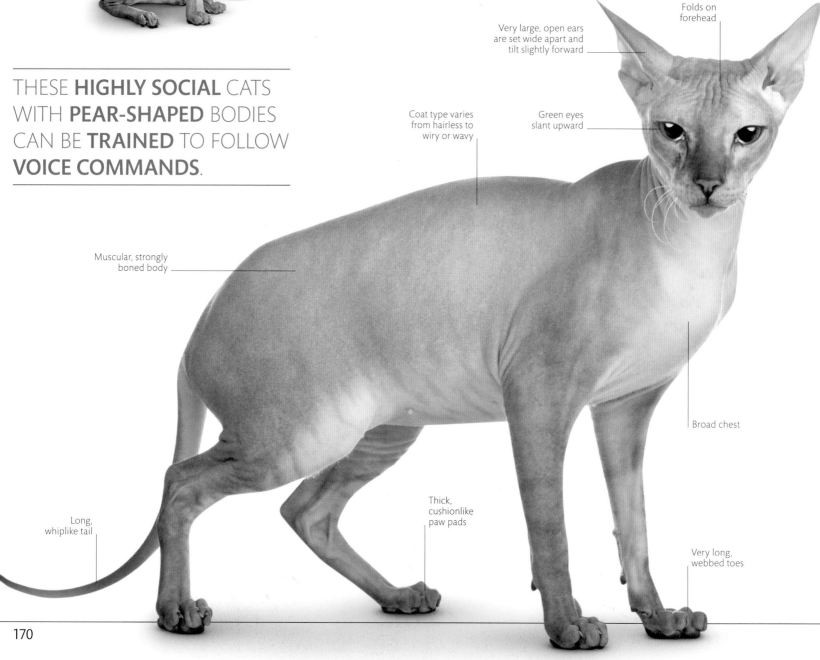

Folds on forehead

Very large, open ears are set wide apart and tilt slightly forward

Coat type varies from hairless to wiry or wavy

Green eyes slant upward

Muscular, strongly boned body

Broad chest

Long, whiplike tail

Thick, cushionlike paw pads

Very long, webbed toes

Peterbald

PLACE OF ORIGIN Russia, 1990s
BREED REGISTRIES FIFe, TICA
WEIGHT RANGE 8–15lb (3.5–7kg)

GROOMING 2-3 times a week
COLORS AND PATTERNS All colors, shades, and patterns.

This elegant, graceful breed has a variety of coat types, is vocal and friendly, and loves to be the center of attention.

Originating in Russia, the Peterbald is a fairly new breed created by crossing the Oriental Shorthair (see pp. 91–101) with the Donskoy (see opposite). This cat is highly variable, and may be completely hairless, covered with a fine soft down, or possess a dense, stiff coat with a brushlike texture. Kittens born with a coat may become hairless as they mature, sometimes retaining downy-coated points. The Peterbald has a pleasant temperament and makes a good family cat. Hairless or very thin-coated varieties need protection from the elements and are probably best kept indoors. The skin of hairless types may have a sticky feel and needs to be washed regularly.

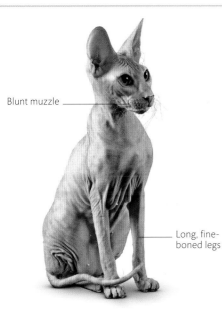

Blunt muzzle

Long, fine-boned legs

PETERBALD **OWNERS** OFTEN **DESCRIBE** THE **CAT'S PLAY** AS **"AERIAL BALLET."**

Huge, flared ears with broad bases

Straight nose runs from flat forehead

Long, triangular head with high cheekbones

Whiskers kinked and broken

Firm, graceful body

Long, whiplike tail

Oval paws with long, flexible toes

Ural Rex

ORIGIN Russia, 1980s
BREED REGISTRIES Other
WEIGHT RANGE 8–15lb (3.5–7kg)

GROOMING 2–3 times a week
COLORS AND PATTERNS Various colors and patterns, including tabby.

Upright ears set high on head

Large, oval eyes set wide apart

Prominent cheekbones

This unusual-looking rex breed is not yet widely known, but its adaptable temperament makes it suitable for most homes.

The first of these wavy-coated cats was born near Yekaterinburg, a major Russian city set in the foothills of the Ural Mountains. Carefully developed over three decades, the Ural Rex is very popular among cat fanciers in Russia and is also now being bred in Germany. This breed's fine, dense, double coat may be short or semi-long; the distinctive, close-lying waves, which have an elastic quality, can take up to two years to develop fully. Grooming is not difficult but must be carried out regularly. The Ural Rex is described as a quiet and good-natured cat that makes an excellent household companion.

THE COAT OF THE URAL REX **KITTEN** HAS **HALF-CLOSED CURLS** THAT LATER TURN INTO **EVEN WAVES**.

Broad, flat forehead

Fine, silky black-smoke coat lies close to body in loose curls

Short, wedge-shaped head

Slim, muscular, relatively short body

White chest, underparts, and legs

Medium-length, moderately thin tail

Slender legs with small paws

LaPerm

ORIGIN US, 1980s
BREED REGISTRIES CFA, GCCF, TICA
WEIGHT RANGE 8–12lb (3.5–5.5kg)

GROOMING 2–3 times a week
COLORS AND PATTERNS All colors, shades, and patterns, including colorpoint.

This bright and inquisitive cat enjoys human contact and has a kittenish energy that it retains into adulthood.

This rex-coated breed originated on a farm in Oregon and was later developed into both shorthaired and longhaired (see pp. 250–51) versions. The LaPerm has a highly strokable coat that may be either wavy or curly and has a light, springy texture. Outgoing and not shy about asking for attention, this cat makes a loving and lively pet. LaPerms adapt themselves easily to homes of all types and become deeply attached to their owners. They need company and should not be left alone for too long. Gentle combing or the occasional shampoo and towel dry are recommended as the best ways of maintaining the coat.

Long, broad nose

Slightly rounded, wedge-shaped head

Tabby pattern evident on head

Very long, wavy whiskers

Large, expressive gold eyes

Firm chin

Curly ruff

Medium-long, muscular body

Medium-long legs

Rounded paws

Selkirk Rex

ORIGIN US, 1980s
BREED REGISTRIES CFA, TICA
WEIGHT RANGE 7–11lb (3–5kg)

GROOMING 2–3 times a week
COLORS AND PATTERNS All colors, shades, and patterns.

A happy "teddy bear" of a cat, this breed is loving and patient and enjoys being in the company of its human companions.

This cat takes its name from the Selkirk Mountains near its place of origin in Montana. Created in the late 1980s, the breed had its beginnings in an animal shelter, where a curly-coated kitten appeared among an otherwise straight-coated litter born to a feral cat. This kitten became the founding female of the Selkirk Rex. As the breed was developed, planned matings with pedigree cats produced both the Selkirk Rex shorthair and a longer-coated type (see p. 248) that was the result of crosses with Persians. Straight-coated variants are common in litters of both types. The dense, soft coat of the Selkirk Rex falls into random curls or waves, rather than in the neat lines sometimes seen in other rex breeds. A greater degree of curl often occurs around the neck and belly. The whiskers are sparse and curly and tend to snap off easily. Grooming a Selkirk Rex is not difficult but a light touch is advisable, since overly vigorous brushing can flatten out the curls. Though calm and tolerant, this cat is far from staid and loves a hug. Selkirks stay kittenish for years and always enjoy games.

BECOMING CURLY

The curls of a Selkirk Rex can take two years to develop fully. It is immediately obvious which of a litter of kittens will be curly, since their whiskers are curly from birth. In kittens born with a rexed coat, the fur—but not the whiskers—usually straightens for a few months before beginning to curl again when the cat is about eight months old. The best coats appear in spayed females and in adult males, whether they are neutered or not.

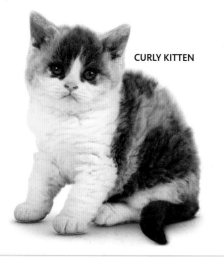

CURLY KITTEN

Curls lie flat against tail

KITTEN

Round, smooth skull

Broad-based, wide-set ears

Rectangular, muscular body

Plush, curly black-and-white coat

Short, square muzzle

Large eyes with sweet expression

Curly, brittle whiskers

Medium-long, heavily boned legs

Large, round paws

Cornish Rex

ORIGIN UK, 1950s
BREED REGISTRIES CFA, FIFe, GCCF, TICA
WEIGHT RANGE 6–9lb (2.5–4kg)

GROOMING Weekly
COLORS AND PATTERNS All solid and shaded colors and patterns, including tabby, tortie, colorpoint, and bicolor.

TWO TYPES

The first Cornish Rex cats bred in the UK were much stockier than those seen today, because the sturdy British Shorthair predominated among other breeds used as outcrosses. When the Cornish Rex appeared in the US, bloodlines from more slender Oriental cats were introduced. Although British and American versions of the breed are both now slimline, they have developed into two distinct types, distinguished by the more athletic build and "tucked up" waistline of the American cat (pictured below).

This inquisitive, athletic cat has a curled coat that extends from the whiskers to the tail, and is a lively and energetic pet.

The founder member of this striking breed was a male cat named Kallibunker, born on a Cornish farm in the UK in 1950. Unlike his siblings, he had the now-classic wavy coat, slim body, long legs, bony face, and large ears. One theory has it that the wavy coat and other Rex features were a mutation caused by radiation from nearby tin mines. In fact, the mutation is due to a recessive gene. Early breeders used in-breeding to preserve the Cornish Rex features, but this led to health problems in the offspring. Therefore, Kallibunker's descendants were crossed with other breeds— including American (see p. 113) and British Shorthairs (see pp. 118–27) and the Siamese (see pp. 104–09)—improving the stamina and genetic diversity of the Cornish Rex and adding a wide variety of colors. With its superfine, rippled coat and streamlined body, this cat stands out from all the rest. It is an extrovert with a large repertoire of amusing antics and a kittenish outlook on life, but turns into an affectionate lap cat when play is over. Because of its thin coat, the Cornish Rex is vulnerable to temperature extremes and should be groomed with a light touch.

KITTEN

Outer ear is hairless

Fairly small, wedge-shaped head

High, chiseled cheekbones

Short, fine, white coat forms tight, uniform waves

Straight nose

Large, oval eyes are set wide apart

Long, slender tail tapers at end

Slim, elongated, muscular body

Finely boned, long, slender legs

Small, oval paws

Growing a full coat
Cornish Rex kittens are born with wavy coats, but some lose them for a few weeks and have a temporary, suedelike covering. By three months the waves seen on this adult cat would have been fully formed.

Devon Rex

ORIGIN UK, 1960s
BREED REGISTRIES CFA, FIFe, GCCF, TICA
WEIGHT RANGE 6–9lb (2.5–4kg)

GROOMING Weekly
COLORS AND PATTERNS All colors, shades, and patterns.

Nicknamed the "Pixie cat," this mischievous breed has an abundance of energy and possesses doglike qualities.

A curly-coated feral tom and an adopted stray tortoiseshell were the founders of this highly specialized breed, which originated in Buckfastleigh, Devon, UK. A litter produced by this unlikely pair included a curly-coated kitten, which was used in the first program to develop the breed. To begin with, it was assumed that this new Devonian line could be crossed with the Cornish Rex (see pp. 176–77), another wavy-coated breed discovered a short distance away and a few years earlier. When only normal-coated kittens resulted from the matings, it was realized that two different recessive genes, arising in surprisingly close geographical proximity, had produced slightly different rexed coats (see panel, below). The coat of the Devon Rex is fine and very short, with few guard hairs. Ideally, the waves should be loose and distributed evenly over the body, but the degree of wave or curl varies from cat to cat and may alter with seasonal shedding of hair or as a cat matures. The whiskers are crinkly and tend to be brittle, breaking off before reaching full length. Because of their thin coats, these cats can seem warmer to the touch than most breeds, but they easily become chilled and need draft-proof accommodation. A Devon Rex's coat usually needs little more than a wipe-down to keep it in good condition; these cats will also tolerate gentle bathing, provided they are introduced to water when they are young kittens. Despite its slender, leggy appearance, the Devon Rex is far from fragile, and it possesses boundless energy for playing games and scaling heights. This cat adores attention and is not suitable for a family that will be away from the home all day.

Firm, muscular body

Long, tapering tail

REX COATS

Although the curly coat of one breed of Rex cat can be much like that of another, the gene mutation that produces it is different in each breed. Recessive genes need to be inherited from both parents for it to be expressed in the kittens, whereas a dominant gene only needs to be inherited from one of them. Despite the geographically close origin of the Devon Rex and Cornish Rex (see pp. 176–77), their coats are the result of a mutation in different recessive genes. For example, the Cornish Rex gene mutation affects the shape of the hair follicle, making it oval rather than round, resulting in curly hair.

CORNISH REX

KITTEN

Comparatively small head set on long neck

Exceptionally large ears, very wide at base

Short muzzle with curly whiskers

Nose has distinct stop

Wide cheekbones

Fine, curly silver tabby coat has few guard hairs

Long, slender legs with small, oval paws

German Rex

PLACE OF ORIGIN Germany, 1940s
BREED REGISTRIES FIFe
WEIGHT RANGE 6–10lb (2.5–4.5kg)

GROOMING 2–3 times a week
COLORS AND PATTERNS All colors, shades, and patterns.

This breed bonds well with its owner and needs plenty of "quality time" with its human family.

A feral cat adopted in Berlin just after the end of World War II was the founding female of this breed. As the German Rex was developed, cats were imported to other parts of Europe and to the US. The wavy coat of this cat arises through the same mutant gene that appears in the Cornish Rex (see pp. 176–77), which for some years was included in German Rex breeding programs; in some countries, the two breeds are not recognized as separate. A good-natured and friendly cat, the German Rex will play with anyone but also likes quiet times staying close to its owners. Since the short coat does not absorb natural oils efficiently, regular bathing is necessary.

Short, curly whiskers

Short, wavy coat with velvety texture

KITTENS

Rounded paws

CATS WITH **PALER** COAT **COLORS** MAY NEED **SUN SCREEN** ON THE EARS DURING **SUMMER**.

Brilliant blue eyes

Broad-based ears

Cream coat shaded with sepia in places

Round head with defined cheekbones

Medium-length, strongly built body

Sepia pointing on tail, legs, and head

Strong, rounded chest

Medium-length, moderately fine legs

American Wirehair

PLACE OF ORIGIN US, 1960s
BREED REGISTRIES CFA, TICA
WEIGHT RANGE 8–15lb (3.5–7kg)

GROOMING Weekly
COLORS AND PATTERNS Variety of solid colors and shades in various patterns, including bicolor, tabby, and tortie.

This versatile, quiet, and friendly cat is happy indoors or outdoors and with people of all ages.

In New York State, in 1966, a wire-haired kitten appeared in a litter born to two domestic cats with normal coats. This was the founder of the American Wirehair breed, which was later developed by using American Shorthairs (see p. 113). The genetic mutation that produced the distinctive coat is not known to have occurred anywhere outside the US. In a Wirehair, each hair is crimped and bends over or forms a hook at the end, resulting in a harsh, springy texture that has been likened to steel wool. In some cats the coat can be brittle, so grooming—preferably by bathing—should be gentle to prevent damage.

Springy brown-and-white classic tabby coat with crimped hairs and coarse texture

Curly whiskers

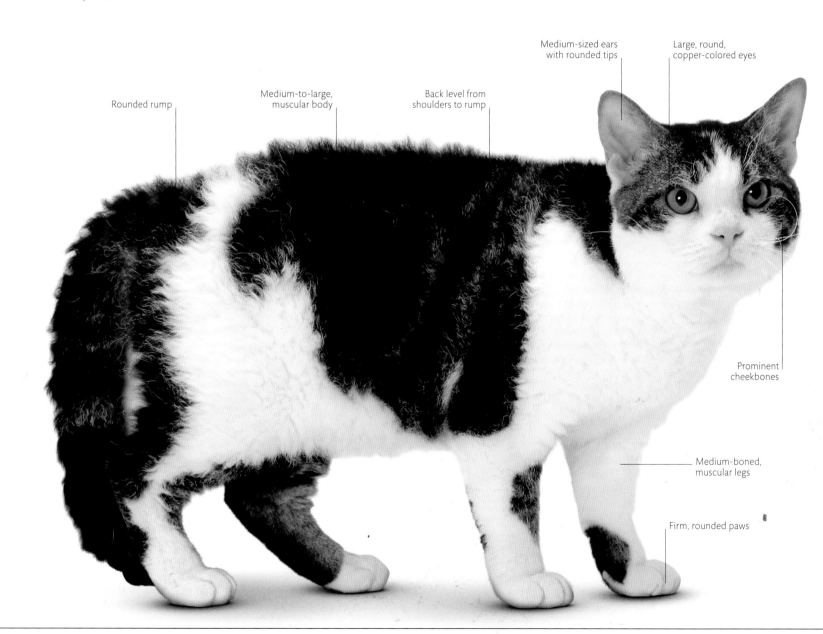

Rounded rump

Medium-to-large, muscular body

Back level from shoulders to rump

Medium-sized ears with rounded tips

Large, round, copper-colored eyes

Prominent cheekbones

Medium-boned, muscular legs

Firm, rounded paws

House cat—shorthair

These hardy cats are very popular all over the world and make excellent, easy-to-keep pets.

The first domestic cats had short coats, and the type still predominates wherever in the world cats are kept as house pets. Random-bred shorthairs occur in nearly every possible color permutation, with tabbies, torties, and traditional self colors being the most common. The majority of these cats are solidly in the middle range when it comes to body shape. Selective breeding, which has created some extreme lines, has largely bypassed the shorthaired house cat, although occasionally a hint of, for example, the lean Oriental shape suggests an out-of-the-ordinary parentage.

Blue mackerel tabby and white
While tabbies with white markings are very common, the blue variation would be a lucky find in a random-bred cat. This one's markings are indistinct against the background color.

Red classic tabby and white
Large size and a dense coat could point to British or American Shorthair in the history of this handsome cat. However, his green eyes may be part of a different inheritance.

Blue and white
In house cats white markings are rarely as symmetrical as those considered desirable in pedigrees. However, a solid color splashed with white is always striking, and a random effect adds individual charm.

Irregularly spaced ring markings on tail

Black and red markings intermingled

Brown tabby
The broken stripes on this cat are, in fact, intermediate between mackerel and spotted tabby patterns. Tabby markings often occur in domestic cats and show up well on short coats.

Calico
Tortoiseshell, or tortie, patterning occurs in many color forms, black and red being the traditional combination. A tortie with white areas over more than half its body is known as a calico cat.

Character counts
Inevitably, looks attract when it comes to choosing a cat as a companion. However, the majority of owners value a pet's personality over perfect coloring or conformity to a breed standard.

A coat for cold weather
The long, thick coat of the Norwegian Forest Cat keeps the cold out and the warmth in. This coat is typical of cats found in cold climates, where the weather conditions can be very harsh.

LONGHAIRS

It is thought that long hair in domestic cats arose as a natural genetic mutation, most likely in response to cold climates. Where this advantageous gene was passed on among cats living in isolated areas, such as mountain regions, longhaired populations would have arisen. Wildcats with long coats are a rarity and have no role in the ancestry of domestic longhairs.

TYPES OF LONGHAIR

The first longhaired cats seen in Western Europe arrived some time in the 16th century. These were the Angoras, a slender, silky-coated Turkish breed that enjoyed a certain popularity until they were usurped by a new type of longhair, the Persian, in the 19th century. Sturdier than the Angoras, Persians had longer, thicker fur, immense tails, and round faces. By the end of the 19th century they were the longhair of choice for cat lovers. The Angora vanished, not to be seen again until the breed was re-created by enthusiasts in the 1960s. The Persian remains a steady favorite, but since the 20th century other longhairs have been attracting attention. These include cats described as semi-longhaired, which have long coats but a less dense, fluffy undercoat than the Persian.

One of the most magnificent of the semi-longhairs is the Maine Coon, native to North America. Huge and handsome, this breed has a shaggy look due to the variable length of the hairs in its topcoat. Almost equally striking is the big blue-eyed Ragdoll, while the brush-tailed Somali has the graceful lines of the Abyssinian cat from which it was developed. More in the style of the original Angoras is the beautiful Balinese—a semi-longhair version of the Siamese—which has silky, flowing, close-lying fur.

Striving for yet more variety, breeders have crossed longhairs with some of the more unusual shorthairs. Bobtails, curled-ear and folded-ear breeds, the wavy-coated Selkirk Rex and Devon Rex, and the LaPerm with its fleecelike curly fur are all now found with luxuriantly long coats.

GROOMING LONGHAIRS

Many longhaired cats shed their coats heavily, especially in the warmer seasons, when they can have a much sleeker appearance. Frequent grooming—a daily session may be needed in some breeds—keeps loose hairs to a minimum and prevents the thick undercoat from matting.

Persian Solid

ORIGIN UK, 1800s
BREED REGISTRIES CFA, FIFe, GCCF, TICA
WEIGHT RANGE 8–15lb (3.5–7kg)

GROOMING Daily
COLORS AND PATTERNS Black, white, blue, red, cream, chocolate, and lilac.

This charming, sweet-tempered cat is the original version of the world's favorite longhair, and it needs a committed owner.

By the late 19th century, when pedigree cat shows were starting to attract worldwide interest, the Persian (sometimes referred to as the Longhair) was already very popular in the US and the UK. This luxuriously coated cat came to the show benches after a long but obscure history in Europe, and it is not known whether the true ancestors of the breed did, in fact, originate in Persia (modern-day Iran). The first recognized Persians were solid-colored, that is, they had coats in one solid color throughout.

The earliest known examples of the breed were pure white, often with blue eyes—a color combination commonly associated with deafness unless breeding is carefully managed. Crossbreeding with solid Persians in other colors produced orange eyes, and white Persians with orange, blue, or odd-colored eyes (one of each color) became accepted. Queen Victoria can be given credit for making blue Persians popular—they were her favorite cats—

and black and red were other early solid colors. Since about the 1920s onward, further solid varieties have been developed, including cream, chocolate, and lilac.

Characteristically, a Persian has a round head with a flat face, snub nose, and large, round, appealing eyes. The body is compact and sturdily built, and the legs are short and strong. The magnificently thick, long coat is a major commitment for the owner of a Persian. Daily grooming is a must to prevent the fur from tangling or developing impenetrable mats that are hard to remove.

Persians are renowned for their gentle, affectionate temperament and home-loving personality. These are definitely not all-action cats, although they can be charmingly playful if offered a toy.

The flattened features of the Persian, overemphasized in modern breeding programs, have led to health issues. Breathing difficulties and problems with the tear ducts are common in this cat.

KITTEN

Short nose with break between eyes

Full cheeks

Long, thick, fine-textured white coat

DISTINGUISHED HISTORY

In the late 19th century, there was a rush of enthusiasm for breeding traditional Persians (sometimes known as "doll face" Persians) among women of the British upper classes. One such aristocratic breeder was Lady Marcus Beresford, founder of the Cat Club of England, whose prize-winning blue Persian "Gentian" (right) was among her many notable successes. The Beresford Club in the US, named in Lady Beresford's honor, sponsored one of the earliest American cat shows.

Large head with broad skull

Small, rounded ears with long tufts

Body stocky and deep-chested

Orange-colored eyes

Deep ruff

Short, sturdy legs

Persian—Blue- and Odd-eyed Bicolor

ORIGIN UK, 1800s
BREED REGISTRIES CFA, FIFe, GCCF, TICA
WEIGHT RANGE 8–15lb (3.5–7kg)

GROOMING 2–3 times a week
COLORS AND PATTERNS White with various solid colors, including black, red, blue, cream, chocolate, and lilac.

These uncommon Persians are hard to find but their popularity is on the rise.

Accepted in the cat-fancy world only since the late 1990s, the Blue- and Odd-eyed Bicolor and Tricolor are variations of the Persian Bicolor (see p. 204). The Odd-eyed is less common than the Blue-eyed, although its enchantingly different look is increasing in popularity. In this cat, one eye is blue and the other copper, with both eyes equally brilliant in color. The mismatch is difficult to produce, since a successful mating between two odd-eyed cats does not guarantee a litter of odd-eyed kittens.

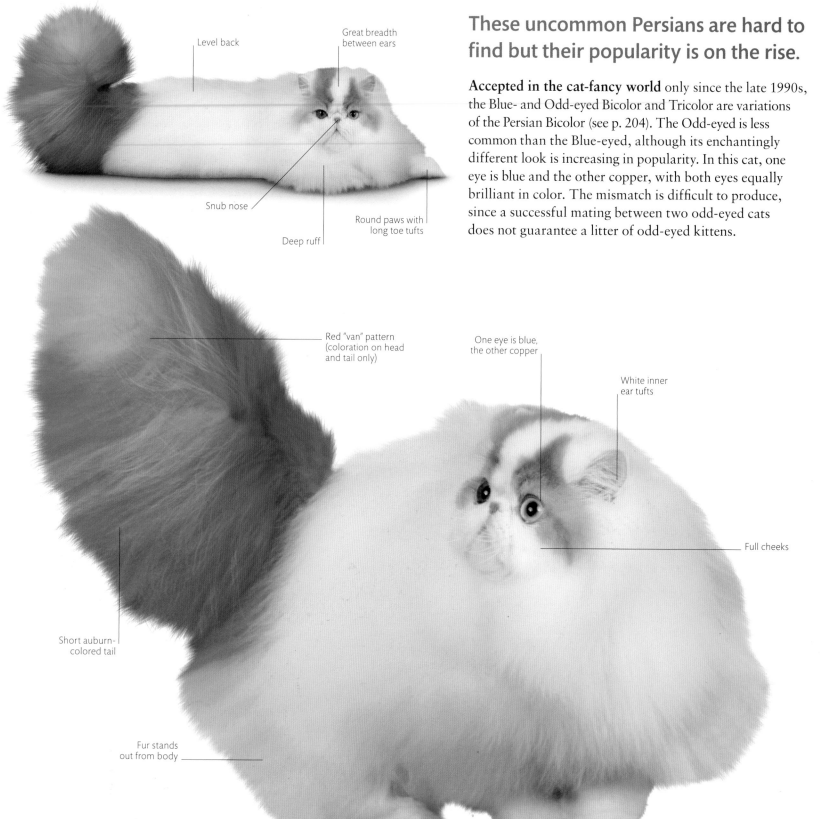

Level back

Great breadth between ears

Snub nose

Deep ruff

Round paws with long toe tufts

Red "van" pattern (coloration on head and tail only)

One eye is blue, the other copper

White inner ear tufts

Full cheeks

Short auburn-colored tail

Fur stands out from body

Persian—Cameo

ORIGIN US, Australia, and New Zealand, 1950s
BREED REGISTRIES CFA, FIFe, GCCF, TICA
WEIGHT RANGE 8–15lb (3.5–7kg)

GROOMING Weekly
COLORS AND PATTERNS Red, cream, black, blue, lilac, and chocolate solid colors and tortie patterns.

This breed has softly blended colors in a rippling coat that requires regular grooming.

Regarded by many cat fanciers as the most glamorous of all the Persian colors, this version was developed in the 1950s by crossing Smoke (see p. 196) and Tortoiseshell (see pp. 202–03) Persians. The fur of a Cameo is white with color carried at the ends of the hair shafts to varying degrees. In the "tipped" variety the color appears only at the very tip of each hair, but extends to up to one-third of the hair shaft in "shaded" cats. Cameo gives the effect, especially as the cat moves, of a coat rippling with changing hues.

Ears set toward side of head

Deep copper eyes

Pink nose leather

Cream-shaded cameo coat

Lighter shading on legs

Main area of color on back and flanks

Pale inner ear tufts

Darker markings on face

Underside of plumed tail lighter in color

Paler fur on chest and underparts

Hair shorter on lower legs

Persian—Chinchilla

ORIGIN UK, 1880s
BREED REGISTRIES CFA, FIFe, GCCF, TICA
WEIGHT RANGE 8–15lb (3.5–7kg)

GROOMING Daily
COLORS AND PATTERNS White, tipped with black.

This silvery-coated breed with its movie-star looks is renowned for its beauty and is a popular choice for a pet.

The first Chinchilla appeared in the 1880s, but it was the "James Bond" series of films, starting in the 1960s, that brought this cat fame when it was seen on screen as the pet of the superspy's archenemy, Blofeld. Chinchillas have a shimmering, silvery- white coat in which each hair is tipped with black. The breed's name derives from the likeness of its coat coloration to that of a small South American rodent called the chinchilla, once a victim of the fashion trade for its beautiful, soft fur.

Red nose leather

BLACK OUTLINING AROUND THE EYES MAKES CHINCHILLAS **LOOK AS THOUGH** THEY ARE **WEARING MAKEUP.**

Black outlines around eyes, nose, and lips

Silvery sparkle to coat

Long white tufts of hair

Blue-green eyes

Black tipping evenly distributed over white coat

Pure white on chest and belly

Shorter coat on lower legs

Persian—Golden

ORIGIN UK, 1920s
BREED REGISTRIES CFA, FIFe, GCCF, TICA
WEIGHT RANGE 8–15lb (3.5–7kg)

GROOMING Daily
COLORS AND PATTERNS Apricot to golden with seal-brown or black tipping.

Once regarded as the "wrong" color, this cat is now considered to be one of the prettiest Persians.

Recognized as a new breed in the US since the 1970s, the Golden Persian has a gloriously colored coat of rich apricot to golden fur that is widely admired. Yet the first Golden Persians, which appeared in the 1920s in litters born to Chinchillas (see opposite), were regarded as rejects as far as the pedigree cat world was concerned. They were known generally as "brownies" and, though barred from the show bench, made appealing pets. Later, breeders saw the potential of Goldens and worked to develop this lovely Persian variation.

Eyes, lips, and nose rimmed with black

Rose-pink nose leather

Domed head

ADULT AND KITTEN

Lightest coloring on chest and belly

SOME GOLDENS ARE **BORN** WITH WONDERFUL, **RICH COLOR**, WHILE IN **OTHERS** IT MAY TAKE **TWO TO THREE** YEARS TO **DEVELOP**.

Golden coat with rich coloring on back

Long pale apricot tufts of hair

Blue-green eyes

Paler underside to tail

Thick ruff around neck

Darker coloration on legs due to seal-brown tipping

Persian—Pewter

ORIGIN UK, 1900s
BREED REGISTRIES CFA, FIFe, GCCF, TICA
WEIGHT RANGE 8–15lb (3.5–7kg)

GROOMING Daily
COLORS AND PATTERNS Very pale with black or blue tipping.

This copper-eyed cat's beautiful flowing coat and calm personality combine to make it a very popular pet.

Years of careful breeding, at first using crosses with Persian Chinchillas (see p. 190), produced the two current variations of Pewter. These cats, originally referred to as Blue Chinchillas, have pale, almost white, coats with blue- or black-tipped hairs. This coloration gives the effect of a mantle extending from the top of the head and down the back. Pewter kittens are born with traditional tabby markings, which gradually fade in intensity but are still retained to some degree in adult cats. The very special look of this breed is enhanced by its characteristic deep orange to copper-colored eyes.

Ghost tabby "M" marking on forehead

Dark-rimmed, copper-colored eyes

Very pale chest

Darkest tipping on back and flanks

Faint tabby markings on legs

Dark tip to tail

Face lightly tipped only

Nose break between eyes

Black pewter coat

Persian—Cameo Bicolor

ORIGIN US, New Zealand, and Australia, 1950s
BREED REGISTRIES CFA, FIFe, GCCF, TICA
WEIGHT RANGE 8–15lb (3.5–7kg)

GROOMING Daily
COLORS AND PATTERNS Red, cream, blue-cream, black, blue, lilac, and chocolate colors with white; tortie pattern with white.

Pale tufts of hair

Deep copper eyes

Short, rounded body

This lovely breed is truly a Persian—an elegant, graceful, and gentle cat distinguished by its remarkable coat.

The color combinations of this version of the Cameo (see p. 189) are almost endless. In addition to the shading and tipping that characterize the Cameo coat, in which the hair shafts are colored only partway along their length, the addition of both bicolor and tricolor patterns make this breed seem like many different cats. Shades of red are common, but black, blue, chocolate, cream, and tortoiseshell (black and red, or blue and cream) also appear, all with extensive areas of white. The contrast between the patches of sparkling white and color of varying intensity is stunning.

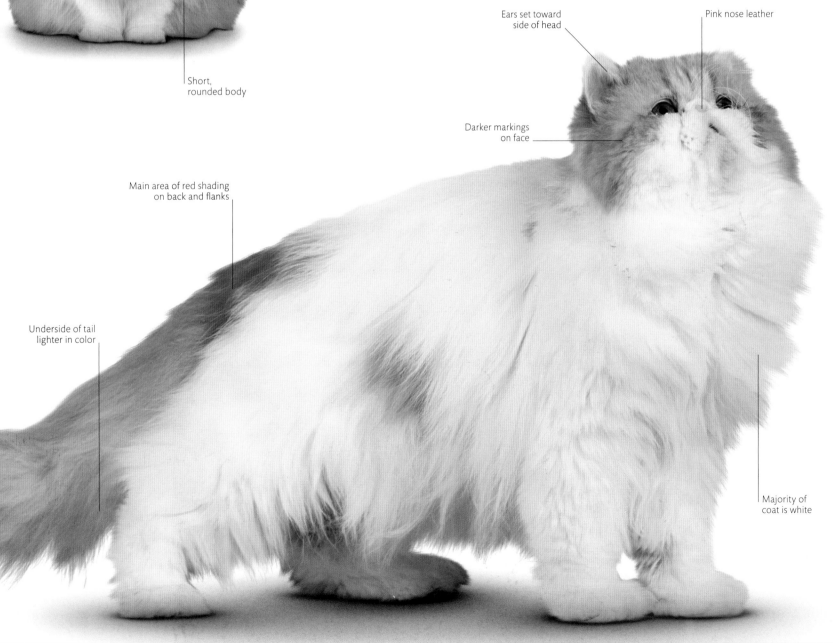

Ears set toward side of head

Pink nose leather

Darker markings on face

Main area of red shading on back and flanks

Underside of tail lighter in color

Majority of coat is white

Persian—Shaded Silver

ORIGIN UK, 1800s
BREED REGISTRIES CFA, FIFe, GCCF, TICA
WEIGHT RANGE 8–15lb (3.5–7kg)

GROOMING Daily
COLORS AND PATTERNS White with black tipping.

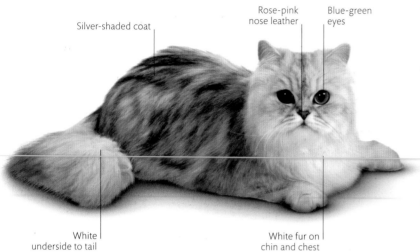

Silver-shaded coat

Rose-pink nose leather

Blue-green eyes

White underside to tail

White fur on chin and chest

This exquisite cat has a placid temperament and is sometimes livelier than the other Persians.

This Persian bears some resemblance to the Chinchilla (see p. 190), both breeds having white coats tipped on the ends of the hairs with a darker color. At one time, these cats were described as "silvers." However, over decades of development from the 20th century onward, Chinchillas have become paler and the Shaded Silver can now usually be distinguished by having the darker coloring of the two. In particular, breeders of Shaded Silvers strive to achieve the characteristic dark mantle that falls over the back.

WITH A **DOGLIKE PERSONALITY**, THIS CAT ENJOYS FOLLOWING ITS OWNER AROUND.

Eyes, nose, and lips are black-rimmed

Well developed nose stop

Short, sturdy legs

Mantle of black tipping, darkest on back, flanks, and tail

Persian—Silver Tabby

PLACE OF ORIGIN UK, 1800s
BREED REGISTRIES CFA, FIFe, GCCF, TICA
WEIGHT RANGE 8–15lb (3.5–7kg)

GROOMING 2–3 times a week
COLORS AND PATTERNS Silver tabby; tortie silver tabby; all with white patches.

A silky, silvery-coated version of the traditional tabby, this is one of the most attractive longhairs.

Some of the most delicately colored Persians of all are the Silver Tabbies. These cats have well-defined tabby coat patterns, but the warm coppery ground colors of the traditional tabby are replaced by a silvery- or bluish-white undercoat. Bicolor Silver Tabby cats have clear white areas, preferably as a minimum on the muzzle, chest, underparts, and sometimes legs. In the Tricolors an additional color, such as a shade of red or brown, is blended into the coat.

IN THESE TABBY CATS, AN **INHIBITOR GENE** RESTRICTS COLOR TO THE **TIPS** OF THE HAIRS.

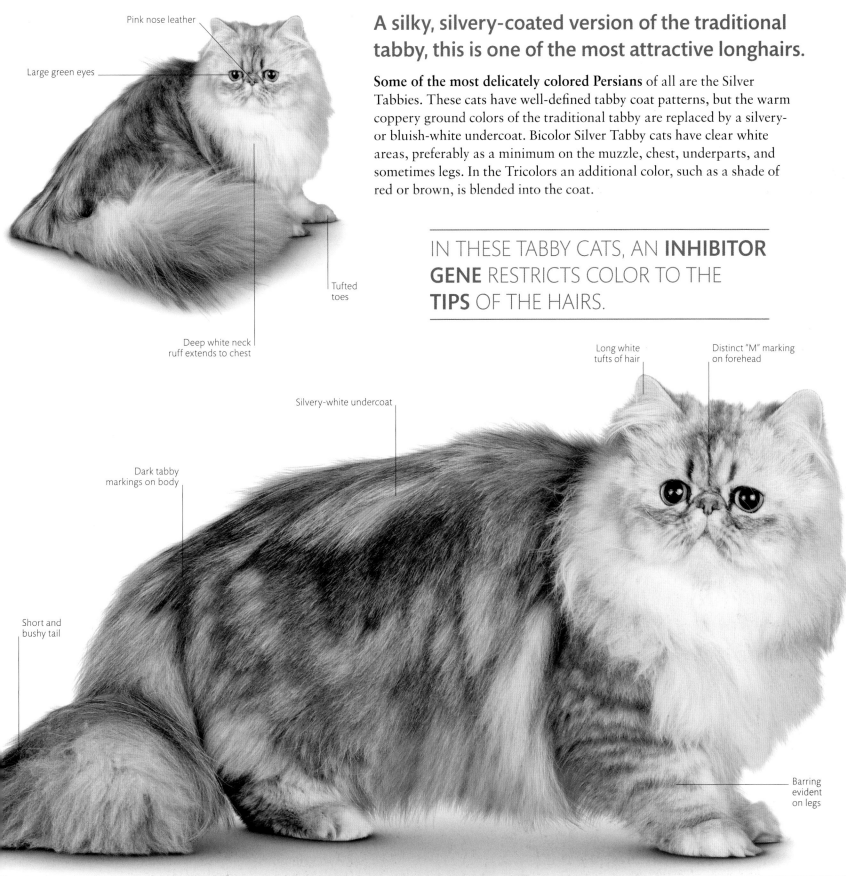

Pink nose leather

Large green eyes

Tufted toes

Deep white neck ruff extends to chest

Silvery-white undercoat

Dark tabby markings on body

Short and bushy tail

Long white tufts of hair

Distinct "M" marking on forehead

Barring evident on legs

Persian—Smoke

ORIGIN UK, 1860s
BREED REGISTRIES CFA, FIFe, GCCF, TICA
WEIGHT RANGE 8–15lb (3.5–7kg)

GROOMING Daily
COLORS AND PATTERNS White deeply tipped with color, including black, blue, cream, and red, and in tortie patterns.

One of the most striking Persian patterns, this rare-colored breed has been brought back from the brink of extinction.

In the coat patterning of the Smoke, each hair is pale at the base, becoming darker by degrees along its length. Smoke kittens are born without any apparent sign of this coloring, which does not start developing until the cat is several months old. Smoke Persians were recorded as early as the 1860s, but they have never been common. By the 1940s this breed had all but disappeared. Fortunately, a few enthusiasts continued to develop the Smoke, creating new interest in the breed and extending its range of colors.

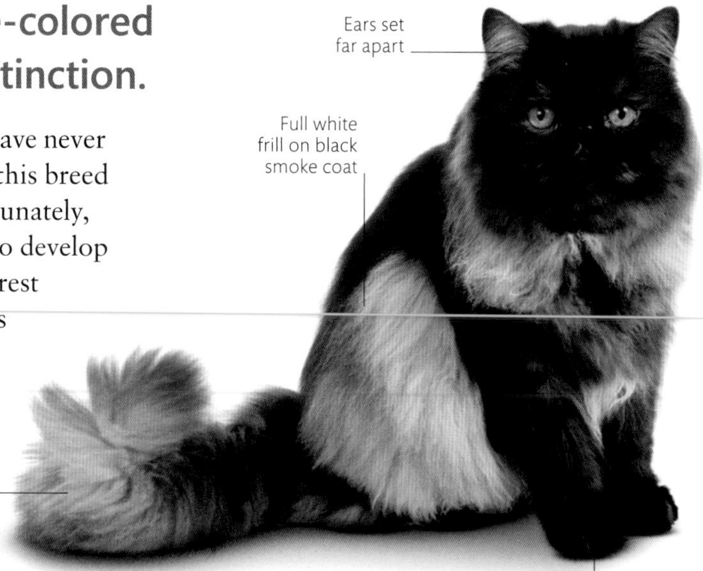

Ears set far apart

Full white frill on black smoke coat

Short, bushy tail

Legs are solid color

Typical cobby Persian body

Blue smoke coat

Dark blue mask and ears

Black nose leather

White undercoat, more apparent in motion

Lighter underparts

Persian—Smoke Bicolor

ORIGIN UK, 1900s
BREED REGISTRIES CFA, FIFe, GCCF, TICA
WEIGHT RANGE 8–15lb (3.5–7kg)

GROOMING Daily
COLORS AND PATTERNS White with smoke colors, including blue, black, red, chocolate, lilac, and various tortoiseshells.

Black nose leather

Deep chest with pure white ruff

Placid and sweet-tempered, this cat's beautifully blended colors make it one of the prettiest of all Persians.

This multihued breed has a coat combining areas of white with various smoke colors, in which each hair is colored for most of its length but is white at the base. Smoke produces greater depth of color than in shaded or tipped coats, and the pale base may not be apparent until the cat moves. Bicolored Smoke Persians can have areas of black, blue, chocolate, lilac, and red smoke with white, while the Tricolors include several tortoiseshell smokes, such as blue and cream tortie.

FOR PERSIAN BREEDS, **EYE COLOR DIFFERS** WITH **COAT COLOR**. SMOKE BICOLORS HAVE **COPPER-COLORED EYES**.

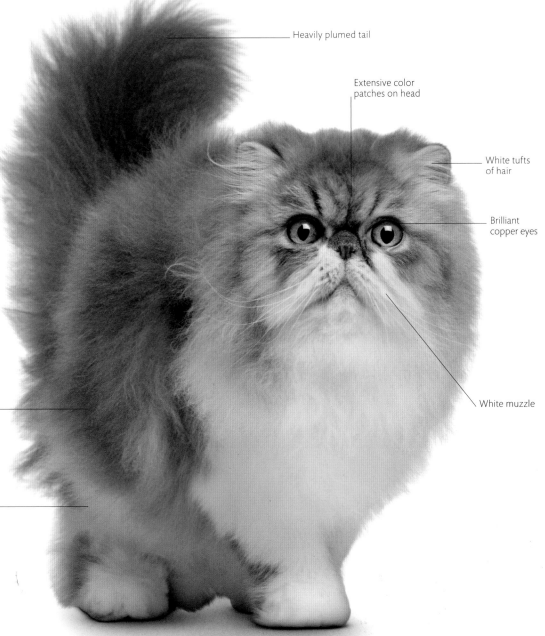

Heavily plumed tail

Extensive color patches on head

White tufts of hair

Brilliant copper eyes

Softly blended blue smoke coat

Long guard hairs

White muzzle

Persian—Tabby and Patched Tabby

ORIGIN UK, 1800s
BREED REGISTRIES CFA, FIFe, GCCF, TICA
WEIGHT RANGE 8–15lb (3.5–7kg)

GROOMING Daily
COLORS AND PATTERNS Many colors also with silver tipping in tabby and patched tabby patterns.

This cat is generally happy-go-lucky, but perverse if its wishes are not fulfilled.

The tabbies have a longer history than many of the other Persians. Brown tabbies appeared in some of the earliest cat shows in the UK in the 1870s, and one of the first purebred cat fancy clubs was established to promote the breed. Since those days, the Persian Tabby has been developed in several colors, and three pattern types are accepted: classic (or blotched), mackerel (with narrow streaks), and spotted. In Tortie-Tabbies (sometimes known as patched tabbies) the tabby markings overlay a bicolored ground coat.

Nose has sharp break between eyes

Black line runs from corner of eye

Barring on legs

Brown classic tabby coat

Full, brushlike tail

Dense black markings on body

Round copper-colored eyes

Tabby "M" mark on forehead

Red nose leather

Short, sturdy legs with large, round paws

Necklace markings on upper chest

Persian—Tabby Tricolor

ORIGIN UK, post 1900
BREED REGISTRIES CFA, FIFe, GCCF, TICA
WEIGHT RANGE 8–15lb (3.5–7kg)

GROOMING 2–3 times a week
COLORS AND PATTERNS Classic and mackerel tabby pattern, in various colors with white.

A breed with rich tabby coloring, this gentle cat loves to be the center of attention.

This lovely variation of the Persian combines sparkling white with the warm colors of the tabby. Two types of markings are accepted: classic tabby (sometimes called blotched tabby), in which the markings appear as large, smudged areas; and mackerel tabby, which is marked with thinner dark streaks or stripes. Tabby Bicolor and Tricolor Persians were first given championship status in the 1980s, and their beautiful markings, softly blurred by the lush coat, have made them firm favorites with cat breeders and owners.

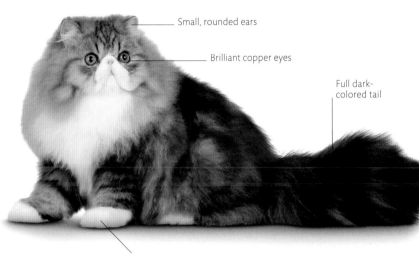

Small, rounded ears

Brilliant copper eyes

Full dark-colored tail

White mittens on paws

TO **CONFORM** TO THE **BREED STANDARD**, THE **WHITE** SHOULD **EXTEND** OVER THE **FEET**, **LEGS**, **UNDERSIDES**, **CHEST**, AND **MUZZLE**.

Body set low on legs

Tricolor with soft classic tabby markings

White muzzle and chest

Pink nose leather

Shorter hair on forehead and face

Perennial favorite
There is no mistaking a Persian, with its long, lush fur, flattened muzzle, and enormous owl eyes. The breed has enjoyed great popularity since its debut at cat shows in the 19th century.

Paintbox pattern
A splash of red tabby added to black and white creates a vivid mix of colors. Calico (also known as Tortie and White) is particularly dramatic when seen on the long, silky hair of a Persian.

Persian—Tortie and Calico

ORIGIN UK, 1880s
BREED REGISTRIES CFA, FIFe, GCCF, TICA
WEIGHT RANGE 8–15lb (3.5–7kg)

GROOMING Daily
COLORS AND PATTERNS Tortoiseshell (black and red), chocolate tortoiseshell, lilac-cream, and blue-cream; also with white patches.

These rare and sought-after Persians come in a wonderful palette of colors, but they can be difficult to breed.

Tortoiseshell cats—frequently called torties—have a coat of two colors, traditionally black and red, forming a pattern of striking patches or more subtle mottling. A more recent variation is the Chocolate Tortie, with brown and red coloring. There is also a tricolored version of this Persian, the Calico (also known as Tortie and White). Both Torties and Calicos have bright copper-colored eyes. Persian Torties have been known since the late 19th century, but it took time for tortoiseshell to be accepted as a true Persian coat color. The US Cat Fanciers' Association finally established a breed standard for Persian Torties in 1914. Torties have always been difficult to breed consistently. Their genetic makeup means that nearly all cats with tortie coloring are females and the few males that do occur are sterile. Like other types of Persian cat, Torties are equally at home in the home or the show ring. However, they are said to be more confident and outgoing than other Persians.

CALICO KITTEN

PEKE-FACED CATS

The Persian's distinctive flattened face has in recent decades been taken to extremes by breeders who have developed cats with exaggeratedly squashed features. This so-called "peke-faced" look, originally a naturally occurring mutation, is popular on the show bench but has exacerbated health problems already common among Persians. These include breathing problems, a poor bite that can affect feeding, and runny eyes due to blocked tear ducts.

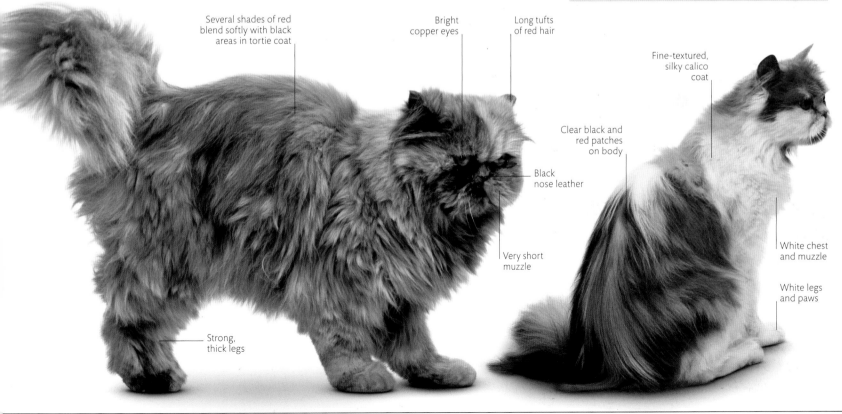

Several shades of red blend softly with black areas in tortie coat

Bright copper eyes

Long tufts of red hair

Fine-textured, silky calico coat

Clear black and red patches on body

Black nose leather

White chest and muzzle

Very short muzzle

White legs and paws

Strong, thick legs

Persian—Bicolor

ORIGIN UK, 1800s
BREED REGISTRIES CFA, FIFe, GCCF, TICA
WEIGHT RANGE 8–15lb (3.5–7kg)

GROOMING Daily
COLORS AND PATTERNS White with various solid colors, including black, red, blue, cream, chocolate, and lilac, and with tortie patterns.

This longhair cat's coat has bold color patches that give it extra glamour and requires thorough grooming.

Up until the 1960s, bicolored Persians were of little interest to breeders, and they were considered suitable only as pets. Today, they are challenging the solid colors in popularity on the show benches. One of the first bicolors to be recognized was black and white, once referred to as "magpie"; now many other solid colors combined with white are accepted. In producing bicolor and tortie-and-white cats, breeders aim for clearly defined, symmetrical markings—an ideal that is difficult to achieve.

Chocolate color on head

Black nose leather

Color patches well defined and symmetrical

Copper-colored eyes

Long hair at base of ears

White muzzle

Chocolate-colored tail

Chocolate and white, fine-haired, silky coat

White chest and underside

White legs and paws

WATERING EYES MAY CAUSE **DARK DISCOLORATION** OR **TEAR MARKS** IN THIS BREED.

Himalayan

ORIGIN US, 1930s
BREED REGISTRIES CFA, FIFe, GCCF, TICA
WEIGHT RANGE 8–15lb (3.5–7kg)

GROOMING Daily
COLORS AND PATTERNS Solid, colored, and tortie and tabby patterned points.

This cat has show-stopping good looks, with beautiful blue eyes and a wide variety of point colors.

Known as the Colorpoint Persian in the UK, the Himalayan is the result of more than a decade of breeding programs aimed at producing a longhair with Siamese markings. Round-faced and snub-nosed, with large eyes, a short, sturdy body, and long, lush fur, the Himalayan has all the typical Persian characteristics. It is a cat that loves to be loved, although as a companion it is quiet and undemanding. Daily grooming is a must for this breed, since the dense, double coat is inclined to mat without regular attention.

Face mask of contrasting seal color

Seal point coat

Round face with broad skull

Broad, stocky body

Short, snub nose with pronounced stop between eyes

Long, thick ivory-colored coat over entire body

Large blue eyes

Small ears with rounded tips

Short, brushlike tail with seal pointing

Deep ruff

Large, round paws with long tufts between toes

Balinese

ORIGIN US, 1950s
BREED REGISTRIES CFA, FIFe, GCCF, TICA
WEIGHT RANGE 6–11lb (2.5–5kg)

GROOMING 2–3 times a week
COLORS AND PATTERNS Seal, chocolate, blue, and lilac self colorpoints.

Refined in appearance but with hidden steel, this special cat is loving, highly social, and sensitive to its owner.

A longhaired version of the Siamese, the Balinese is an exquisite cat with the slender, graceful outlines of its relation draped in a flowing, silky coat. Records show that longhaired kittens have appeared occasionally among shorthaired Siamese litters for many decades, but it was not until the 1950s that some breeders began to develop the new look. The Balinese has an outgoing personality and is bursting with energy and curiosity. Although not as loud-voiced as the Siamese, it is attention-seeking, and it also has a strong streak of mischief—owners of a Balinese would be advised not to leave this cat to its own devices over long periods.

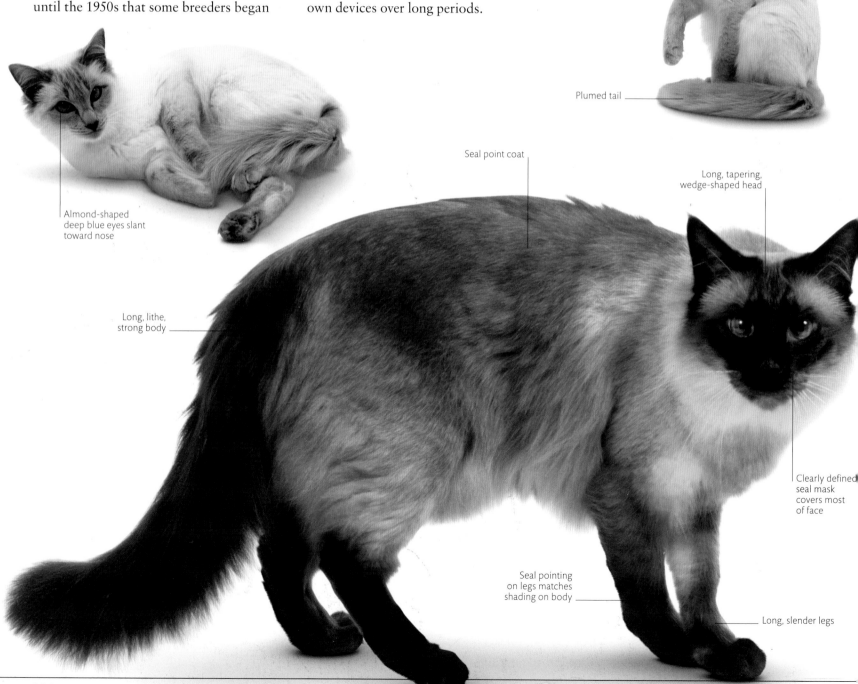

Very large, wide-based ears

Long, straight nose with no break

Long, fine, close-lying lilac point coat

Plumed tail

Almond-shaped deep blue eyes slant toward nose

Seal point coat

Long, tapering, wedge-shaped head

Long, lithe, strong body

Clearly defined seal mask covers most of face

Seal pointing on legs matches shading on body

Long, slender legs

Balinese-Javanese

ORIGIN US, 1950s
BREED REGISTRIES CFA
WEIGHT RANGE 6–11lb (2.5–5kg)

GROOMING 2–3 times a week
COLORS AND PATTERNS Many point colors, in tabby and tortie patterns.

Insatiably curious and fearless, this confident, talkative, and attention-seeking cat demands a place in the family.

This enchanting cat is a development of the Balinese (see opposite), the longhaired relation of the Siamese, with which it shares an identical breed standard in terms of conformation and coat quality. The difference between the two is the range of additional colors and patterns in the Javanese, which were acquired mostly through crosses with the Colorpoint Shorthair (see p. 110). Lithe and athletic despite its delicate appearance, the Javanese has a strong character to match. An affectionate, communicative cat, it loves to follow its owner around—when it is not prying into every nook and cranny of the house. The silky coat does not mat and is relatively easy to groom.

Long, thin, plumed tail

Fine, silky, seal tortie-tabby point coat

Clear, vivid blue eyes

Small, neat, oval paws

Large, pointed ears

Long, wedge-shaped head with flat skull

Shoulders and hips are same width

Slender, elegant neck

Ivory coat with seal tortie pointing

Long, graceful, muscular body

Long, slim-boned, legs with oval paws

York Chocolate

ORIGIN US, 1980s
BREED REGISTRIES Other
WEIGHT RANGE 6–11lb (2.5–5kg)

GROOMING 2-3 times a week
COLORS AND PATTERNS Solid color: chocolate, lavender; bicolor: chocolate and white, lavender and white.

This sweet and loving cat makes an excellent hunter outdoors—quick and sure, it enjoys the chase and hunt.

The founding female of the York Chocolate breed came from New York State and was a dark chocolate brown, hence the breed's name. When kittens born to this cat had the same rich coloring, their owner developed an enthusiasm for continuing the line. Although still comparatively rare, the York Chocolate has attracted much attention at cat shows in North America. The breed includes bicolors with patches of chocolate or lavender. It is a gentle lap cat with an affectionate temperament and loves to be petted. In the home this soft-voiced breed will quietly make its presence felt by following its owner everywhere and joining in with anything that is going on.

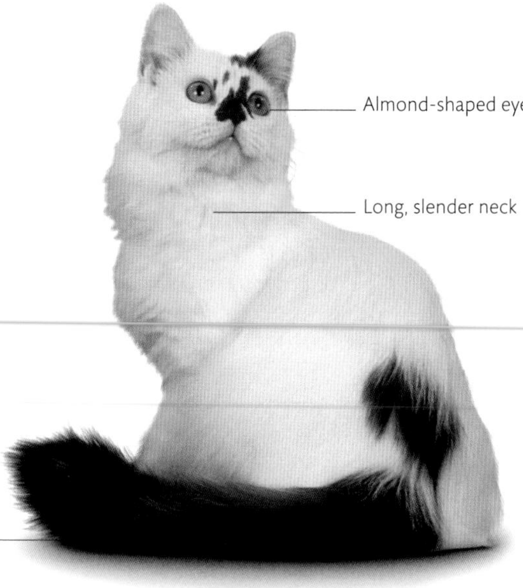

Almond-shaped eyes

Long, slender neck

Plumed tail tapers to a point

THE KITTEN THAT GAVE RISE TO THIS BREED WAS PRODUCED BY **TWO MIXED BREED** CATS, ONE OF WHICH CARRIED A **LATENT SIAMESE GENE**.

Rounded head

Large, pointed ears

Medium-long muzzle

Long, well built but not heavy body

Semi-long, silky chocolate and white coat with thin undercoat

Paws tufted between toes

Oriental Longhair

ORIGIN UK, 1960s
BREED REGISTRIES CFA, FIFe, GCCF, TICA
WEIGHT RANGE 6–11lb (2.5–5kg)

GROOMING 2–3 times a week
COLORS AND PATTERNS Many colors, including solid, smoke, and shaded; tortie, tabby, and bicolor patterns.

A typical Oriental, this cat is ideal for people who want an active and engaging pet and a devoted companion.

Known originally as the British Angora, the Oriental Longhair was renamed in 2002 to avoid confusion with the Turkish Angora (see p. 229). The breed was developed in the 1960s in an attempt to re-create the silky-haired Angora cats that were favored pets in Victorian households until ousted by the up-and-coming Persians. Breeding programs included various longhaired Oriental cats, such as the Balinese (see pp. 206–07), producing what is in essence a longhaired Siamese—lithe-bodied and elegant but without color points. Curious, playful, and highly active, the Oriental Longhair loves to be the center of family attention, but often chooses one person with whom to form a close bond.

Striking, almond-shaped green eyes

Fine, silky, semi-long coat with no undercoat

Long, elegant neck

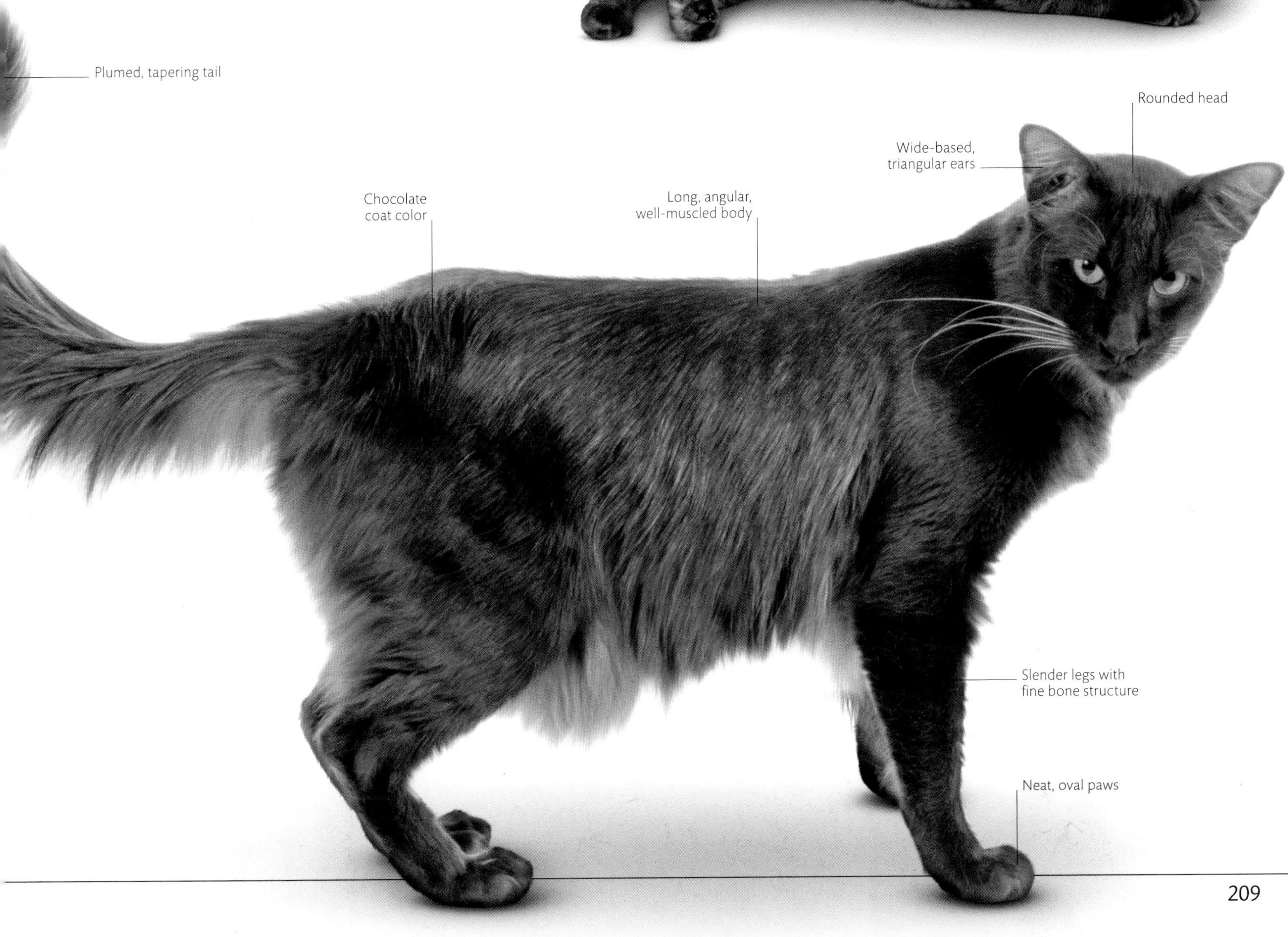

Plumed, tapering tail

Rounded head

Wide-based, triangular ears

Chocolate coat color

Long, angular, well-muscled body

Slender legs with fine bone structure

Neat, oval paws

Tiffanie

ORIGIN UK, 1980s
BREED REGISTRIES GCCF
WEIGHT RANGE 8–14lb (3.5–6.5kg)

GROOMING 2–3 times a week
COLORS AND PATTERNS All solid and shaded colors; tabby and tortie patterns.

Bright and fun-loving, this breed makes an ideal companion and will happily wait for its owner to come home.

Formerly called the Asian Longhair, this cat is often confused with an American breed that has been known variously as the Tiffany, Chantilly, or Chantilly/Tiffany (see opposite). It first appeared by chance as a longhaired variant of the Burmilla, a breed that itself originated as a happy accident following an unplanned mating between a European Burmese (see p. 87) and a

Persian Chinchilla (see p. 190). The Tiffanie is a gentle, cuddly cat with a hint of mischief inherited from the Burmese side of its family. This cat is good at amusing itself with its own games, but is pleased if a human wants to join in. Sensitive and intelligent, the Tiffanie is said to be highly responsive to the moods of its owner.

Medium-long, silky coat darkens toward base of tail

Broad, wedge-shaped head

THE **ORIGINAL TIFFANIES** WERE ESSENTIALLY **SEMI-LONGHAIRED** **BURMILLAS** WITH SHADED COATS.

Fairly large, wide-based ears

Yellow-green eyes set well apart

Thick ruff around neck

Compact body with straight, muscular back

Blue-tipped silver coat

Strong, medium-length legs

Oval paws

Long, plumed tail

KITTEN

Chantilly/Tiffany

ORIGIN US, 1960s
BREED REGISTRIES Other
WEIGHT RANGE 6–11lb (2.5–5kg)

GROOMING 2–3 times a week
COLORS AND PATTERNS Black, blue, lilac, chocolate, cinnamon, and fawn; various tabby patterns.

A relatively rare breed with a soft, full, richly colored coat, this loyal, easygoing cat is not overly demanding.

The history of the Chantilly/Tiffany starts with a litter of chocolate-brown kittens born to two longhaired cats of unknown origin. A once widespread belief that the Burmese was included in the breed's ancestry has now been discounted. The various names registered for this cat during its development—Foreign Longhair, Tiffany, and Chantilly—caused considerable confusion, and the dual name is now the most commonly accepted. Although very attractive and possessing a sweet personality, the Chantilly/Tiffany has not yet achieved great popularity. It loves human companionship but asks for it politely, attracting attention with a soft trill.

High cheekbones

Longer ruff around neck

Medium-long body

Silky, semi-long chocolate coat has minimal undercoat

Ears with rounded tips

Almond-shaped eyes slightly angled

Nose slopes to broad muzzle

Legs strong but not heavy

Long tail is thickly plumed

211

Birman

ORIGIN Myanmar (Burma)/France, c.1920
BREED REGISTRIES CFA, FIFe, GCCF, TICA
WEIGHT RANGE 10–18lb (4.5–8kg)

GROOMING 2–3 times a week
COLORS AND PATTERNS All color points, with white feet.

This cat is quiet and gentle but highly responsive to an owner's attention, and it makes a loving companion.

With its distinctive color points, this exquisite cat has the appearance of a longhaired Siamese, but the two breeds are unlikely to be closely related. According to legend, Birmans inherited their coloring from a cat belonging to a priest in ancient Myanmar (Burma). One day the priest was attacked by robbers; as the cat guarded the dying priest, he gained a gold-tinted coat and deep blue eyes like the goddess whom the priest served. In reality, the breed was probably created in France in the 1920s, although the foundation cats may have been acquired from Myanmar. Long-bodied and sturdily built, the breed is notable for its "Roman" nose (having a slightly curved profile) and its white paws. The Birman has silky-textured hair that does not mat. Birmans are gentle, easygoing, sociable cats with soft voices. They love human company and usually get along well with children and other pets.

KITTEN

DESIGNER'S MUSE

German fashion designer Karl Lagerfeld's Birman cat Choupette enjoys the lifestyle of a supermodel. She travels by private jet and has two personal assistants to cater to her every need and to take care of her beauty routine. Choupette has even featured in numerous magazine "interviews." She is also the inspiration behind a collection of cat-themed Lagerfeld accessories that include knitted hats, scarves, gloves, and leather goods.

KARL LAGERFELD AND CHOUPETTE FIGURINE

Tail medium in length

Roman nose

Round, blue eyes

Silky blue point coat

Strong, elongated body

Full cheeks and round muzzle

Well developed jaw

Thick ruff around neck

Sturdy legs

Paws have white mittens and socks

Maine Coon

ORIGIN US, 1800s
BREED REGISTRIES CFA, FIFe, GCCF, TICA
WEIGHT RANGE 9–17lb (4–7.5kg)

GROOMING 2–3 times a week
COLORS AND PATTERNS Many solid colors and shades in tortie, tabby, and bicolor patterns.

An impressively large cat that is kind-natured and easy to keep, this breed is intelligent and makes a devoted pet.

Regarded as America's native cat, the Maine Coon is named after the New England state where the breed was first recognized. Exactly how the breed first arrived there has been explained in various entertaining but mostly improbable tales. Wilder versions of the Maine Coon's history put forward the theory that it descends from Scandinavian cats brought in by the Vikings, or claim that several cats of this type were sent to the US by Queen Marie Antoinette, anxious to preserve her pets during the French Revolution. The suggestion that the Maine Coon was originally a hybrid between feral cats and raccoons can definitely be discounted as a scientific impossibility, although the cat's

bushy tail makes it easy to see how the idea might once have had credibility. Huge and handsome, the Maine Coon has a thick, shaggy, waterproof coat that served it well in its earlier role as a farm cat, leading an outdoor life through harsh North American winters. Once highly regarded for its skills as a vermin-catcher, this breed has become a popular pet since the mid-20th century. Maine Coons have many endearing characteristics, including a tendency to act like kittens all their lives. Their voice, described by some as a birdlike chirrup, sounds surprisingly small for such a big cat. These cats are slow to mature and do not usually reach their full magnificent growth until about their fifth year.

KITTEN

LITTLE NICKY

In 2004, a Maine Coon named Little Nicky was the first pet animal to be cloned commercially. His Texas owner paid $50,000 to have a "carbon copy" created of her much-loved cat Nicky, which died at age 17. Nicky's DNA was transplanted into an egg cell and the resulting embryo was carried by a surrogate mother cat. The highly controversial procedure produced a kitten identical in appearance and personality to the original.

Red coat with smooth, silky texture

Long, thick-furred tail

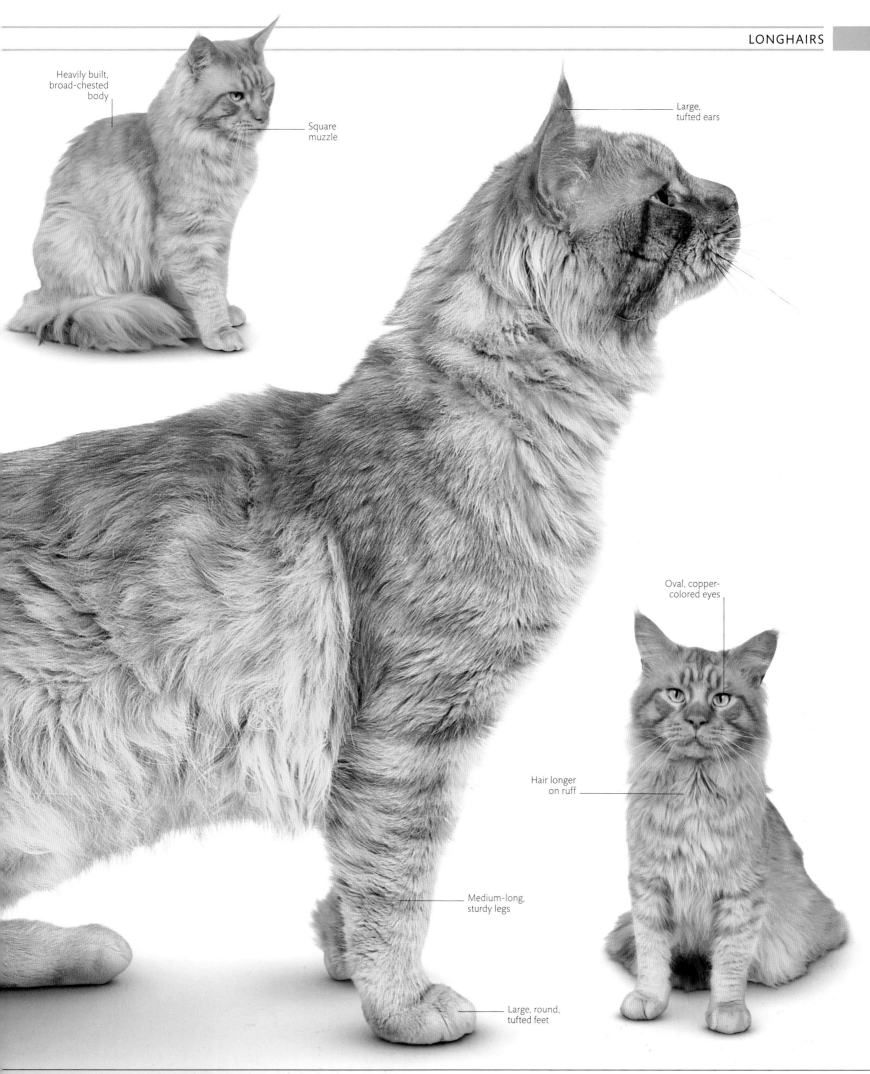

Heavily built, broad-chested body

Square muzzle

Large, tufted ears

Oval, copper-colored eyes

Hair longer on ruff

Medium-long, sturdy legs

Large, round, tufted feet

Ragdoll

ORIGIN US, 1960s
BREED REGISTRIES CFA, FIFe, GCCF, TICA
WEIGHT RANGE 10–20lb (4.5–9kg)

GROOMING 2–3 times a week
COLORS AND PATTERNS Most solid colors in tortie and tabby patterns; always pointed and bicolor or mitted.

This large, laid-back cat is remarkably well-behaved and amenable, making it perfect for people with busy lifestyles.

The name is well chosen, since few cats are easier to handle or more ready to sit on a lap than a Ragdoll. One of the largest of all cat breeds, this cat has a confused history—supposedly, the original Ragdolls were developed from a litter of kittens, born in California, that became unusually limp and "floppy" when picked up. These cats love human company, will happily play with children, and are usually well disposed toward other pets. Ragdolls are not particularly athletic and, once past kittenhood, mostly prefer their games to be gentle. Moderate grooming is enough to keep their soft, silky fur free from tangles.

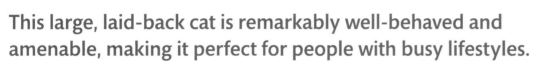

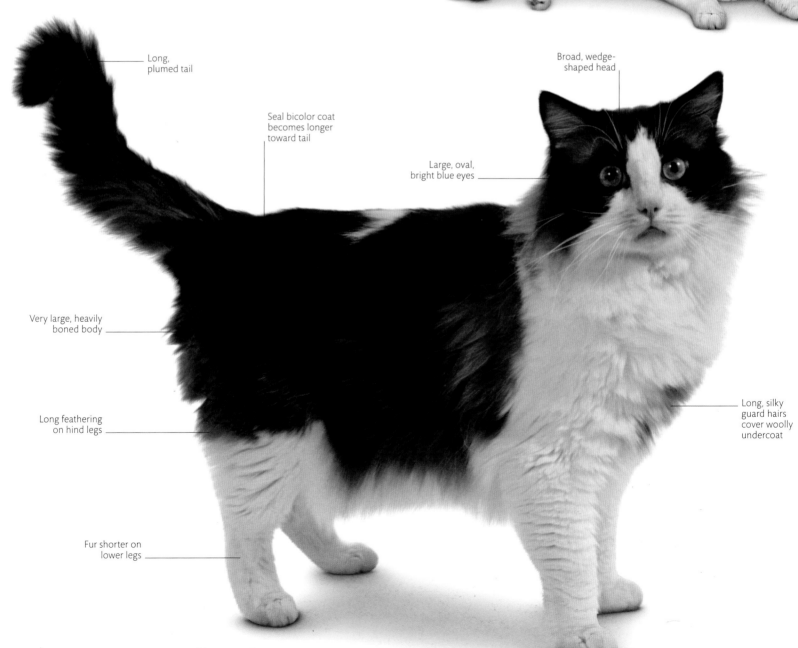

Wide-set ears

Blue and white bicolor coat

Long, plumed tail

Broad, wedge-shaped head

Seal bicolor coat becomes longer toward tail

Large, oval, bright blue eyes

Very large, heavily boned body

Long feathering on hind legs

Long, silky guard hairs cover woolly undercoat

Fur shorter on lower legs

Ragamuffin

ORIGIN US, late 20th century
BREED REGISTRIES CFA, GCCF
WEIGHT RANGE 10–20lb (4.5–9kg)

GROOMING 2–3 times a week
COLORS AND PATTERNS All solid colors
in bicolor, tortie, and tabby patterns.

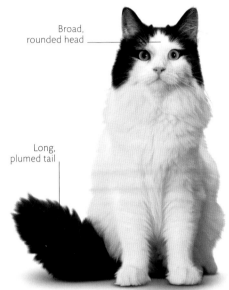

Broad, rounded head

Long, plumed tail

This massively built, big-hearted, and delightfully calm cat forms strong bonds and loves to please its owner.

This comparatively recent breed has a complicated history but it emerged as a new development of the better-known Ragdoll (see opposite). The Ragamuffin is a huge cat, a true gentle giant that fits in placidly with families of all types. It thrives on affection and its docile temperament makes it an excellent pet for children. The Ragamuffin is not without a sense of fun and is easily persuaded to play with toys. This cat's dense, silky fur is not prone to matting, and short, regular grooming sessions will keep the coat in good condition.

Thick, silky black and white coat does not mat easily

Heavily built, rectangular body

Wide-set ears with rounded tips

Dip in nose

Large eyes with characteristic sweet expression

Full cheeks

Somali

PLACE OF ORIGIN US, 1960s
BREED REGISTRIES CFA, FIFe, GCCF, TICA
WEIGHT RANGE 8–12lb (3.5–5.5kg)

GROOMING 2–3 times a week
COLORS AND PATTERNS Various colors, some with silver tipping; tortie pattern; silver hairs always ticked.

This cat with dramatic looks, gorgeous coat, and a colorful personality makes an attention-seeking yet loving pet.

This beautiful breed is a longhaired descendant of the shorthaired Abyssinian (see pp. 132–33). At first, breeders of Abyssinians had rejected longhaired kittens (see panel, right); other people, however, found these cats attractive, and breeders started to produce them intentionally. The US Cat Fanciers' Association accepted the Somali as a breed in 1979. The "ticked" coat of the Somali comes in a variety of colors, from rich, earthy red to blue, with each hair having bands of lighter and darker color; a dark stripe runs along the back and tail.

It can take up to 18 months for a young cat to develop its full coat color. The Somali's most striking feature is the long, plumed tail. The cat also has a ruff around the neck (fuller and more pronounced in males), giving a regal appearance. Lively and insatiably curious, the Somali makes an entertaining pet. Although highly affectionate and family-friendly, this is not generally a lap cat; the Somali has too much energy to sit still for long. Its confident temperament makes the breed ideally suited to the show ring.

KITTEN

EARLY REJECTS

When a gene for long hair occurred by chance in Abyssinian cats, the longhaired kittens that appeared alongside shorthaired siblings initially found little favor with breeders. There was no interest in developing the trait, and the longhairs were sold as pets. When a few pioneer breeders recognized the potential for a new cat, they made slow progress; the first Somalis received scant attention at shows from exhibitors and judges. But with determination came success, and in 1979 Somalis achieved full recognition.

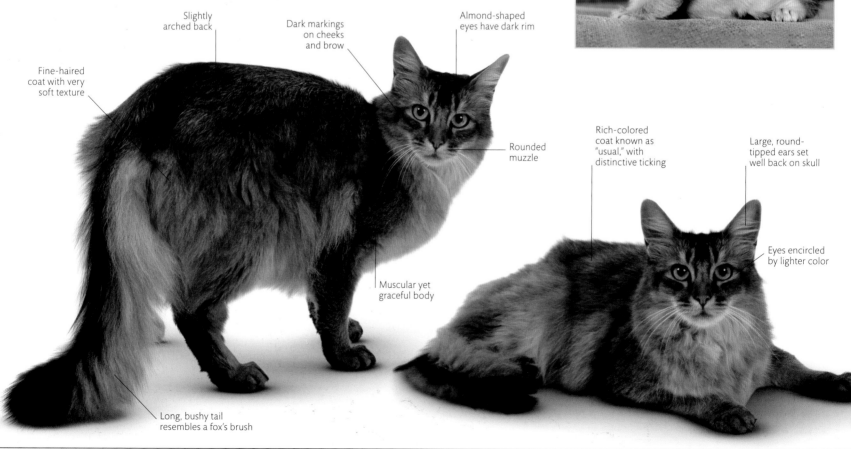

Slightly arched back

Dark markings on cheeks and brow

Almond-shaped eyes have dark rim

Fine-haired coat with very soft texture

Rounded muzzle

Rich-colored coat known as "usual," with distinctive ticking

Large, round-tipped ears set well back on skull

Eyes encircled by lighter color

Muscular yet graceful body

Long, bushy tail resembles a fox's brush

Winter coat
In the winter, the Somali grows a full coat and ruff. Despite the coat, it is not well suited to cold weather, although it will insist on being let out in the snow.

British Longhair

ORIGIN UK, 1800s
BREED REGISTRIES TICA
WEIGHT RANGE 9–18lb (4–8kg)

GROOMING 2–3 times a week
COLORS AND PATTERNS Same colors and patterns as recognized in the British Shorthair.

This chunky, handsome cat has a long, flowing coat and a happy-go-lucky nature.

Known as the Lowlander in the US and the Britanica in Europe, this cat is the longer-haired cousin of the British Shorthair (see pp. 118–27). The two are identical in body shape, sharing the same sturdy build, massive head, and round face, and both come in the same range of colors. Not all pedigree cat registries regard the British Longhair as a separate breed. Regardless of its official status, this cat makes an excellent pet, since it has a calm, easygoing, people-loving temperament. The long coat needs moderate grooming to keep it tangle-free.

Short, broad nose

Full neck ruff

Short, thick, brushlike tail

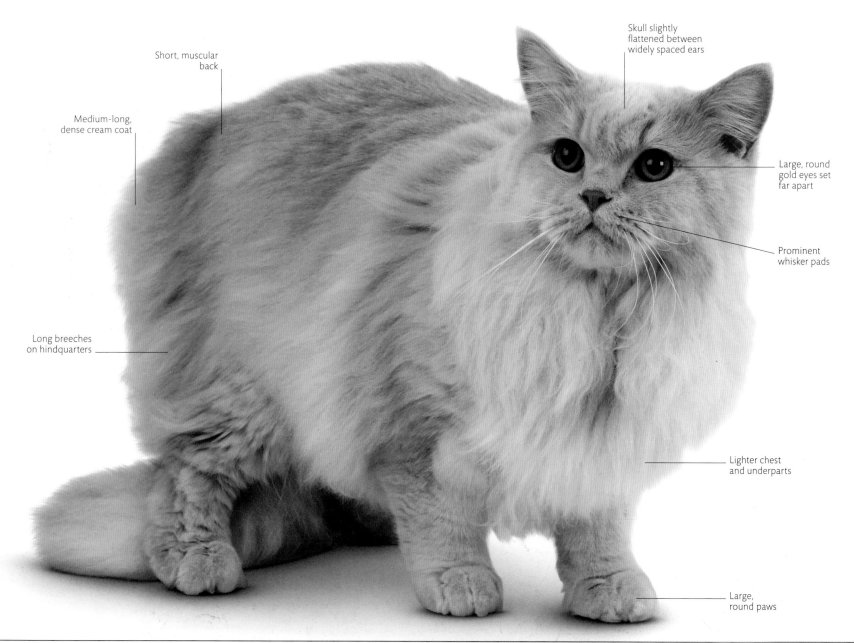

Short, muscular back

Medium-long, dense cream coat

Long breeches on hindquarters

Skull slightly flattened between widely spaced ears

Large, round gold eyes set far apart

Prominent whisker pads

Lighter chest and underparts

Large, round paws

Nebelung

ORIGIN US, 1980s
BREED REGISTRIES GCCF, TICA
WEIGHT RANGE 6–11lb (2.5–5kg)

GROOMING 2–3 times a week
COLORS AND PATTERNS Blue, sometimes silver-tipped.

An affectionate breed that likes a secure routine, this cat prefers the company of its family and is shy with strangers.

Long, graceful body

Prominent whisker pads

Silver-tipped blue coat has soft sheen

Developed in Denver, Colorado, in the late 20th century, the Nebelung is an outcross from the Russian Blue (see pp. 116–17), deliberately bred to re-create the longhaired blue cats that were popular in the Victorian era. The breed's name, taken from the German word *nebel* meaning haze or mist, is appropriate due to its softly glistening coat. Naturally reserved and preferring a quiet environment, this cat may not settle well in a family of boisterous children. With sensitive handling, however, the Nebelung makes a devoted pet, anxious to keep its owners in sight and loving a lap to sit on.

Feathering behind ears

Large ears continue wedge-shaped line of head

Slightly oval yellowish green eyes

Heavily plumed tail

Ruff around neck

Shorter fur on lower legs

Hair tufts between toes

Norwegian Forest Cat

PLACE OF ORIGIN Norway, 1950s
BREED REGISTRIES CFA, FIFe, GCCF, TICA
WEIGHT RANGE 7–20lb (3–9kg)

GROOMING 2–3 times a week
COLORS AND PATTERNS Most solid colors, shades, and patterns.

THE SKOGKATT

In Norway, folktales and legends featuring enormous longhaired cats have been repeated for centuries. Because of its size and powerful build (as can be seen in the image below), the Norwegian Forest Cat—or "Skogkatt," as it is known in its native country—was once even believed to be a cross between a cat and a dog. Despite its long history, by the latter part of the 20th century the Forest Cat was all but forgotten, until a determined project in the 1970s revived interest in the breed.

Contrary to its big, tough, and burly appearance, this cat is gentle and well-mannered and loves to stay at home.

Cats have been known in Scandinavia since Viking times, being kept as pest destroyers in homesteads and villages and on board ships. The Norwegian Forest Cat was developed fully as a breed only in the 1970s, but its characteristics are recognizably those of the cats familiar for centuries on Norwegian farms. These semi-wild cats bred with no human interference and hunted for themselves. They became tough, intelligent, and courageous; only the fittest survived the harsh environment. They featured in

Norwegian legends (see panel, right), and today they are officially recognized as the national cat of Norway. The breed is still large and sturdy; notably, it takes up to five years to reach physical maturity. The double coat, a natural insulation against bitter northern winters, may become much thicker in colder months as the undercoat reaches full density. Surprisingly, this does not mean extra winter grooming, although shedding is likely to be heavy in spring. Despite their wild ancestry, these cats are gentle and fun-loving.

KITTEN

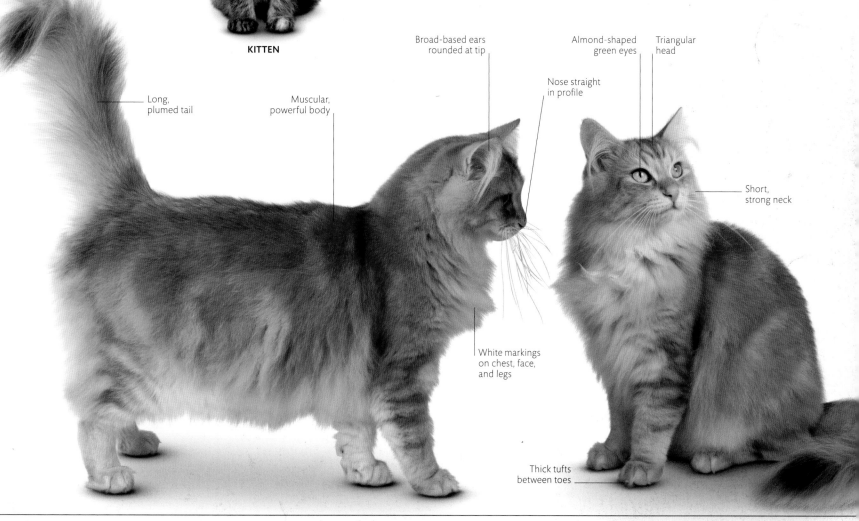

Long, plumed tail

Muscular, powerful body

Broad-based ears rounded at tip

Nose straight in profile

Almond-shaped green eyes

Triangular head

Short, strong neck

White markings on chest, face, and legs

Thick tufts between toes

Ready for anything
Splendidly rugged and powerful, the Norwegian Forest Cat is not too dignified to appreciate some fun. The breed makes an excellent pet but likes to have plenty of freedom outdoors.

Turkish Van

ORIGIN Turkey / UK (modern breed), pre-1700
BREED REGISTRIES CFA, FIFe, GCCF, TICA
WEIGHT RANGE 7–19lb (3–8.5kg)

GROOMING 2–3 times a week
COLORS AND PATTERNS White with darker colors on head and tail.

A playful breed said to have a liking for water games, this energetic cat can be tireless in its search for amusement.

The predecessors of this cat, named after the Lake Van area of eastern Turkey, may have existed for hundreds of years in southwestern Asia. The breed is now a regional treasure in Turkey. The modern Turkish Van was first developed in the UK in the 1950s, and breeding cats have since been exported to other countries, although they remain uncommon. The breed is noted for its soft, semi-longhaired, water-resistant coat, distinctive markings, and quiet, bleating voice. A Turkish Van is an intelligent, affectionate companion, but perhaps is not the ideal choice for an owner who wants a peaceful lap cat—zestful and fun-loving, this cat needs plenty of exercise. It loves human company and enjoys a game, especially if the family joins in. Many

Turkish Vans are said to love water, paddling in puddles and pouncing at dripping faucets. The claims that these cats are confident swimmers have led to their nickname, the "swimming cats."

KITTEN

ODD-COLORED EYES

The odd-colored eyes seen in this breed are caused by the white-spotting gene (see p.53), which prevents melanin (pigment) from reaching the iris (colored part) of one eye. All Turkish Van kittens are born with pale blue eyes that then gradually acquire their adult color. In some, both eyes become amber (see below), but in others one eye remains blue. Turkish Vans can have two blue eyes too, but those affected by the white-spotting gene have eyes that are different shades of blue.

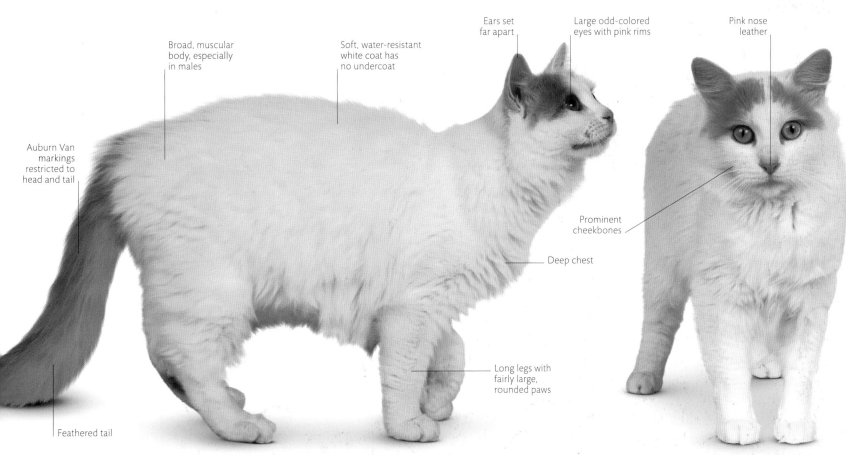

Broad, muscular body, especially in males

Soft, water-resistant white coat has no undercoat

Ears set far apart

Large odd-colored eyes with pink rims

Pink nose leather

Auburn Van markings restricted to head and tail

Prominent cheekbones

Deep chest

Long legs with fairly large, rounded paws

Feathered tail

Turkish Vankedisi

ORIGIN Eastern Turkey, pre-1700
BREED REGISTRIES GCCF
WEIGHT RANGE 7–19lb (3–8.5kg)

GROOMING 2-3 times a week
COLORS AND PATTERNS Pure white only.

This rare breed, an all-white variant of the Turkish Van, is friendly and needs little encouragement to play.

This cat has its origins in the same region of Turkey as the Turkish Van (see pp. 226–27), and it is distinguished from that breed only by the lack of the typical Van markings on its snow-white coat. In all other respects, it shares the characteristics of its relation. The Turkish Vankedisi is rare anywhere in the world and is much prized in its native country. Like many all-white cats, the breed has a tendency to inherit deafness but it is nonetheless strong and active. Its pleasant temperament makes this cat an affectionate companion, but it demands plenty of attention.

Fairly broad, wedge-shaped head

Long, straight nose

Silky, snow-white coat

Long hair inside ears

Pink rim around eyes

Long, bushy tail

Long, muscular legs

Round, tufted paws

Turkish Angora

ORIGIN Turkey, 16th century
BREED REGISTRIES CFA, FIFe, TICA
WEIGHT RANGE 6–11lb (2.5–5kg)

GROOMING 2–3 times a week
COLORS AND PATTERNS Many solid colors and shades; patterns include tabby, tortie, and bicolor.

This breed may look delicately built, but it has a strong character and enjoys lots of family interaction.

Records indicate that this native Turkish breed probably reached France and the UK some time around the 17th century. Widely used in the development of other longhaired cats such as Persians, especially during the early 20th century, the Turkish Angora as a breed became so diluted that it almost ceased to exist, except in its own country. In Turkey, the cat had been given greater protection, and by the 1950s purebred Angoras were being sent around Europe and to the US. Still rare, the Angora is one of the most exquisite of all longhaired cats, with its fine bone structure and exceptionally soft, glistening coat.

Slender, graceful neck

Small, rounded paws are usually tufted between the toes

Small-to medium-sized head

Large, tufted ears are set high on head

Almond-shaped, slightly slanting green eyes

Fine-boned, slender yet muscular body

Fine, silky, shimmering black coat, with no undercoat

Long, tapering, brushlike tail

Long legs

Siberian

ORIGIN Russia, 1980s
BREED REGISTRIES CFA, FIFe, GCCF, TICA
WEIGHT RANGE 10–20lb (4.5–9kg)

GROOMING Daily
COLORS AND PATTERNS All colors and patterns.

Russia's national cat, this large, heavy-coated breed is very agile and loves to play, but it is slow to reach full maturity.

Although the Siberian is considered to be a relatively recent breed, longhaired Russian cats were first recorded in Russia as early as the 13th century. The breed still shows its adaptation to the harsh Russian climate in its dense, waterproof coat, bushy tail, and tufted paw pads. Many Siberians also have thickly furred ears with tufted tips like those of a lynx. Breeding Siberians to standard did not begin until the 1980s, and full breed recognition did not come until a decade later, after a number of cats had been imported to the US. Although still rare, the Siberian cat is gaining popularity for its handsome looks and engaging personality.

It may take five years or more for a Siberian to attain full growth. Despite its moderately hefty build in adulthood, this breed is highly athletic and loves to leap and play. It is intelligent, inquisitive, and friendly, and is said to be highly loyal to its owners. The Siberian also has a melodious chirping voice and a deep, resonant purr.

KITTEN

RUSSIAN LONGHAIR

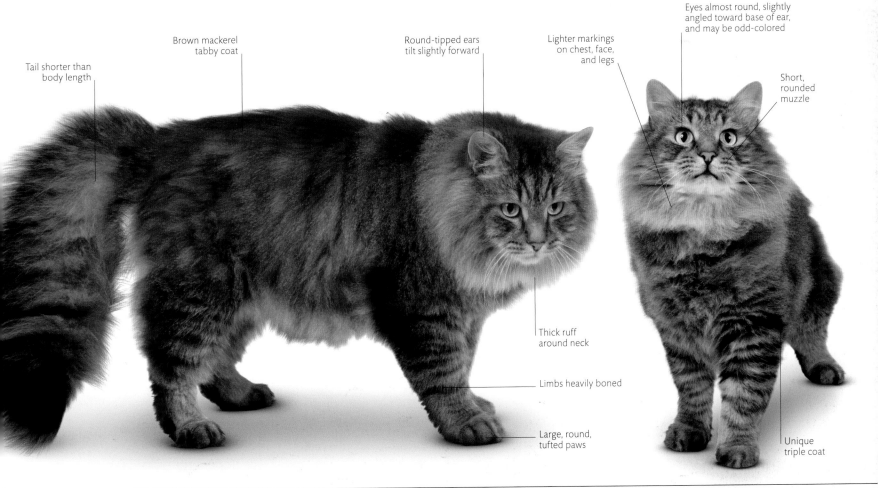

Tail shorter than body length

Brown mackerel tabby coat

Round-tipped ears tilt slightly forward

Lighter markings on chest, face, and legs

Eyes almost round, slightly angled toward base of ear, and may be odd-colored

Short, rounded muzzle

Thick ruff around neck

Limbs heavily boned

Large, round, tufted paws

Unique triple coat

Neva Masquerade

ORIGIN Russia, 1970s
BREED REGISTRIES FIFe
WEIGHT RANGE 10–20lb (4.5–9kg)

GROOMING 2–3 times a week
COLORS AND PATTERNS Various colorpoints, including seal, blue, red, cream, tabby, and tortie.

A magnificent colorpointed cat with an ultra-thick coat, the breed is calm and fearless, with an easygoing nature.

This breed is the colorpoint version of the Siberian (see pp. 230–31), a forest cat that has a long history in Russia. The Neva Masquerade is named after the Neva River in St. Petersburg, where it was first developed. Combining strength with gentleness, this substantially built cat makes an excellent family pet and has a reputation for becoming particularly attached to children. The immensely thick coat of the Neva Masquerade, which has a double-layered undercoat, is not inclined to form mats or knots, so grooming is not a difficult task, although it does need to be done regularly.

Very thick, long, weatherproof, triple coat

Seal tabby pointing on tail, legs, and head

Tufted ears set to side of head

KITTEN

Darker ears and mask

Large, slightly oval blue eyes

Broad, round muzzle

Substantially boned, strong, muscular body

Dense white ruff around neck

Tabby markings evident on legs

Long, fluffy breeches

Large paws tufted between toes

Munchkin

ORIGIN US, 1980s
BREED REGISTRIES TICA
WEIGHT RANGE 6–9lb (2.5–4kg)

GROOMING 2–3 times a week
COLORS AND PATTERNS All colors, shades, and patterns.

Despite its very short legs, this active little cat has a full zest for living, and it enjoys a good game with the family.

The extraordinarily short legs of the Munchkin are the result of a chance mutation. This breed appears to have escaped the spinal problems sometimes associated with very short legs in dogs such as the Dachshund, and having a low-to-the-ground stature does not inhibit its general mobility. In fact, Munchkins can run extremely fast, and they are energetic and playful. These confident and inquisitive cats make sociable family pets. In addition to the silky, semi-longhaired version, there is also a shorthaired Munchkin (see pp. 150–51), and both come in an almost endless variety of colors and patterns. The Munchkin longhair needs regular grooming to prevent the coat from matting.

Walnut-shaped golden eyes set wide apart, have an alert expression

Defined cheekbones

Exceptionally short legs

VARIOUS COLORS AND PATTERNS HAVE BEEN INTRODUCED THROUGH OUTCROSSING, WHICH MAINTAINS THE MUNCHKIN'S GENETIC DIVERSITY.

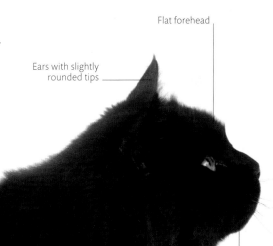

Flat forehead

Ears with slightly rounded tips

Tail is same length as body, with rounded tip

Silky, weather-resistant coat

Muscular body

Whisker pads often prominent

Shaggy breeches

Kinkalow

ORIGIN US, 1990s
BREED REGISTRIES TICA
WEIGHT RANGE 6–9lb (2.5–4kg)

GROOMING Weekly
COLORS AND PATTERNS Many colors and patterns, including tabby and tortie.

Soft, sleek white coat

Rounded paws

This new and rare breed is said to be intelligent and playful, and it enjoys its owner's lap.

Like its shorthaired relative (see p. 152), the Kinkalow Longhair is an "experimental designer breed." This hybrid was created by crossing the Munchkin (see p. 233) with the American Curl (see pp. 238–39). The cats have the Munchkin's short legs and the American Curl's turned-back ears. However, some Kinkalow litters include kittens born without one or both of these features. Both forms of Kinkalow have soft, silky fur, but the longhaired version has a semi-long, shaggy coat. The coats occur in a variety of colors and patterns. Kinkalows are lively, intelligent, friendly cats who enjoy interacting and playing with their owners. As with any longhaired breed, the Kinkalow Longhair will need (and appreciate) grooming two or three times a week.

IN SOME KINKALOWS, THE **TAIL** MAY BE **LONGER THAN** THE **BODY**.

Pink nose leather

Curled-back ears inherited from American Curl

Tail long in comparison with body

Short, compact body feels heavy for size

White chest

Forelegs particularly short

Skookum

ORIGIN US, 1990s
BREED REGISTRIES None
WEIGHT RANGE 6–9lb (2.5–4kg)

GROOMING Weekly
COLORS AND PATTERNS All colors
and patterns.

Despite being one of the smallest of all breeds, this cat is agile, athletic and full of confidence, and loves to play.

As a cross between the Munchkin (see p. 233) and the LaPerm (see pp. 250–51), this little cat has inherited two striking features: extremely short legs and a soft coat, either long or short, that stands away from its body in exuberant curls or waves. The curly coat is not generally prone to matting and is easy to groom. The Skookum has been developed in several countries, initially in the US, and also in the UK, Australia, and New Zealand. However, it is still rare and has not yet achieved universal recognition. This is an active, playful cat, able to run and jump just as well as longer-legged breeds.

Ears very wide at base

Walnut-shaped eyes look large for head

Lighter colored chest and underparts

Sturdy body

THE **CHINOOK** JARGON WORD
SKOOKUM MEANS **POWERFUL**,
OR **GREAT** AND CAN **SIGNIFY**
GOOD HEALTH OR **GOOD SPIRITS**.

Rounded, wedge-shaped head

Chocolate tortie tabby coat

Soft, springy curls stand out from body

Slight stop between eyes

Very short legs

Neat, round feet

Napoleon

ORIGIN US, 1990s
BREED REGISTRIES TICA
WEIGHT RANGE 7–17lb (3–7.5kg)

GROOMING Daily
COLORS AND PATTERNS All colors, shades, and patterns, including colorpoint.

This short, round cat has a luxurious fur coat and is gentle, very affectionate, and well-suited for family life.

A sturdy, low-to-the-ground cat, the Napoleon longhair is a hybrid specially bred to combine the very short legs of the Munchkin (see p. 233) with the luxuriant fur of the Persian (see pp. 186–205), including versions with a colorpointed coat. There is also a shorthaired variant of the Napoleon. This breed is very active, despite its short stature, and it has plenty of character. The Persian influence has ensured that the Napoleon likes spending time as a lap cat, too, and it loves to be made a fuss of, although it is not overly demanding.

THIS BREED HAS THE GENTLENESS OF A PERSIAN AND THE ENERGY AND CURIOSITY OF A MUNCHKIN.

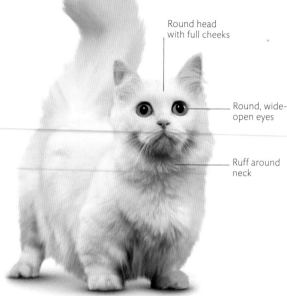

Round head with full cheeks

Round, wide-open eyes

Ruff around neck

Long, plumed tail

Semi-long white coat stands out from body

Short nose with defined stop

Smallish ears with rounded tips

Muzzle fairly short with round whisker pads

Shaggy breeches

Short, firm legs

Scottish Fold

ORIGIN UK/US, 1960s
BREED REGISTRIES CFA, TICA
WEIGHT RANGE 6–13lb (2.5–6kg)

GROOMING 2–3 times a week
COLORS AND PATTERNS Most solid colors and shades; most tabby, tortie, and colorpoint patterns.

This charming, sociable cat, with a delightful "owl-faced" appearance, thrives on attention.

The tightly folded-down ears of this rare breed and its shorthaired relative (see pp. 156–57) are due to a genetic mutation seen in no other cat. Descended from a folded-ear Scottish farm cat, the Fold is not recognized as a breed by the leading cat registry in the UK because of concerns about genetically linked health problems, although it has been more successful in the US. The diverse coat colors of the Scottish Fold come from the many different outcrosses, including domestic non-pedigree cats that were selected to develop the breed. The dense coat is of variable length and is enhanced by a thick ruff and a huge, plumed tail.

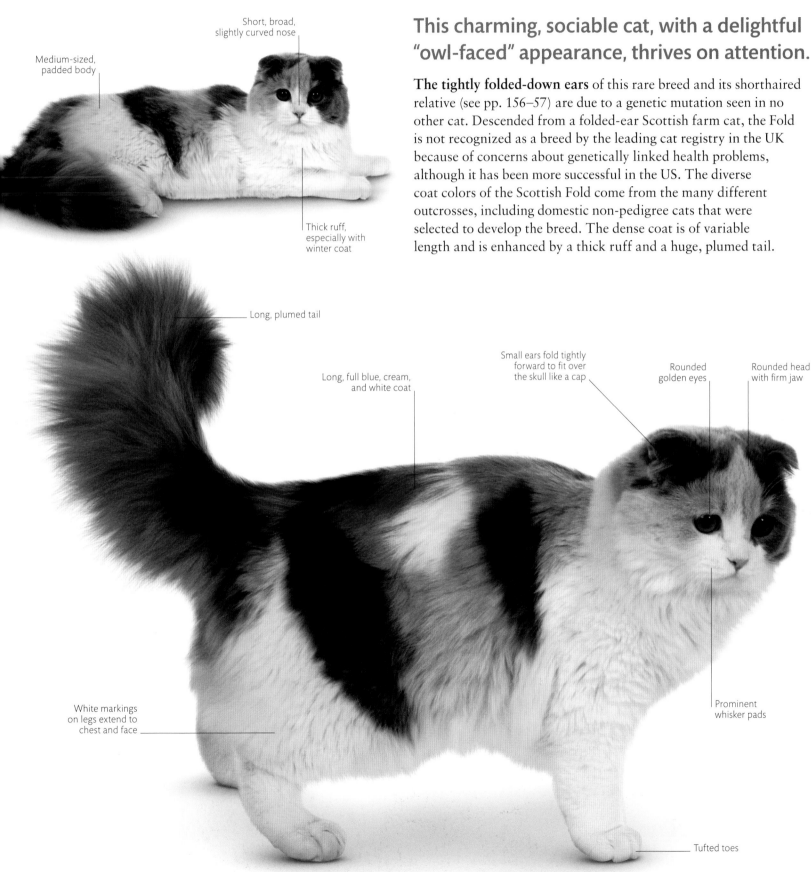

Short, broad, slightly curved nose

Medium-sized, padded body

Thick ruff, especially with winter coat

Long, plumed tail

Long, full blue, cream, and white coat

Small ears fold tightly forward to fit over the skull like a cap

Rounded golden eyes

Rounded head with firm jaw

Prominent whisker pads

White markings on legs extend to chest and face

Tufted toes

American Curl

PLACE OF ORIGIN US, 1980s
BREED REGISTRIES CFA, FIFe, TICA
WEIGHT RANGE 7–11lb (3–5kg)

GROOMING Weekly
COLORS AND PATTERNS All solid colors and shades; patterns include colorpoint, tabby, and tortie.

A rare breed with highly distinctive curled-back ears, this gentle, soft-voiced cat makes a wonderful pet.

This breed has its origins in a stray cat with a long, black coat and oddly curled ears that was adopted off the street by a family in California in 1981. The cat, a female, went on to produce a litter of curly-eared kittens, and the rare mutation aroused widespread interest among both breeders and geneticists. Programs for the planned development of the American Curl, in both longhaired and shorthaired (see p. 159) variants, began remarkably quickly, and the future of the new breed was secured. In an American Curl, the ears curve backward to a greater or lesser extent, the arc of the curl ideally somewhere between 90 and 180 degrees. The cartilage is firm, not floppy, and the ears of these cats should never be manipulated. At birth, all Curl kittens have straight ears, but in about 50 percent of them the characteristic curve begins to take shape within a few days, reaching its full arc by the time the cat is about three or four months old. Cats whose ears remain straight are of value in breeding programs, since their use helps to keep the American Curl genetically healthy. The longhaired Curl has a silky coat that lies close to the body. There is very little undercoat, which makes grooming easy and means minimal shedding. An additional embellishment in the longhair is the lovely, long, plumed tail. Alert, intelligent, and affectionate, the American Curl has an attractive personality and is an excellent family pet. This cat is gentle and soft-voiced, but not at all shy about pestering its owner for attention.

Tufted ears curl backward

Long, plumed tail

Fine, silky coat with very little undercoat

Moderately strong
yet slender body

Seal tortie point
with white coat

HEALTHY MIX

The American Curl is one of the newest cats to
emerge in a continuing trend to create breeds
with unusual features. The perpetuation of
natural mutations for the sake of appearance
has not been without controversy in the cat
fancy world. However, the Curl remains free of
the health problems that can arise in cats with
genetic variations. The only outcrosses allowed
in this breed are nonpedigree domestic cats,
which provide a large and robust gene pool.

Walnut-
shaped eyes

Rounded
muzzle

Medium-
length legs

KITTEN

Highlander

ORIGIN North America, 2000s
BREED REGISTRIES TICA
WEIGHT RANGE 10–25lb (4.5–11kg)

GROOMING Daily
COLORS AND PATTERNS All colors in any tabby pattern, including colorpoints.

Sloping forehead

Prominent whisker pads

Substantial, solidly boned legs

This rare breed with striking looks is family-loving, playful, and extremely energetic and enjoys a game of chase.

With its thick, almost shaggy coat, the Highlander longhair looks like a small lynx, although there are no wildcats in its breeding. This curly-eared newcomer on the cat scene is large and powerfully built, but moves with grace. Full of life and energy, the Highlander longhair is not content to stay in the background,

and owners—and other pets—will be pestered constantly to play. Nonetheless, this is a gentle, affectionate cat that gets along well with children. The heavy coat requires regular grooming to prevent mats and tangling. There is a shorthaired version (see p. 158) of the Highlander that is easier to maintain.

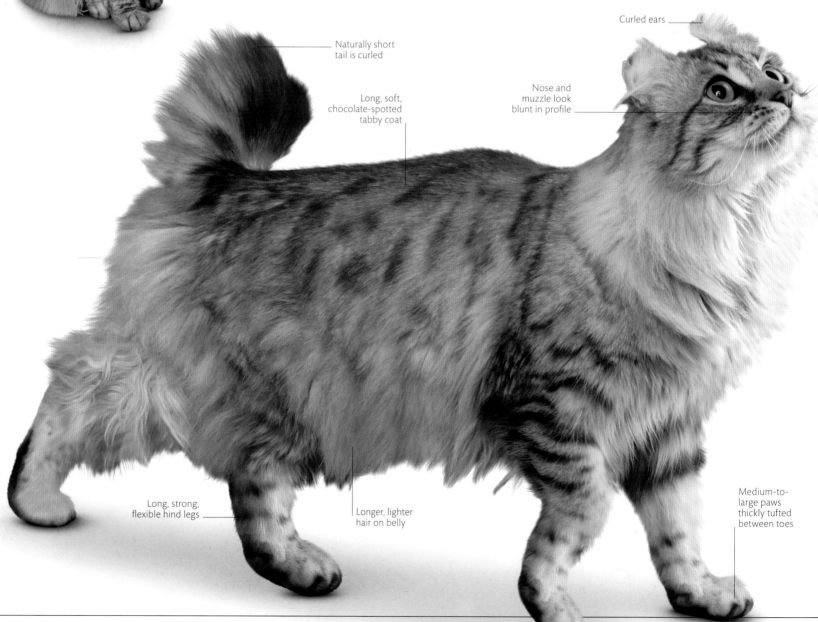

Naturally short tail is curled

Long, soft, chocolate-spotted tabby coat

Curled ears

Nose and muzzle look blunt in profile

Long, strong, flexible hind legs

Longer, lighter hair on belly

Medium-to-large paws thickly tufted between toes

Japanese Bobtail

ORIGIN Japan, c.17th century
BREED REGISTRIES CFA, TICA
WEIGHT RANGE 6–9lb (2.5–4kg)

GROOMING 2–3 times a week
COLORS AND PATTERNS All solid colors in bicolor, tabby, and tortie patterns.

This "talkative" and inquisitive breed is always on the go and loves to explore, but loyally returns to its family.

Both longhaired and shorthaired (see p. 160) Japanese Bobtails appear to have been favored pets in Japan for several hundred years. In the 1960s, the first of these charismatic and unusual cats were imported to the US, where the modern breed was developed. Japanese Bobtails are loving and lovable, but with their outgoing and energetic natures they are not for the owner who wants a lap cat. There are many variations on the short, plumed tail, which can curve or bend in any direction. The longhaired coat falls softly over the body and is relatively easy to groom.

Long nose with slight stop

Unique kinked "rabbit" tail

Long coat parts along top line

Brown mackerel tabby color patches

Elegantly sculpted head with high cheekbones

Ears set wide apart

Large, oval eyes set at a slant

Longer coat on hindquarters

Hind legs longer than forelegs

Soft, silky white coat with minimal undercoat

Long, slender legs with oval paws

Kurilian Bobtail

ORIGIN Kuril Islands, North Pacific, 20th century
BREED REGISTRIES FIFe, TICA
WEIGHT RANGE 7–10lb (3–4.5kg)

GROOMING 2–3 times a week
COLORS AND PATTERNS Most solid colors, shades, and patterns, including tabby.

This rare, short-tailed breed is said to thrive on company and affection, and it is highly intelligent and trainable.

This solidly handsome cat takes its name from the Kuril Islands, an archipelago of volcanic islands in the North Pacific, where it is thought to have its origins. Since both Russia and Japan have laid claim to several of these islands, it is uncertain from which country the Kurilian Bobtail longhair really comes. Although it is considered a modern breed, the forebears of the Kurilean Bobtail have been popular on the Russian mainland since the 1950s, as has the shorthaired version (see p. 161), but it is uncommon elsewhere and particularly rare in the US. The breed is known for its distinctive short tail, which is highly variable (see panel, right). The Kurilian Bobtail adores family life and can never get enough fuss and attention from its owner, although it also has a strong streak of independence.

KITTEN

(see p. 161)

POM-POM TAIL

Each Kurilian Bobtail has its own personal version of the breed's trademark pom-pom tail, and no two are ever quite alike. Through natural genetic diversity, the vertebrae in the tail kink and bend in any direction, and can be rigid or flexible. Between two and 10 vertebrae may be affected, with any combination of curve and mobility. In the breed standard, different tail forms are variously described as "snag," "spiral," or "whisk," depending on their structure.

Short tail is kinked

Stocky body shape

Silky, blue with white classic tabby coat

Medium-sized ears wide at base

Large, rounded head

Bright, oval gold eyes

Prominent whisker pads

Banding on legs

Medium-length legs with round paws

Pixiebob

ORIGIN US, 1980s
BREED REGISTRIES TICA
WEIGHT RANGE 9–18lb (4–8kg)

GROOMING 2–3 times a week
COLORS AND PATTERNS Brown-spotted tabby only.

This large, athletic breed resembles the wild bobcat found in North America, but it bonds well with its human family.

This relatively new breed has a similar appearance to the bobcat, native to the mountains of North America's Pacific coast. The resemblance is deliberate—the Pixiebob's characteristics having been developed by breeders catering to a growing fashion in domestic cats that look like their wild cousins. Lynxlike features include a thick, double tabby-spotted coat that stands out from the body; tufted ears; a heavy brow; and facial hair that grows in "sideburns." The tail varies in length and may be long and brushlike, although only short-tailed cats are eligible for showing. A shorthaired variation of the Pixiebob (see p. 166) creates much the same wildcat illusion. The founding father of this breed was an exceptionally tall, bobtailed tabby that bred with an ordinary domestic female cat and sired bobtailed kittens with a special look—one of them, christened "Pixie," passed her name to the breed. Powerfully built, with a swaggering air, Pixiebobs are active and athletic. However, they are also relaxed and sociable cats that take happily to family life, enjoy playing with older children, and they are usually tolerant of other pets. Pixiebobs like being with people and many enjoy outdoor walks on a leash.

Brown-spotted tabby markings muted by ticking

Short tail

Slightly rounded ear tips with small tufts

Small spots on coat merge together along spine

Large, polydactyl paws

EXTRA TOES

Cats usually have five toes on their front paws and four on the back. In Pixiebobs, the paws often have extra toes—a naturally occurring genetic mutation known as polydactyly. In other cat breeds, the characteristic is regarded as a fault for showing purposes. However, it is so common in the Pixiebob that the standard for the breed permits cats to have up to seven toes on each paw. Polydactyly is most likely to occur on the front paws.

KITTEN

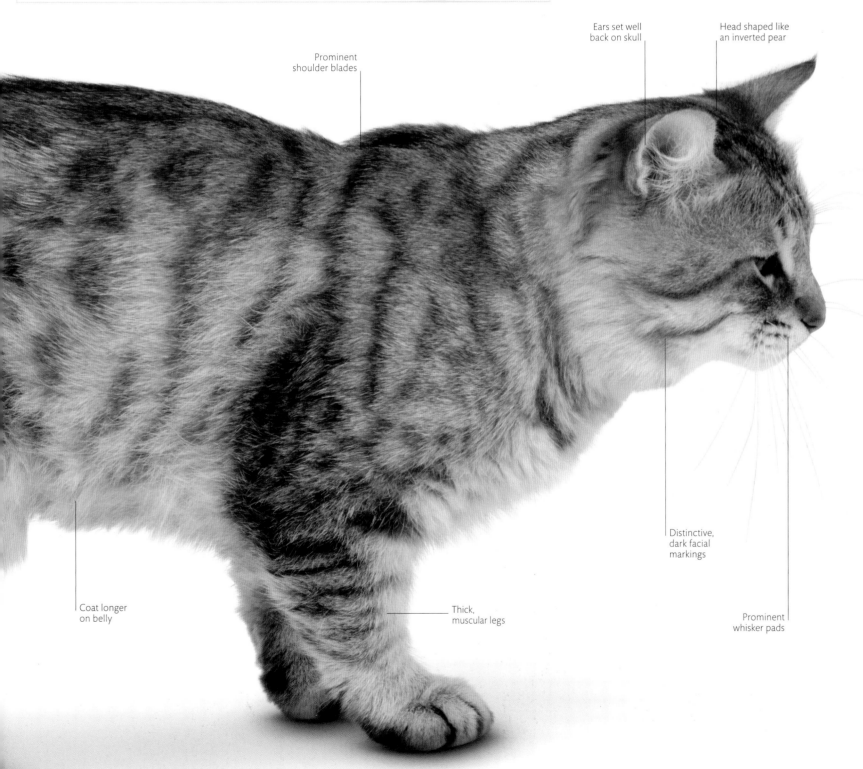

Ears set well
back on skull

Head shaped like
an inverted pear

Prominent
shoulder blades

Distinctive,
dark facial
markings

Coat longer
on belly

Thick,
muscular legs

Prominent
whisker pads

Cymric

ORIGIN North America, 1960s
BREED REGISTRIES FIFe, TICA
WEIGHT RANGE 8–12lb (3.5–5.5kg)

GROOMING 2-3 times a week
COLORS AND PATTERNS All colors, shades, and patterns.

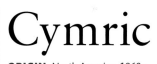

An excellent family companion, this calm and intelligent cat can easily be persuaded to play.

Developed in Canada, the Cymric is a long-coated variant of the tailless Manx (see pp.164–65). Sturdy and round-bodied, the breed, which is sometimes referred to as the Longhaired Manx, differs from its relative only in the length of its silky coat. Muscular hindquarters and long hind legs give the Cymric a powerful jump—it can spring up onto high places with ease. Cymrics have an affectionate nature, frequently forming close attachments to their human family. They make intelligent and entertaining companions and appreciate plenty of attention from their owners.

Thick breeches on hind legs

Coat shorter on lower legs

Ruff around neck extends to shoulders

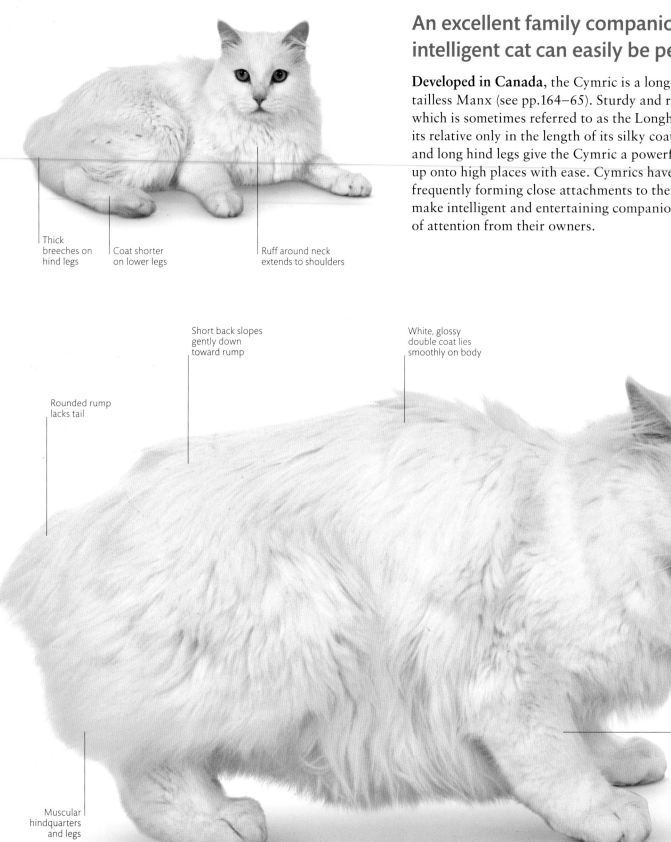

Short back slopes gently down toward rump

White, glossy double coat lies smoothly on body

Large, round eyes slightly angled

Rounded rump lacks tail

Prominent whisker pads

Sturdy forelegs shorter than hind legs

Muscular hindquarters and legs

American Bobtail

ORIGIN US, 1960s
BREED REGISTRIES CFA, TICA
WEIGHT RANGE 7–15lb (3–7kg)

GROOMING 2–3 times a week
COLORS AND PATTERNS All colors, shades, and patterns.

This wildcat look-alike has a home-loving personality, is affectionate and loving, but not too demanding on its owner.

According to a widely accepted opinion, the origins of this true native American cat can be traced to the naturally short-tailed, feral cats found free-roaming in various US states. The breed also has a short-coated cousin (see p.163). The large, powerfully built Bobtail longhair has the alert air of a wildcat, but it is entirely benign and a good family pet. It is renowned for being tolerant of children and staying calm and friendly even with strangers. The Bobtail's long coat does not mat, so moderate grooming is all that is required.

Large, deep-set, almost almond-shaped eyes

Chocolate-spotted tabby coat

Short, slightly curved tail

Distinct brow above eyes

Non-matting, easy-to-groom, classic brown tabby coat

Well-built, muscular body

Alert "wildcat" expression

Hips as wide as chest

Prominent whisker pads

Legs substantially boned

Selkirk Rex

ORIGIN US, 1980s
BREED REGISTRIES CFA, TICA
WEIGHT RANGE 8–11lb (3.5–5kg)

GROOMING 2–3 times a week
COLORS AND PATTERNS All colors, shades, and patterns.

This easygoing and patient breed's wild curly coat and endearingly huggable personality make it a lovable pet.

The breed originated with an odd curly-coated female kitten, discovered among an otherwise normal litter in an animal rescue center in Montana. Adopted as something of a curiosity, this cat went on to produce curly offspring and lay the foundations for the Selkirk Rex. Through planned matings with both Persians and short-coated breeds, longhaired and

shorthaired (pp. 174–75) lines were developed. These sweet-tempered, placid cats are almost irresistibly cuddly, and fortunately they are very happy to accept attention. Regular grooming of the Selkirk Rex longhair is essential, but owners should avoid overly vigorous brushing, since this can straighten the curls.

Nose has well-defined stop

Round-cheeked, broad head

Brittle curly whiskers

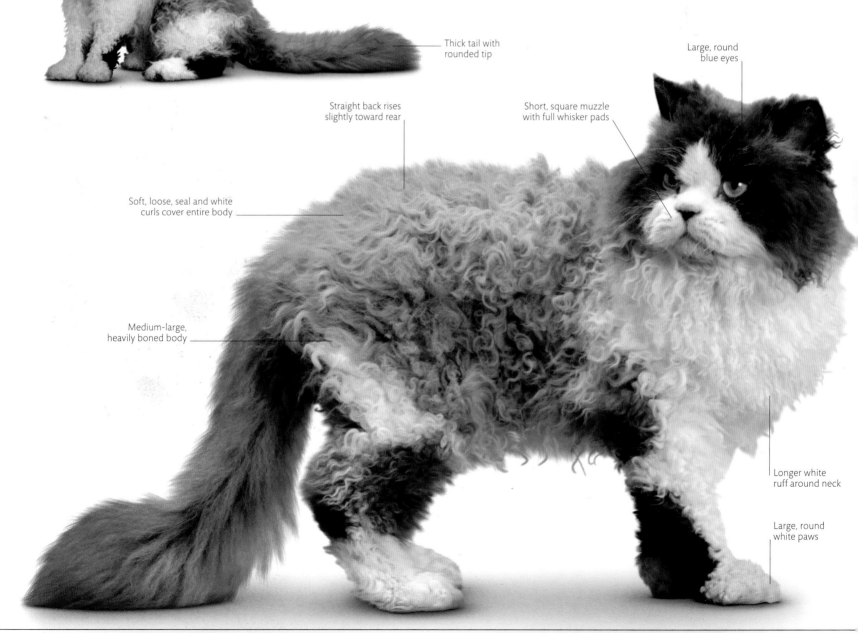

Thick tail with rounded tip

Large, round blue eyes

Straight back rises slightly toward rear

Short, square muzzle with full whisker pads

Soft, loose, seal and white curls cover entire body

Medium-large, heavily boned body

Longer white ruff around neck

Large, round white paws

Ural Rex

ORIGIN Russia, 1940s
BREED REGISTRIES Other
WEIGHT RANGE 8–15lb (3.5–7kg)

GROOMING 2–3 times a week
COLORS AND PATTERNS Various colors and patterns, including tabby.

This little-known breed with a cheerful and balanced temperament is said to be quiet and good with families.

Although this cat was not generally recognized until fairly late in the 20th century, it is possibly one of the oldest of the rex breeds and is thought to have been in existence in the Ural region of Russia since the late 1940s. The Ural Rex longhair has a medium-long coat that falls in waves over its entire body. This rare cat comes in a shorter-haired version (see p. 172), which is also far from common. As test breeding has shown, the genetic mutation responsible for the Ural Rex's wavy coat appears to be very different from that found in other, better-known, rex cats, such as the Cornish Rex (see pp. 176–77) and Devon Rex (see pp. 178–79).

Large, slanted, oval eyes

Slender, relatively short muscular body

Oval white paws

Short, broad, wedge-shaped head

Ears have rounded tips

Pronounced cheekbones

Tail tapers to rounded tip

Semi-long chocolate coat lies in loose, elastic waves

Slim legs

DESPITE BEING ONE OF THE **OLDEST REX BREEDS,** IT IS STILL ONE OF THE **LEAST WELL-KNOWN.**

LaPerm

ORIGIN US, 1980s
BREED REGISTRIES CFA, TICA
WEIGHT RANGE 8–11lb (3.5–5kg)

GROOMING 2–3 times a week
COLORS AND PATTERNS All colors, shades, and patterns.

This clever, captivating cat is gentle and affectionate and adores human company, making it an ideal family pet.

An ordinary farm cat in Oregon in 1982 produced the original curly-coated kitten that led to the development of the LaPerm. This cat bred naturally with other cats on the farm, and more curly-coated offspring appeared. Cat breeders then started to take an interest in the unusual coats, and a new breed was born. The coat of this shaggy but graceful cat varies considerably from soft waves to bouncy, corkscrew curls.

There is also a shorthaired version (see p. 173). Long-legged and agile, LaPerms are active cats, but will readily accommodate their owners by switching from playing games to purring on a lap. The breed is gratifyingly responsive to affection and welcomes being fussed over. Its long, strokable, curly coat is not difficult to groom, since it has very little undercoat to shed or mat. Regular combing is the best way to keep the curls in good order.

KITTEN

WHISKERS AND CURLS

The bouncy texture of the LaPerm's fur is created by the shape of the curls and a mixture of three hair types: the soft down hairs of the undercoat; intermediate fawn hairs; and longer guard hairs, which form the topcoat. The tightest ringlets appear on the neck, ruff, and along the plumy tail. The LaPerm is unique among cats with rex (curly) coats in having very long whiskers; in other rex breeds, the whiskers are short and brittle.

Large, cupped ears with tufts

Almond-shaped, gold eyes

Nose has slight dip

Springy curls on lilac coat are soft and light to the touch

Prominent whisker pads with long, flexible whiskers

Broad muzzle

Curly plumes on tail

Longest, tightest curls occur in ruff

Medium-long legs

House cat—longhair

Regardless of their ancestry, these cats have undeniable glamour and are sought-after pets.

Nonpedigree cats with long hair are less common than their shorthaired counterparts. In some of them, the clues to their origins are obvious. A dense, woolly undercoat, stocky body, and a round, flattened face are likely to be inherited from a Persian. The ancestry of others remains a mystery in a confusion of variable coat lengths, mixed colors, and indeterminate patterns. Longhaired house cats rarely have the extravagantly thick coats seen in the show ring, but many of them are very beautiful.

Silver and white
Rarely seen in the domestic house cat, silver is the effect of a white coat tipped with darker color at the end of each hair. Depending on their degree of tipping, pedigree silver cats are sometimes known as chinchillas.

Faint tabby markings

Cream and white
Cream—a diluted form of red—is an unusual color in the average house cat. This one has "ghost" tabby markings, which cat fanciers try to eliminate in pedigrees by breeding only the very palest creams.

Red-and-white tabby
Most owners of a red tabby are likely to refer to their pet as a "ginger" cat. This color is much sought-after and can often be just as deep and rich in nonpedigree cats as it is in purebreds.

Greenish-gold eyes

Brownish tinge to ruff

Thick, medium-long hair on body

Black
Jet-black was among the first colors to be popular in longhairs. In random-bred cats there are likely to be slight tinges of brown or tabby pattern in the coat. Black coats may have a grayish or brownish hue.

Brown tabby
Long fur tends to blur tabby patterning. This cat has a semi-long coat marked with the pattern known as "classic" tabby, which on a shorter coat would appear as boldly defined, dark whorls.

Appealing mixture
A longhaired cat can be a show-stopper even without a pedigree. Many attractive house cats combine a medley of colors with long, lush fur, often the result of a Persian cross somewhere in their history.

CHAPTER 5

CARING FOR YOUR CAT

Preparing for arrival

Getting a new pet is a big event and all concerned are bound to feel a little anxious and excited. Make sure your house is ready for a cat or kitten. A little preparation will turn your home into a safe environment for the new arrival. Plan ahead and stay calm—most cats settle in very quickly and will soon act as if they own the place.

FIRST CONSIDERATIONS

Before making the decision to buy or adopt a cat, think carefully about how he will fit into your lifestyle. Bear in mind, too, that your responsibilities may be long-term—a cat can live for up to 20 years.

Can you give a cat daily attention? Most cats are relatively independent but some dislike being left alone all day. Never leave a cat unattended for more than 24 hours; in an emergency, make sure that someone is able to look in on him. If you regularly stay away from home, a cat may not be right for you.

Is a cat suitable for the whole family? Often, a cat that was not raised with young children will find living with them stressful; and if family members suffer from allergies or have restricted vision or mobility, a cat around the house is a potential hazard.

Do you want a kitten or an adult cat? Kittens need extra care and supervision, so be realistic about how much time you can allow for such things as litter-box training and feeding up to four times a day. If you take on an adult cat, his previous experiences will influence how well he fits into your home. For example, a cat that is unused to children or other pets could find living with them stressful. Rescue shelters that place adult cats do their best to avoid such mismatches.

Will your cat live indoors or outdoors? Keeping a cat inside is generally safer (see pp. 258–59), but few homes can provide all the stimulation that most cats require; adult cats that have always had access to the outside may not adapt well to an indoor lifestyle (see pp. 260–61). Cats are hunters, so if your cat goes outside you must accept that he might bring home prey. In the house, a cat inevitably sheds hairs everywhere and may leave claw marks on the furniture.

Would you prefer a quiet cat or a lively one? If you choose a pedigree, breed can indicate a cat's likely temperament, but a random-bred cat is more of an unknown quantity. In both cases, individual personality can be influenced by early life experiences and the temperaments of the cats' parent.

Do you want a male or female cat? Generally, neutered cats show little difference in behavior and temperament. Unneutered toms may roam and spray urine, while females in heat may be restless.

ESTABLISHING A ROUTINE

In order to allow your cat to settle in and make him feel secure, it is best to set out a routine in the early days. Once the cat has found his place in your house, he will develop his behavior patterns and routine around your family's daily schedule.

Try and plan your routine around regular activities such as grooming (see pp. 276–79), feeding (see pp. 270–73), and playtime (see pp. 284–85). Make sure this does not interfere with your other commitments,

OWNER RESPONSIBILITIES

- Providing food and clean water
- Meeting the cat's needs for companionship
- Offering a choice of resources, such as beds and litter boxes
- Providing enough stimulation to ensure the cat stays fit and happy
- Grooming (and bathing) when necessary
- Socializing kittens so that they are confident in any situation
- Seeking veterinary care when needed
- Microchipping the cat and fitting him with a quick-release safety collar and ID tag

Window on the world
Cats kept indoors from birth will rarely want to venture out because they see your home as their territory. However, to give your cat a breath of fresh air and exercise, install a catflap that he can use without your help.

A place in the sun
Provide your cat with plenty of spots in the yard to bask and doze. A gardening basket makes an ideal bed for a laid-back cat.

because you will need to be consistent for many months. Cats do not like change and get stressed if they are subjected to it frequently. This may result in behavioral problems and aggression. A regular routine will also help you observe any changes in your cat's behavior and health (see pp. 300–01). Predictability means safety to your cat.

It will help to decide the mealtimes for your cat at the outset. Always make sure to put the food and water bowls in the same place. This will help you check his appetite. You will get to know when he is hungry, which in turn will prove useful for training.

Cats do not particularly enjoy grooming, but they will tolerate it if they know it is only for a short duration. If your cat needs regular grooming, aim to do this at the same time each day. Grooming just before feeding or playtime will act as an incentive for your cat to be nearby and to cooperate with the process.

Having a fixed time for play will give your cat something to look forward to and reduce the likelihood of him going crazy and running around the house looking for attention. Ensure that the playtime activity is a worthwhile experience for your pet. Plan it in a way that you add in plenty of variety and devote sufficient time solely to your cat.

BECOME CAT-AWARE

Cats are inquisitive and athletic, and you should take this into account when evaluating your home. If you regularly leave doors and windows open, assess whether your cat could escape through them or enter areas you want to keep cat-free. Also, start looking behind you when going through a door, since a cat can easily slip through a gap at your feet. Close the doors of washing machines and dryers when not in use, and always check the whereabouts of your cat before turning on the machines.

SAFETY INDOORS

Cats love climbing, so remove breakable or valuable objects from low tables or shelves. Be aware of possible pathways that would allow your cat to reach high shelves or work surfaces, and move furniture accordingly. Stools, standing lamps, wall hangings, and curtains are all scalable to a cat. Consider temporarily putting double-sided tape, plastic sheeting, or aluminum foil around the edges of furniture you want to remain off limits until your cat learns to leave them alone; cats dislike the textures and will avoid them. Climbing and scratching are entirely natural behaviors for a cat, so make sure you provide outlets for these

activities, such as a scratching post and something safe for him to climb on. Beware of leaving small objects lying around: cats can swallow or choke on things such as toys, bottle caps, pen lids, and erasers. Tuck away wiring on electrical appliances and pull up dangling cords so that your cat cannot drag a lamp or iron on to himself.

SAFETY OUTDOORS

After assessing your home, conduct a "safety audit" of your yard (see pp. 260–61). Remove sharp, potentially harmful objects and prevent access to sheds and greenhouses. Even if you try to secure your yard from animal intruders, you will always have some "visitors." Foxes are usually wary of mature cats and their claws, but they may harm kittens. Snakes are an issue in some places, mainly because cats prey on them and sometimes get bitten in the process. There are cat-friendly snake-repellent products on the market. Always examine your pet carefully after a fight with a neighborhood cat, in case he has injuries that need a vet's attention. In urban areas, the greatest threat will be from traffic, so do your best to prevent your cat from being able to reach the road.

Naturally curious
Cats will inspect and explore whatever and wherever they can. Make sure cupboards cannot be entered, and always put away sharp knives, scissors, pins, and tacks.

Living indoors

If you decide that the indoor life will best provide your cat with long-term security and happiness, you must take stock of your home surroundings and lifestyle. While you cannot make a house completely cat-proof, you will need to take certain precautions. You must also be prepared to organize your cat's exercise and entertainment.

INDOOR CATS

Your cat is likely to live longer and face fewer hazards if he is kept indoors rather than allowed to roam outside (see pp. 260–61). However, indoor life is not entirely problem-free; it will be your responsibility to keep your cat safe, happy, and active.

If you are out at work all day, your cat will need a regular playtime (see pp. 284–85) or, better still, a companion. Bored cats grow frustrated and stressed and will constantly pester you for attention when you get home. Without enough exercise, indoor cats can become overweight and unhealthy, and stress may manifest itself in unwanted behavior (see opposite).

HAZARDS IN THE HOME

Cats left alone in the house usually sleep a great deal of the time, but in their wakeful periods they may amuse themselves by going exploring. Make sure that nothing likely to be investigated by an inquisitive cat can cause any harm.

Most potential dangers to your cat are found in the kitchen. Never leave anything unattended that your cat could jump on or knock over, such as a switched-on burner, an iron, or sharp utensils. Keep the doors of washing machines or dryers closed (but first make sure your cat is not inside), and double-check before you switch on the appliance.

Cats are less inclined than dogs to steal food, raid the garbage bin, or chew up forbidden items such as electric cords, but they still need to be protected from substances that could make them sick. Keep them away from wet paint and chemical cleaners, which are easily transferred from walls and floors to fur, and then licked off and swallowed. Check that there are no dangers lurking in the carpet, such as thumbtacks, needles, or shards of broken glass or china.

Keep small pet animals and birds out of temptation's way, especially while you are out. A predatory cat may not be able to resist harassing the occupants of a hamster cage or investigating a fish bowl, causing damage and distress for all concerned.

INDOOR PLANTS

Many common indoor plants, including lilies, geraniums, cyclamen, and various potted bulbs such as daffodils, are toxic to cats if eaten. Keep houseplants off the floor and low tables, and cover the soil in the pot with chippings or pebbles to discourage digging. If your cat likes to nibble your houseplants, buy him his own special cat grass from a pet store or garden center—or grow it yourself from seed—and place it away from other plants. If all else fails, you could try spraying around houseplants with a citrus-scented cat repellent.

CALL OF THE OUTDOORS

Despite their natural instincts, most cats kept indoors from birth will rarely want to venture out because they see your home as their territory. Once they get a taste for going

Window screens
Installing a window screen will enable you to leave windows open for ventilation, safe in the knowledge that your cat cannot jump or fall out.

INDOOR CHECKLIST

■ Never leave heated kitchen appliances, such as stovetops and irons, unattended
■ Do not leave sharp utensils and breakables within the cat's reach
■ Shut the doors of cupboards and appliances such as washing machines and dryers
■ Keep your cat away from wet paint or surfaces wet with cleaning chemicals
■ Protect open fires with a guard
■ Ensure that your cat cannot jump out of upper-floor windows
■ Do not place toxic houseplants where your cat could eat or brush against them

KITTENS WILL EXPLORE HOUSEHOLD PLANTS

Household chemicals
Keep household chemicals securely shut away in places your cat cannot reach. Mop up spills right away. Also check whether any products are toxic to cats—for example, carpet cleaners and insect control sprays.

KEEPING ACTIVE

Physical and mental activity is vital for your cat's health. If he lives permanently indoors, you will have to organize this for him.

Indoor cats need space to play, so they should have access to several rooms if possible, especially if you have more than one cat—like us, cats need "personal space." To give your cat a breath of fresh air you could screen off a porch, patio, or balcony that he can access through a catflap (see p. 261). If you live in an apartment, consider allowing your cat out into the hallway for a run-around game. First check that all doors leading to the outside are closed.

Even a cat that spends his life indoors will retain his natural instinct to stalk and catch prey. Without an outlet for his hunting instinct, a cat may turn to "catching" and

out, however, they may want to do it more frequently and take any chance to escape. If so, you will have to be vigilant about closing windows and doors. Be extra careful in a high-rise apartment—despite their balance and agility, cats have died after falling from an open window or jumping over a balcony while chasing birds or insects.

chewing household objects. To prevent this, give him plenty of interesting toys to play with (see pp. 284–85). Toys that allow you to interact with your cat are just as important as those that will keep him occupied when you are out. Set aside some time each day to give your cat your undivided attention.

UNWANTED BEHAVIOR

Other types of "outdoor" behavior can be a problem in the home. A cat scratches to stretch and keep its claws healthy (see p. 278) and also to make visual and scented territorial markings. To prevent your sofa from being used as a substitute for a tree or a fence, buy a scratching post (see p. 263) or mat to satisfy your cat's natural need.

Indoor cats may also exhibit stress-related behavior such as biting, spraying, or inappropriate urinating (see pp. 290–91). Pheromone therapy in the form of a spray or plug-in dispenser uses a synthetic version of natural feline pheromones that may reduce the anxiety that leads to such problems.

Keeping company
If you are away from home during the day, getting two cats might be a good idea. If introduced to each other at an early age, cats may enjoy each other's company.

Going outdoors

Cats are independent and prefer to live on their own terms. But as an owner it is your responsibility to decide whether your cat can be allowed to roam outdoors. There are hazards on the far side of the catflap, such as traffic and other animals, that you can do little to protect your cat from once he is out there on his own. What you can do is try to make territory close to home as safe and inviting as possible.

CALL OF THE WILD

Domestic cats were once wild animals, adapted to living and roaming in open spaces. Many of their wild instincts remain, but the world that cats inhabit has changed dramatically. Many cat owners live in urban environments, surrounded by busy roads, buildings, people, and other animals, and an outdoor cat will have to contend with all these hazards. So should you allow your cat to go outdoors as and when he pleases?

Take your pet's personality into account when deciding on the limits of his freedom. Confining an active and inquisitive cat indoors can lead to havoc in the house, but on the other hand you must consider the greater risks outdoors. Not all cats develop good road sense, and some will inevitably fall victim to passing cars. If you let your

Natural behavior
Allowing your cat freedom to roam means he will have no restraints on his natural instincts, which will probably include stalking and killing small rodents and birds.

cat go out after dark, buy him a collar with reflective patches that can be picked up in vehicle headlights. Cats are naturally more active at dawn or dusk—which are often the peak rush hour periods on the roads. Try to keep your cat indoors at these times.

Given his freedom, your cat is likely to roam beyond your yard. This leaves him vulnerable to encounters with other cats, wild animals, and possibly even cat thieves.

CREATING A BACKYARD SANCTUARY

High fencing could deter your cat from wandering, but it is an expensive option. The best way to keep an outdoor cat close to home is to make your yard a cat-friendly sanctuary. Plant bushes to provide shade and shelter as well as a few scented plants that cats love—such as catnip, mint, valerian, heather, and lemongrass—in sunny places for your cat to bask among. If you habitually spray your grass and plants with chemicals, leave an untreated clump of cat grass for your pet to snack on.

Make the yard as safe as possible for wildlife, too. Attach a bell to your cat's collar to warn birds and other creatures of

Border patrol
Cats like to take up elevated positions from which they can view their territory. Shed roofs, fence posts, and walls are ideal lookout points.

his presence. Bird tables and scattered food are a magnet for predators, so ensure that all bird feeders are placed out of reach of the most determined cat.

TERRITORIAL DISPUTES

Once your yard is cat-friendly, it will undoubtedly attract other cats. Feline disputes are certain to break out because cats are territorial animals. Make sure your cat is neutered; this reduces aggression among tomcats and avoids constant pregnancies among females. Neutered cats need smaller territories, but that will not stop your cat from straying or an unneutered feral tom from invading your cat's territory and picking a fight. Make sure that your cat is immunized against common diseases, because fights inevitably lead to bites and scratches that can become infected.

RESPECTING THE NEIGHBORS

Appreciate that not all of your neighbors are cat lovers. Some people are allergic to cats and go to great lengths to avoid them. Even the best-trained cats have bad habits—they dig up flowerbeds to defecate, chew on plants, spray, rip open garbage bags, chase birds, and wander into other homes uninvited. If your cat has been neutered, there is at least the advantage that neutered cats bury their droppings and their urine is less smelly.

HAZARDS IN THE GARDEN

While cats rarely nibble anything but grass, it is wise to find out whether your yard contains any toxic plants. Be cautious where

Solitary nature
Domestic cats have retained much of the solitary nature of their wild ancestors. There is likely to be conflict if your cat crosses paths with other cats in his own or a neighboring yard.

you put down common toxins such as slug bait and rodent poisons. While some products are formulated to be safe for use with pets, others can be lethal. You should ensure that your cat does not come into contact with or try to eat the remains of animals that have ingested poison.

Ponds and wading pools are also potential hazards, especially for young kittens. Until a kitten knows his way around, allow him out only under careful supervision. As a precaution, cover fishponds with netting—which will also

stop older cats from poaching fish—and empty out wading pools when not in use.

Keep shed and garage doors shut to prevent your cat from coming into contact with chemicals and sharp tools. Make sure that you do not accidentally shut your cat in, too.

If you have a greenhouse in your yard, you should keep it closed at all times. A cat trapped inside is at risk of heatstroke (see p. 304).

Do not forget to protect your yard against the cat. Children's sandpits and soft soil make inviting litter trays, so cover up the sandpit and scatter cat deterrents around precious plants.

CATFLAPS

A catflap is a handy way to allow your cat freedom of movement between your house and the outside. Cats will quickly learn to use a flap once they have been shown how it works. Install a catflap that recognizes your cat's microchip (see p. 269) or a magnet on your cat's collar, to prevent other cats from entering your home. All catflaps should be lockable—for when you go on vacation, and also if you want to keep your cat indoors, such as at dawn, dusk, and evenings when there are firework displays.

OUTDOOR HAZARDS

■ Cats with white coats or patches of white can be susceptible to sunburn, especially on the nose, eyelids, and tips of the ears. As in humans, persistent sunburn can lead to the development of skin cancers, so keep your pet's sensitive areas covered with a sunblock formulated for cats.

■ Shut your cat indoors during firework displays and mask the noise with music. Let your cat hide if he wants to. Do not reassure him, since this may be taken as a sign that you are afraid, too.

■ Other cats and sometimes dogs may be threats to your cat. Fox attacks on cats are occasionally reported but are relatively uncommon. In some regions, venomous snakes can be a danger.

SUNBURN (WHITE CATS)   FIREWORKS   OTHER CATS   FOXES   SNAKES

Essential equipment

If you are a new cat owner, you will need to buy a certain amount of equipment for your pet's comfort and well-being. These items include a bed, litter box, and feeding bowls. You may be tempted by the latest designer cat accessories but think first about whether your pet really needs them. Start with good-quality basic items that are within your budget, since the initial outlay on your cat will soon mount up. You can indulge in more sophisticated products later on.

COMFORT FIRST

Cats are good at making themselves comfortable and have an unerring eye for the best places to curl up in and snooze. They are more than willing to share your favorite armchair or pillows, or the comforter on your bed, if that is permitted. Most people delight in seeing their cat make free use of the home—and will be prepared to forgive the nest made in a pile of newly laundered towels. However, cats do need a safe and special bed that is indisputably their own territory.

There is a wide range of cat beds on the market, from baskets and roofed-in tent-style beds to bean bags and hammocks.

From an owner's point of view, whether the bed looks attractive and is easy to wash may be priorities. From your cat's point of view, soft fabrics that generate warmth—such as fleece—are desirable, as are beds with soft sides to snuggle up against. Cats usually prefer to sleep somewhere fairly compact that gives them a sense of wraparound security.

FOOD AND WATER BOWLS

Your cat needs separate bowls for food and water, and if you have more than one cat each should have his own set. Bowls can be plastic, ceramic, or metal, and should be stable enough not to tip over if stepped on. They should not be too deep and must be wider than the cat's whiskers. Wash bowls at least once a day and remove any leftover "wet" food after the cat has finished eating. There are also automatic feeding stations available that operate on a timer. These have a lid that prevents the food from becoming stale and flips open at your cat's mealtime—a useful asset if you are going out and don't want to break the cat's routine.

LITTER BOXES

A cat likes a litter box to himself, so more than one cat means more than one box. Open, covered, manual, automatic, and self-cleaning boxes are all available. Whichever type you choose should be fairly large and have sides high enough to prevent spills when the cat scrapes the litter around. Litter materials made of clay or absorbent biodegradable pellets are the most convenient to use because when wet they form clumps that are easy to scoop up. You may have to experiment with various materials to find the type your cat prefers. Litter deodorizers help to prevent odors, but avoid using scented products, since these may deter a cat from using the box.

Cats can pick up infections from prey, so pregnant women should not handle litter to prevent passing toxoplasmosis to her unborn child.

Hanging around
A hammock-style bed suspended from a radiator or mounted on the wall provides your cat with a cozy, draft-free retreat. It also has cat appeal as a good vantage point from which to survey the room.

Tagged for security
A collar with a snap fastening is a must for an outdoor cat. Your ID can be sealed in a pendant cylinder or engraved on a disk. To help protect birds, add a bell to the collar to give warning of your cat's approach.

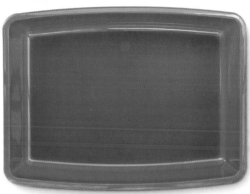

Sleeping in style
A tent bed, or "igloo" (top), keeps out drafts and gives your cat the security of a roof over his head. Soft fabric, basket-style beds (above) are good for snuggling into; check that the material is easy to wash.

Litter requirements
Cats can be fussy about litter boxes and materials, so finding the types to meet both your cat's approval and your requirements for cleaning may involve some trial and error. A plastic scoop is useful for removing soiled litter.

Choosing a bowl
There are many cat bowls to choose from. Those with shallow sides are the most comfortable for your cat to use. A rubber base can help stop the bowl from sliding around the floor while your cat is eating.

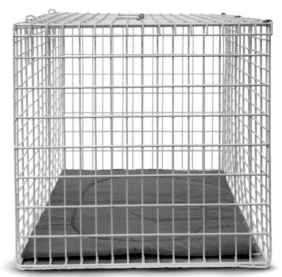

COLLARS AND MICROCHIPS

It is important to get your cat tagged with a microchip, so that he can be identified if he strays. These devices, the size of a rice grain, are inserted by a vet under the loose skin at the back of the neck. Each chip has a unique number that can be detected by a scanner. All outdoor cats should also have a collar with an ID tag giving your contact details. The collar must be loose enough to slip two fingers underneath and have a quick-release snap that tugs open if the collar becomes snagged. Collars with elastic inserts are unsafe because they may stretch enough to become stuck around the head or a leg.

SCRATCHING POSTS

Providing a place for your cat to scratch is essential if you don't want your furniture or carpets ruined. Cats need to scratch every day to help wear away the outer sheaths of their claws and to mark their territory. Scratching posts usually comprise a flat, rough-carpeted base and an upright post covered in coiled rope, often topped by a carpeted platform. Locate the post close to where your cat usually sleeps, since cats do most of their stretching and scratching immediately after waking up.

CARRIERS

A cat carrier is the safest way to transport your cat. Whether it is made of plastic, wire, or traditional basketwork, it must be large enough for your cat to turn around in. A familiar-smelling blanket or pillow can be put inside to keep him comfortable. To get your cat used to going in a carrier, leave it somewhere accessible and encourage him to use it as a refuge. If he regards the carrier as a safe place he will be happier to travel in it, even if journeys usually end at the vet.

Safe transportation
A carrier must be easy for your cat to enter and exit. Most cats object to being confined, so it is important to choose a carrier with a wide grid opening. Your cat may travel better in a cage, which lets him see out all the way around, although this may require a large car for transport.

First days

When a new cat arrives in your home, you will want him to feel comfortable as soon as possible. Naturally, everyone involved is going to be excited, especially any children in the house, but with a little advance planning you can keep the occasion calm and stress-free. Most cats soon adapt to new surroundings and settle down in a remarkably short time.

THINKING AHEAD

In the days before you bring your cat home, check the house and yard for obvious hazards (see pp. 258–59 and pp. 260–61). Think about both his immediate and future needs. For example, rather than stocking up on one kind of cat food, buy several varieties so that you can find out what he likes best.

Plan his arrival on a day when your house is likely to be calm and quiet, so that you can give him all your attention. If you have children and this is their first pet, make it clear that a cat is not a toy that can be played with whenever they want.

TRANSPORTING YOUR CAT

To travel safely, your cat needs a secure box or cat carrier. Reduce his anxiety by giving him a familiar piece of bedding with a smell he recognizes, and cover the carrier so that he can see only out of one end. Strap the carrier in the car with a seatbelt, or place it in a footwell to stop it from flying around.

WELCOME HOME

Begin by bringing your cat into the room where he will be spending his first few days. It is best to restrict him to one or two rooms until he has settled in and appears relaxed.

Check that any doors and windows are closed. If you already have other pets, make sure they are out of the way in another room. Put the carrier on the floor and open the door. Allow your cat to venture out in his own time; be patient, and do not try to remove him yourself. Curiosity will eventually get the better of him, and he will leave the carrier and start to explore.

Part of your cat's acclimatization involves introducing him to the essential elements of his new life: his basket, the litter box, feeding station, and scratching post. Make sure that these are in easily accessible places

Stepping out
Do not lift your cat from his carrier or start urging him to come out the moment you arrive home. Just leave the door open, keep family excitement to a minimum, and wait until the cat emerges in his own good time.

New and strange
Your cat will soon have the confidence to go exploring his new territory. Set the boundaries of where you can allow him to go and then let him choose his favorite corners.

but are away from busy areas of the house. It is best to start with the litter box—with any luck your cat will use it right away. If the litter box is in a separate room, make sure that he can always get to it. Feeding bowls should be put in a place where it is easy to clean up any spills.

MEETING THE RESIDENTS

It will be hard to keep small children away from something as exciting as a new cat or kitten. However, shouting and rushing around may frighten your cat, so make sure they understand this. Show them how to hold the cat correctly and let them stroke or cuddle him; if he looks unhappy, then be swift to intervene—a scratch could put a child off a new pet for a long while.

An older cat already in the household will almost certainly take a dim view of a stranger encroaching on his personal territory, although adult cats are less likely to be aggressive toward a kitten than to another adult cat. Never place litter boxes or food bowls side by side, and expect the resident and the newcomer to sort it out for themselves. Keep them apart to begin with but allow them to become accustomed to the other's scent by swapping food bowls or moving them into one another's rooms. After a week or so, introduce them, but do not leave them alone together until they at least tolerate one another.

Introductions between dogs and cats are not necessarily a problem. For the first few meetings, keep the dog on a leash and give the cat space to back off. Again, never leave the two alone until you are confident that the relationship is going to be peaceful. Small pets such as hamsters or rabbits are probably best not introduced at all but kept permanently out of the cat's sight and smell.

SETTING A ROUTINE

Start as you mean to go on by establishing some ground rules right from the beginning, especially about eating and sleeping. If you give your cat titbits, for example, he will always expect them, and if you let him sleep

on your bed "just this once" it will be hard to stop him from doing it again. Cats are creatures of habit, so setting a routine in the early days will help your cat or kitten to settle in and feel secure. Eventually, he will develop his own patterns of behavior around your daily schedule.

Base your routine around regular activities such as feeding, grooming, and playtime. You need to be consistent with this for some months, so make sure that it fits in with your own commitments and lifestyle. Constant change stresses cats and may cause behavioral problems such as chewing and biting, or clawing furniture. A regular routine also helps you to keep an eye on any changes in your cat's health and general well-being.

Fix regular mealtimes for your cat and always put his bowls in the same place. By doing this, you can monitor his feeding—and if you know when he is likely to want food, you can use his hunger as an aid to teaching such things as coming to call.

If your cat needs daily grooming, aim to do this at a regular time. Grooming may not be your cat's favorite activity, but if you always do it just before feeding or playtime it will give your cat an incentive to be near at hand and to cooperate with the process.

Having a regular playtime is also a good idea. It gives your cat something to look forward to and reduces the likelihood of "crazy time," when your cat rushes around the house or pesters everyone for attention. Make sure that playtime is a worthwhile experience with plenty of variety and a decent amount of time devoted solely to your cat.

Using a litter box
Most cats and kittens already know how to use a litter box by the time you bring them home. However, an unfamiliar litter box can cause a few setbacks in the early days, especially if your cat takes a dislike to a type of litter that feels strange to him.

Catnap
Young kittens need lots of sleep to recharge their batteries. A warm, soft bed will be comforting to a kitten in a new home away from the company of its mother and siblings.

First vet check-up

For the best possible start, take your new cat to a vet as soon as you can for a comprehensive check-up. This first visit is the time to have the protective vaccinations that will help to keep your pet safe from most serious feline infections. You can also speak to the vet about neutering and microchipping. Follow up the visit with annual health checks throughout your cat's life.

Before bringing a new cat home, look for a veterinary practice that is local to you. The breeder of your cat may be able to recommend one. Alternatively, consult friends, look at local newspaper and internet advertisements, or ask a local shelter or one of the cat breed organizations (see p. 64) for suggestions. Visiting local practices to find out how they are organized can be useful; check to see if they have arrangements that reduce stress for nervous pets, such as separate access and waiting areas for cats and dogs, and raised areas to place cat baskets.

THE FIRST VISIT

If you buy a pedigree kitten, he should have had his first vaccinations (see opposite) before you take him home at about 12 weeks. The breeder will give you the vaccination certificate, which you should show the vet on your initial visit. An early health check at the vet is still important. A cat adopted from a rescue shelter should ideally have had a vet examination. If not, arrange for him to have a full check-up as soon as you take ownership.

Going to the vet is stressful for most cats, because they encounter strange people and animals. Take your cat in a carrier, and keep its door facing you in the waiting room so that he can see you and be reassured.

At this first appointment the vet will assess your cat's general health by giving him a thorough all-over examination. If your kitten has not been vaccinated and is more than nine weeks old, he will be given his first vaccinations now.

Be ready with a list of questions, since the vet will be able to answer any questions on general cat care and offer advice on the control of common parasites such as worms, fleas, and mites. Now is also the right time to ask the vet about microchipping (see p. 263) and neutering, if these procedures have not already been performed.

Having your cat microchipped means that he can be easily identified if he strays or is involved in an accident.

NEUTERING

Vets usually recommend that kittens be neutered at around four months of age, before they reach sexual maturity. Neutering is a procedure performed under general anesthesic to remove the ovaries and uterus in females and the testicles in males. Aside from preventing unwanted litters, having your cat neutered has other benefits.

Thorough examination
During a routine check-up, the vet will examine your cat from head to tail, feeling for any tenderness or lumps. The vet will also listen to his heart and breathing, to ensure there are no irregularities.

Initial vaccinations
Cats should have their first vaccinations against infectious diseases, such as cat flu and feline leukemia, between 9 and 12 weeks of age, followed by annual boosters for the rest of their lives.

Unneutered males, or toms, often roam far from home and have the habit of spraying urine around their territory, even in the house, as a calling card to receptive females. These roving toms can be very aggressive. Unneutered females, or queens, are at risk of frequent pregnancies that can sap their general health, and when in heat they become agitated, calling constantly to attract males, which is stressful for cats and owners alike. After neutering, these sexual behaviors either disappear or never develop in the first place.

Neutering also reduces the chances of sexually transmitted infections being passed between cats, and it removes the risk of cancer of the reproductive organs.

After neutering, your kitten will stay at the vet for only a few hours and will usually recover within a few days. A female kitten may have a few stitches in the skin, or none at all. The vet will tell you whether the stitches are dissolvable—in which case they should gradually disappear—or whether they need to be removed, usually about 10 days after the operation.

VACCINATIONS
By having your cat immunized against infectious diseases that may be caught from the environment or from other cats, you can improve his chances of a long and healthy life. Vaccines work by stimulating the

Microchipping
A microchip is a tiny device, about the size of a rice grain. The vet inserts the microchip by injecting it under the skin at the back of the neck. At later visits, your vet can check with a microchip reader that it is in place and working.

immune system so that it is ready to put up a defense if exposed to an infection. All cats should be immunized against feline panleukopenia virus (FPV), feline calicivirus (FCV), and feline herpes virus (FHV). Cats at high risk for feline leukemia virus (FeLV), *Chlamydophila felis*, and rabies may also need immunization. Kittens have their first routine injections from around nine weeks old (12 weeks for rabies) and should have a full booster vaccination 12 months later (except for rabies).

FPV, caused by feline parvovirus, is also called feline infectious enteritis or feline distemper. It easily spreads between cats and attacks the white blood cells, weakening the immune system. If kittens are infected just before or after birth they may die or suffer brain damage.

FCV and FHV cause up to 90 percent of upper respiratory infections, or "cat flu." Even when they have recovered from the flu, cats may still carry the virus and pass it to others. Vaccination will not prevent the diseases, but it can make them less severe.

The potentially deadly feline leukemia virus (FeLV) is shed in saliva, other body fluids, and feces. Pregnant or nursing cats can pass it to their kittens. Some cats may overcome the virus, but it can take hold in kittens or in cats that are already sick. The virus attacks the immune system, destroying white blood cells, and may cause blood cancers such as lymphoma or leukemia. It may also destroy developing red blood cells, causing anemia.

The bacterium *Chlamydophila felis* mainly causes conjunctivitis, with sore, inflamed inner eyelids and excess tears. It can also cause mild cat flu. Vets may advise vaccination for cats living in groups. Rabies is a highly dangerous viral infection

UNPLANNED PREGNANCIES
If you do not plan to breed from your cat, neutering is essential. Unspayed females can produce up to three litters a year and you will be responsible for finding each kitten a home. Many unwanted kittens wind up in rescue shelters or are put down.

that can also be passed to humans. It is a global problem; only a few countries, such as the UK, are unaffected. The virus is transmitted in saliva, usually by a bite from an infected animal. Immunization against rabies is very effective.

One of the most lethal viruses to infect cats is feline infectious peritonitis (FIP). This usually fatal disease is an uncommon mutation of feline coronavirus, an infection that may cause only mild gastroenteritis, or no signs of illness at all. Protection is difficult to provide, as immunization against FIP can be given only to kittens over 16 weeks old, by which time many will already have been exposed to coronavirus infection. FIP is most likely to occur within breeding groups and among very young or old cats.

FOLLOW-UP VISITS
Most cats and kittens come through their initial check-up with a clean bill of health, but health issues inevitably arise over the years. Rather than waiting until things go wrong, book your pet an annual veterinary visit for booster vaccinations and a check-up so that potential problems can be identified and dealt with early on.

Food and feeding

A well-fed and well-nourished cat is a happy cat. Although the occasional mouse caught outside may supplement your cat's diet, he will rely on you almost exclusively for his food. And that reliance places great responsibility on you. Providing your cat with a healthy, balanced diet will help him to grow and develop as he should, and give him the best chance of living a long life, free of illness.

ESSENTIAL NUTRITION

Meat is the natural diet for cats. They eat meat because they cannot convert the fats and proteins found in vegetable matter into the amino acids and fatty acids necessary for their bodies to function properly and stay healthy. Meat protein contains everything they need plus an important amino acid that they cannot make—taurine. Insufficient taurine in a cat's diet can lead to blindness and heart disease. Taurine is added to all processed cat food. It is impaired by cooking, so if you cook your cat's food yourself, you will also need to provide him with a regular taurine supplement. Regardless of your own food preferences, you cannot turn your cat into a vegetarian without putting his health, and even his life, at risk. A feline digestive system is not designed to process large amounts of vegetable matter, although it is usual for cats to chew a little grass now and then.

Prey caught in the wild supplies not just meat protein but also essential fats, vitamins, minerals—such as calcium from bones—and fiber. Domestic cats are unlikely to have to hunt for their meals, and they are not natural scavengers, so they rely on us to supply the correct nutrients, whether in ready-made or home-cooked food. Cats are notoriously picky eaters, so you may have to experiment with different types, textures, and flavors of food before you hit on the ones that bring your pet hurrying to his feed bowl.

VITAMINS AND MICRONUTRIENTS

The vitamins needed for essential cat nutrition include D, K, E, B, and A (cats cannot manufacture vitamin A). They also need vitamin C, but intake of this vitamin should be monitored, as cats can develop bladder stones if they have too much. Cats also require certain micronutrients—for example, phosphorus, selenium, and sodium. Although these are only needed in tiny quantities, a lack of them can lead to serious health problems. A source of calcium is vital,

A healthy appetite
Your cat knows what he likes, but it is important that his favorite foods contain the right balance of nutrients to maintain good health.

DRY FOOD

WET FOOD

HOME-COOKED FOOD

Natural fiber
Cats need fiber in their diet, which should be supplied by correct feeding. In the wild, a cat will obtain the necessary fiber from prey.

Dry, wet, and home-cooked food
Dry food will not spoil, but wet food is more like a cat's natural diet. Homemade meals are freshest, but avoid single-protein diets.

too, as calcium only occurs in small quantities in meat. Most commercial cat food contains all of these essential vitamins and micronutrients.

TYPES OF FOOD
Supermarket shelves offer a huge selection of prepared cat food in almost every gourmet flavor imaginable. So which ones should you choose? Most commercial cat foods are complete foods, that is, they provide all necessary nutrients and do not need anything else added. However, some products may be labeled "complementary," in which case they need to be combined with other foods to provide balanced nutrition. Check the information on the package to be sure which type you are buying.

Most prepared cat food is described as "dry" or "wet." Dry food has been pressure-cooked and then dried. In some cases, it is sprayed with fat to make it palatable, but this may require preservatives to be added. Dry food usually includes antioxidants such as vitamin C and E, which are natural and beneficial to your cat. Although you should not give your cat dry food all the time, it does have some advantages. It can, for example, be left out during the day without spoiling. You may want to give dry food in the morning and reserve the wet food for the evening.

Wet food comes in airtight cans or pouches, so it does not need preservatives to keep it fresh. Although tasty, wet food is soft in texture, so it provides little resistance to keep teeth and gums healthy. If wet food is not eaten immediately, it will soon become unappealing to your cat.

HOME-COOKED FOOD
For home-cooked meals, use meat and fish that is fit for human consumption. Make sure it is well cooked to kill bacteria or parasites. Homemade meals are a good way of introducing cooked bones as a calcium source, but remove small, splintery bones and do not offer bones if your cat eats too quickly. The scraping action of bones keeps teeth in good shape; without them, your cat's teeth will require regular cleaning.

WATER
Your cat needs constant access to clean water, both indoors and outdoors, especially if his diet consists mostly of dry food. Water helps dilute the urine and is absorbed by fiber in the intestines. Keep water bowls apart from the feeding bowls to avoid any contamination from scattered food. You need to change the water daily, and remember in particular to check that water bowls left in the yard are not full of debris.

FOODS TO AVOID

■ Milk and cream can cause diarrhea, as most cats do not have the necessary enzymes to digest milk products. Special-formula "cat milk" is available.
■ Onions, garlic, and chives cause gastric upsets and may lead to anemia.
■ Grapes and raisins are thought to cause kidney damage.
■ The alkaloid theobromine in chocolate is highly toxic to cats.
■ Raw egg may contain the bacteria that causes food poisoning. Uncooked egg white disrupts vitamin B absorption, leading to skin problems.
■ Raw meat and fish may contain harmful enzymes and also cause fatal bacterial poisoning.
■ Small, splintery bones in cooked food can become lodged in the throat or farther down the digestive tract, causing blockage and tearing the intestinal lining.

Drinking water
Your cat needs constant access to clean water. Cats fed a dry-food diet will require more water than those given wet food. Always keep drinking water in the same place so that your cat can find it easily.

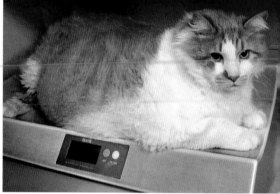

Eating the right amount
Your cat knows what he likes, but it is important that his favorite foods contain the right balance of nutrients to maintain good health. Make sure that your cat is eating the right quantity for his age and weight. If necessary, monitor his intake at regular intervals.

Weight watching
Almost overflowing the veterinary scales, this overindulged cat could be heading for serious health problems unless his weight is reduced by adjustments to his diet.

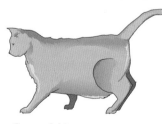

WHEN AND HOW MUCH TO FEED

Generally, your cat should be fed twice a day at regular times, usually once in the morning and once in the evening. This will allow him to build up an appetite and you to regulate how much he eats. Once you have established a regular feeding regime, it will be easy to tell if your cat has lost his appetite and is unwell. The feeding levels for your cat may need to be increased or decreased depending on your cat showing signs of being under- or overweight. As a guideline, you should be able to feel your cat's ribs easily but not see them (see panel, right). Make sure you never feed an adult cat food intended for kittens or dogs—kitten food contains too much protein and will be bad for an adult cat's kidneys; conversely, dog food does not contain enough protein for a cat. To prevent infections or health problems, make sure your cat's food and water bowls are always washed thoroughly after use.

THE RIGHT BALANCE

Cats enjoy variety, and it is important that they are fed a mix of different foodstuffs to ensure they get adequate nutrition. Make any changes to your cat's diet gradually, so that he can build up enough bacteria in his gut to digest the new food. Once you've found a varied and balanced diet that your

cat likes, stick to it. Constantly changing his food may encourage him to become a fussy eater. Cats can hold out for days until you give them what they want.

LIFE CHANGES

Cats have different nutritional needs at different times of life in terms of both type and quantity of food. Kittens need a high-protein diet to sustain their rapid development (see pp. 292–93), and there are many commercial brands of food

specially formulated for them. In their first few months, kittens should be fed smaller amounts at more frequent intervals than adult cats; four to six tiny meals a day would be the average for a kitten that has just started on solids. Later, you can increase the portions and reduce the number of meals. Initiate any new feeding regime in easy stages, because a rapid change can cause digestive upsets. To introduce a new foodstuff, replace 10 percent of the original food with the new food, increasing the

ASSESSING CONDITION

You cannot always judge by appearance alone whether a cat is too fat or too thin, especially if he is longhaired. Learn to assess his weight by the feel of his body, gently running your hands

around his back, ribs, and belly. A regular assessment of your cat's weight can be of great help in the long run. It allows you to take the necessary action to ensure the health of your pet.

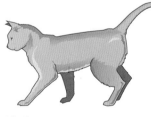

Underweight
There is little or no fat over the ribs, spine, and hip bones. The cat's belly is "tucked up," and there is a noticeable hollow behind the rib cage.

Ideal weight
The ribs can be felt through a thin layer of fat, and there is a slight narrowing of the body behind the rib cage. The belly has only a small covering of fat.

Overweight
The ribs and spine cannot be felt through a thick layer of fat. Heavy pads of fat cover the belly and there is no discernible "waistline" behind the rib cage.

DIET AND LIFESTYLE FEEDING GUIDE

Adult weight	4lb (2kg)	8½lb (4kg)	13lb (6kg)	22lb (10kg)	26lb (12kg)
Inactive lifestyle	100–140kcal (4oz [120g] wet/ 1oz [30g] dry)	200–280kcal (8oz [240g] wet/ 2oz [60g] dry)	300–420kcal (12oz [360g] wet/ 3oz [90g] dry)	400–560kcal (1 lb [480g] wet/ 4oz [120g] dry)	500–700kcal (1½ lb [600g] wet/ 5oz [150g] dry)
Active lifestyle	140–180kcal (6oz [160g] wet/ 1½oz [40g] dry)	280–360kcal (12oz [320g] wet/ 3oz [80g] dry)	420–540kcal (1 lb [480g] wet/ 4½oz [120g] dry)	560–720kcal (1½ lb [640g] wet/ 6oz [160g] dry)	700–900kcal (2 lb [800g] wet/ 7oz [200g] dry)
Pregnant female	200–280kcal (8oz [240g] wet/ 2oz [60g] dry)	400–560kcal (1 lb [480g] wet/ 4oz [120g] dry)	600–840kcal (1½ lb [720g] wet/ 6oz [180g] dry)	800–1,120kcal (2 lb [960g] wet/ 8oz [240g] dry)	1,000–1,400kcal (2½ lb [1,200g] wet/ 10oz [300g] dry)

proportion by 10 percent daily until your kitten is eating only the new food by the tenth day—this will prevent diarrhea. If he does get an upset stomach, revert to a higher proportion of the old food and take longer to make the switch.

Most adult cats in good health do well on two meals a day. However, as a cat ages, his appetite may diminish and you may need to revert to feeding him little and often again. The commercial cat food market caters to seniors just as it does to kittens.

A pregnant cat needs extra protein and vitamins, and will want to eat more in the final stages of pregnancy. This may mean giving her smaller portions more frequently if she cannot eat as much as usual in one meal. She will also have increased nutritional requirements when nursing.

A vet's advice is essential when controlling a cat's weight or if a special diet is required for a medical condition. You may also want to consult your vet on your cat's diet during a pregnancy and while she is nursing.

Food allergies in cats are rare, but when they occur the only way to find the cause is through a food-elimination trial supervised by your vet.

AN IDEAL WEIGHT

By checking your cat's weight and girth regularly, you will soon recognize if he is getting fat or becoming too thin (see panel, opposite). If you have any concerns, take your cat to the vet to be weighed.

It's mealtime
Regular mealtimes will allow you to know when your cat is likely to be hungry, which is the best time to attempt to teach your cat new tricks.

It is hard to refuse a cat who appears to be ready for a second helping, but overfeeding soon leads to obesity. Being overweight is just as unhealthy for cats as it is for humans. Appetite is not necessarily linked to a high-energy lifestyle; many inactive cats are capable of packing away enormous meals. Indoor cats have the highest risk of obesity—some types are naturally sedentary and need encouragment to climb down from the sofa now and then. Outdoor cats are more likely to burn up the energy they get from food.

Packaged foods give some guidelines on how much to feed, but the amounts suggested are only approximate. If your pet is becoming rotund, even though you are careful with portion sizes, suspect him of scrounging meals elsewhere. A conversation with the neighbors may solve the mystery.

Weight loss without a change in diet should never be ignored, since it can be an early sign of illness. Very elderly cats do tend to become thinner with age, but you should ensure that there are no underlying problems such as loose teeth. Have your cat checked by the vet if he is refusing food or has difficulty chewing.

GIVING TREATS

Whether given as rewards in training or to aid bonding with your cat, try to ration treats to keep your cat from gaining weight.

Treats are largely unnecessary, but if you do give them make sure that they make up no more than 10 percent of your cat's calorie intake and adjust meals accordingly. Some treats may give nutritional benefits, but others contain "filler" ingredients with little nutritional value and lots of fat.

Handling your cat

Cats are notoriously choosy about who they will allow to touch them, let alone pick them up and pet them. Some cats simply do not like being picked up at all, and will struggle to get free. There are right and wrong ways to handle a cat—learn how to do it correctly and the chances are your cat will enjoy the opportunity to get closer to you. If a cat is comfortable with being held, grooming and any necessary health checks will be made much easier.

START EARLY

The best time to get a cat used to being handled is when it is a kitten. Early and routine contact from about two or three weeks old helps kittens not only to develop faster but also to grow into more contented cats that are happy to be handled by humans. If you have children, teach them to be gentle. Mishandled kittens grow into nervous cats who keep their distance from people and never really learn to enjoy fussing and petting. Cats have long memories and will always avoid children who have handled them too roughly.

Some cats are simply less demonstrative than others, regardless of their early experiences. If your pet likes to maintain a friendly distance, respect his wishes.

Stress relief
There is something about cats that makes us want to stroke them. Research has shown that petting cats is good for reducing stress in humans—and fortunately most cats like it, too.

HOW TO PICK UP A CAT

Cats rarely enjoy being picked up, so only lift your cat when necessary, unless you are sure he welcomes it. Handle him calmly and quietly, stroking his head, back, and cheeks to relax him. If he wants to be put down again, he will make his feelings clear.

A very young kitten can be picked up by the scruff of his neck, like his mother does, but he will need more support as he gets older and heavier. When his mother stops picking him up like this, so should you. From then on, the correct way to pick up your cat will be to approach from the side and place one hand flat against his rib cage, just behind his front legs. Use the other hand to support him under his hind quarters. Hold him upright, as cradling him in your arms can increase his sense of insecurity.

DIFFERENT STROKES

Cats are more independent than most other pet animals and although many like stroking and cuddles, they still appreciate their own space. Do not try to stroke your cat unless he clearly shows that he is willing to be touched. Put out a hand or finger for him to sniff. If he touches you with his nose or rubs his cheek or body against you, he is in the mood for contact. If he shows no interest, leave it until another time.

Once your cat is amenable to being petted, begin by stroking him along his back in a slow, continuous motion. Always go from head to tail, never the other way against the direction of the fur. Stop when you reach the base of his tail. If your cat is enjoying it, he may arch his back to increase the pressure of your hand.

Learn how your cat likes to be petted. The top of the head, especially between and behind the ears, is often a favorite place.

It is thought that being stroked in this particular spot reminds cats of when their mother used to lick them there. Some cats also like being stroked under the chin. Rubbing the cheeks with a circular motion is popular with many cats, because it helps them spread their scent on to your fingers. Your cat may like being raked gently with the fingers, but do not stop and scratch him in one place. Most cats dislike being patted, especially along the flank.

When your cat jumps on to your lap and lies down, pet him once to see if he wants attention or just a warm place to snooze.

The right spot
Cats often respond with pleasure to having their heads scratched. Be slow and gentle and try to find the spot that your cat enjoys most.

Tactful handling
Hold your cat as upright as possible when you pick him up. Put one hand under his "armpits," place the other under his rear, and hold him securely. Do not cradle your cat on his back; this position is unnatural and will make him feel vulnerable and uneasy.

If he fidgets or his tail twitches, stop stroking. A cat that is enjoying being petted may change his position so that the part he wants stroking is uppermost and closest to your hand.

ROUGH AND TUMBLE

Some cats like rough play and will grab and "play bite" at a hand that tries to rub their belly. If your cat sinks his claws in, keep still until he disengages. Pushing farther in toward him may surprise him enough to let go. In general, when you stop, so will he. If he kicks with his back legs at your hand, do not assume that he wants his paws touched. Try stroking one foot lightly with a finger in the direction of his fur; if he pulls his foot away, flattens his ears, or walks off, let him be.

KNOWING WHEN TO STOP

Watch your cat's body language and stop petting him if he seems to be getting angry (pp. 280–81). One of the early warning signs that a cat is feeling ill at ease is lip-licking. Be careful if he is lying on his back exposing his belly, since this is not necessarily an invitation to pet, although he may tolerate you touching his head. Even in a normally docile cat, presenting the belly may be an aggressive defense posture that leaves him free to kick, bite, or claw.

If you misjudge his mood and are rewarded with a bite or a scratch that breaks the skin, wash the wound with soap and water and treat it with antiseptic. See your doctor if the area around the bite swells or reddens and starts oozing. Occasionally, infection acquired through a cat scratch can cause symptoms in other parts of the body and, uncommonly, a flulike illness.

APPROACH WITH CAUTION

Never try to pick up or pet a cat that does not know you. Give him time to sniff and investigate you, and try stroking him while talking in a calm tone. If he gets used to you being friendly he may let you handle him on further acquaintance. If he seems at all nervous, back off, since he may lash out.

Be especially cautious about attempting to pick up or even stroke feral cats (see pp. 20–21), however much you feel they are in need of affection. Although the most likely response of a feral cat to well-meant approaches from humans is to run off— unless perhaps food is involved—an animal that feels cornered or threatened may instinctively resort to aggression. In certain countries, a bite from a feral cat could carry the risk of infection with rabies.

Meeting and greeting
Your cat may actively seek out contact with you, especially if you have been out of the house for a time. Even if he is simply reminding you that it is dinnertime, accept his attentions as a compliment and reciprocate his greeting.

Grooming and hygiene

A clean coat is healthy and comfortable, and staying well-groomed comes naturally to cats. By giving your cat additional grooming—especially important if you own a longhaired breed—you can help him to look good and enjoy a bonding experience at the same time. To ensure your cat stays in peak condition, it is also important to give him assistance with basic hygiene, such as teeth cleaning and occasional bathing.

NATURAL CLEANING

Cats spend a large part of their day self-grooming. This is important to them because a sleek, conditioned coat is waterproof, keeps a cat warm, and protects the skin from infection.

Your cat will always groom himself in the same order. He begins by licking his lips and paws, then uses his wet paws to clean the sides of his head. The saliva removes the scent of recent meals, making him "odorless" to natural enemies that hunt by scent. Next, your cat will use his rough tongue to groom his front legs, shoulders, and sides. The surface of the tongue is covered in tiny hooks that can sweep up skin debris and loose hairs, as well as get rid of mats and smooth out tangles in the coat. The tongue also spreads the natural oils secreted by glands in the skin that condition and waterproof the coat. Your cat will nibble away any stubborn tangles using his small incisors. His flexible spine then allows him to attend to his anal region, back legs, and tail, working from its base to the tip. He uses his back paws like a wide-toothed comb to scratch his head. In fact, cats are so particular about daily grooming that it may not seem necessary to give them any extra help.

Neat and clean
Cats are naturally clean and spend much of their time methodically grooming themselves. They begin at the head and work down the body in an unvarying routine.

Basic grooming tools
Combs and bristle brushes remove tangles, and a slicker brush sweeps up loose hair and debris. Ask a professional for advice on the correct use of equipment such as tick removers and nail clippers.

TICK REMOVER

NAIL CLIPPERS   **SLICKER BRUSH**   **FINE COMB**   **SOFT-BRISTLED BRUSH**

GROOMING SESSIONS

Helping your cat maintain his coat is essential for several reasons. For a start, grooming sessions will enable you to maintain a close bond with your cat and also give you a chance to check his body for problems such as parasites, hidden injuries, lumps and bumps, and changes in weight. When you groom your cat, you will help reduce the amount of hair he swallows while grooming himself. This hair is usually coughed up as harmless fur balls, but some fur balls pass through the stomach and may become lodged in the intestine, causing serious problems. Cats become less efficient at grooming themselves as they get older, so elderly cats can benefit greatly from a helping hand. The sudden neglect of self-grooming in cats of any age is a warning sign that all is not well, and it should be investigated by a vet.

If you accustom your cat to grooming sessions from an early age, he will come to view you as a parent figure and enjoy the experience. Always begin a grooming session by stroking your cat and talking in a soothing voice to help him relax. Remember to be patient and on the lookout for signs that he is uncomfortable, such as a flicking tail or whiskers turning forward. In such cases, stop and try again later or the next

GROOMING A SHORTHAIRED CAT

Begin the session by loosening dead hairs and skin, drawing a fine-toothed metal comb from head to tail along the lie of your cat's coat. Take extra care when grooming around particularly sensitive areas such as the ears, the underside (armpits, belly, and groin), and the tail.

Remove the loosened debris by working over your cat's body with a slicker or soft-bristled brush, again drawn along the lie of the fur. For a super-sleek and shiny look, finish the grooming session by "polishing" the coat with a soft cloth such as a piece of silk or a chamois leather.

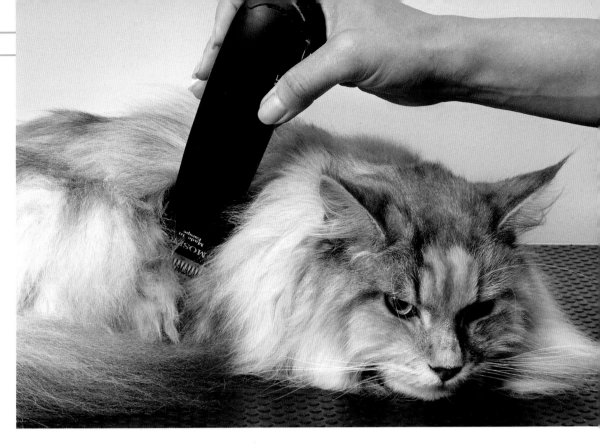

day. Make sure you also check his ears, eyes, nose, and teeth—and clean them if necessary; you may also need to clip his claws and give him a bath (see pp. 278–79). Always end a grooming session with praise and a treat.

COAT TYPES

In longhaired cats such as Persians, the undercoat can be massively thick. The coat not only collects debris from around the home and yard but tends to form tangles that no amount of licking can remove. Neglected tangles can easily turn into impenetrable mats, especially behind the ears and in parts of the body where there is friction, such as under the armpits, and in the groin area.

Even the most fastidious longhaired cats simply cannot keep a coat of this type in good order by their own efforts, so owners need to provide additional grooming. In extreme cases, there will be no option but to cut the matted hair away—a task that needs the skill of a professional groomer or a vet. Longhairs are also at greater risk than shorthairs of collecting large fur balls. If you own a longhaired cat, a daily grooming session is necessary (see below).

Semi-longhaired cats, which include Maine Coons (see pp. 214–15) and the Balinese (see pp. 206–07), have a silky topcoat and a minimal undercoat, so their fur remains free from tangling. Weekly brushing and combing is all that is required.

Some cats have fine, wavy, or rippled coats, as seen in the Cornish Rex (see pp. 176–77), and a few breeds sport longer curls. Such coats do not shed heavily and are not very difficult to maintain. Overly vigorous grooming can spoil the appearance of the fur, so bathing rather than brushing is often recommended for this type of cat. Shorthaired cats have a

topcoat of sleek guard hairs and a soft, downy undercoat of varying thickness. Although the undercoat may shed quite heavily, especially in warm weather, these cats are generally very easy to maintain. Grooming once a week is usually sufficient for shorthairs (see opposite).

Hairless cats such as the Sphynx (see pp. 168–69) are not usually entirely bald but have an overlay of fine fuzz. This thin covering is not enough to absorb the natural body oils that are secreted through the skin, so regular bathing is needed to prevent a greasy buildup that can be transferred to owners' clothes and furniture.

GROOMING A LONGHAIRED CAT

Begin by gently combing the cat through from head to tail with a wide-toothed comb, following the natural direction of the fur. Do not tug at knots or tangles—tease them out with your fingers, using unscented talcum powder formulated for cats. The powder will also absorb excess body oils.

Using a slicker brush with fine pins or a soft-bristled brush, work along the lie of the fur to collect the loosened hairs, skin debris, and any remaining talcum powder from both the topcoat and the undercoat. This will help to make the coat look full and shiny.

To end the grooming session, fluff up the coat with a brush or wide-toothed comb, and comb through long plumes on the tail. If your cat is a Persian, comb the neck fur up into a ruff. Ideally, to keep a longhaired coat in good condition, you should spend 15–30 minutes on this routine every day.

Extending the claws
When clipping your cat's claws, very gently press down on the bone just behind each claw with your finger. This will make the claw extend fully. If your cat is not in the mood and struggles, let him go and try again the next day.

TRIMMING THE CLAWS

Cats naturally keep their claws worn down by exercise, scratching, and climbing, and also by biting them. Indoor and especially older cats often do not get much claw-wearing exercise and are at risk of growing long claws that curl into the pads of the paws, causing discomfort. To prevent this, regularly check your cat's claws and cut them with clippers about every two weeks. To trim the claws, keep a firm hold on your cat and make sure you remove just the very tip of the claw. Any farther down and you might cut into the pink region, or "quick," and cause pain and bleeding—which will make your cat extremely resistant to having his claws clipped in future.

Accustom your cat to having his claws clipped from an early age. If you find the task too difficult, ask your vet to do it instead.

CLEANING THE FACE

The inside of your cat's ears should be clean and free of odor. Remove excess earwax with cotton or tissue. If you see dark, gritty specks in the ears, which indicate ear mites, or any discharge, take your cat to the vet. Damp cotton can also be used to clean around the eyes and nose. Mucus may collect in the corners of the eyes of long-muzzled cats, such as Siamese. Short-faced cats, such as Persians, often suffer from tear overflow, which leaves mahogany stains on the fur around the eyes. Consult your vet if you find any discharge from the eyes or nose, or prolonged redness of the eyes.

TEETH CLEANING

Brushing your cat's teeth once a week will give you the opportunity to check for signs of oral disorders. Problems that need the attention of your vet include discolored teeth, inflamed gums, and bad breath.

To clean the teeth, use a soft child's toothbrush or a specially made cat's toothbrush that fits over your finger. Alternatively, wrap your fingertip in gauze. Always use specifically formulated cat toothpastes; your cat will probably enjoy the meat-flavored ones. Never use a brand of toothpaste intended for humans.

Hold your cat's head firmly and gently lift his lips. Starting with the back teeth, brush each tooth carefully in a circular motion and massage the gums.

If your cat will not allow you to brush his teeth, ask your vet for oral antiseptics, which you apply directly to the cat's gums. Antiplaque solutions for cats are also available from pet stores or your vet. These products are simply added to your pet's

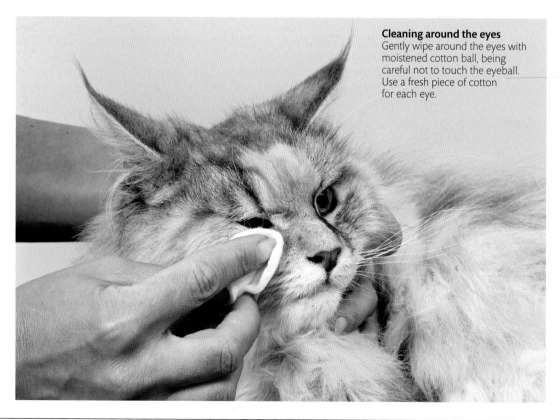

Cleaning around the eyes
Gently wipe around the eyes with moistened cotton ball, being careful not to touch the eyeball. Use a fresh piece of cotton for each eye.

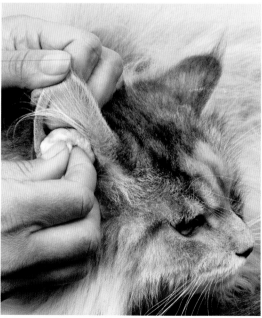

Cleaning the ears
Use a piece of cotton wool moistened with water or a cleaning solution formulated for cats to wipe carefully inside each ear. Use a fresh piece for each ear and never push anything into the cat's ear canal.

drinking water and have a palatable flavor. You will need to change the water and add fresh solution every day.

BATHING YOUR CAT

Outdoor cats occasionally give themselves a dust bath, in which they roll in dry dirt to clean their coat of grease and parasites, such as fleas. You can buy dry shampoos for cats, which work in a similar way. A shorthaired cat may need a wet bath if it becomes covered in oil or a pungent substance. A longhaired cat requires more regular bathing. Use only a shampoo made for cats, and keep it out of your pet's eyes, ears, nose, and mouth—especially if you are applying a medicated shampoo to treat a skin problem.

Few cats enjoy being bathed, and it is easier for both of you if you accustom your cat to the experience from an early age. You will need to be patient. Use soothing words throughout the session and give treats to your cat afterward as a reward.

CLEANING UNDER THE TAIL

All cats wash their anal area, but additional cleaning may be necessary, especially in older or longhaired cats. Check beneath the tail as part of your grooming routine, and gently wipe the area with a damp cloth if needed.

BATHTIME You can wash your cat in a bathtub or a sink using a shower attachment, but make sure the water flow is very weak. Before you begin, close all doors and windows and make sure the room is warm and free of drafts. Prior to bathing your cat, brush his coat thoroughly. Line the bottom of the bathtub or sink with a rubber mat for your cat to grip, so that he feels secure and also to prevent him from slipping.

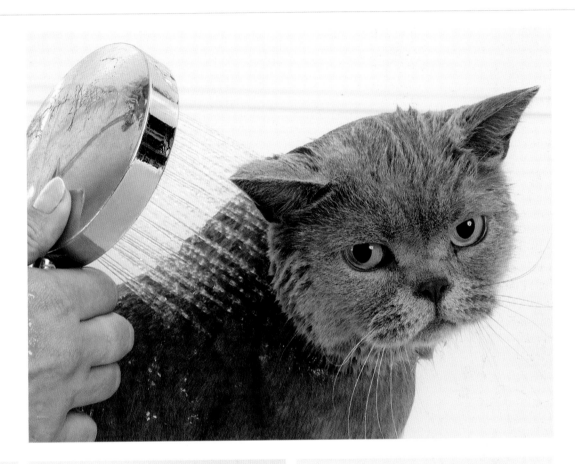

1 Slowly lower your cat into the sink or bathtub, talking to him soothingly. Spray him with warm water that is as near body temperature (101.5°F / 38.6°C) as possible. Soak his fur thoroughly.

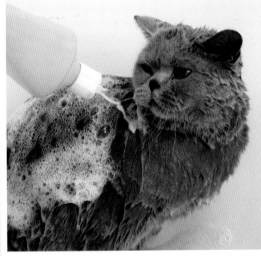

2 Use special cat shampoo, never products formulated for dogs or humans, which may contain toxic chemicals. Be careful not to get shampoo in your cat's eyes, ears, nose, or mouth.

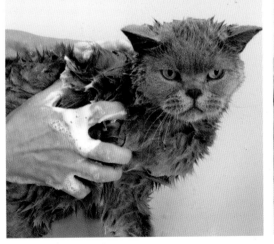

3 Lather in the shampoo thoroughly, then rinse it off completely. Repeat the shampoo wash or rub in a conditioner and then rinse off again. Keep comforting your cat throughout.

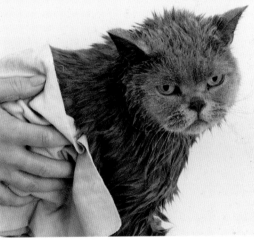

4 Towel-dry your cat, or use an hair dryer on a low setting if the noise does not upset him. Brush his coat and allow him to finish drying off in a warm room.

Understanding your cat

Cats are generally solitary animals. Highly independent, they have developed subtle and complex ways of behaving and communicating that often send confusing messages to their owners. Cats do, however, have a range of other signals that you can learn to interpret.

FACIAL EXPRESSIONS AND BODY LANGUAGE

Your cat will give you signals using his ears, tail, whiskers, and eyes. Ears and whiskers usually work together. Normally, the ears are erect and facing forward and the whiskers are to the front or sides, showing that your cat is alert and interested. When his ears are rotated back and flat and his whiskers are forward, he is feeling aggressive. Ears out to the sides and whiskers flat against the cheeks mean that your cat is scared.

Cats do not like eye contact, which is why your cat will often make for anyone in the room who ignores him: this is interpreted as friendly behavior. Once your cat is used to those around him, he will find eye contact less threatening. Dilated pupils can mean he is interested and excited or fearful and aggressive, so look for other signals to read his behavior.

BODY POSTURE

Your cat's posture tells you one of two things: "go away" or "come closer." Lying down, sitting in a relaxed manner, or coming toward you indicates that he is approachable. A cat on his back exposing his belly is not being submissive like a dog: this is usually a fight posture that allows him to wield all his claws and teeth. If he is also rolling from side to side, you can assume that he is in a playful mood, but avoid touching his belly too much or you may get scratched or bitten. Wiggling the rump is another sign that he is up for a play. When your cat is crouching—either looking sideways or with his tail wrapped

Warning stance
When your cat stands with rump raised or back arched, he is feeling threatened and warning that he is about to attack. The hair on his body may also be raised.

around his body—he is looking for a chance to escape, pounce, or go on the offensive.

SMELL AND TOUCH

Cats have a superb sense of smell and use urine and scent to mark territory and leave messages for other cats. They head-rub to deposit scent in areas where they feel relaxed and spray urine where they feel threatened. A cat that is not neutered will spray to warn other cats of his presence, threaten any rivals, and announce that he is ready to mate. If a neutered cat still sprays, he is probably feeling anxious so investigate what is triggering this behavior.

Cats also spread scent from glands on their cheeks, paws, and tail by rubbing them on surfaces or other cats. These scents mark territory and help cats to form social bonds. Cats that live together will rub each other along the flanks or the head, creating a group scent that alerts them to the presence of strangers. Your cat will also rub the members of your family to mark you all as part of his "gang." Cats sniff nose-to-nose when they

Intimidating eye contact
Cats use eye contact as a form of intimidation to avoid a fight. Staring is perceived as a threat, and two cats will try to out-stare each other until one looks away or slinks off.

TAIL SIGNALS

The most obvious signs of your cat's mood are the visual signals he sends out. Although he will give you signals with all parts of his body, one of the best barometers of his emotional state is his tail. When you look at your cat, the way he is carrying and moving his tail will be a clear expression of the way he is currently feeling. Try to learn these different tail configurations and their meanings. Remember that a cat's mood can change in an instant. Recognizing tail talk is valuable because behavior problems often arise as a result of poor communication.

Flicking from side to side	Your cat is telling you that he is mildly irritated	
Thumping on the floor	A sign of frustration or a warning signal	
Curved like an "N" or low to the ground and flicking	With this tail shape and action, your cat is advertising the fact that he is feeling aggressive	
Strong lashing movements	Stand back—your cat is not happy and he may become aggressive if approached	
Hair fluffed out and standing on end	A sign of increased anxiety and that your cat is feeling threatened	

Arched over the back	A warning sign that he is poised ready to strike	
Tucked between the legs	This tail position is designed to express submission	
Horizontal or slightly low to the floor	Everything is all right—he is feeling calm and relaxed in a situation	
Erect, sometimes with a curl at the tip	He is feeling friendly and interested in making contact with you	
Pointing straight up and vibrating	Your cat is quite literally quivering with joy and excitement	

Cat making contact
Your cat may often make the first move himself, by bumping or brushing up against you. If it is not convenient for you to pet him, at least stroke your cat once or twice so that he knows he is not being ignored.

meet; unfamiliar cats end the encounter there, but friendly cats progress to rubbing heads or licking each other's face or ears. Scratching is another way of leaving scent, as well as being a visual signal of a cat's presence.

CAT VOCALIZATIONS

Wild cats are solitary, predatory animals that patrol a territory they regard as theirs. Consequently, most cat communications are designed to ward off intruders. Learning what the noises he makes mean will help you understand what he is trying to tell you.

Chief among cat noises are hissing, growling, miaowing, and purring. Hisses and growls—sometimes accompanied by a flash of teeth or show of claws—are warnings to usurpers trespassing on the cat's territory or to humans who get too close. Meows—rarely used between adult cats—are mainly a way for kittens to signal to their mother. Domestically, your cat will use meowing to announce his presence. Short and high-pitched chirps and squeaks usually signal excitement or a plea for something, but drawn-out and low-pitched sounds express displeasure or

Cat language
Speak cat, not human. If you hiss or make a spitting noise when you say "no" to unacceptable behavior, your cat will understand that he is doing something wrong. This will prove much more effective than shouting.

a demand. Rapid, intense, and loud repeated sounds often signify anxiety. Long, drawn-out cries and shrieks indicate that the cat is in pain or fighting. Mating cats produce long wails known as caterwauls. Purring is usually a sound of contentment, but cats also purr as a way of comforting themselves when they are in pain or anxious.

Socializing your cat

By nature, cats are solitary creatures, although some cats are able to live quite happily in groups. Bringing a new cat into your home may change his whole outlook on the people and other animals around him. If you make introductions carefully and sensitively, your cat will grow into a confident, friendly animal that can cope with a variety of social situations.

START EARLY
Socialization should start in kittenhood. Give your kitten plenty of opportunities to meet new people, cats, and dogs, and make it a fun and rewarding experience. Introduce him to friends, neighbors, and the vet at an early stage; keep initial encounters brief and reward your kitten with treats for good behavior. A cat that is not exposed to new situations as a kitten may grow up to be timid and fearful and will likely react badly to being touched or approached by strangers or other animals.

It is important that your kitten gets used to being handled and that it is given plenty of play designed to hone his predatory skills, but let him sleep when he wants to.

SOCIALIZING AN ADULT CAT
If you are adopting an adult cat, it will take longer than a kitten to adapt to new people and surroundings. Changes in routine are

upsetting for an older cat. Try to get as much information as possible from the previous owner or animal shelter about the cat's habits, personality, and favorite food and toys. Familiar objects can help him to settle in, so try to bring some of his old bedding or toys to make him feel more secure. Provide him with a refuge, such as a carrier or box, to which he can retreat and feel safe.

An older cat may initially be wary of contact with his new owners and may resist being touched. Let him explore his surroundings in his own time. Talk to him in a low, soothing tone so that he gets used to your presence and the sound of your voice. One of the chief problems with poorly socialized cats is that they play too rough, biting and scratching to get what they want. If that is the case, simply stop playing with him, say "no" in a firm voice, and give him a toy instead. Give plenty of praise when your cat is playing nicely with you, but also praise him when

he takes his aggression out on a toy. That way, he will learn that he can play hard with toys but not with you.

Instead of forcing your cat to meet strangers, let him approach them when he is ready; once he realizes that nothing bad is going to happen, he will become more confident and trusting. If you have to leave your cat to be looked after by friends or neighbors, get him used to the new people before asking them to come to your home.

INTRODUCING A NEW BABY
If your cat has always been the center of attention, he may become jealous of the competition for affection when a new baby

Socializing mother
Kittens start to learn social skills from their mother between 8 and 12 weeks of age. Adopting a kitten less than 12 weeks old is not recommended, since it still needs a lot of socialization time with its mother, who will teach it essential life skills.

Getting used to children
A new cat will be an irresistible attraction to children in your family. Teach them the correct way to approach and handle a cat, and make sure you supervise their initial encounters.

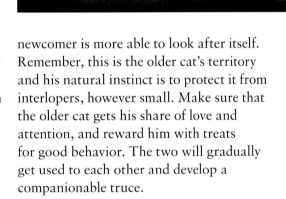

arrives. Some careful preparation can help prevent this. Before the birth, allow your cat to examine the baby's room and equipment, but make it clear that he is not allowed in on his own and that the crib, baby basket, and stroller are off limits. If your cat has any behavioral problems that you need to address, now is the time to do it, since they may get worse when the baby arrives.

When you bring the baby home for the first time, allow your cat to sit next to the baby and give him treats for good behavior so that he associates the baby with a positive experience. Never leave the baby and cat alone together. Close the door to the room where your baby is sleeping. Try to keep your cat's routine as normal as possible and make sure he gets his share of attention from someone in the family.

OTHER CATS IN THE HOME
Your cat sees your home as his territory and bringing another adult cat into the house may be seen as a threat. A new kitten, however, is more likely to be tolerated by the resident cat. Keep a lookout for bullying and jealousy on the part of the adult cat. If it looks like the older cat is picking on the kitten, keep the two apart until the

newcomer is more able to look after itself. Remember, this is the older cat's territory and his natural instinct is to protect it from interlopers, however small. Make sure that the older cat gets his share of love and attention, and reward him with treats for good behavior. The two will gradually get used to each other and develop a companionable truce.

MEETING OTHER PETS
Whether you are introducing a new cat to a dog or a new dog to a cat, similar methods of socializing them can be used. When you first bring your new cat home, put him in a room that the dog does not need to access until the cat has settled in. Alternatively, put up a barrier or put the dog in a crate. While the cat is getting used to his new surroundings, let the dog smell the cat's scent by rubbing the dog with

Learning to be friends
Cats and dogs are not natural allies. Make sure the dog does not get overexcited when he meets that cat, so that the cat will feel safe when he is around.

Good company
If they are not siblings, companion cats are best introduced early in their lives. They will provide company and a playmate for each other if you are out at work all day.

a towel that you have previously rubbed on the cat or letting the dog sniff your hands after handling the cat. Do the same with the cat. Once the dog is familiar with the cat's scent, put the dog on a leash and bring him to the door of the cat's room. Do not allow any bad behavior such as barking, scratching, or lunging. If the dog behaves properly, try letting him off the leash. Sadly, some dogs may never be safe to leave with a cat. If that is the case, you will have to keep them separate or supervise their encounters at all times.

Feline hunting instincts are very close to the surface, so small pets such as hamsters or rabbits are best left out of introductions to your new cat.

Importance of play

Cats need some excitement in their lives to ensure their physical and mental well-being—especially indoor pets that are left alone at home all day. With a little thought and commitment, you can give your cat a fun home life. Playing games together is a positive way of interacting with your cat, but you should also encourage him to play alone.

Play is an important outlet for your cat's excess energy. Any cat that is deprived of opportunities to hunt and stalk is likely to become bored and stressed, and this may lead to behavioral problems (see pp. 290–91). The mental and physical stimulation derived from play is just as important to adult cats as it is for kittens. Most cats, especially if neutered, will retain their sense of playfulness as they get older.

Lack of stimulation can be a real problem with indoor cats, which after a dull day with no company will constantly pester their owners for attention when they get home. Outdoor cats have a riskier but more stimulating and active lifestyle (see pp. 260–61). With plenty of space to run and jump around and exposure to new experiences, they can give free rein to their natural instincts for exploring, chasing, and hunting. Even indoors, a cat needs to let off steam regularly. Often, this takes the form

Learning natural skills
Dangling or dragging a piece of ribbon along will appeal to your kitten's natural urge to hunt and stalk. This form of play also helps your kitten to learn essential skills for survival that it would normally need in the wild, such as catching and biting prey.

of a "crazy moment," when the cat rushes around the room, leaping on to furniture and climbing the curtains before bolting off. This is perfectly natural behavior, but uncontrolled sessions like this run the risk

of damaging your home and causing injury to your cat. To prevent manic bursts of activity, channel your cat's predatory instincts with interactive toys and constructive play.

A VARIETY OF TOYS
Cats like toys that appeal to their chasing, stalking, and pouncing instincts (see panel, opposite), so satisfy your cat's need to hunt by providing him with a convincing substitute. Interactive toys, such as play wands with a dangling feather or catnip mouse, give your cat something to grab or bat with his paws, or to chase after when trailed along the ground. A play wand also keeps your hands at a safe distance from claws and teeth when your cat attacks his "prey."

You should not be the sole source of fun for your cat, so be sure to offer him toys that he can play with on his own. Toys that move, have an interesting texture, or are scented with catnip are most likely to catch

Hiding and exploring
Paper bags and cardboard boxes appeal to a cat's sense of curiosity, giving him something to investigate, or hide in if he is feeling insecure. Monitor your cat to make sure he can get out whenever he wants to.

Outdoor games
Even the most pampered cat retains its desire to hunt and the need for mental stimulation. A cat that is allowed outdoors has plenty of opportunity to follow its instincts.

his attention. Most cats find windup or battery-operated toys that move around the floor particularly exciting.

Make sure that toys are in good condition, with no pieces that could fall off and be swallowed. You should supervise your cat's use of anything that could be chewed or shredded. Bits of string and fabric can cause intestinal blockages, while sharp edges can damage a cat's mouth.

SIMPLE PLEASURES

You do not need to buy your cat expensive accessories or toys. Cats can make their own amusement from simple, everyday items such as crumpled newspaper, thread spools, pencils, pinecones, corks, and feathers. Cats love hiding, so provide yours with somewhere to play hide-and-seek, such as an old cardboard box or a paper bag. Never let a cat play with a plastic bag— a cat can suffocate inside or strangle itself if it gets trapped in the handles.

Make sure that curtain and window-blind cords are not allowed to dangle within easy reach of your cat, since he is likely to view them as a great opportunity to play. As agile as your cat may be, he could easily become entangled and strangle himself.

KEEPING YOUR CAT STIMULATED

One way to make playtime with your cat more interesting is to teach him a new trick (see pp. 288–89). Unlike a dog, which will learn tricks to please its "pack leader," a

cat needs a different motivator—food. The best time to teach your cat is just before a meal, when he is hungry. Select a quiet spot with no distractions, but do not spend more than a few minutes on each training session. You may need to repeat the training a few times each day for several weeks, depending on your cat's age and the difficulty of the trick. Reward your cat's progress in getting the trick right with small treats and give him plenty of praise. Your cat will be happy to participate only if he is having a good time: Do not try to force him to do something he does not want to, and do not get upset if he decides that he is not interested.

Even if your cat is not ready to cooperate by learning tricks, you can still have fun with food by buying or making a puzzle feeder. Your cat has to paw and nose the feeder to make the food fall out. You can also scatter dry food around the house so that he has to "hunt" for it, instead of just eating from a bowl.

Raised platform where cat can perch

Hanging toys for cat to bat and catch

Wide base stops post from toppling over

Activity center
Cats like to explore their environment from every angle, so it is essential to provide some places for your cat to investigate or perch on. A sturdy scratching post with a raised platform gives your cat an outlet for his need to jump and climb.

TOY PARADE

There is a wide variety of playthings available for cats. Most toys are designed to stimulate the cat's desire to hunt and stalk prey. Suitable toys include small, lightweight balls and bean bags, felt or rope pretend mice, pom-poms, and feathers. Many pet stores also stock catnip-scented toys and hollow balls in which a treat or small amount of food can be hidden. A scratching post, play station, or cat gym will stimulate the cat's natural inclination to climb on to a higher surface. Multiactivity centers provide plenty of variety for your cat, with a cozy hiding place, scratching post, somewhere to sit, and hanging toys to play with.

PLAY BALLS

FURRY MICE

PLAY STATION

CATNIP BRAID

FEATHER

Fun time
Most cats enjoy play all through their lives and into old age. They are capable of amusing themselves, but benefit from the extra stimulus provided by constructive games with their owners.

Training your cat

Cats are naturally active and need plenty of stimulation to ensure both mental and physical well-being. Teaching your cat good behavior and playing games are positive ways of interacting with your cat. Kind, effective training involves setting up house rules, rewarding "good" behavior, and ignoring "bad" behavior. This in turn will make it easier for you to control and manage your pet.

ANYTHING FOR FOOD

Cats are happy to learn if there is an edible reward. Unlike dogs, cats do not respond to discipline. Simply calling to your cat will not teach him to sit or come to you, but a tasty titbit—such as a dried chicken treat or a dehydrated shrimp—and lots of gentle praise will help. Cats learn best when hungry, so try training just before meals. Break treats into small portions—too many too soon and your cat will stop feeling hungry and lose interest.

Cats learn best from about four months old. Young kittens lack concentration; old cats are generally not interested. Active shorthaired cats, such as Siamese (see pp. 104–09), are generally easier to train than other breeds.

NAME TRAINING

Your cat cannot be trained unless he has a name—preferably a short name of one or two syllables that he will find easy to recognize and respond to. If you've adopted an adult cat, it's best not to change his name, even if you dislike it. Training sessions should last for one or two minutes, never much longer, and preferably in a quiet room free of distractions.

To get a cat to come to you, call him by his name while tempting him with a treat. As he approaches, take a step back and say "Come." When he has walked up to you, give the treat immediately and praise him. Repeat this, increasing the distance each time until he will run to you from another room on hearing your command. If you then phase out the treats, he should still respond to your call.

Once your cat has learned to come when called, you can try training him to meow on cue. Hold a treat in your hand and call to him, but withhold the treat until he meows—even if he tries to swipe the morsel from your hand. As soon as he meows, say his name and at the same time hand over the treat. Practice both with and without giving a treat to reinforce the behavior, until your cat always meows at the sound of his name.

CLICKER TRAINING

If you want to teach your cat some basic tricks—for example, going into his carrier—clicker training is very effective. A clicker is a small device with a metal tab that clicks when pressed. By clicking when your cat is doing the "right" thing, and immediately offering

him a treat, you can train him to associate a click with something good and to perform the desired behavior on request.

REALISTIC EXPECTATIONS

Domestic life can frustrate a cat's natural predatory instincts. Cats are motivated to hunt, climb, jump, and scratch, so be prepared to accept these as normal behavior. However, if you find any of these problematic, try to provide safe and acceptable alternatives, such as interactive toys or a scratching post. Never punish your cat or forcibly restrain him from behaving naturally, but use physical barriers if there is a risk he might harm himself or damage property.

Using a catflap
If your cat is to be truly independent, install a catflap so that he can come and go as he pleases. Otherwise, you will be perpetually opening doors and windows to see whether he wants to go in or out.

Scratching post
A post must be sturdy enough not to topple over and have a surface that will not catch claws. Some models double as activity centers.

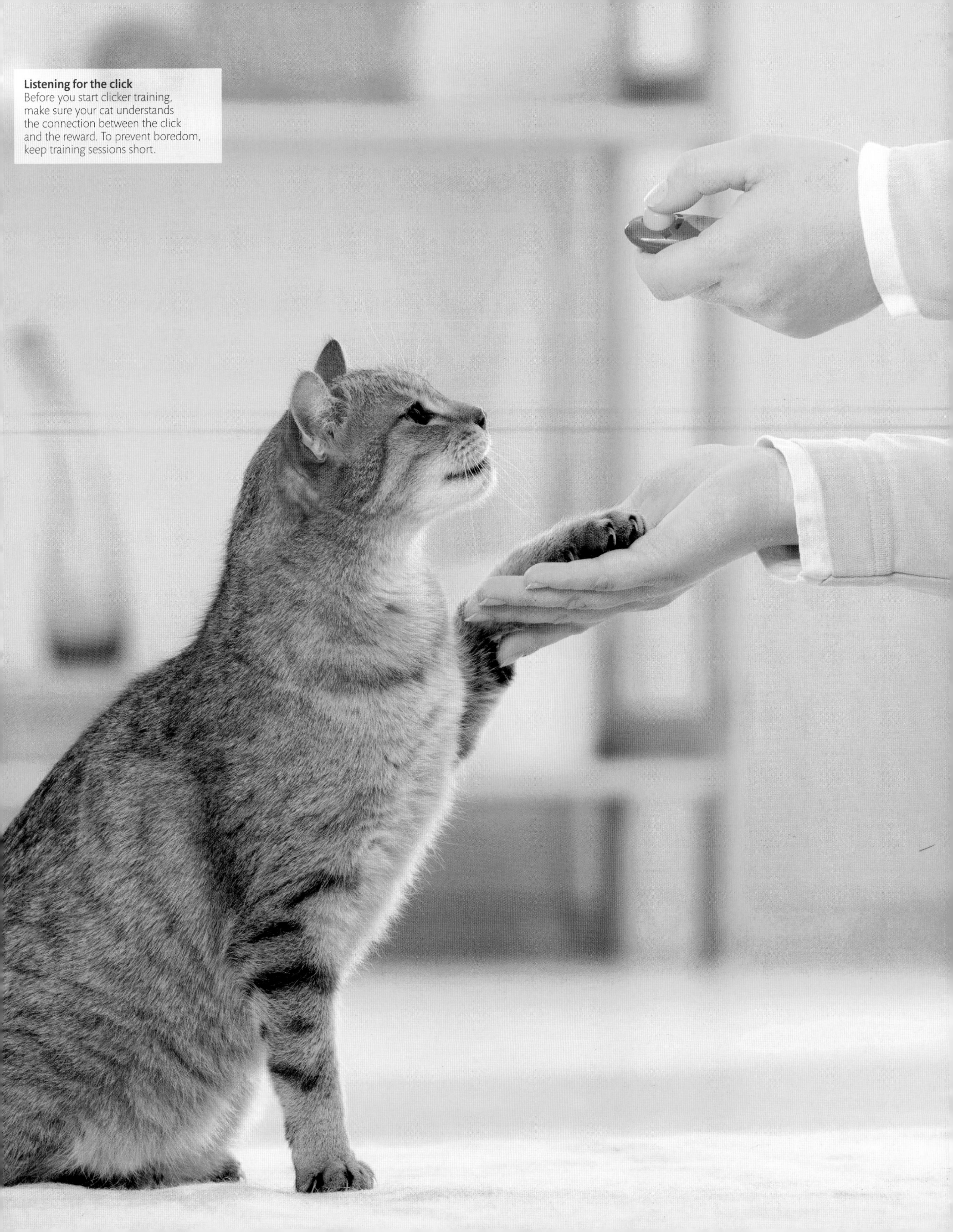

Listening for the click
Before you start clicker training, make sure your cat understands the connection between the click and the reward. To prevent boredom, keep training sessions short.

Behavioral problems

Unacceptable behavior in a pet cat—such as scratching furniture, inappropriate soiling, or sudden displays of aggression—should be investigated. It may be a sign that a cat has issues that are affecting his welfare and possibly his physical health. Your job as an owner is to try to find out whether the behavior is caused by illness, stress, or boredom, or just a case of a cat following his natural instincts. You should, with patience, be able to solve or minimize the problem.

KEY STRATEGIES FOR RESOLVING A PROBLEM

■ Have your cat's health checked by a vet to rule out underlying medical problems
■ Try to find out what first initiated the behavior and identify factors that trigger it now
■ If possible, protect your cat from the triggering factors
■ Never punish your cat for inappropriate behavior or give him attention for it
■ Redirect normal cat behavior, such as scratching, on to more appropriate targets
■ Ask your vet to refer you to a qualified and experienced feline behavior expert

Fighting it out
Cats are innately threatened by others that are not part of their social group. Conflicts of interest often result in fighting, especially among cats that are forced to share resources such as feeding areas or a litter box.

AGGRESSION

If your cat bites or scratches when you are playing with him, stop the game immediately. He is probably becoming overexcited or does not want you touching a sensitive area, such as his belly. Don't use your hands as "toys" when playing with him, since this will encourage him to bite or scratch them. Rough play may trigger aggression, so make sure your children play gently and know when to leave the cat alone. Also train pet dogs not to tease your cat to prevent a backlash. If your cat likes to ambush ankles or jump on shoulders, anticipate this and distract him with a toy.

Should your cat become aggressive for no obvious reason, he may be lashing out because he is in pain, so take him to the vet. Long-term aggression may result from your cat not having been socialized properly as a kitten. He may always remain wary of humans, but be patient and you may eventually gain his trust. In general, cats are much more docile after neutering.

CHEWING AND SCRATCHING

Boredom may lead to stress and destructive behavior. A cat that spends his life indoors, especially if he is often alone, may chew household objects to relieve the tedium. If this sounds like your cat, give him plenty of toys to play with and make sure you set aside some special time each day when you give him your full attention.

Scratching is a natural way for a cat to sharpen his claws and make a visible and scented sign of his territory. If your sofa is becoming heavily scratched, buy a scratching post as an alternative for your cat to mark his territory. Most posts are covered with

Claiming territory
Cats urine-mark to stake a claim in disputed territory. They may do this in the house as well as the yard if there is conflict with another cat using a particular area. Stress, perhaps caused by noise or a change in environment, can also lead to a cat to spray in inappropriate places.

Furniture at risk
Scratching is natural behavior that cats use to keep their claws in good condition and also as a way of leaving messages. If your cat scratches in areas of potential conflict with other cats, he may be leaving territorial marks because he feels insecure about his status.

rough rope or burlap, which provide an inviting texture. Place the post close to where your cat has been scratching and rub some catnip into it to tempt him if he is reluctant to use it. If he prefers to claw at the carpet, provide a horizontal scratching mat instead. If he persists in scratching the furniture, deter him further by cleaning the scratched area to take away his scent. Then cover the area in something that cats dislike the feel of, such as double-sided tape.

Another possible solution to scratching is to treat the targeted furniture with a spray containing a synthetic copy of the facial hormone that cats use naturally to mark their territory. This product, which also comes in the form of a plug-in diffuser, is said to help reduce anxiety and stress-related behavior by sending out a reassuring message to your cat.

SPRAYING
Like scratching, spraying marks territory, too, but this behavior usually disappears once a cat is neutered. It may recur if your cat becomes stressed by a change in his environment, such as the arrival of a baby or another pet.

To combat indoor spraying, distract your cat the moment you see him raise his tail to spray. Push his tail down or throw him

a toy to play with. If there is an area he sprays repeatedly, cleanse it thoroughly and place his food bowls there to deter further spraying. Use only safe biological cleaning agents, avoiding ammonia or other strong-smelling chemicals. You can also line sprayed areas with aluminum foil as a deterrent, because cats dislike the sound of their urine hitting it.

LITTER-BOX PROBLEMS
If your cat experiences pain when relieving himself, he may associate his discomfort with the litter box and go elsewhere. So when he relieves himself outside the litter

box, seek a vet's advice. An all-clear from the vet will mean that the problem is probably about something else. If waste is not removed from the litter box frequently, your cat may find the odor overpowering. Similarly, adding a cover to the box, to shield the smell from you, may make the smell inside too much for him. Switching to a new type of litter can also cause problems, since your cat may find its texture unpleasant.

Responsible breeding

Breeding pedigree cats may sound like an enjoyable, and potentially lucrative, endeavor, but it is a serious commitment. Most successful breeders have years of experience behind them. If you decide to go ahead, be ready to spend a lot of time and money on research, preparation, and caring for your pregnant cat and her newborn kittens. You will also have to plan ahead for the kittens' future.

A BIG DECISION

Do not consider breeding from your cat unless you have good reason to believe that you will be able to find a home for every kitten (see p. 269).

Before starting, get as much advice and detailed information as possible. The breeder from whom you bought your pedigree female cat will be able to give you valuable tips, including where to find a suitable pedigree tom. You will need a good understanding of cat genetics, especially coat colors and patterns (see pp. 51–53), because the litter may have a mix of characteristics. You must also be aware of genetic diseases associated with your breed (see pp. 296–97). Pedigree kittens sell for hundreds of dollars, but most of this income will be offset by stud and veterinary fees, heating for the kittens, registration fees, and extra food for both the mother and the kittens once they are weaned.

PREGNANCY AND PRENATAL CARE

If your cat has mated successfully, one of the first signs will be a slight reddening of her nipples, which appears about the third week of pregnancy. In the following weeks she will steadily gain weight and change shape. Never try to perform investigations of her condition yourself, as this could be harmful.

Expecting
A domestic cat's pregnancy usually lasts for between 63 and 68 days.

An expectant cat needs plenty of nourishment; your vet can give you guidance on feeding and will suggest supplements if necessary. It is also vital to have your cat checked for parasites (see pp. 302–03), since she could pass these on to her kittens. The vet may test a sample of your cat's stools for intestinal worms and can give you advice on flea treatments if necessary.

If your cat is naturally active, there is no need to stop her from jumping or climbing, but she should stay indoors during the last two weeks of pregnancy. Do not pick her up unless absolutely necessary and tell children to handle her gently.

Well before your cat is due to give birth, prepare a kittening box for her in a quiet corner. This can be bought ready-made,

STAGES OF DEVELOPMENT

Newborn kittens are blind, deaf, and completely dependent on their mother, but they develop rapidly. Within a few weeks helpless infants turn into lively individuals that have learned all the basic lessons about being a cat. As soon as they find their feet, at around three weeks of age, they start copying their mother and use the litter box when she does. By four weeks, the kittens are starting to make the change from their mother's milk to solid food and imitate the way the mother feeds from her bowl. They become less and less dependent on their mother for nutrition and are usually fully weaned at eight weeks old. A cat is generally full-grown at around 12 months, although some cats take longer. Cats reach sexual maturity before adulthood and kittens can be neutered as early as four months of age.

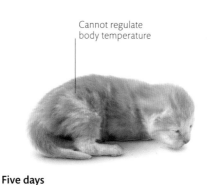

Cannot regulate body temperature

Five days
The kitten has some sense of the surrounding world, even though the eyes are not yet open. The ears lie flat against the head and hearing is still not fully developed. Kittens in the first week of their lives stay close to their mother and do little more than feed and sleep.

Eyes are open but not yet permanent color

Two weeks
The eyes have opened but vision is imperfect. For a few weeks, all kittens have blue eyes that gradually change to the permanent color. The sense of smell is improving and the kitten will react defensively to unfamiliar scents by hissing or spitting.

First wash
As soon as a kitten is born, the mother licks it clean, using her tongue vigorously to remove the surrounding membrane and stimulate the kitten's breathing.

you about what will happen at each stage of the birth. In most cases, kittens are born without difficulty and the mother cat knows instinctively what to do, even if it is her first litter.

THE FIRST WEEKS

Until they have been weaned, kittens need to stay with their mother and siblings all the time. The mother cat is not only a protector and source of nutrition, but a teacher of feline behavior as well. It is through interaction with brothers and sisters that kittens practice their social and life skills. No kitten should be removed from the family group unless absolutely necessary.

Kittens start playing as early as four weeks of age and benefit from a few stimulating toys. Objects that roll around are popular, but don't offer anything that could snag tiny claws. Games often become rough and tumble, but even if the entire litter becomes a tussling furball there is no need to separate them. They are unlikely to harm each other and these mock fights are part of their

development. Keep a constant eye on the whereabouts of kittens once they are mobile and can climb out of the kittening box. They will wander everywhere and can easily end up being stepped on or hurting themselves. Keep them indoors until they have been fully vaccinated.

FINDING HOMES

Kittens are ready for new homes at 12 weeks old. It will be hard to part with a litter that you have tended to since birth and even if you had not planned to keep any of them, you may not be able to resist. Before entrusting a kitten to a new owner, do all you can to ensure that it is going to the best possible home. Arm yourself with a list of questions and do not come to an agreement unless you are fully satisfied with the answers.

Dropper feeding
On rare occasions a kitten needs to be hand-reared and fed artificially. It is vital to use the correct equipment, milk formula, and technique, so always ask your vet for advice.

but a sturdy cardboard box serves just as well. It should be open at one side for easy access, but not so low that newborn kittens can roll out. A thick lining of plain paper that your cat can tear up will provide warmth and comfort and is easily replaced when soiled. Encourage your cat to spend time in the box so that she feels at home in her kittening area and, hopefully, will go there when labor begins.

GIVING BIRTH

When the time for birth arrives, your role is simply to keep a close watch and contact a vet if problems arise. Make sure that you know what to expect—your vet can advise

Four weeks
Up and running, tail held erect as a balancing pole, the kitten starts exploring. Sight and hearing are well developed. Some of the baby teeth have come through and the digestive system can cope with solid food. The mother cat will start the weaning process.

Learning how to self-groom

Eight weeks
Very active and fascinated by anything and everything, the kitten is instinctively adopting characteristic feline habits such as self-grooming and will practice hunting by pouncing on toys or siblings. Weaning should be fully completed around this stage.

Ten weeks
Not quite a cat—but almost—the kitten has already developed an independent character and will soon be ready to leave home. Bold experiments with jumping and climbing will need some supervision. It is important for first vaccinations to be given by this age.

Inherited disorders

Inherited disorders are genetic problems that are passed on from one generation to the next. There are certain disorders associated with particular breeds; a few of the most important are described here.

WHY DO GENETIC PROBLEMS OCCUR?

Inherited disorders result from faults in a cat's genes—sections of DNA inside cells that hold the "instructions" for a cat's development, body structures, and functions. Genetic disorders usually develop in small populations, or result from the mating of animals that are too closely related. For this reason, such disorders are more common in pedigrees. Sometimes, screening tests are used to identify cats with inherited disorders.

BREED-SPECIFIC PROBLEMS

Because the gene pool may be quite small for each cat breed, faulty genes can have a greater influence than they would in a larger mixed-breed population, where such genes usually vanish after a few generations. A disease such as hypertrophic cardiomyopathy (HCM) is mainly associated with the Maine Coon (see pp. 214–15) and Ragdoll (see p. 216), and is linked to one faulty gene. The disorder causes the heart muscle to become thicker and less elastic, which reduces the space inside the heart's chambers and the volume of blood that the heart can pump. This eventually leads to heart failure. Some cat breeds are actually characterized by inherited disorders—for example, in the past the crossed eyes of classic Siamese cats were the result of a visual problem.

An inherited disorder may be present when a kitten is born or may develop later in a cat's life. Some cats may have a faulty gene but never develop symptoms. These cats are called carriers and can produce kittens with the inherited disease if they breed with another cat carrying the same faulty gene.

Many cat diseases are thought to be genetic in origin, but have not yet had faulty genes identified to explain them. The disorders listed in the table (see opposite) have all been confirmed as genetic. For some of them, screening tests are available to identify whether or not a cat has the faulty gene.

WHAT CAN OWNERS DO?

To help eradicate inherited disorders, responsible breeders should avoid using any cats known to have or to carry an inherited disorder for breeding by having them neutered.

If your cat has, or develops, a genetic disorder, try to find out as much information as possible about the condition. Most inherited disorders are not curable, but careful management can reduce symptoms and allow a good quality of life for your pet.

Checking heartbeat and breathing
Vets use a stethoscope to listen to a cat's heartbeat and breathing rate. This helps them to detect any unusual noises in the chest, which may be an indicator of inherited diseases.

Kidney disorders
Persians (see pp. 186–205) are at risk of a number of inherited disorders, including polycystic kidney disease. In this disorder, fluid-filled cysts develop in the kidneys, eventually causing kidney failure.

BREED-SPECIFIC INHERITED DISORDERS

Disease	Description	Can it be screened for?	Managing the disease	Breeds of cat affected
■ Primary seborrhea	Flaky or greasy skin and hair.	No specific screening test is available.	Wash the affected cat frequently with medicated shampoo.	Persian, Exotic
■ Congenital hypotrichosis	Kittens are born with no hair and are susceptible to infection.	No test is currently available for this rare disorder.	No treatment. Keep the cat in a warm indoor environment, away from potential sources of infection.	Birman
■ Bleeding disorders	Excessive or abnormal bleeding after injury or trauma.	Yes. There are tests available for some types of bleeding disorder.	Look for non-healing wounds on your cat. Try to staunch blood flow and seek veterinary advice.	Birman, British Shorthair, Devon Rex
■ Pyruvate kinase deficiency	A condition that affects the number of red blood cells, leading to anemia. Reduces lifespan.	Yes. A genetic test is available.	Affected cats may need blood transfusions.	Abyssinian, Somali
■ Hypertrophic cardiomyopathy	Thickening of the heart muscle, usually results in heart failure.	Yes. A genetic test is available.	Drugs may be given to minimize the effects of heart failure.	Maine Coon, Ragdoll
■ Glycogenosis	Inability to metabolize glucose properly, leading to severe muscle weakness then heart failure.	Yes. A genetic test is available.	No treatment. Affected cats will need short-term fluid therapy.	Norwegian Forest Cat
■ Spinal muscular atrophy	Progressive muscular weakness, beginning in the hind limbs. Appears in kittens from 15 weeks old.	Yes. A genetic test is available.	No treatment. In some cases, the cat may survive with an adequate quality of life if given support.	Maine Coon
■ Devon Rex myopathy	General muscle weakness, an abnormal gait, and problems with swallowing.	No. Disorder first appears in kittens at 3–4 weeks old.	No treatment. Give affected cats small, liquid meals to avoid risk of choking.	Devon Rex
■ Hypokalaemic polymyopathy	Muscle weakness, associated with kidney failure. Affected cats often have a stiff gait and head tremors.	Yes. A genetic test is available for Burmese cats.	The condition can be managed with oral potassium.	Burmese, Asians
■ Lysosomal storage disease	Any of various enzyme deficiencies that affect many body systems, including the nervous system.	Yes. Some types of the disease can be screened and tested for.	No effective treatment. Affected cats usually die young.	Persian, Exotic, Siamese, Oriental, Balinese, Burmese, Asians, Korat
■ Polycystic kidney disease	Pockets of fluid (cysts) develop in the kidneys, eventually causing kidney failure.	Yes. A genetic test is available.	No cure. Drugs can be given to ease the workload of the kidneys.	British Shorthair, Persian, Exotic
■ Progressive retinal atrophy	Degeneration of the rods and cones in the retina of the eyes, leading to early blindness.	Yes. There is a test available for one form of the disorder, found in Abyssinians and Somalis.	No cure. Affected cats should be kept as safe as possible, away from potential hazards.	Abyssinian, Somali, Persian, Exotic
■ Osteochondrodysplasia	Painful degenerative joint disorder, leading to the fusion of tail, ankle, and knee bones.	No. To prevent, cats with folded ears should only be crossed with cats with normal ears.	Palliative treatment can help ease pain and swelling of joints.	Scottish Fold
■ Manx syndrome	A condition where the spine is too short, leading to spinal-cord damage and affecting the bladder, bowels, and digestion.	No. There is no specific test for this severe form of taillessness.	No treatment. Most kittens are euthanized when the disease becomes apparent.	Manx

A healthy cat

From the very first day, get to know your cat's usual physical condition and normal behavior so that you recognize good health and can quickly detect any signs of illness. By monitoring your cat for changes in activity or behavior, you can spot illness or injury at an early stage. Similarly, a vet can assess your cat's condition at regular check-ups and keep records of any problems.

APPEARANCE AND BEHAVIOR

It is normal for a cat to be shy at first, but as he gets used to you his personality will emerge. In general, your cat should look alert and happy, whether he is naturally outgoing or more reserved. Note how he moves (fast or leisurely)

HEALTHY BEHAVIOR

- Expression bright and alert
- Runs and jumps freely
- Friendly or calm with people
- Grooms self easily
- Eats and drinks normal amounts
- Urinates and defecates normally

and what sounds he makes (meowing, chirruping). Watch how he interacts with you and your family—he should come to trust you and be happy to see you, especially once he has realized that you provide the food.

Note how your cat eats and drinks—he should have a good appetite and eat without difficulty. Cats prefer to eat little and often (see pp. 270–73). Since they get most of their moisture from food, cats will not drink as often as they eat, but they may drink more if fed solely on dry food.

If your cat uses a litter box, remove waste from it several times a day. This way you will learn how often your cat normally passes feces and urine. Finally, watch for unusual behavior, such as excessive licking of a body part, pawing the face, or shaking the head. These activities could suggest a wound, parasite infestation, or something stuck in the skin or coat.

HOME CHECKS

Perform regular head-to-tail checks. With a new cat, do this every day; once you know your cat, every two or three days should be enough. If necessary, split the task into several mini-checks of a few minutes each.

First, run your hands over your cat's head, body, and legs. Gently squeeze the abdomen to feel for lumps or sore spots. Move his legs and tail to ensure that they move freely. Feel the ribs and look at the waist to check that he is not becoming too fat or thin.

Examine the eyes. Watch the blink rate: cats normally blink more slowly than we do. Check that the pupils respond correctly to light and dark and that the third eyelid is barely visible. Check that the cat is not holding his ears or head at a strange angle. Check the ears for soreness, parasites, or dark wax. Check that the nose is cool, damp, and free of excess mucus.

Look inside the mouth to check the gums for inflamed areas or bleeding. The breath should not smell bad. Press the outer gum briefly: it should go pale, but quickly turn pink when you stop.

The coat should feel smooth and not greasy. Look and feel for lumps, wounds, bald spots, or parasites. Gently lift the scruff of the neck and then let go; the skin should quickly return to normal.

Check the claws. They should be almost totally hidden when they are retracted and should not catch on carpets and other surfaces.

Look under the tail to check the area is clean and has no redness, swelling, or sign of worms.

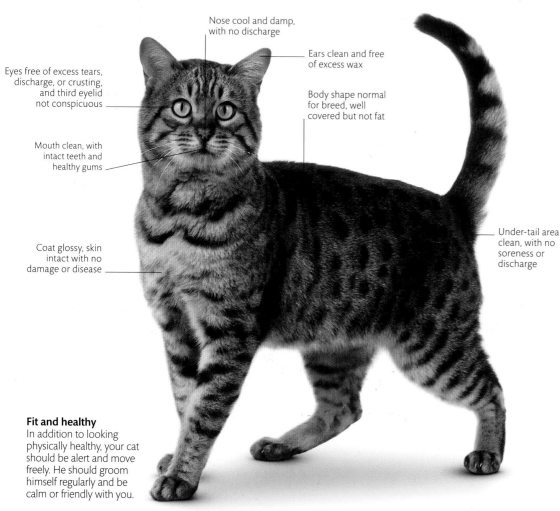

Nose cool and damp, with no discharge

Ears clean and free of excess wax

Eyes free of excess tears, discharge, or crusting, and third eyelid not conspicuous

Body shape normal for breed, well covered but not fat

Mouth clean, with intact teeth and healthy gums

Under-tail area clean, with no soreness or discharge

Coat glossy, skin intact with no damage or disease

Fit and healthy
In addition to looking physically healthy, your cat should be alert and move freely. He should groom himself regularly and be calm or friendly with you.

DETECTING PROBLEMS

Cats are notorious for hiding any signs of pain, illness, or injury (see pp. 300–01). In the wild, their survival would depend on not showing weakness to avoid attracting the attention of predators. This ruse also means, however, that owners might not notice problems until they have become severe.

If your cat seems more hungry or thirsty than usual, refuses to eat, or loses weight, you need to consult a vet. If your cat cries or strains when passing urine or feces, or has accidents in the home, it could signify an internal disorder and may require the immediate attention of a vet.

Changes in behavior could also indicate problems. Your cat may be reluctant to come to you or may hide himself away. He may be less active or may sleep more than usual. He may become abnormally timid or aggressive. Consult the vet immediately if you notice any of these signs.

ANNUAL CHECK-UPS

Your cat should have a regular health check at least once a year. The vet will assess his condition by checking the cat from head to tail, feeling for any tenderness or lumps. A booster vaccination may be given. The vet will also inspect your cat for parasites and give you advice on administering worming and flea treatments. Your vet may clip your cat's claws, if necessary, especially if he is a house cat or elderly.

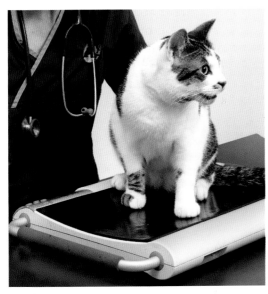

Cat being weighed
It is important to keep accurate records of a cat's weight, since this is a good indicator of general health. Consult the vet if your cat is overweight or loses weight suddenly.

ROUTINE CHECKS

Eyes
Check that the eyes are moist and clean. Gently pull the eyelids away from the eye; the conjunctiva (inner lining) should be pale pink.

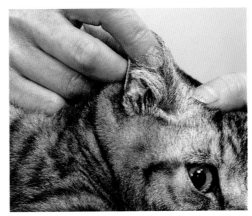

Ears
Look in the ears. The interior should be clean and pink, with no wounds, soreness, discharge, parasites, or dark wax. There should be no bad smell.

Teeth and gums
Gently lift the lips to check the teeth and gums, and look inside the mouth. The teeth should be intact and the gums pale pink.

Claws
Press each paw gently to expose the claws; look for any damaged or missing claws and then check the skin between the toes for any wounds.

Weight
Assess your cat's weight by gently running your hands around his back, ribs, and belly. You should be able to feel your cat's ribs easily but not see them.

Signs of illness

Cats instinctively hide signs of pain or illness because in the wild signs of weakness attract the attention of predators. With domestic cats, however, this behavior can make it hard for owners to recognize problems until they are severe. Regularly monitor your cat for changes in appearance or behavior so that you can spot health issues early on.

COMMON HEALTH PROBLEMS

Every cat will experience health problems during his lifetime. Some complaints, such as a one-time incident of vomiting or diarrhea, are not a major cause for concern and do not require treatment by a vet. Other problems, such as intestinal worms or fleas, can be treated easily enough at home, following instructions from your vet. More serious disorders requiring urgent veterinary attention include: repeated vomiting or diarrhea—often a sign of an underlying disorder; urinary tract infections or obstructions, which can cause painful urination; eye problems, such as conjunctivitis or a visible third eyelid; abscesses from fights with other cats; and dental problems that prevent eating.

WARNING SIGNS

Cats tend to suffer in silence and do not draw attention to themselves when they are feeling vulnerable. One of your

RECOGNIZING HEALTH PROBLEMS

- Lethargy, hiding away
- Unusually fast, slow, or difficult breathing
- Sneezing or coughing
- Open wound, swelling, bleeding
- Blood in feces, urine, or vomit
- Limping, stiffness, inability to jump on to furniture
- Unintentional weight loss
- Unexpected weight gain, especially with a bloated abdomen
- Change in appetite—eating less, walking away from food, voraciously hungry, or having difficulty eating
- Vomiting, or unexplained regurgitation of undigested food shortly after eating
- Increased thirst
- Diarrhea, or difficulty passing a motion
- Difficulty passing urine, crying
- Itchiness
- Abnormal discharge from any orifice
- Coat changes, excessive loss of fur

responsibilities as an owner is to be vigilant, keeping an eye out for any changes in your cat's routines and behavior that might suggest he needs veterinary attention.

Lethargy is difficult to spot because cats generally spend much of their time sleeping or resting, but decreased levels of activity, including a reluctance to jump, and reduced alertness are often signs that your cat is sick or in pain. Lethargy is also often linked to obesity, so it may disappear when a cat loses his excess weight.

Changes in appetite are usually a sign of an underlying condition. Loss of appetite may be due to mouth pain, such as toothache, or a more serious illness, such as kidney failure. Weight loss despite an increased appetite, together with increased urination and increased thirst, may be the result of an overactive thyroid or diabetes mellitus.

Abnormal or labored breathing may occur after a chest injury or as a result of an obstruction in the airway, an upper respiratory tract infection, or shock. Wheezing may be due to asthma or bronchitis. Breathing difficulties always require an emergency trip to the vet.

Dehydration is life-threatening and has various causes, including vomiting, diarrhea, increased urination, and heatstroke. You can perform a simple test to check if your cat is dehydrated. Gently lift up the skin on the back of

Not hungry
It is a cause for concern when a cat that normally has a good appetite loses interest in food. He may be in pain or have an illness requiring prompt veterinary attention.

Changes in behavior
Illness in a cat may not be immediately obvious, but you can pick up clues from his behavior. If an active cat becomes lethargic, or a lazy one is less responsive than usual to attention, there may be a health problem.

Time for the vet
If you are worried about your cat's health, do not hesitate to get in touch with a vet. In the event of sudden severe illness or a serious injury, call the practice immediately so that the staff can be ready when you bring the cat in.

his neck. If the skin springs back into position, your cat is healthy, but if it returns slowly this is a sign of dehydration. Feel the gums with a finger—dry, tacky gums also indicate dehydration. Emergency rehydration involves a vet injecting fluids under the skin or directly into a vein.

The color of a cat's gums can indicate good health or one of several serious disorders. A healthy cat has pink gums. Pale or white gums indicate shock, anemia, or blood loss; yellow gums are a sign of jaundice; red gums are caused by carbon-monoxide poisoning, fever, or bleeding in the mouth; blue gums suggest poor oxygenation of the blood.

Other indicators of poor health include lumps on the skin, which you can check for regularly during grooming sessions

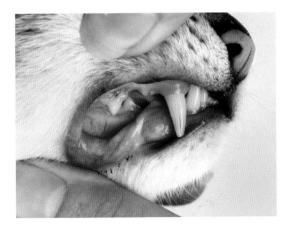

Checking gums
Changes in gum color indicate changes in health. Ask your vet to explain the correct way to examine a cat's gums and teeth, and make regular mouth checks part of your pet's normal care and hygiene routine.

(see pp. 276–79). Neglect of self-grooming, changes in coat texture, fur loss, and a refusal to use the litter box can also be signs that all is not well with your cat.

RECOGNIZING AN EMERGENCY

If you suspect your cat has a serious health problem, acting quickly can mean the difference between life and death. Keep the telephone numbers for your vet and the emergency vet service where you can easily find them. Call a vet immediately if your cat has any of the following signs:
- Loss of consciousness (always check to make sure the airway is not obstructed)
- Seizures
- Rapid breathing, panting, or struggling for breath
- Fast or weak pulse—feel the inner side of a back leg, near the groin area (a normal pulse is 110–180 beats per minute)
- Hot or cold temperature—feel the ears and pads of the paws
- Pale gums
- Limping, difficulty in walking, or paralysis
- Difficulty in standing, or collapse
- Serious injuries—a cat that has had an accident should be seen by a vet even if there are no visible injuries, since there could be internal bleeding

Health and care

Your greatest responsibility as a cat owner is the health of your pet. It is up to you to ensure that your pet has regular vaccinations and check-ups with a vet and recognize any changes in his body or behavior that may require a trip to the vet. Educate yourself about common disorders and learn how to care for your cat when he is ill, recovering from surgery, or in the case of an emergency.

Every cat will experience health problems during his lifetime. However, cats tend to suffer in silence and do not draw attention to themselves when feeling vulnerable. Keep an eye out for any changes in your cat's routines and behavior, such as lethargy or changes in appetite, which might suggest he needs veterinary attention. Regular home checks (see pp. 300–01) will help you spot common signs of illness or discomfort, but your cat will also need annual check-ups from a vet, and some conditions will require additional tests.

PARASITES AND DISEASES

Some health issues—such as external and internal parasites, infectious diseases, and tooth and gum disorders—are easily dealt with if caught early.

External parasites, also called ectoparasites, are tiny creatures—such as fleas, ticks, and a variety of mites—that infest a cat's skin. Saliva from their bites can irritate the skin, and some parasites, such as tapeworm, can also transmit infections. Ticks are sometimes carriers of Lyme disease.

Some parasites live in a cat's internal body tissues, usually in the intestines, but also in other areas, such as the lungs. Your vet will prescribe medicine or suggest a treatment for external or internal parasites, and may also advise on preventative medication.

Your cat may catch infectious diseases from the environment or from other cats. Although these diseases can be serious, especially in older cats or kittens, vaccinations will help to protect your pet. Cats kept in large groups or those that come into contact with other cats can pick up infections from fighting, mutual grooming, or from sharing litter boxes and food bowls.

Cats use their mouths for eating and for grooming themselves. The mouth usually keeps itself healthy by producing saliva, but regular checks and even brushing the teeth will prevent problems such as a buildup of plaque.

DISORDERS AND INJURIES

If you notice any signs of injury or illness, contact your vet. Only give your cat medicine prescribed by a vet and follow instructions carefully. Serious disorders that require urgent veterinary attention include repeated vomiting or diarrhea; urinary tract infections; eye problems, such as conjunctivitis or a visible third eyelid; skin abscesses; and dental problems that prevent your cat from eating.

Disorders and injuries may affect the structures of the eye or the eyelids, or both. All eye problems in a cat need prompt investigation by a vet, since even minor disorders can become sight threatening if left untreated.

Excessive scratching
If your cat excessively scratches or licks himself, it may be an indication of a skin or coat disorder. Scratching may further aggravate itchy skin, and bacteria on the cat's claws can infect the affected area.

Parasites
Cats can easily pick up parasites from their environment or from other cats. The four most common external parasites are shown here.

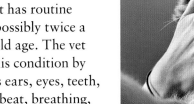

FLEA   TICK   EAR MITE   HARVEST MITE

A wide range of ear problems can affect cats, from external injuries to disorders of the inner ear that can cause issues with balance. Cats can also suffer from deafness due to genetic disorders.

Cats by nature keep their coat and skin healthy by grooming themselves. However, skin disorders can still affect them. Symptoms such as flaky skin or greasy coat are usually easy to spot, and will need prompt attention from a vet.

The digestive system of a cat breaks down food, releasing nutrients to be converted into energy by the body's cells. Any problem with the cat's eating, digestion, or waste elimination can have an overall impact on his health.

Abnormal or labored breathing may occur after a chest injury or as a result of an obstruction in the airway, an upper respiratory tract infection, or shock. Wheezing may be due to asthma or bronchitis. Breathing difficulties always require an emergency trip to the vet.

If your cat is injured, you may need to administer first aid (see pp. 304–05) as an emergency measure before seeing the vet.

CHECK-UPS AND TESTS

It is good practice to ensure that your cat has routine check-ups, possibly twice a year in his old age. The vet will assess his condition by checking his ears, eyes, teeth, gums, heartbeat, breathing, and weight, and feel all over for abnormalities. The vet may recommend additional tests to diagnose some disorders.

Inherited disorders (see pp. 296–97) may be associated with certain breeds. Screening tests may be available for some genetic disorders.

Disorders of the musculoskeletal system include injuries such as fractures and torn ligaments, but cats may also develop arthritis. If your vet suspects the presence of a musculoskeletal problem, your cat may be sent for a scan or an X-ray.

Problems with a cat's heart, blood vessels, or red blood cells can cause weakness or even make the cat collapse.

Blood tests
The vet may take blood samples to detect an underlying illness for a range of symptoms—for example, seizures as a result of epilepsy—or to diagnose diabetes.

Hormones are body chemicals that control particular functions. They are produced by glands and carried in the bloodstream. Any over- or underproduction of hormones may cause disorders, such as diabetes mellitus and hyperthyroidism.

Giving ear drops
Ear drops may be prescribed to treat an infection. To administer the drops, hold the cat's head so that the ear that is to be treated faces upward. Squeeze in the drops, then massage the base of the ear.

Medicine for constipation
Laxatives, which relieve constipation, may be supplied as a paste, gel, or liquid, which you feed to your cat on your finger or by syringe. Only vet-prescribed medicine should be given to the cat.

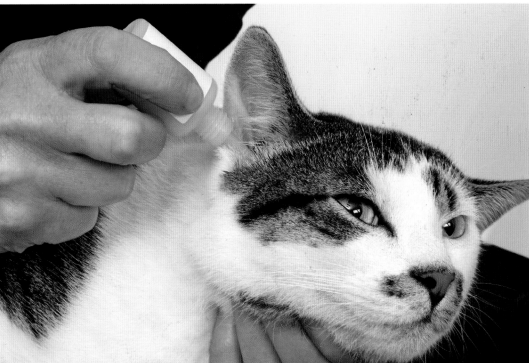

HANDLING AN INJURED CAT

Check the cat for broken bones and open wounds or bleeding, but try not to move him. Take care—even the most loving pet may bite or lash out if it is in severe pain.

If the cat has a fracture or severe wound, lay him on a blanket with the injury uppermost and wrap the wound up gently. Do not try to splint broken bones yourself.

If your cat has a hemorrhage (severe bleeding), raise the bleeding area above the level of the cat's heart, if possible, and apply direct pressure with a pad of cloth to stem the blood flow.

Lift the cat carefully, with one hand under the shoulders and the other under the hips, and place him in a carrier.

FIRST AID

If your cat is injured, you may need to administer first aid before he has a chance to be seen by a vet. Wounds that are bleeding profusely need prompt veterinary attention, as do bites and scratches from other animals (since these could become infected). Remember to call the vet before leaving.

To stop bleeding, apply pressure on the wound with a gauze pad or clean cloth soaked in clean, cold water. Do not use tissue because it will stick to the wound. If the bleeding does not stop after two minutes, cover the wound with a clean, dry pad (or cloth) and bandage in place.

For very heavy bleeding or a severe wound, keep the material in place, even if it becomes soaked with blood, until you see the vet. Removing an object embedded in a wound could cause more bleeding—leave

Overheating
A greenhouse, sun room, or a room with big windows can get very hot in direct sunlight. A cat trapped in a room like this will be at risk of heat stroke.

it in place for your vet to treat. For an eye wound, cover the eye with a gauze pad and tape in place.

If you find your cat unconscious, make sure his airway is not obstructed, listen and look for breathing, and feel for a pulse with a finger on one of the femoral arteries, which can be found on the inner side of his hind legs, where they meet the groin. If there is no breathing, attempt artificial respiration by gently blowing air into your cat's lungs down the nostrils. If there is no heartbeat, alternate two breaths of artificial respiration with 30 chest compressions at two compressions per second. Keep this up for 10 minutes, after which time it is unlikely to be successful.

MINOR WOUNDS

Small cuts and grazes can be treated at home. Look for bleeding, moist fur, or a scab, or the cat licking an area intensely.

Treating shock
A cat in shock may suffer from heat loss. Wrap him loosely in a blanket or fleece until he is assessed by a vet.

NORMAL VITAL SIGNS

Temperature	100.5–102.5°F (38–39°C)
Pulse	110–180 beats per minute
Respirations	20–30 per minute
Capillary refill time*	Less than two seconds

*Time for gum to regain pink color after being blanched by gentle pressure with finger

Gently wipe away blood and dirt using a cotton ball moistened in saline solution—a teaspoon of salt stirred into 2 cups (500ml) of clean, warm water. Cut away hair around the wound using blunt-ended scissors.

Small skin wounds can sometimes occur with more extensive internal damage. Check for heat, swelling, or discolored skin around the wound, and watch for signs of pain or shock. Small wounds can also become infected, so look for signs of abscess formation, such as swelling and pus.

BURNS

Cats may suffer burns from fires, hot surfaces, scalding liquids, electrical appliances, or chemicals. These injuries can be very serious, with damage to deep tissues, and they require urgent veterinary attention.

For a burn or scald, remove the cat from the heat source without endangering yourself. Flood the affected area with clean, cold water for at least 10 minutes, then cover it with a moist sterile dressing. Keep the cat warm during the journey to the vet.

If your cat has been electrocuted (for example, by chewing through a power cord), turn off the power first, or use a wooden broom handle to move the power source away from the cat. Perform first aid and take the cat to the vet immediately.

For chemical burns, call the vet at once and say which chemical is responsible. If the vet advises rinsing, put on rubber gloves to avoid contaminating yourself, and flush the area carefully with water.

STINGS AND BITES

If your cat has been stung, move him away from any other bees or wasps to avoid further stings. Call the vet for advice, and take the cat in if he develops breathing difficulties or

Bandaged leg
A leg wound should be bandaged by a vet. Keep your cat inside if he has a bandaged limb. If the dressing becomes dirty, wet, loose, or uncomfortable, take your cat back to the vet for it to be changed.

becomes unsteady on his feet. If your cat goes into shock, take him to the vet immediately.

For a bee sting, bathe the area in baking soda mixed in warm water. A wasp sting should be bathed with vinegar diluted in water.

Most cats will suffer only minor irritation from small biting insects, such as mosquitoes and gnats. However, some cats may suffer a severe allergic reaction to mosquitoes. If your cat is hypersensitive to mosquito bites, prevent exposure to these flying insects by keeping the cat indoors at dawn and dusk.

VENOMOUS ANIMALS

Cats may be bitten by other cats, but bites from venomous animals can be more serious. Dangers from snakes, toads, scorpions, and spiders vary between countries. Venomous snakes found in the US include rattlesnakes, copperheads, water moccasins, and coral snakes. Captive exotic reptiles can also be a hazard.

Snake bites can cause serious swelling, nausea, vomiting, and dizziness, and are potentially fatal; your cat may lick the area, and you may see two puncture wounds in the skin. Some snake vaccines are available, although even if your cat has been vaccinated a snake bite is an emergency.

Some toad species secrete toxins on to their skin, which can cause inflammation in a cat's mouth and perhaps retching.

If your cat has been affected, call the vet immediately and report what kind of animal was involved (or take a photo if you can) so that the vet can obtain the correct antivenom. The cat should be taken to the vet as soon as possible.

CHOKING AND POISONING

Cats can choke on a variety of objects. Some objects, such as bird bones, may get wedged in the mouth; others, such as pebbles, may block the throat (airway). Items such as ribbon, string, or thread can get tangled around the tongue or, if swallowed, cause

problems in the intestines. A choking cat will cough, drool, and gag, and paw frantically at its mouth. If the airway is blocked, the cat will struggle to breathe and may pass out.

Call the vet and take the cat in. Wrap the cat in a towel. Holding the top of the head with one hand, open the lower jaw with the other. Look inside the mouth. If the object is easy to dislodge, try to remove it with tweezers.

Cats may ingest poisons from prey animals, toxic plants, household chemicals, medicines, or even some human foods. If you think your cat has been poisoned, even if he is showing no signs, contact your vet. If you see any signs of poisoning, take the cat to the vet, together with a sample of what he has swallowed.

INJURIES AND SHOCK

A cat that has had an accident, such as being hit by a car, should be seen by a vet even if he has no visible injuries, since there could be internal bleeding, which can lead to shock. Shock is a life-threatening condition in which there is reduced blood flow, and tissues become starved of nutrients. Symptoms of shock include irregular breathing, anxiety, pale or blue gums, and a lowered body temperature. A cat in shock should be kept warm and the hindquarters elevated to increase blood flow to the brain while you take him to a vet.

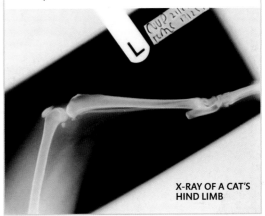

X-RAY OF A CAT'S HIND LIMB

CREATING A SICK ROOM

You will need to keep a sick or injured cat indoors so that you can easily monitor him. Keep your cat confined in a warm, quiet room or even in a wire crate. Provide food and water, and a litter box in an area away from the food. Make up a warm bed on the floor for easy access; you can use a cardboard box, which can easily be replaced if soiled. Cut one side away, line the bottom with newspaper, and add cozy blankets and perhaps a hot-water bottle.

Check on your cat regularly and change the bedding if it becomes soiled. If you have an outdoor cat, make sure he is kept indoors during his recovery and has easy access to bowls of water and a litter box.

HANDLING YOUR CAT

A sick or injured cat may want to hide himself away and try to avoid the extra stress of having medicine or other treatment. Handle your cat gently and in a calm, unhurried, and confident way—any anxiety on your part could make him stressed and uncooperative. Your cat may feel comforted if you spend time just talking quietly to him and petting him (if he will accept this), so that he does not associate you solely with receiving medicine.

If your cat is ill or recovering from surgery or an accident, you must resist the temptation to stroke and cuddle him. He will most

Safe space
A wire crate should be large enough to let the cat walk around. Line it with newspaper, and add food, a water bowl, a bed, and a litter box.

likely not enjoy being handled in the early stages of convalescence. Stroke or pet your cat only if he clearly wants the attention. Provide him with a warm bed, where he can be left in peace to recuperate.

ADMINISTERING MEDICINE

Only give your cat medicine that has been prescribed by a vet. It is also essential both to follow your vet's directions on giving medication and to complete the full course, especially with antibiotics. If you are unsure, ask your vet to demonstrate how to administer eye or ear drops or dose the cat with a syringe (see p. 303).

You can try hiding a pill in a ball of meat or mold a sticky treat around it, but only if your cat is allowed to take food with his medicine. If not, or if he rejects or coughs up the pill, you will need to place it in his mouth. This is best done with a helper to hold your cat

Caring for a convalescing cat
Provide a cozy bed, in a quiet location, with a microwavable heating pad or a hot-water bottle wrapped in a towel.

while you insert the pill (see panel, opposite). If you are on your own, immobilize your cat by wrapping him in a towel, leaving his head exposed.

Liquid medicines are also widely available and should be instilled into the mouth, between the back teeth and cheek, using a plastic medicine dropper or a plastic syringe without a needle. Drops for the eyes or ears can be administered while gently immobilizing your cat's head. Make sure that the dropper does not ever come into contact with his eyes or ears.

If your cat is completely resistant to being given any kind of medicine at home, take him to your veterinarian each day or have him kept at the practice until the course of treatment is over.

FOOD AND CARE

A cat may lose interest in food when sick or if his sense of smell is impaired. Call a vet if your cat has gone for more than a day without eating, especially if he is overweight, since lack of food can harm the liver. Let food come to room temperature, or warm it slightly in the oven, to increase its smell and make it more appetizing. In addition, offer small pieces of strong-smelling, tasty foods. If your cat is struggling to eat properly, you may need to feed him by hand.

If your cat is vomiting or has diarrhea, call your vet. To prevent your cat from becoming dehydrated, offer a teaspoon every hour of bland food such as poached skinned chicken or an appropriate prescription diet. Once the gastric upset ceases, you can gradually increase portion size and keep your cat on this diet for three or four days, before weaning back to normal meals. Provide your cat with cooled, boiled drinking water at all times.

Your cat may need help with grooming. In particular, wipe away discharge from the eyes, keep the nose and mouth clean to help the cat breathe and smell food, and clean under the tail if the cat has diarrhea. Use a cotton wool ball moistened in clean, warm water. For itchy skin or minor wounds, bathe the area with saline solution—a teaspoon of salt dissolved in 2 cups (500ml) of warm water. If the cat resists, wrap him in a towel, leaving the sore part exposed.

Elizabethan collar
After surgery your cat may have to wear an cone collar for several days to prevent him from licking or chewing a wound that may have been stitched.

AFTER AN OPERATION

A cat that has had a general anesthetic may be groggy for a while. Stay with him until he is fully alert. Keep him indoors until any surgical wound has healed and dressings or stitches have been removed. Your vet may fit a cone to prevent your cat from worrying at a wound, and you may have to remove this to let the cat eat. For small wounds on the limbs, the vet may cover the area with "anti-lick" strips impregnated with a taste that cats dislike. Check a dressing or a plaster cast several times a day to ensure it is clean and dry. If the cat seems in pain, or if the wound looks sore or has a discharge when you change the dressing, contact your vet.

GIVING A PILL Medication should always be given by a responsible adult. Give the pill by hand to make sure the cat swallows it and that other pets do not take it. It may help to crush the pill into a small amount of tasty food. Do not let your cat feel cornered during the process, and reward him with praise and a treat once he has taken the medication.

1 Hold your cat's head with your forefinger and thumb on either side of his mouth. Gently tilt his head back and ease open his jaws.

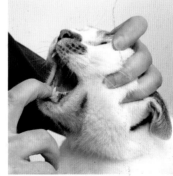

2 Grip your cat's head with one hand, and with the other hand keep his jaws open. If the cat resists, get a helper to hold the head while you give the pill.

3 Place the pill as far back as possible on his tongue to trigger swallowing. Give him gentle encouragement while doing so.

The aging cat

Most well-cared-for pet cats can live to age 14 or 15, with some occasionally reaching 20. Life expectancy is increasing due to advances in disease prevention, a better understanding of diet, improved drugs and treatments, and more cats being kept indoors away from traffic hazards.

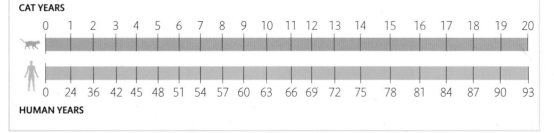

SENIOR YEARS

By about age 10, your cat may begin to show signs of aging: weight loss (or gain), deteriorating eyesight, dental disease, a decrease in mobility, less fastidious grooming, and a thinner, less shiny coat. His personality may change, too, with your cat becoming easily irritated and noisier, especially at night. As a senior, he may occasionally feel disorientated and relieve himself outside the litter box.

The older cat will need more frequent health checks. You may want to start increasing his routine visits to the vet to twice a year. Many veterinary practices now offer clinics for older cats, to detect and deal with age-related problems. There are many treatments now available to help manage chronic conditions—even senility.

HOME CARE

You may need to make adaptations to your cat's diet and living conditions to maximize his comfort and well-being as he ages. Your vet may recommend a "senior" diet, which

Catering for a smaller appetite
Many older cats lose the robust appetite of their youth. To ensure that your senior maintains a healthy intake of nutrients, you may have to tempt him to eat by offering frequent small meals and a few extra tasty treats.

will supply the correct nutrients for the changes in your cat's metabolism and digestive processes. Your cat may prefer to eat smaller meals more often during the

day. If he seems less interested in eating, try warmer or tastier foods to tempt him. It is also helpful to weigh your cat every two weeks; older cats can gain excess weight due to inactivity, or lose weight due to difficulty with eating or conditions such as hyperthyroidism, a common hormonal disorder in seniors.

As your cat's body becomes less supple, he may need help with grooming hard-to-reach places. Gentle brushing a few times a week will keep him clean and make him more comfortable. His claws can grow harder with age and become overgrown if he is not very active, so clip them regularly or ask your vet to do it for you.

If your cat is not as agile as he used to be, make sure he doesn't have to jump up to reach his food and water bowls. Keep bowls and litter boxes on each floor of the house, in quiet places where he won't be disturbed. Use boxes or furniture to make "stepping-stones," so that he can still reach his favorite perches or windowsills.

Have several warm, comfortable cat beds around your home, in places where your cat already enjoys sleeping, so that he does not have to go far to find a cozy corner. If your cat is having trouble with soiling, use washable beds or cardboard boxes lined with newspaper that can be thrown away.

Even if your cat still prefers to urinate and defecate outdoors, it is wise to have litter boxes in the house. Older cats are often less willing to go outdoors, either because they want to avoid confrontation with other cats or because they no longer have the urge to hunt and explore.

Even an old cat still likes to have fun, so provide him with toys. Playing with your cat helps to keep his mind active and lets him express his natural instincts, although you will have to play more gently than before.

COMPARING LIFESPANS

It is popularly said that one year of a cat's life equates to seven years of a human's. But this is not a reliable comparison, particularly since life expectancy for pet cats has risen in recent years. It also does not take into account the very different rates at which cats and humans develop into adulthood: a one-year-old cat can breed and raise

kittens, which is a far more advanced stage of maturity than that of a seven-year-old child. By about three years of age, a cat is roughly equivalent to a person in their early 40s. Each cat year from then on corresponds to about three human years. Use the chart below to find an approximate "human age" for your cat.

CAT YEARS

0	1	2	3	4	5	6	7	8	9	10	11	12	13	14	15	16	17	18	19	20
0	24	36	42	45	48	51	54	57	60	63	66	69	72	75	78	81	84	87	90	93

HUMAN YEARS

Getting around
Going up and down stairs can be a big effort for an elderly cat whose joints are beginning to stiffen. Make sure your senior pet has access to bowls, beds, and keep litter boxes on all floors.

WARNING SIGNS

You need to keep a closer eye on an older cat to detect any alterations in his normal habits. In particular, let your vet know if you notice any of the following changes.

Watch for any increase in appetite, with your cat seeming ravenously hungry but losing weight even with regular meals.

Unusual drinking habits
Let your vet know if your cat is drinking more water than usual, including from puddles or dripping faucets. Excessive thirst may be due to any one of various disorders commonly found in older cats.

In contrast, if your cat is obviously hungry but turns away from certain foods (especially hard foods), or paws at his mouth, he may have problems with loose or painful teeth or difficulty swallowing.

Increased thirst may cause your cat to use the litter box more than usual and to start drinking from odd places such as ponds and bathroom faucets. An elderly cat may also become dehydrated. Check by grasping the scruff of the neck and letting go. The skin should fall back instantly; if it does not, the cat may not be getting enough liquid.

Alert your vet promptly if your cat is straining or crying when he passes feces or urine, or if he starts having "accidents" in the home. He may need investigations for bowel or bladder disorders.

Many older cats develop stiff joints or arthritis that cause difficulty with running and jumping, and your cat may struggle to climb stairs. Elderly cats may also lose vision, causing them to bump into things or misjudge heights.

A cat that is feeling very sick or showing signs of dementia may become more withdrawn or aggressive, hide away, or meow more than usual.

EUTHANASIA

For a very old or sick cat, sometimes the kindest thing to do is to give him a dignified, peaceful ending. Euthanasia is usually carried out in a veterinary practice, but it can be done at home (you will need to book in advance). The vet will give an injection of anesthetic—in effect, an overdose—into a front leg vein. The procedure is painless and the cat will become unconscious before passing away. There may be involuntary movements, and the bladder or bowels may empty.

You can ask for your cat to be cremated, or take the body home. Many owners wish to bury their pet in the yard, perhaps in one of his favorite places, while others opt for burial in a pet cemetery.

Glossary

Familiar shape
All cats have the same basic body design, although some natural variations do occur. Selective breeding has further developed some variations, such as short-legged breeds and bobtails.

Pinna (external part of ear)

Cheek

Neck

Back

Base of tail

Whisker pad

Chest

Abdomen

Foreleg

Paw

ALBINISM—Lack of the pigment that gives color to skin, hair, and eyes. In cats, true albinism is very rare, but partial albinism gives rise to pointed coat patterns, as in the Siamese, and color variations such as silver tabby.

ALMOND-SHAPED EYES—Oval eyes with flattened corners, seen in breeds such as the Abyssinian and Siamese.

AWN HAIRS—Slightly longer bristly hairs that, together with the soft down hairs, constitute the undercoat.

BICOLOR—Coat pattern combining white with another color.

BLOTCHED TABBY—Alternative term for Classic Tabby.

BLUE—Light to medium-gray coat color, a dilute form of black. Blue-only cat breeds include the Russian Blue, Korat, and Chartreux.

BRACELETS—Dark horizontal bands on the legs of a tabby cat.

BREAK—see Stop

BREECHES—In longhaired cats, extra-long hair on the upper back part of the hind legs.

BREED STANDARD—Detailed description produced by a cat registry that defines the required standards for a pedigree cat's conformation, coat, and color.

CALICO—Tortoiseshell with a high proportion of white fur; known as tortie and white in the UK.

CAMEO—Red, or its dilute form cream, where white covers two-thirds of the hair shaft.

CARNIVORE—Meat-eating animal.

CAT FANCIER—Enthusiast for breeding and showing pedigree cats.

CAT REGISTRY—Organization that sets breed standards and registers the pedigrees of cats.

CFA—The Cat Fanciers' Association, the world's largest registry of pedigree cats, based in North America.

CHOCOLATE—Pale to medium-brown coat color.

CHROMOSOME—Threadlike structure within a cell nucleus, containing genes arranged along a strand of DNA. Domestic cats have 38 chromosomes arranged in 19 corresponding pairs (humans have 46, arranged in 23 pairs).

CLASSIC TABBY—see Tabby

COBBY—UK term to describe compact, muscular, heavy-boned body type.

COLORPOINT—see Pointed

CROSSBREED—see Hybrid, also cross of two different breeds.

CURLED EARS—Ears that curve backward, as in the American Curl.

DILUTE/DILUTION—Paler version of a color caused by the dilution gene, for example, when black becomes blue and red becomes cream.

DOMESTIC CAT—Any member of *Felis silvestris catus*, pedigree or mixed breed. Also commonly known as a housecat.

DOMINANT—Describes a gene inherited from one parent that overrides the effect of a recessive gene inherited from the other parent. For example, the gene for a tabby coat is dominant.

DOWN—Short, soft, fine hairs that form an undercoat in some breeds.

DOUBLE COAT—Fur consisting of a thick, soft undercoat covered by a protective topcoat of longer guard hairs.

FAMILY—The taxonomic rank Family, as in Family Felidae, belongs to Order Carnivora and Class Mammalia. All animals fit into a taxonomic hierarchy that becomes more exclusive as you move from class to order, then family, genus, and species level.

FEATHERING—Longer hair on areas such as legs, feet, and tail.

FERAL—Describing a domesticated species that has reverted to a wild state.

FIFe—Fédération Internationale Féline, the leading European federation of cat registries.

FOLDED EARS—Ears that fold forward and downward, seen in breeds such as the Scottish Fold.

GCCF—The Governing Council of the Cat Fancy, the leading organization for the registration of cats in the UK.

GENE POOL—The complete collection of genes within an interbreeding population.

GHOST MARKINGS—Faint tabby markings on the coat of a self-colored cat that show up in certain lights.

GROUND COLOR—Background color in tabbies; there are many variants: brown, red, and silver are among the most common.

GUARD HAIRS—Longer, tapering hairs that form a cat's topcoat and provide weatherproofing.

HYBRID—Offspring of two different species—for example, the Bengal, which is a cross between the domestic cat (*Felis silvestris catus*) and the Asian leopard cat (*Felis bengalensis*).

LEATHER—Hairless area at the end of the nose. Color varies according to coat color and is defined in the breed standards for pedigree cats.

LILAC—Warm pink-gray color, a dilute form of brown.

MACKEREL TABBY—see Tabby

"M" MARK—Typical "M"-shaped mark on the forehead of tabby cats; also known as a "frown" mark.

MARBLED—Variation of the Classic tabby, mostly seen in wildcat hybrids such as the Bengal.

MASCARA LINES—Dark lines running from the outer corners of the eyes, or encircling the eyes.

MASK—Dark coloration on the face, usually around the muzzle and eyes.

MITTED—Color pattern in which the paws are white. Also called mittens or socks.

MUTATION—Change in a cell's DNA, arising by chance; effects of genetic mutations in cats include hairlessness, folded or curled ears, curly coats, and short tails.

PARTI-COLOR—General term for a coat pattern that has two or more colors; often one being white.

PATCHED TABBY—Tortoiseshell with tabby markings.

PEDIGREE—Purebred.

POINTED—Coat pattern in which a cat has pale body fur with darker extremities (head, tail, and legs); typically seen in the Siamese.

POLYDACTYLY—Extra toes produced by a genetic mutation; polydactyly, or polydactylism, is common in certain breeds, but only in the Pixiebob is the trait accepted in the breed standard.

RANDOM-BRED—Cat of mixed parentage.

RECESSIVE—A gene that can produce an effect only when inherited from both parents. If a recessive gene from one parent is paired with a dominant gene from the other parent, its effect will be overridden. The genes for certain eye colors and long fur in cats are recessive.

RED—Reddish brown, used to describe a coat color in Abyssinian and Somali cats; also known as sorrel.

REX COAT—Curly or wavy coat, as seen in Devon and Cornish Rex cats.

RUDDY—A color of Abyssinian cats—known as usual in the UK.

RUFF—Frill of longer hair around the neck and chest.

SELECTIVE BREEDING—Mating of animals that possess desired traits, such as a particular coat color or pattern.

SEMI-LONGHAIR—Medium-long coat, usually with a minimal undercoat.

SEPIA—Dark brown ticking on a paler ground color.

SHADED—Coat pattern in which the final quarter of each hair is colored.

SINGLE COAT—Coat with just one layer, usually the topcoat of guard hairs, seen in such cats as the Balinese and Turkish Angora.

SMOKE—Coat pattern in which each hair shaft is pale at the base and colored for about half of its length.

SOLID—Coat in which a single color is distributed evenly along the hair shaft; also known as self.

SPOTTED TABBY—see Tabby

STOP—Indentation between the muzzle and the top of the head; also known as a break.

TABBY—Genetically dominant coat pattern that comes in four types: Classic tabby has a blotched or whorled pattern; Mackerel tabby has "fishbone" stripes; Spotted tabby has spots or rosettes; Ticked tabby has a faint pattern on a ticked coat.

TEMPERAMENT—The character of a cat.

TICA—The International Cat Association, a genetic registry for pedigree cats worldwide.

TICKED—Coat pattern in which each hair shaft has alternate bands of pale and darker colors; also known as agouti. See also Tabby.

TIPPED—Coat pattern in which just the tip of each hair is strongly colored.

TOPCOAT—Outer coat of guard hairs.

TORTIE – Common abbreviation for tortoiseshell.

TORTIE AND WHITE— Alternative term used for calico in the UK.

TORTIE-TABBY—Tortoiseshell with tabby markings; term used in the UK.

TORTOISESHELL—Coat pattern in which black and red hairs, or their dilute forms, are mixed in patches.

TRICOLOR—Term sometimes used to describe a coat of two colors plus white.

TUFTS—Clusters of longer hairs that are seen, for example, between the toes or on the ears.

UNDERCOAT—Layer of hair beneath the topcoat, usually short and often woolly.

VAN PATTERN—Pointed coat pattern in which the color is restricted to the head and tail only, as in the Turkish Van.

WEDGE—Triangular facial conformation seen in most cats except the flat-faced Persian; the shape is elongated in breeds such as the Siamese and Orientals.

WHISKER PADS—Fleshy pads on either side of a cat's muzzle where the whiskers are placed in rows.

WIREHAIR—Rare coat type, caused by a genetic mutation, in which the hairs are twisted or bent at the tips, giving a coarse, springy texture; seen in the American Wirehair cat.

Index

Main entries in **bold**

A

abscesses 300, 302, 304
Abyssinian 49, 64, 66, 70, **132–3**, 185
  inherited disorders 297
  see also Somali
accidents
  bowel/bladder 309
  emergencies 301
  road traffic 21, 257, 260, 305
acclimatization 264–65
activity centers 285
activity levels, changes in 298, 299, 300
Adam 29
adders 305
adoption fees 67
adrenal gland 43
adrenalin 62
adult cats
  diet and feeding 273
  and new kitten 283
  socialization 282–83
  versus kittens 67, 256
advertising 39
Aesop's Fables 28
Africa, cat species in 12
African wildcat (*Felis silvestris lybica*) 13, 14, 65, 145
age
  and choice of cat 256
  elderly cats 308–09
aggression 282, 290, 299
agility 26–27, 48, 57, 64
  reduced 308
agouti fur 51, 52
airway, obstructed 30, 300, 301, 303, 305
Akbar, Emperor 15
albinism 70
alertness, reduced 300
Alice's Adventures in Wonderland (Carroll) 30, 39, 123
allergies
  in cats 62–63, 305
  food 273
  to cats 256
almond-shaped eyes 45
aluminum foil 257, 291
alveoli 58, 59
American Bobtail
  longhair **247**
  shorthair **163**

American Burmese **88**
American Curl
  longhair **238–39**
  shorthair **159**
American Ringtail 49, 167
American Shorthair 71, **113**
American Wirehair 67, **181**
amino acids 270
Anatolian 128
anatomy 42–63
anemia 269, 297, 301
anesthetics 307
Angora 33, 65, 185, **229**
antiplaque solutions 278–79
antibiotics 306
antibodies 62, 63
antihistamines 63
antioxidants 271
aorta 59
appetite
  changes in 299, 300, 302, 309
  in elderly cats 308
Arabian Mau **131**
archeology 14–15
Arctic Curl 65
art, cats in 32–7
arteries 58
arthritis 301, 303
artificial respiration 304
Asia, cat species in 12
Asian
  Burmilla **78**, 79, 80–81
  inherited disorders 297
  Longhair *see* Tiffanie
  Self and Tortie **82**
  Smoke **79**
  Tabby **83**
  Tortie **53**
Asian Leopard Cat 9, 65, 70, 143
Assyrians 15
asthma 62, 300
athleticism 258
Atlantic Ocean 19
Australia 19
Australian Mist **134–35**
autoimmune disorders 62, 63
automatic feeding stations 262
awn hair 50, 51

B

B-lymphocytes 62
babies, cats and 282–83
bacteria 272
bad habits 290–91
balance 45
  problems with 303

Balinese 185, **206**
  grooming 277
  inherited disorders 297
Balinese-Javanese **207**
ballet, cats in 39
balls 285
Balthus 34–35
Bambino 66, **154–55**
bandages 305, 307
barn cats 21
Bartolo, Domenico di 32
Bastet 24, 37
bathing 277, 279
  hairless cats 170, 171
bay cat group 12
beds and bedding 262, 263, 264, 265
  for elderly cats 308
  for pregnancy and birth 292–93
  for sick or injured cats 306
bee stings 305
behavior
  changes in 290, 298, 299, 300, 301, 302
  healthy 298
  problems 257, 258, 259, 265, 281, 282, **290–91**
  see also training
bells 260, 263
belly, presentation of 275
Benedictine 65
Bengal 64, 65, 66, 67, 70, **142–43**
Beresford, Lady Marcus 187
Bering land bridge 11, 12
bibs 53
bicolors 53, 101, 188, 197,
big cats 8, 12, 59
  domesticating 15
bile 61
biofeedback loop 43
biology, feline 40–67
bird feeders/tables 261
birds
  catching 55
  chasing 260–61
  endangered 21
  pet 258
Birman 67, **212–13**
  inherited disorders 297
birth, giving 292
bites, animal/insect 305
biting 257, 258, 265, 275, 282, 284, 290
"The Black Cat" (Poe) 31
black color 26, 52
bladder 61, 309
  stones 270

Blake, Sir William 25
bleeding 300, 304
  disorders 297
  heavy 304, 305
  internal 301
blood 59
  disorders 297, 303
  loss 301
  tests 303
  types 58
  vessels 58, 59, 303
blotched tabby 199
Blue Chinchilla 192
blue color 52, 116–17, 182, 188, 192
boarding kennels 269
bobcats 59, 64, 244
Bobtail 19, 49, 185
  American **163, 247**
  Japanese **160, 241**
  Kurilian **161, 242–43**
  Mekong **162**
body language 275, 280–81
body shapes 48–49, 49
Bombay 66, 82, **84–85**
bones
  broken 303, 304
  eating 271
  skeleton **48–49**
Bonnard, Pierre 34
boredom 258, 284, 290
Bosch, Hieronymus 32, 33
bowels 60, 61, 309
bowls, food and water 262, 263
  hygiene 271, 272
  sharing 259, 262, 302
brain 42–43, 59
breakages 257
breathing
  artificial respiration 304
  difficulties 300, 301, 303, 305
  irregular 301, 305
  respiratory system **58–59**
breed registry 67
breeders
  choice of 67
  and genetics 296
  questions to ask 67
  recommendation of vets by 268
  reputable 66, 67
breeding
  responsible **292–93**, 296
  selective 19
  see also reproduction
breeds
  characteristics 64
  choice of 66–67

creation of 64
definition of 64
development of 64
guide to 68–253
and health problems 296–97
hybrid and future 65
longhairs 184–253
outcrossing 65
shorthairs 70–183
understanding 64–65
Britanica 220
British Angora *see* Oriental
   Longhair
British Longhair **220**
British Shorthair 66, 67, 71,
   122–23
   Bicolor **121**
   body shape 49
   coat 53, 64, 123
   Colorpointed **120**
   inherited disorders 297
   Smoke **124**
   Solid **118–19**
   Tabby **125**
   Tipped **126**
   Tortie 53, **127**
bronchi 58
bronchioles 58, 59
brushes
   grooming 276, 277
   tooth 278
Buddhism 25
Bulgakov, Mikhail 31
Burmese 66, 71
   American 88
   European 87
   inherited disorders 297
   Lilac 78
Burmilla *see* Asian Burmilla
Burmoire 79
burns 305

C

cabbits 165
Cadoc, St 27
cages 263, 306
calcium 270–71
calico color 53, 127
calicoes 53, 182, 202–03
California Spangled 67, **140**
calories 273
cameo color 52, 126, 189, 193
cancer 63
  and neutering 269
canine teeth 8
capillaries 58, 59
caracal 9, 12, 64
Caracat 64
carbon dioxide 58, 59
carbon monoxide poisoning 301
Carbonel (Sleigh) 31
cardiac muscle 54

cardiovascular disease 296,
   297, 303
cardiovascular system **58–59**
carnassial teeth 61
carnivores 8, 10, 60, 64, 270
carriers 263, 264, 268, 282
Carroll, Lewis 30
carrying position 274
cars, traveling in 263, 264
cartilage 48
cartoon cats 38–39
Casey, Paul 140
The Cat Book Poems 100, 104
Cat Club of England 187
cat clubs 19, 67
cat family 64–65
cat fanciers 19, 64
Cat Fanciers Association (CFA) 64
cat flu 269
cat foods 271, 272, 273
cat grass 258, 260
The Cat in the Hat (Seuss) 31
"cat mysteries" 31
cat registries 64, 65
cat repellent sprays 258
cat shelters 67
cat shows 64, 67, 119
cat welfare organizations 20, 21
catching 284
caterwauls 281
catflaps 256, 259, 260, 261, 288,
   290
catnip 260, 284, 285, 291
cats
   aggression to/from other 260,
     261, 290
   ancestors of 10–12
   biology 40–67
   breeds 64–65, 68–253
   caring for 254–309
   choice of 66–67, 256
   in culture 22–39
   domestication 14–15
   evolution 8, 10–12
   feral **20–21**
   genetics 64–65
   health 296–309
   legendary origin of 29
   longhairs 184–253
   meeting other 265, 281, 283
   neighborhood 257, 260, 261
   shorthairs 70–183
   species around the world **8–9**
   spread of domestic **18–19**
   understanding **280–81**
Cats (musical) 39
catteries 269
cave lions 12
cemeteries, pet 309
central nervous system (CNS) 43
cerebellum 42
cerebral cortex 43
cerebrum 42

Ceylon **136**
CFA *see* Cat Fanciers Association
Chantilly/Tiffany **211**
Chartreux 64, 65, 66, **115**
chasing 284
Chausie 49, 64, 65, 67, **149**
check-ups
   annual 268, 269, 299, 303
   first vet **268–69**
cheetah 12, 15, 59
chemical burns 305
chemicals
   garden 260, 261
   household 258, 259, 291
Cheshire Cat 30, 39, 123
chewing 257, 259, 265, 285, 290
children
   involvement with cat 283
   learning how to handle cat
     265, 274, 283
   meeting new cat 264, 265, 283
   playtime 290
China 15, 19, 27
chinchilla fur 52
Chinchilla Shorthair *see* British
   Shorthair, Tipped
Chinese Li Hua **77**
Chlamydophila felis 269
chocolate, eating 271
chocolate color 208
choking 257, 305
Choupette 213
Christianity 25
Chulalongkorn (Rama V), King
   of Thailand 75
Cimolestes 10, 11
cinnamon color 52, 95
circuses, cat 39
classic tabby 53, 123
claws
   checking 298, 299
   elderly cats 308
   retractable 8, 54, 64
   showing 281
   sinking in 275
   trimming 278
clay litter 262
clicker training 288, 289
climate
   and body shape 49
   and long coats 184, 185
climbing 55, 257, 284, 285, 288
clippers, nail 276, 278
clock, internal 43
cloning 214
clouded leopard 8
coats
   changes to 300
   color and pattern 51, **52–53**, 64
   double-layered 71
   in elderly cats 308
   foreign bodies in 298
   genetics 64–65

grooming **276–79**
health checks 298
heat-sensitive enzyme and
   point coloration 53, 107
single 71
types of 50–51
undercoats 71, 185
see also curly coats; longhairs;
   shorthairs
collars 260, 263
   cone-shaped 307
colonies, feral cat 20–21
colonization 19
color 52–53
Colorpoint Shorthair 110, **120**
combs 276
coming when called 288
commercial foods 271, 272, 273
communication 280–81
companionship
   human 256
   of other cats 258, 259, 283
compass, directional 43
condition, assessing 272
congenital hypotrichosis 297
conjunctivitis 269, 300, 302
consciousness, loss of 301
conservation, wildlife 140
constipation 303
convalescence 306–07
Cornish Rex 19, 66, 71, 168,
   176–77, 178, 180
   coat 51, 178, 277
   two types of 176
cortical folding 42, 43
cortisol 43, 62
cost, of cat ownership 262
cougar 59
coughing 300
crates 306
cream, drinking 271
cremation 309
creodonts 10, 11
Cretaceous period 10, 11
crossbreeds 19, 65
culture, cats in 22–39
cupboards 257, 258
curiosity 257, 264
curled ears 185
   American Curl 159, **238–39**
   Highlander **158**
   Kinkalow **152**
   see also folded ears
curly coats 51, 71, 185
   American Wirehair **181**
   Cornish Rex **176–77**
   Devon Rex **178–79**
   German Rex **180**
   Kinkalow **152, 234**
   LaPerm **173, 250–51**
   Skookum **103**
   Slekirk Rex **174–75, 248**
   Ural Rex **172, 249**

Cymric 165, **246**
see also Manx
Cyprus 14–15

D

da Vinci, Leonardo 32
dairy products 271
dark, going out after 260
deafness 91, 303
dehydration 300–01, 306, 309
dementia 309
dental care/problems 300, 301, 302
dermis 50
designer cats 67, 140, 152, 154–55
destructive behavior 290–91
the Devil 25, 27
Devon Rex 71, 168, **178–79**, 185
   blood group 58
   inherited disorders 297
diabetes 300, 303
diaphragm 58
diarrhea 273, 300, 302, 306
Dickens, Charles 31
diet **270–73**
   balanced 272
   carnivorous 8, 270
   changes through life 272–73
   for elderly cats 308
   and lifestyle 273
   for pregnant cats 292
   special 273
   and weight problems 272–73
digestive system **60–61**, 270, 303
digging 257, 261
disabled cats 67
discharges, abnormal 278, 300, 307
disease *see* health; inherited disorders
disks, ID 263
dog food 272
dogs
   contact with 29, 290
   meeting resident 265, 283
   socialization **283**
   threat from 261
doll faces 49
domestic cats 8, 65, 71
   crossing with wildcats 64–65
   evolution of 12
   spread of **18–19**
domestication 14–15, 71
dominant genes 64, 65
Donskoy (Don Sphynx) **170**
doors, and safety 259
down 50, 51
Dragon Li **77**
dressings 305, 307
drinking 271, 298
   increased 299, 300, 309
dropper feeding 293
drops, eye and ear 303, 306

dryers 257, 258
dry food 271
dry shampoos 279
dust baths 279
dwarf cats
   Bambino **154–55**
   Kinkalow **152**
   Lambkin Dwarf **153**

E

ear mites 278
ears
   cleaning 277, 278
   drops 303, 306
   examining 298, 299
   hearing 44–45
   independent rotation 45
   problems with 303
   shape 45, 67, 185
   signals from 45, 280
   see also curled ears; folded ears
Eastern colors 52
eggs, raw 271
Egypt, Ancient 14, 15, 18–19, 24, 32, 36–37, 130, 132, 168
Egyptian Mau 66, 67, **130**
elderly cats
   caring for **308–09**
   diet for 273
   from rescue centers 67
   grooming 276
   vet's check-ups 303
electrical flexes 257, 258, 305
electrocution 305
Elf 19
Eliot, T.S. 31, 39
Elizabethan collars 307
emergencies, recognizing 301
endocrine system 42
endorphins 62
energy 58
entertainment, cats in **38–39**
environmental problems 21
enzymes
   deficiencies 297
   heat sensitive 56, 107
Eocene epoch 10
eosinophils 62
epidermis 50
epilepsy 303
epinephrine 62
equipment
   essential 262–63
   grooming 276
escape routes 257, 259, 260, 261
eumelanin 51
Eurasian lynx 9
Europe, cat species in 12
European Burmese **87**
European Shorthair **114**
euthanasia 309
evolution 8, **10–12**

exercise
   for elderly cats 308
   for indoor cats 259
Exotic Shorthair 71, **72–73**
   inherited disorders 297
exploring 284, 285
external parasites 302, 303
extinction 11–12
eyelids, visible third 298, 300, 302
eyes
   checking 298, 299
   cleaning 277, 278, 306
   color and shape 45, 292
   drops 306
   large 8, 44, 64
   night vision 44
   problems 269, 300, 302–03, 305
   signals from 280
   vision 44

F

face
   cleaning 278
   facial expressions 280
   shapes 49
faeces
   blood in 300
   burying 261
   digestive system 61
   infected 269
   normal passing of 298
   pain passing 299, 309
fairy tales 28–29
falls 55
farm cats 15, 21
fat, dietary 273
fatty acids 270
fawn color 52, 95
feeding **270–73**
   automatic feeding stations 262
   difficulties 300
   kittens 293
   routine 256, 257, 265
   unwell cats 306
   see also diet; food
Felidae 8, 12, 64
Felinae 8, 11, 12
feline calcivirus (FCV) 63, 269
feline coronavirus 269
feline enteritis 63
feline herpes virus (FHV) 63, 269
feline immunodeficiency virus (FIV) 63
feline infectious peritonitis (FIP) 269
feline leukemia virus (FeLV) 63, 269
feline panleukopenia 269
Felis attica 10, 12
Felis lunensis 10, 12
Felis manul 10
Felis silvestris 9, 12, 14–15, 16–17

Felis species 10, 12
Felix the Cat 38
femoral arteries 304
feral cats **20–21**, 247, 261
   handling 275
Fertile Crescent 14, 15, 18
fertility 147
fibre 271
fights 257, 280, 281, 290
   and infection 259, 261, 302
   injuries from 300
film, cats in 38–39, 168
fireworks 39, 261
first aid 30, 300, 302, 304
fish
   in diet 271
   eating raw 271
   garden 261
flat faces 49
flats, living in 259
fleas 62, 63, 268, 292, 299, 300, 302, 303
flehman response 45
flexibility 48–49, 54, 55
folded ears 185
   Scottish Fold **156–57**, 237
   see also curled ears
folklore **28–29**
food
   allergies 62–63, 273
   commercial 271, 272, 273
   in convalescence 306
   dangerous 271, 305
   for elderly cats 273, 308
   and feeding **270–73**
   fussy eaters 270, 272
   and health problems 298, 299
   for kittens 272
   and learning tricks 285
   as motivation 285
   for pregnant cats 273, 292
   refusing 300
   regular mealtimes 256, 257, 272
   for sick cats 306
   special diets 273
   stealing 258
   and training 288
   types 271
food bowls 263, 265, 271, 272, 291
Foreign 99
foreign bodies
   in skin or coats 298
   in wounds 304
fossils 11, 12
founder effect 64
foxes 257, 261
fractures 303, 304
Fragonard, Jean-Honoré 33
freedom, limits to 260
French Revolution 214
Freud, Lucian 35
Freya 24–25

friends, looking after cat 282
Fritz the Cat 39
fur *see* coats
fur balls 276, 277
furniture 256, 257, 284, 290–91
fussy eaters 270, 272

G

gaits 54, 55
gall bladder 61
garages 261
garbage bags 261
gardens, cat-friendly 257, 260–61
garlic 271
gastroenteritis 269
Gauguin, Paul 34
gender, and choice of cat 256
genealogy 10
genetic analysis 12
genetic disorders *see* inherited
  disorders
genetic screening 296–97, 303
genetics 64–65, 292
Gérard, Marguerite 33
German Rex **180**
Gertrude, St. 25
Gethers, Peter 156
glands
  hormone-producing 303
  scent-producing 50
  sebaceous 50, 51
  sweat 50
glucose, inability to metabolize
  297
glycogenosis 297
The Gods and their Creators
  (Long) 36–37
Golden Siamese 90
grain 15
grapes, eating 271
grass, eating 270, 272
Gray, Thomas 31
grazes 304
Greeks, ancient 18
greenhouses 257, 261
greetings cards 35
Grimm, Jacob and Wilhelm 28
grooming **276–79**
  change in habits 301
  in elderly cats 308
  and flexibility 48, 55
  hairless cats 155
  longhairs 185, 277
  mutual 259, 302
  regular time for 256, 257, 265
  self- 276, 279, 303
  shorthairs 71, 276
  for sick/injured cats 306
  time required for 67
ground rules, establishing 265
growling 281
guard hairs 50–51, 277

gums
  blue 301, 305
  checking 278, 298, 299, 301
  disorders 302
  pale or white 301, 305
  red 301
  yellow 301

H

hair
  disorders 297
  follicles 51
  loosening old 276
  shafts 51
  shedding 71, 185
  types of 50–51
hair dryers 279
hairless cats 67, 71
  Bambino **154–55**
  Donskoy **170**
  grooming 277
  Peterbald 71, **171**
  Sphynx 71, **168–69**
hammock-style beds 262
hand rearing 293
handling **274–75**, 282
  feral cats 275
  in pregnancy 292
  sick or injured cats 304, 306
Havana 66, 94, 95, 99, **102**
Havana Brown 94, 102
hazards
  home 256, 257, 258, 259, 285
  outdoor 260–61
head shapes 49
health 296–309
  caring for older cats **308–09**
  common problems 300, 302
  feral cats 21
  first aid 300
  giving medicine 306, 307
  home checks 298–99
  inherited disorders **296–97**
  looking after sick/injured cats
    306–07
  recognizing an emergency 301
  routine checks 298–99
  signs of ill health 273, 299,
    300–01
  weight problems 273
hearing 8, 44–45, 47
heart
  cardiovascular system **58–59**
  disorders 296, 297, 303
heatstroke 261, 300, 304
Hemingway, Ernest 31
hemorrhage 304
hiding 285, 299
Highlander
  longhair **240**
  shorthair 49, 66, **158**
Himalayan 205

Hinds-Daugherty, Dorothy 112
Hinduism 25
hissing 281
Hockney, David 35
Hodge 31
Hogarth, William 33
home-cooked food 270, 271
homes
  cat-proofing 257, 258
  establishing a routine 256–57
  first days in **264–65**
  for kittens 292, 293
  preparing for cats **256–57**, 258
homing instinct 43
hormones 42, 62
  disorders 303, 308
Horner, Nikki 84
hot-water bottles 306
house-training 256
Housecat
  Longhair **252–53**
  Shorthair **182–83**
household chemicals 258, 259,
  291
houseplants 258
human age, equivalent 308
hunting 8, 20, 43, 54, 55, 64, 71,
  256, 259, 270, 284, 288
hybrids 65, 67, 147
hygiene
  food and water bowls 271, 272
  grooming and 276–79
  litter boxes 298
hyoid bone 48, 59
hyperthyroidism 303, 308
hypertrophic cardiomyopathy
  297
hypokalemic polymyopathy
  297
hypothalmus 42

I

ice age 12
ID tags 256, 263
immune system 50, **62–63**, 269
immunization *see* vaccinations
immunodeficiency 63
Impressionism 34
in season 61
inbreeding 64
Incas 25
incisors 61
India 15
Indian Desert Cats 16–17
indoor cats
  choice of 256
  going outdoors 258–59, 260–61
  living indoors 258–59
  stimulation and play 284
infectious diseases 62, 63, 259, 302
  and handling cats 275
in heat 61

inherited disorders 91, 129, 203,
  292, **296–97**, 303
  and outcrossing 65
injuries 261, 300, 301, 302, 303
insect bites 305
interactive toys 284
internal parasites 302
The International Cat
  Association (TICA) 64, 150
international cat registries 64
internet cats 35, 38, 39
intestines 60, 61
Islam 25
itchiness 300

J

Jacobson's organ 45
jaguar 8
Japan 26, 32, 33
Japanese Bobtail
  longhair **241**
  shorthair **160**
jaws 8
jealousy 282, 283
Johnson, Samuel 31
joints
  disorders 297
  flexible 48–49, 55
  stiff 309
Judaism 29
jumping 55, 284, 285, 288
  reluctance/inability 300
jungle cat 65, 149
Just So Stories (Kipling) 31

K

Kallibunker 176
Kanaani **144–45**
kangaroo cats 150
Keats, John 31
keratin 50, 51
Khao Manee **74–75**
kidneys 60, 61
  disorders 296, 297, 300
Kinkalow
  longhair **234**
  shorthair 67, **152**
Kipling, Rudyard 31
kitchens, hazards in 258
kittening boxes 292–93
kittens
  birth of 293
  breeding 292–93
  choice of 67
  feeding 272–73, 293, 295
  feral 20, 21
  finding homes for 256, 292, 293
  first weeks 293
  handling 274
  health checks 268
  hunting 43

kittens *continued*
immune system 62
neutering 269
and older cats 283
playtime 284
sleep 266
socialization 66, 282, 283
sources of 67
stages of development 292–93
training 288
vaccinations 268, 269
versus adult cats 67
Klee, Paul 34
Korat **76**, 297
Kuniyoshi, Utagawa 32
Kurilian Bobtail
longhair 67, **242–43**
pom-pom tail 243
shorthair **161**

L

Lagerfeld, Karl 213
Lambkin Dwarf 66, 67, **153**
LaPerm
longhair 67, 185, **250–51**
shorthair **173**
whiskers and curls 251
larynx 48, 59
laxatives 303
Lear, Edward 31
leopard cat 9, 12, 65, 70, 143
Leopardette *see* Bengal
leopards 8, 140
lethargy 300, 302
leucocytes 62
leukemia *see* feline leukemia
Li Hua **77**
licking, excessive 298, 302, 304
lifespan 256, 308
feral cats 21
lifestyle 256
ligaments 48, 303
lilac color 78
limbs
back 49, 55
front 48–9, 55
injured 305, 307
limping 300, 301
lions 8, 25, 29, 59
literature, cats in 30–31
litter material, choice of 262, 265, 291
litter boxes 262, 263, 264, 265
accidents 308
problems with 258, 291
regular cleaning 298
training 256
litters 61, 269
Little Nicky 214
liver 61
Lloyd Webber, Andrew 39
Long, Edwin 36–37

long tails 49
longhairs
bathing 279
breeds 184–253
and choice of cat 68
coats 51
genetics 65
grooming 185, 277
origins of 185
types of 185
lookout points 260
Lowlander 220
luck, good 26
lumps 298, 299, 301
lungs 58–59
Lyme disease 302
lymphatic system 62, 63
lynx 9, 12, 65
Lynx Colorpoint 108
lysosomal storage disease 297

M

Machairodontinae 11
mackerel tabby 53, 199
macrophages 62
McSorley, Paul 155
"mad moments" 265, 284
magic 26–27
Maine Coon 19, 64, 66, 185, **214–15**
coat color and pattern 51, 52, 53, 64
grooming 277
inherited disorders 296, 297
Mandalay **89**
Maneki Neko 26
Manet, Edouard 34
Manx 29, 49, 64, **164–65**, 246
inherited disorders 297
tail types 49, 64, 164, 165
see also Cymric
Manx syndrome 297
marbled cat 9
Marc, Franz 34
Marie Antoinette, Queen of France 214
Mary, the Virgin 25
The Master and Margarita (Bulgakov) 31
mating
choice of mate 292
noises made during 61, 281
reproduction 61
matriarchal societies 20–21
Mau
Arabian **131**
Egyptian **130**
Mayans 25
Meadow, Hal 86
mealtimes
number of 272
regular 256, 257, 272

meat 270, 271
medicine, giving 306, 307
Mediterranean 18
Mekong Bobtail **162**
melanin 51
meowing 59, 281
on cue 288
miacids 10
miacines 11
mice, toy 285
microchipping 256, 261, 263, 268, 269
Middle Ages 19, 25, 26, 32
migrations 11, 12
milk
drinking 271
immunity and mother's 62
for kittens 292, 293
minerals 270
Minskin 150, 155
Miocene epoch 10, 11
mites 268, 278, 302, 303
mittens 53
Moche people 25
molting 71, 185
Morland, George 33
mosquitoes 305
mothers
pregnancy and birth 292–93
and socialization 282
mousers *see* rodents
mouth, checking 298, 299
movement 54–55
mucus 278, 298
Muhammed, the Prophet 25
mummification 15, 24, 27
Munchkin 64, 66, 67
longhair 49, **233**
shorthair 49, **150–51**
muscle fibres 54–5
muscles 48, 54–55, 57, 59
muscular disorders 296, 297
musculoskeletal problems 303
The Musicians of Bremen 28–29
mutations 64, 156, 185, 239
myopathy, Devon Rex 297
myths and legends 26, 27, 28, 104, 165, 223

N

nails, clipping 278
names
choosing 288
recognizing 288
Nanus Rex *see* Lambkin Dwarf
Napoleon **236**
natural breeds 64
natural mutations 239
natural selection 64
navigation 45
Nebelung **221**
neck 48

neighbors
attitude to cats 261
feeding cats 273
introducing cats to 282
looking after cats 282
Neolithic Period 14
nerves 43, 50
nervous system 42, 43
neurons 42, 43
neutering 261, 268–69
and behavior and temperament 256
and docility 290
of feral cats 21
and health 269
and playfulness 284
and spraying 268–69, 291
neutrophils 62
Neva Masquerade **232**
New World 19
night vision 44
nimravids 10, 11
nine lives 26–27
noises 281
Norse mythology 24–25
North America, cat species in 11, 12
Norton 156
Norwegian Forest Cat 24, 67, 184, **222–25**
inherited disorders 297
nose
checking 298
cleaning 278
and senses 45
nutrition 270–73
feral cats 21

O

obesity 273, 299, 300
diet for 273
obstructions, urinary 300
ocelots 8, 12, 64, 140
Ocicat **137**
Classic **138**
odd-colored eyes 45, 188
"Ode on the Death of a Favorite Cat Drowned in a Tub of Gold Fishes" (Gray) 31
oils, body 277
Ojos Azules **129**
Old Possum's Book of Practical Cats (Eliot) 31, 39
Oligocene epoch 11
onions, eating 271
operations 307
oral antiseptics 278
Oriental
Bicolor **101**
Cinnamon and Fawn **95**
Foreign White 91, 99
inherited disorders 297

Longhair **209**
Shaded **97**
Shorthair 71, 94, 95, 102
Smoke **96**
Solid **94**, 100
Tabby **98–99**
Tortie **100**
osteochondrodysplasia 297
Our Cats (Weir) 119
outcrossing 65
outdoor cats 256, 258–59,
  260–61, 284
"The Owl and the Pussycat"
  (Lear) 31
owner responsibilities 256, 302
oxygen 58, 59

P Q

Paleocene epoch 10
Panamanian land bridge 12
pancreas 61
Panthera spelaea 12
Pantherinae 8, 11, 12
paralysis 301
parasites 268, 276, 279, 298,
  302, 303
Pardofelis marmorata 9
particolors 53
patched tabby 53, 198
pathogens 50
patterns 52–53
paws 43, 45, 278
pedigree cats 66, 67
  breeding 292
peke-faced cats 203
pelvis 49
pemphigus complex 63
penis 61
peripheral nervous system (PNS)
  43
Perrault, Charles 28
persecution, of cats 25, 26
Persian 64, 67, 185, 186–205, 197
  Bicolor **205**
  Blue- and Odd-Eyed Bicolor
    and Tricolor **188**
  Cameo **189**
  Cameo Bicolor **193**
  Chinchilla **190**, 194
  coat color and pattern 52, 53
  Colorpoint 53, **205**
  face shape 203
  Golden **191**
  grooming 186
  inherited disorders 186, 296, 297
  Pewter **192**
  Shaded Silver **194**
  Silver Tabby **195**
  Smoke **196**
  Smoke Bicolor and Tricolor **197**
  Solid **186–87**
  Tabby and Patched Tabby **198**

Tabby Tricolor **199**
  Tortie and Calico **202–03**
personality, and choice of cat 256
pet quality 67
Peterbald 67, 71, **171**
pets
  meeting other 265, 283
  small 258, 283
petting 274–75
phaeomelanin 51
pheromone treatment 259
Phoenicians 18
phosphorus 270
Picasso, Pablo 34
picking up 274, 275
pigment/pigmentation 51–53, 65
pills, giving 306, 307
pineal glands 42
pinnae 45
pituitary gland 42, 43
Pixie Cat *see* Devon Rex
Pixiebob
  longhair **244–45**
  shorthair **166**
plants
  cats' favorite 260
  dangerous 258, 261, 305
plaster casts 307
plastic bags 285
plastic sheeting 257
platelets 59
play stations 285
playtime 265, 275, 287, 288
  biting and scratching during
    275, 282, 290
  for elderly cats 308
  importance of **284–85**, 290
  kittens 293
  regular 256, 257, 258, 259
Pliocene period 12
Poe, Edgar Allan 31
poetry 31
pointed patterns 53, 104–05,
  107, 108, 109, 110, 120, 205
pointed-tip ears 45
poisoning 305
Pollatschek, Doris 145
polycystic kidney disease 296, 297
polydactylism 19, 166, 245
pom-pom tails 243
ponds 261
portraits 33, 34, 35
post-Impressionism 34
posters 35
posture, signals from 280, 281
potatoes, green 271
Potter, Beatrix 30
pouncing 284
praise 282, 288
pre-Columbian civilzations 25
pregnancy 61, 292–93
  diet in 273
  unplanned 269

prenatal care 292–93
prey 256, 270, 305
primary seborrhea 297
Prionailurus bengalensis 9
Proailurus 11
progressive retinal atrophy 297
protein 270, 272, 273
Pseudailuris 10, 11
pulse 301, 304, 305
puma 8, 12
puma gods 25
punishment 288, 290
pupils 44, 298
purring 8, 59, 281
puss 304
Puss in Boots 28–29, 39
puzzle feeders 285
pyloric sphincter 61
pyruvate kinase deficiency 297
queens 269

R

rabies 269, 275
Ragamuffin 67, **217**
Ragdoll 67, 185, **216**
  body shape 49
  coat color 53
  inherited disorders 296, 297
raisins 271
Realism 34
recessive genes 64, 65, 178
red blood cells 58, 59, 269, 303
reflex, righting 55
refuges 282
registration fees 292
rehydration, emergency 301
religion 15, **24–25**
Renaissance art 32–33
Renoir, Pierre August 34
reproduction 60, 61
rescue centers 26, 67, 256, 268,
  282
respiratory system 58
respiratory tract infections 269,
  300, 303
retina 44
rewards 288, 289
rexed coats 67, 71, 178
  Cornish Rex **176–77**
  Devon Rex **178–79**
  German Rex **180**
  LaPerm **173**, **250–51**
  Selkirk Rex **174–75**, **248**
  Ural Rex **172**, **249**
rib cage 48, 272
righting reflex 55
Ringtail Sing-a-Ling *see*
  American Ringtail
road traffic accidents 21, 257,
  260, 305
roaring 8, 59
rodents 14, 15, 19, 118, 161, 214

Romans, ancient 19, 25
rough play 275, 282, 290
round eyes 45
rounded faces 49
rounded-tip ears 45
Rousseau, Henri 34
routine
  changes to 282, 283, 300, 302
  establishing a 256–57, 265
Russian Blue 67, 71, **116–17**
Russian Shorthair 117

S

saber-toothed cats 10, 11–12
safety
  in the home 257, 258
  outdoors 257, 260–61
  road 260
saliva 60, 302
sandpits 261
Savannah 66, **146–47**
  creation of 49, 65, 67
scalds 305
scavenging 20, 270
scent marking 45, 281, 290, 291
scent-producing glands 50
scoops, plastic 263
scorpions 305
Scottish Fold
  ear shape 64, 65, 67
  inherited disorders 65, 297
  longhair **237**
  shorthair **156–57**
Scottish Straight 156
scratching
  during handling/play 265, 275,
    282
  in the home 256, 257, 259, 263,
    288, 290–91
  of skin 302
scratching posts 257, 259, 263,
  264, 285, 288, 290–91
seafarers 26
sebaceous glands 50, 51
seizures 301, 303
selective breeding 19
selenium 270
Selkirk Rex 65
  longhair **185**, **248**
  shorthair **174–75**
senses 42, 43, 44–45, 47, 50
sensory hairs 50, 51
Serengeti **148**
serval 64, 65, 147
Seuss, Dr. (Theodor Giesel) 31
sexual maturity 269, 292
sexually transmitted
  infections 269
Seychellois 111
shaded fur 51, 52
Shakespeare, William 26
shampoos 279

shape
  body 49
  ear 45
  eye 45
  face 49
  head 49
Shashthi 25
sheds 257, 261
Shell Cameo 126
shell fur 52
ship's cats 19
shock 304, 305
short-legged cats
  Bambino **154–55**
  Kinkalow **152**
  Lambkin Dwarf **153**
  Minskin 155
  Munchkin 49, **150–51, 233**
  Napoleon **236**
  Skookum **235**
short-tailed cats 49
  American Bobtail **163, 247**
  Japanese Bobtail **160, 241**
  Kurilian Bobtail **161, 242–43**
  Mekong Bobtail **162**
  Pixiebob **166, 244–45**
  see also tailless cats
shorthairs
  bathing 279
  breeds 70–183
  and choice of cat 68
  coats 51
  developing 71
  grooming 71, 276, 277
  maintenance 71
shoulder blades 48–49
Siamese 19, 29, 64, 65, 66, 67, 71, **104–09**
  blood group 58
  body shape 49, 104
  coat pattern / color 52, 53, 107
  face shape 104
  Golden 90
  inherited disorders 296, 297
  kittens 105, 106–07
  longhaired 206, 209
  seal points 104
  Solid-Pointed 53, **104–05**
  semi-longhair version 185
  Tabby-Pointed **108**
  Tortie-Pointed **109**
Siberian 67, **230–31**, 232
signals, body 280–81
silk production 27
Silk Road 18
Simon's Cat 39
Singapura 49, 66, **86**
size 66
skeletal muscle 54
skeleton **48–49**, 54
skin
  color of 52–53

dead 276
disorders 62, 63, 279, 297, 298, 303, 306
  hairless cats 170, 171
  lumps on 301
  structure 50
  wounds 304–05
Skogkatt **223**
Skookum 67, **235**
skull 48, 49
  deformities 129
slanted eyes 45
sleep 43, 266
Sleigh, Barbara 31
slicker brushes 276, 277
smell, sense of 45, 47, 280
Smilodon 11
smoked coats 51, 52, 79, 96, 124, 196, 197
smooth muscle 54
snakes 257, 261, 305
sneezing 62, 300
Snow Bengal 70
snow leopards 8
Snowshoe **112**
socialization 20, 256, 282–83, 290
sodium 270
Sokoke 67, **139**
solid coats 51, 52, 82, 94, 104–05, 118–19, 186–87
solid colors 52
solid-white coats 52
solitary nature 282
Somali 185, **218–19**
  inherited disorders 297
  see also Abyssinian
"Sonnet to a Cat" (Keats) 31
South America, cat species in 12
species 8–9
speed 48, 54, 55
Sphynx 64, 67, 71, **168–69**
  grooming 168, 277
  hairlessness 50, 51
spiders 305
spinal cord 42, 43
spinal disorders 165, 297
spinal muscular atrophy 297
spine 42, 48, 55
spotting 53
spraying 259, 268–69, 281, 291, 292
stalking 55, 284
Steinlen, Theophile 35
sterility 127
sterilization see neutering
stiches, surgical 269, 307
stimulation
  of elderly cats 308
  importance of 256, 284, 285, 288
stings 305
stomach 60–61
  upsets 272, 273, 306
Straede, Dr. Truda 135

strangers, introduction to 282
stress
  in cats 62, 258, 259, 265, 284, 290, 291
  cats good for 274
striated muscle see skeletal muscle
stripes 53
Stripey 19
stroking 274–75
Stubbs, George 33
studs 292
suffocation 285
sunburn 261
superstition 26–27
swallowing
  difficulty in 309
  foreign bodies 257, 285
sweat glands 50
swimming 55
swirling patterns 53
Sylvester 38
systemic lupus erythematosus (SLE) 63

T

T-cells 62, 63
tabby coats 25, 51, 53, 64, 83, 98–99, 108, 125, 182, 195, 198–99
tags 21, 263
tailless cats
  Cymric 246
  Manx 49, 165
  see also short-tailed cats
The Tailor of Gloucester (Potter) 30
tails
  and balance 49
  bones 48
  checking under 298
  cleaning under 279
  signals from 49, 280, 281
  types 49
talcum powder 277
The Tale of Samuel Whiskers (Potter) 30
The Tale of Tom Kitten (Potter) 30
tangles 276, 277
tape, double-sided 257, 291
tapetum lucidum 44
tapeworm 302
taste, sense of 45
taurine 60, 270
Tchaikovsky, Pyotr 39
tear overflow 278
Ted Nude-Gent 168
teddy bear cat 73
teeth 61, 64
  carnivorous 60
  checking 298, 299

cleaning 61, 276, 277, 278–79, 302
  disorders 302
  in elderly cats 309
  toothache 300
  and weight loss 273
temperaments, breeds and 66
temperature, body 301, 305
tendons 54
Tenniel, John 30
territory
  disputes over 261, 280, 281
  home as 258, 283
  marking 45, 269, 281, 290, 291
tests, medical 303
Thai **103**
theater cats 39
theft, cat 260
thirst, increased 300, 309
Through the Looking-glass (Carroll) 30
thyroid problems 300
TICA see International Cat Association
tick removers 276
ticked fur 51, 52, 53
ticks 302, 303
Tiffanie **210**
tigers 8, 59
tipped fur 51, 52
toads 305
toes, polydactylism 166, 245
Tom and Jerry 38
tomatoes, green 271
tongue 45
Tonkinese Shorthair 66, **90**, 92–93
toothpaste 278
torties 27, 53, 100, 109, 127, 202–03
tortoiseshells see torties
touch, sense of 45, 51
Toyger **141**
toys 284–85, 290
  for kittens 293
  and socialization 282
  and stimulation 259
trachea 58, 59
traffic accidents 21, 257, 260, 305
training **288–89**
  length of sessions 285, 288, 289
  tricks 285
  unacceptable behavior 281
transportation 263, 264
treats
  as rewards 285, 288, 289
  role of 273
  and socialization 283
tricolors 53, 188, 197
Troubetskoy, Natalie 130
Turkish Angora 19, 128, 185, **229**
Turkish Shorthair **128**

Turkish Van 19, 53, 66, 128, **226–67**
Turkish Vankedisi **228**
tylotrichs 51

U

unconsciousness 304, 305
undercoats 71, 185, 277
unneutered cats 261, 268–69
Ural Rex
  longhair **249**
  shorthair **172**
urinary tract infections 300, 302
urine
  digestive system 60, 61
  and neutering 261
  normal passing of 298
  pain passing 299, 300, 309
  increased amounts of 300
  scent marking 281

V

vaccinations 63, 67, 261, 269, 293, 302
vagina 61
Vans 226–28
vegetable matter 270
venomous animals 305
Venus 28

verbal cues 288
Veronese, Paolo 33
vertebrae 48
veterinary surgeons
  administering medicines 306
  advice on breeders 67
  advice on diet 273
  annual check-ups 269, 299, 303
  and breeding 292
  check-ups for elderly cats 303, 308
  choice of 268
  emergencies 301, 305
  first check-ups 268–69
  introducing kittens to 282
  visiting 302–03
vibrissae *see* whiskers
Vikings 214
viruses 269
vision 43, 44
  color 44
  loss of 309
  night 44, 47
  sensitive to movement 44
vital signs, normal 305
vitamins and micronutrients 60, 270–71, 273
viverravines 10, 11
vocal cords 59
vocalizations 8, 59, 281
vomeronasal organ 45
vomiting 300, 302, 306

W

wading pools 261
Wain, Louis 35
Warhol, Andy 34
washing machines 257, 258
waste, elimination of 59, 61, 303
water, drinking 271, 306
water bowls 262, 263, 271, 272
wavy coats *see* curly coats
weaning 292, 293
wedge faces 49
weight
  assessing/checking 272–73, 299
  and body form 49
  and diet 272, 273
  gain 273, 300, 308
  loss 273, 299, 300, 308
  in pregnancy 292
  problems 299, 300, 308
Weir, Harrison 119
Western colors 52
wet food 271
wheezing 300
whiskers 44, 45, 47, 51
  signals from 280
white blood cells 59, 62, 269
white coats 26, 91, 261
white spotting 53
Whittington, Dick 29
wild animals, encounters with 260, 261

wildcats
  coat length 71, 185
  crossing domestic cats with 64–65
wildcat (*Felis silvestris*) 9, 12
  domestication **14–15**
  kittens 16–17
windows
  escaping through 259
  falling from 258, 259
  screens 258
witchcraft 25, 26
Wordsworth, William 31
worming 67, 268, 292, 299
worms, intestinal 298, 300, 302
wounds 298, 300, 304
  checking 307
  treatment of 304–05, 306

X Y Z

X-rays 303
York Chocolate 208
Zula 132

Acknowledgments

Dorling Kindersley would like to thank the following people for their assistance with this book:
Suparna Sengupta, Vibha Malhotra for editorial assistance; Jacqui Swan, Chhaya Sajwan, Ganesh Sharma, Narender Kumar, Niyati Gosain, Rakesh Khundongbam, Cybermedia for design assistance; Saloni Talwar for work on the Jacket; Photographer Tracy Morgan, Animal Photography, and her assistants Susi Addiscot and Jemma Yates; Anthony Nichols, Quincunx LaPerms, for help and advice on some of the cat breeds. Caroline Hunt for proofreading; and Helen Peters for the index.

The publisher would like to thank the following owners for allowing us to photograph their cats:
Valerie and Rose King, Katsacute Burmese and Rose Valley: Australian Mist Cats (www.katsacute.co.uk); Liucija Januskeviciute, Sphynx Bastet: Bambino cats (www.sphynxbastet.co.

uk); Chrissy Russell, Ayshazen: Burmese and Khao Manee cats (www.ayshazencats.co.uk); Anthony Nichols, Quincunx: LaPerm cats (www.quincunxcats.co.uk); Karen Toner: Munchkin Longhair and Shorthair, Kinkalow, and Pixibob cats (Kaztoner@aol.com); Fiona Peek, Nordligdrom: Norwegian Forest cats (www.nordligdrom.co.uk); Russell and Wendy Foskett, Bulgari Cats: Savannah cats (www.bulgaricats.co.uk); Maria Bunina, Musrafy Cats: Kurilian Bobtail – Longhair and Shorthair, and Siberian cats (www.musrafy.co.uk); Suzann Lloyd, Tansdale Pedigree Cats: Turkish Van and Vankedisi cats (www.tansdale.co.uk).

PICTURE CREDITS
The publisher would like to thank the following for their kind permission to reproduce their photographs:

(Key: a-above; b-below/bottom; c-center; f-far; l-left; r-right; t-top)

2-3 Getty Images: o-che / Vetta. **4-5 Alamy Images:** Vincenzo Iacovoni. **6-7 Corbis:** Mother Image / SuperStock. **8 Dreamstime.com:** Nico Smit / Jeff Grabert (br). **9 Dreamstime.com:** Mirekphoto (tl). **FLPA:** Terry Whittaker (cr). **Getty Images:** Daryl Balfour / Gallo Images (ca). **Science Photo Library:** Art Wolfe (crb). **10 Science Photo Library:** Natural History Museum, London (cr). **11 Dorling Kindersley:** Jon Hughes and Russell Gooday (br); Natural History Museum, London (tc). **12 Science Photo Library:** Mark Hallett Paleoart (tr). **13 FLPA:** Ariadne Van Zandbergen. **14 Corbis:** Brooklyn Museum (tr); The Gallery Collection (b). **15 Alamy Images:** World History Archive / Image Asset Management Ltd. (tr). **Getty Images:** Gustavo Di Mario / The Image Bank (bl). **16-17 Corbis:** Terry Whittaker / Frank Lane Picture Agency. **19 Corbis:** Hulton-Deutsch Collection (cl). **http://nocoatkitty.**

com/: (br). **20 Alamy Images:** Sorge / Caro (crb); Terry Harris (bl). **21 Alamy Images:** Larry Lefever / Grant Heilman Photography (tr); ZUMA Press, Inc. (cr). **Photoshot:** NHPA (bl). **22-23 SuperStock:** Robert Harding Picture Library. **24 Dorling Kindersley:** Christy Graham / The Trustees of the British Museum (r). **25 Alamy Images:** BonkersAboutAsia (br). **The Bridgeman Art Library:** Walker Art Gallery, National Museums Liverpool (tr). **Dorling Kindersley:** Museo Tumbas Reales de Sipan (c). **27 Alamy Images:** Mary Evans Picture Library (bl). **Mary Evans Picture Library:** (r). **28 Getty Images:** Universal History Archive / Universal Images Group (bl). **29 123RF.com:** Neftali77 (tc). **Getty Images:** British Library / Robana / Hulton Fine Art Collection (br). **30 Alamy Images:** Mary Evans Picture Library (tr); Pictorial Press Ltd (bl). **31 Alamy Images:** Mark Lucas (br). **Getty Images:** Tore

Johnson / TIME & LIFE Images (tr). **PENGUIN and the Penguin logo are trademarks of Penguin Books Ltd:** (bl). **32 Alamy Images:** Collection Dagli Orti / The Art Archive (cr). **The Bridgeman Art Library:** Utagawa Kuniyoshi / School of Oriental & African Studies Library, Uni. of London (bl). **Dorling Kindersley:** (tr). **33 The Bridgeman Art Library:** Marguerite Gerard / Musee Fragonard, Grasse, France (tr). **Corbis:** (bl); Blue Lantern Studio (crb). **34 akg-images:** Franz Marc / North Rhine-Westphalia Art Collection (tl). **Getty Images:** Henri J.F. Rousseau / The Bridgeman Art Library (br). **35 Corbis:** Found Image Press. **36-37 Getty Images:** DEA Picture Library. **38 Alamy Images:** AF archive (crb, bl). **39 The Advertising Archives:** (cra). **Alamy Images:** AF archive (bc). **40-41 Alamy Images:** Oberhaeuser / Caro. **46-47 Corbis:** Tim Macpherson / cultura. **49 Dorling Kindersley:** Natural History Museum, London (cla). **Dave Woodward:** (bc). **56-57 Alamy Images:** Juniors Bildarchiv GmbH. **65 Alamy Images:** Blickwinkel (br). **Dorling Kindersley:** Jerry Young (bl). **66 Getty Images:** Mehmet Salih Guler / Photodisc (b). **67 Alamy Images:** ZUMA Press, Inc. (cb). **Dreamstime.com:** Jura Vikulin (br). **68-69 Alamy Images:** Phongdech Kraisriphop. **70 Alamy Images:** Juniors Bildarchiv GmbH. **72 Alamy Images:** Arco Images / De Meester, J. **73 Dreamstime.com:** Isselee (c). **SuperStock:** Biosphoto (cl). **75 Corbis:** Luca Tettoni / Robert Harding World Imagery (tc). **77 Larry Johnson:** (cra, b, tr). **80-81 Animal Photography:** Alan Robinson. **84 Alamy Images:** Tierfotoagentur / R. Richter (ca). **SuperStock:** Biosphoto (cr). **85 Dreamstime.com:** Sheila Bottoms. **88 Ardea:** Jean-Michel Labat (cla, tr); Jean Michel Labat (b). **89 Alamy Images:** Tierfotoagentur (cra, tr, b). **92-93 SuperStock:** imagebroker.net. **97 Animal Photography:** Alan Robinson (cra, tr, b). **98 Alamy Images:** Top-Pet-Pics. **99 Alamy Images:** Juniors Bildarchiv GmbH (c). **102 Animal Photography:** Helmi Flick (cl, tr, b). **103 Alamy Images:** Juniors Bildarchiv GmbH (cla, b, tr). **104 Taken from** *The Book of the Cat* by Frances Simpson (1903): (bl). **106-107 Corbis:** D. Sheldon / F1 Online. **110 Chanan Photography:** (cl, b, tr). **111 Animal Photography:** Alan Robinson (cla, tr). **Chanan Photography:** (b). **113 Animal Photography:** Tetsu Yamazaki (b). **Dreamstime.com:** Vladyslav Starozhylov (cl, tr, cra). **115 Fotolia:** Callalloo Candcy (b). **116 123RF.com:** Nailia Schwarz. **117 Animal Photography:** Sally Anne Thompson (cr). **Dreamstime.com:** Anna

Utekhina (c). **119 Project Gutenberg** (www.gutenberg.org): Taken from *Our Cats and All About Them* by Harrison Weir (tc). **122-123 Alamy Images:** Juniors Bildarchiv GmbH. **128 Alamy Images:** Juniors Bildarchiv GmbH (cra); Tierfotoagentur (tr, b). **129 Animal Photography:** Tetsu Yamazaki (cra, tr, b). **131 Petra Mueller:** (cl, clb, br, tr). **132 Project Gutenberg** (www.gutenberg.org): Taken from *Cats: Their Points and Characteristics, with Curiosities of Cat Life*, and a Chapter on Feline Ailments by W. Gordon Stables (cr). **133 SuperStock:** Biosphoto. **136 SuperStock:** Marka (b, cl, cra, tr). **137 Alamy Images:** Tierfotoagentur / R. Richter (cl). **138 Chanan Photography:** (cla, tr). **Robert Fox:** (b). **139 Animal Photography:** Helmi Flick (cra, tr, c, b). **141 Animal Photography:** Tetsu Yamazaki (cra, tr, b). **Dreamstime.com:** Sarahthexton (cl). **142 Alamy Images:** Sergey Komarov-Kohl (bc). **144 Alamy Images:** Juniors Bildarchiv GmbH. **145 Alamy Images:** Juniors Bildarchiv GmbH (cr, b). **naturepl.com:** Ulrike Schanz (bl). **Rex Features:** David Heerde (fcr). **147 Bulgari Cats / www.bulgaricats.co.uk:** (cla). **148 Animal Photography:** Helmi Flick (b, tr). **SuperStock:** Juniors (cla). **149 Animal Photography:** Helmi Flick (b). **Ardea:** Jean-Michel Labat (cra, tr). **150 Alamy Images:** Idamini (cra). **Barcroft Media Ltd:** (bl). **152 Animal Photography:** Helmi Flick (cra, b, tr). **153 Animal Photography:** Helmi Flick (cra, tr, b). **155 Fred Pappalardo / Paul McSorley:** (cr). **156 Alamy Images:** Life on white (clb). **The Random House Group Ltd:** EBury press (bc). **158 Animal Photography:** Helmi Flick (cla, tr, b). **159 Animal Photography:** Tetsu Yamazaki (cl, tr, b). **160 Animal Photography:** Alan Robinson (cra). **161 Animal Photography:** Helmi Flick (cra, tr, b). **162 Dreamstime.com:** Elena Platonova (tr, b); Nelli Shuyskaya (cla). **163 Animal Photography:** Helmi Flick (cla, b, tr). **164 Animal Photography:** Sally Anne Thompson. **165 Alamy Images:** Creative Element Photos (ca). **Taken from** *An Historical and Statistical Account Of The Isle Of Man:* (cl). **167 Dave Woodward:** (cla, b, tr). **168 Alamy Images:** AF archive (bl). **170 Fotolia:** Artem Furman (cla, tr, b). **171 Fotolia:** eSchmidt (cla, tr, b). **172 Alamy Images:** Tierfotoagentur (cla, tr, b). **173 FLPA:** S. Schwerdtfeger / Tierfotoagentur (b, cla, tr). **176 Animal Photography:** Helmi Flick (cl). **Dreamstime.com:** Oleg Kozlov (cr). **177 Dreamstime.com:** Sikth. **179 Dreamstime.com:** Jagodka (cla). **180 Alamy Images:** Juniors

Bildarchiv GmbH (tr, b); Tierfotoagentur (cla). **181 Animal Photography:** Tetsu Yamazaki (cla, tr, b). **183 Dorling Kindersley:** Tracy Morgan. **184-185 Dorling Kindersley:** Tracy Morgan-Animal Photography. **184 Alamy Images:** Top-Pet-Pics. **187 Image courtesy of Biodiversity Heritage Library. http://www.biodiversitylibrary.org:** Taken from *Cats and All About Them*, by Frances Simpson (tc). **188 Chanan Photography:** (b, tr, cla). **193 Alamy Images:** Juniors Bildarchiv GmbH (b). **Dreamstime.com:** Petr Jilek (cla, tr). **195 Chanan Photography:** (b, cla, tr). **197 Dreamstime.com:** Isselee (cla, tr, b). **199 Chanan Photography:** (b, tr, cra). **200-201 Dreamstime.com:** Stratum. **202 Alamy Images:** Petra Wegner. **203 123RF.com:** Vasiliy Koval (c). **Getty Images:** Martin Harvey / Photodisc (cr). **208 Chanan Photography:** (tr, cra, b). **210 Alamy Images:** Petographer (clb). **212 Alamy Images:** PhotoAlto. **213 Corbis:** Maurizio Gambarini / epa (cra). **214 123RF.com:** Aleksej Zhagunov (cra). **Press Association Images:** Tony Gutierrez / AP (bl). **217 Animal Photography:** Tetsu Yamazaki (cla, tr, b). **218 Dreamstime.com:** Nataliya Kuznetsova (cr). **Photoshot:** MIXA (ca). **219 Getty Images:** Lisa Beattie / Flickr Open. **220 Alamy Images:** Petra Wegner (cra, tr, b). **221 Animal Photography:** Tetsu Yamazaki (cla, tr, b). **223 Alamy Images:** Juniors Bildarchiv GmbH (c). **Caters News Agency:** (cra). **224-225 Corbis:** Envision. **231 Project Gutenberg (www.gutenberg.org):** Taken from *Our Cats and All About Them*, by Harrison Weir (cr). **232 Animal Photography:** Tetsu Yamazaki (cra, b, tr). **Dreamstime.com:** Jagodka (cla). **235 Alamy Images:** Idamini (cra, tr, b). **236 Animal Photography:** Helmi Flick (cra, tr, b). **239 Dreamstime.com:** Eugenesergeev (tr); Isselee (br). **240 Alamy Images:** Idamini (cla, tr, b). **241 Chanan Photography:** (cla, tr, b). **245 www.ansonroad.co.uk:** (tr). **247 Animal Photography:** Helmi Flick (tr, b); Tetsu Yamazaki (cra). **248 Animal Photography:** Tetsu Yamazaki (cla, tr, b). **249 Olga Ivanova:** (cla, tr, b). **251 Alamy Images:** Tierfotoagentur / L. West (ca). **Corbis:** Rachel McKenna / cultura (cra). **252 Dreamstime.com:** Nataliya Kuznetsova. **253 Dreamstime.com:** Ijansempoi. **254-255 Corbis:** Silke Klewitz-Seemann / / imagebroker. **256 Fotolia:** Tony Campbell (tr). **257 Alamy Images:** imagebroker (br). **258 Dorling Kindersley:** Kitten courtesy of The Mayhew Animal Home and Humane Education Center

(br). **Dreamstime.com:** Joyce Vincent (bl). **259 Getty Images:** Marcel ter Bekke / Flickr (b). **260 Dreamstime.com:** Celso Diniz (b). **SuperStock:** Biosphoto (tr). **261 Corbis:** Michael Kern / Visuals Unlimited (fbr). **Dorling Kindersley:** Rough Guides (bc/Fireworks); Jerry Young (br). **Getty Images:** Imagewerks / Imagewerks Japan (bc). **262 Dorling Kindersley:** Kitten courtesy Of Betty (tr). **Dreamstime.com:** Stuart Key (b). **264 Alamy Images:** Isobel Flynn (bl). **265 Corbis:** Image Source (tr). **266-267 Corbis:** C.O.T / a.collectionRF / amanaimages. **268 Getty Images:** Fuse (bl). **269 Photoshot:** Juniors Tierbildarchiv (cra). **270 Alamy Images:** Juniors Bildarchiv GmbH (b). **271 Dreamstime.com:** Llareggub (tr). **272 Alamy Images:** Tierfotoagentur / R. Richter (tl). **Corbis:** Splash News (br). **273 Alamy Images:** Juniors Bildarchiv GmbH (crb). **274 Alamy Images:** Bill Bachman (bl). **275 Alamy Images:** Juniors Bildarchiv GmbH (crb). **280 Fotolia:** Callalloo Candcy (bl). **281 Alamy Images:** Juniors Bildarchiv GmbH (bl). **282 Alamy Images:** Tierfotoagentur / R. Richter (tr). **283 Alamy Images:** Juniors Bildarchiv GmbH (tr). **Dorling Kindersley:** Kitten courtesy of Betty (tl). **284 Dorling Kindersley:** Kitten courtesy of Helen (c). **Dreamstime.com:** Miradrozdowski (bl). **286-287 Alamy Images:** Arco Images / Steimer, C. **288 Getty Images:** Les Hirondelles Photography (bl). **289 Alamy Images:** Juniors Bildarchiv GmbH. **290 Alamy Images:** Juniors Bildarchiv GmbH (b). **291 Alamy Images:** Juniors Bildarchiv GmbH (tr); Rodger Tamblyn (tl). **294-295 Corbis:** Mitsuaki Iwago / Minden Pictures. **296 Alamy Images:** Juniors Bildarchiv GmbH (b). **300 Fotolia:** Callalloo Candcy (bl). **301 Alamy Images:** Graham Jepson (tl). **Fotolia:** Kirill Kedrinski (cr). **302 Alamy Images:** FB-StockPhoto (bl). **303 Alamy Images:** Nigel Cattlin (tc/Tick); R. Richter / Tierfotoagentur (bl). **Corbis:** Bill Beatty / Visuals Unlimited (tc); Dennis Kunkel Microscopy, Inc. / Visuals Unlimited (tc/Ear Mite). **Dreamstime.com:** Tyler Olson (tr). **304 Alamy Images:** Brian Hoffman (tc). **306 Alamy Images:** FLPA (tc). **307 Getty Images:** Danielle Donders - Mothership Photography / Flickr Open (t). **308 Dreamstime.com:** Brenda Carson (ca). **309 Fotolia:** Urso Antonio (bl). **Getty Images:** Akimasa Harada / Flickr (t). **310 Animal Photography:** Tetsu Yamazaki

All other images © Dorling Kindersley
For further information see:
www.dkimages.com